The
People's
Work

A Social History
of the Liturgy

Frank C. Senn

Fortress Press ⌁ Minneapolis

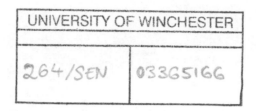
THE PEOPLE'S WORK
A Social History of the Liturgy

Cover image: The Feast of Corpus Christi © Kenneth Zammit Tabona/SuperStock
Cover design: Laurie Ingram
Book design: Jill Carroll Lafferty

Library of Congress Cataloging-in-Publication Data

Senn, Frank C.
  The people's work : a social history of the liturgy / by Frank C. Senn.
    p. cm.
  Includes bibliographical references (p.   ) and index.
  ISBN 0-8006-3827-1 (alk. paper)
  1. Liturgics—History. 2. Social history. I. Title.
  BV178.S46 2006
  264'.009—dc22

                        2005036142

The paper used in this publication meets the minimum requirements of American National Standard for Information Sciences—Permanence of Paper for Printed Library Materials, ANSI Z329.48-1984.

Manufactured in the U.S.A.

10   09   08   07   06   1   2   3   4   5   6   7   8   9   10

Contents

 Illustrations

A gallery at the center of this book includes the following illustrations. Captions for each plate are listed before and after the gallery.

ACKNOWLEDGMENTS

My thanks to Immanuel Lutheran Church in Evanston, Illinois, for granting me a three-month sabbatical in 2004. Part of the time was used to put the finishing touches on this book. My thanks also to the Lilly Endowment, Inc., for a Clergy Renewal grant that made it possible to have this sabbatical and travel to Australia and New Zealand.

Some of this material was shared in lecture form before it was honed into book form. Part of chapter 3 was shared with pastors of the Southern Wisconsin District of the Lutheran Church–Missouri Synod in May 2000. Part of chapter 7 was shared with pastors of the Evangelical Lutheran Church in Canada in Calgary in the spring of 2001. Parts of chapters 10 and 11 were shared with pastors in the Diocese of Växjö, Sweden, in November 2001. Parts of chapters 11 and 14 were shared with pastors in Skálholt, Iceland, in July 2002. Some material in chapters 16, 17, and 18 was shared with audiences in Brisbane, Melbourne, and Adelaide in October 2004 in lectures on worship and culture. Finally, I presented the concept of this book as a case study at the 2005 Congress of Societas Liturgica, held in Dresden, Germany, and received helpful suggestions, especially from Gordon Lathrop. I was grateful for the opportunity to share this material with receptive audiences and garner responses that helped shape this book.

Finally, my thanks to Michael West of Fortress Press for his interest in this project and to Joshua Messner for his careful work on the text.

To Mary Elizabeth,
who has a very good sense about what's
really going on in the Liturgy.

What Is a Social History of the Liturgy?

Social history has emerged as an important aspect of historical study. What is it? Social history has been described as history with politics left out. It is less interested in tracking major historical events than it is in discovering how people lived their daily lives in different periods of history. It is about the structures of everyday life, including sex and family, occupations and commerce, religion and culture.

Social history has made a significant contribution to biblical studies as Bible scholars have probed the social worlds in which the ancient Hebrews and early Christians lived. Wayne Meeks has been a pioneer in this aspect of biblical studies.[1] Also, some liturgists, John Baldovin among them, have shown an interest in the social historical setting of the liturgy.[2]

Liturgical study as a whole may actually be viewed as one aspect of the social history of a community of faith, since it studies what the people of God have done when they have gathered in public assemblies to do their work of worship and proclamation before God and the world and with one another. Liturgical studies also include rites of passage such as initiation, vocation, marriage, and death, which are very much a part of the social history of a people.

However, liturgical studies have tended to concentrate on official rites. The liturgical books alone may not tell us about the people who did their liturgy or how they did it. If social history is about the structures of everyday life with the politics left out (surely a tongue-in-cheek definition), then a social history of the liturgy is more about the politics of worship than about the structures liturgists have usually studied—not the social structures but the liturgical structures. By liturgical structures, I mean orders, texts, rubrics, and so on. In a social history of the liturgy, the orders, texts, and rubrics are important only insofar as they affect the behavior of the worshiping people, either positively (in terms of faith formation) or negatively (in terms of provoking reaction). In other words, a social history of the liturgy is more concerned with what the orders, texts, and rubrics meant to the people who used them than what they mean in themselves. We know that certain texts, actions, and symbols rallied the people to the defense of their faith, as did the use of icons during the iconoclastic controversy in the Byzantine Empire. In other instances, the imposition of official liturgy was met with hostility, if not outright resistance, by the people—for instance, the rebellion in Devonshire and Cornwall against the prayer book of King Edward VI.

I have already written a major history of the liturgy that primarily analyzes documents.[3] The studies in this book try, as far as possible, to inquire about who used those documents and how they were used. What was actually done in liturgical assemblies that may have used (or not used) the official texts or observed (or not observed) the official rubrics? What cultural expressions influenced liturgical rites, and what were the social consequences of the liturgies that were performed? This kind of data is much more difficult to get at, because how liturgy was actually performed or received is not something one will find in official liturgical books. We can observe today that liturgies can be performed quite differently in different congregations, even though these congregations use the same worship book. What makes the worship of each assembly unique is not so much the material they use as the way they use it.

A focus on liturgical books does tell us something about the people who produced and used them, but it doesn't tell us everything. It may not always tell us the most interesting things about liturgy as it was actually done. Moreover, some liturgical books that are important to study may never have been used in actual assemblies. For example, much attention has been given to the liturgical material in ancient church orders such as *The Didache*, *The Apostolic Tradition* attributed to Hippolytus of Rome, and *The Apostolic Constitutions*. Yet many liturgical scholars have questioned whether these were actual liturgies that were actually used in actual assemblies. More likely they were model liturgies compiled by authors who disagreed with what was being done in liturgical assemblies.

Liturgical Books and Liturgical Practice

The result of textual preoccupation is that we miss much of what is actually happening in the liturgical assembly, since assemblies do not always or strictly follow the script. Let me give several examples of things that we know were or are actually done in liturgies but for which there is no provision in official books:

- No medieval missal has a rubric calling for the passing and kissing of the pax board, yet it was one of the most popular features of the late medieval mass in England and France.

- In recent years, the Advent wreath with its four candles, lit progressively on the four Sundays of Advent, was brought from private homes into the public assembly and has become the subject of much liturgical catechesis. Yet none of the official worship books have, up until now, had rubrics calling for the use of an Advent wreath in the liturgy.

- Special music not provided for in the rubrics is added to a service in various places within the order.

- Special events occur within the liturgy that may be a major focus for that day but are not mentioned in worship books. In the case of special music or special events, however, worship bulletins would mention them and their location within the order of service. Worship bulletins have really become primary sources for the study of liturgy, since today many congregations use folders rather than worship books.

While rubrics in official worship books are often observed in the breach, sometimes we need to pay closer attention to rubrics in order to appreciate how liturgy was actually performed. For example, liturgy in ancient Rome, Constantinople, Jerusalem, and other cities was stational liturgy; it involved processions from one place to another, during which psalms and litanies were sung.[4] Historically, liturgy is not necessarily confined to one place, even within a church building. Historic liturgies of the East and West had a processional character. Processional liturgy survived into the Middle Ages. "Beating of bounds" of the parish by a procession around the perimeter of the parish territory during the three Rogation Days before Ascension Day while singing the Great Litany was such a popular feature of late medieval English life that it survived the Protestant Reformation.[5] It matters that liturgical material once used while the congregation was walking is now used while it remains standing (or sitting) in place. The whole dynamic associated with use of the textual material is changed.

Not only do we miss popular elements in the liturgy if we look only at the orders and texts or fail to study the rubrics carefully enough, but we also miss the dynamics of liturgical change—and how changes were received by the people—when we stick too closely to the liturgical script. For example, recent studies have shown how often the liturgical reforms of the Reformation were simply imposed on the people. This also puts the so-called conservatism of a Martin Luther or a King Gustav Vasa of Sweden into perspective; their desire to "go slow" with reform so as not to put people in "bad faith" (Luther) or provoke them to revolt (Gustav Vasa) may have been a pragmatic rather than an ideological conservatism. Not all reformers, kings, or pastors restrained their enthusiasm to replace old orders with new ones. Yet liturgy has a basic conservative character, as many leaders have discovered to their regret when they try to effect change too precipitously. The liturgy really is "the people's work," and the people have ways of guarding what belongs to them.

The story of Christian liturgy has seldom been told from the perspective of the worshiping people. This is understandable. They didn't prepare the liturgical texts or organize the liturgical actions. But we can take the data we have about the community and see what kind of social group that community was. For example, early Christian assemblies that met in members' homes to celebrate banquets such as were common in the Greco-Roman world (i.e., symposia) give us a very different impression of Christian worship than ancient communities that met in a public hall (i.e., basilica) to celebrate "awesome mysteries." Sometimes lay people and clergy wrote down what they witnessed and experienced. For example, the Spanish nun Egeria kept a diary of her pilgrimage to the Holy Land in the fourth century, and Bishop John Chrysostom of Constantinople often complained about the deportment of the people during the liturgy.

The Character of Social History

Social history—reconstructing how something might actually have been done in an earlier period in history—requires a bit of imagination. This is because historical sources don't always spell out everything that a historian might need in order to be able to reconstruct an event and tell what its actors did. Certainly the historian wants to avoid being imaginary while being imaginative. But I don't believe one can go too far wrong by extrapolating from human behavior as we experience it today to human behavior in earlier times. Given what we know about the dynamics of social behavior from the studies of the behavioral sciences, it is highly likely that people in earlier times acted similarly to the ways people act today.

Also, because social history describes the ordinary life of the people, it has appealed to Marxist historians. When Marxists have written social history, because of their view of history as a process of class struggle, they have used the history to oppose the daily life and aspirations of ordinary people to the people's rulers or political leaders. Thus, social history in the hands of such authors as Vilhelm Moberg[6] or Howard Zinn[7] became a history of these nations from the obverse perspective of the usual histories; it is history written "from below" rather than "from above." Instead of glorifying kings, Moberg championed peasants. The kings, in fact, received a bad rap. Instead of chronicling the efforts of plutocratic political leaders, Zinn told the stories of Native Americans and slaves, of women and laborers of all nationalities. But social history does not have to be written only from a Marxist perspective; one of my seminary professors, Arthur Vööbus, an ardent anti-Communist, wrote a social history of the Estonian people[8] that tells the story of a culturally suppressed and politically oppressed people struggling against a succession of foreign occupiers of their land.

In some situations, the people and their local leaders are actually in the same situation vis-à-vis higher authorities. This is often the situation of parish pastors and their congregations. Eamon Duffy's story of the priest and people of Morebath during the vicissitudes of the English Reformation is an example of this.[9] With each change of royal administration, there were liturgical changes. The priest and people of Morebath held on to as much of the tradition as they could as the country moved from being lavishly Catholic to starkly Protestant during the tenure of Sir (as English priests were called) Christopher Trychay from 1530–1580. The story of the priest and people of Morebath may have been replicated thousands of times across northern Europe, since there was not a wholesale change in parish clergy during the Reformation.

A third quality of social histories is that they have often depended on a binary opposition. They contrast the oppressed with the oppressors, the "people" (e.g., peasants, proletariat, subjects) with the "elite" (e.g., landowners, employers, conquerors). In writing a social history of the liturgy, one could follow the same model and contrast the laity with the clergy, or popular religion with official liturgy. Where these contrasts are noteworthy, I will note them. But it would also be misleading to identify official liturgy with the clergy and popular religion with the laity. That would falsify history. The people have never lacked a role in the liturgy, not even in the height of the Western Middle Ages, and the clergy, from popes down to parish priests, have promoted popular devotions. For these reasons, I don't approach the social history of the liturgy with a series of binary oppositions. I know from personal experience that the performance of liturgy can and often has degenerated into a tug-of-war between competing offices and factions in the church (e.g., clergy versus musicians, adherents of traditional liturgy versus promoters of contemporary worship, bishops versus liturgical reformers). Yet I also know from experience that—thankfully—this does not have to be the case.

Whose Liturgy?

It is perhaps also necessary to assert that Christian liturgy as acts of rite and prayer instituted by Jesus the Christ and inspired by the Holy Spirit in the history of the church is also the work of God (*opus Dei*), that in fact it is the work of God's people only because it is the work of God. It is a work done in faith. The people assemble to hear words that are God's word and to celebrate signs that are Christ's sacraments. Precisely because it is a "divine liturgy," no group or individual within the assembly should "own" the liturgy or "control" it. When there is an attempt on the part of a group to wrest control of the liturgy for doctrinal or ideological purposes, worship wars can result. In the annals of history, these worship wars could be real wars or occasions of civil strife, such as the great iconoclastic controversy that ripped apart the Byzantine Empire in the eighth century or the Cornishmen's revolt against the prayer book of King Edward VI in 1548, which I have already mentioned. Even the English Civil War was a contest between

Anglican "episcopalian" prayer book users and Anglican "puritan" anti-prayer-book churchmen.

A reliable social history of the liturgy will be sensitive to and record instances of conflict within the liturgical assembly in the effort to "control" the liturgy for doctrinal or ideological purposes. But we do not have to assume that there are always conflicts over control of the liturgy. It would be false both to historical data and to ordinary experience to present the social history of the liturgy as a continuing class struggle in the church. It would also be false to ignore the impact of clergy-lay divisions on liturgical performance and participation. The clergy did come to the point of dominating the performance of the liturgy. The hierarchy did find ways of controlling the liturgy in order to fence it off from false doctrine or excessive piety. But the more interesting story is how the people found ways of claiming their rightful place in the assembly and participating according to their inclinations and means of expression. So, for example, we have conventionally assumed that the people were shut out of the official liturgy in the Western Middle Ages and therefore turned to paraliturgical devotions. But we will see that they also figured out how they could participate actively in the liturgy without requiring speaking parts.

Because social history sometimes relies on the tools and insights of anthropology and sociology, it is often regarded as reductionistic when applied to Christianity. I have no bias against a theological approach to the study of liturgy. Liturgy, like any phenomenon, yields whatever we are looking for when we study it. If we are looking for theological meaning, we will find it in liturgical structures and texts, as I demonstrated in *New Creation: A Liturgical Worldview*. My aim in this work, however, is to venture off the beaten path of documentary studies to explore the impact of the people on the performance of their "public work," by means of which they signified their hopes and aspirations, expressed their devotion to God, and acted out their human relationships in the presence of the Judge of all.

It is perhaps also necessary to say that my treatment of the church, the *ekklesia*, as a social body in this study does not mean that I don't acknowledge its theological meaning as the mystical body of Christ. With the eminent ecclesiologist Jean-Marie-Roger Tillard, who has promoted a communion ecclesiology, I agree that the church is "a graft of communion on the wounded body of humankind."[10] But the dynamics by which the church is established as a fellowship of love through participation in a meal also operate according to observable sociological principles. The incarnational principle of Christian theology suggests that we do not need to avoid observing the way the church really operates as a human institution in order to affirm its meaning as a community created by the Holy Spirit in the image of the Triune God.

The history of the liturgy is vast and multifaceted. The terrain of social history is seemingly limitless. While I have gone through two thousand years of history, one person could not possibly write *"the* social history of the liturgy" or even *"a* social history of the liturgy." Many times and places are not covered, and everything else is covered in a cursory way, since this is a survey rather than an in-depth study of particular times, places, peoples, or practices. I have chosen to follow the historical path I took in *Christian Liturgy—Catholic and Evangelical* because it is a path I already know, perhaps shedding more light on that history in the process. Accordingly, I will look at the social history of the liturgy in the early church, the Western Middle Ages, the Reformation, and modern periods. I have come to see as much continuity as discontinuity between the medieval and Reformation periods and as much discontinuity as continuity between the Reformation and modern periods, and that will be reflected here. Especially in modern times (from the seventeenth century on), it is exceedingly difficult to do justice to the wide diversity of liturgical traditions and practices on six continents. I have focused on four strains that flow through these centuries: popular religion in Catholicism and Protestantism, the worship awakenings of revivalism, romantic liturgical restoration, and the modern liturgical renewal movement. Because life goes on, I conclude with a brief sketch of a new movement that is under way in some parts of the world: postmodern liturgical retrieval.

Given my limited time and accessibility to libraries to do research as a parish pastor, I can only paint a picture using broad strokes. I invite others to color in the details of particular traditions and local worshiping communities.

CHAPTER 1

Sociologically Speaking, What Kind of Group Was the Christian Assembly?

Modern scholarship commonly holds that Christianity began as a Jewish sect in the cities and villages of Judea and Galilee in the first century *annos Domini* (A.D.) or in the years of the Common Era (C.E.). However, we need to understand what we mean by "sect." When the nineteenth-century sociologists Max Weber and Ernst Troeltsch first began using the term *sect*, they opposed it to *church*. A sect was defined as a deviant group within a cohesive religious culture. But first-century Judaism bears little resemblance to "church," especially if one has in mind the model of Christendom. No one particular Jewish group dominated the land of Israel in the monopolistic way that the state churches dominated European territories. Some Jews at the time of Jesus belonged to parties called the Sadducees (a priestly aristocracy), the Pharisees (students of the Torah who dominated the synagogues), the Essenes (a quasi-monastic "sanctuary for Israel"), and the Zealots (a nationalist party);[1] undoubtedly many Jews adhered to none of these parties. Within the spectrum of Jewish life, Christians—who confessed their founder, Jesus, to be the Jewish Messiah—took their place as one party among others. They shared certain convictions with all Jewish parties, were allied with some parties in some of their views, and had their own unique beliefs. But this could be said of every one of the Jewish parties. So if Christianity is to be identified as a Jewish sect at the time of its origin, we must have a different definition of sect than that given by Weber and Troeltsch.

One possible definition is presented in the analysis of Peter Berger, who observed, "The attitude toward the world largely determines the inner social structure of the sect."[2] In other words, Berger defines a sect in terms of its relationship vis-à-vis the world rather than vis-à-vis the dominant religious group. Under this definition, Christianity would be classified as a sect not because of its opposition to other Jewish parties in the land of Israel, such as the Pharisees or the Sadducees, but because of its attitude toward the world, including the worlds of Judaism, Hellenism, and Rome. Under this definition, the Essenes may also be classified as a sect, while the Pharisees and the Sadducees are not because they were more accommodating to the world. Jewish Christianity, or rather the Christian Jews for whom the Gospel of Matthew was written, lived in the same relationship to the Jewish, Hellenistic, and Roman worlds as the Essenes. In a sect, under this definition, the boundary between the pure community and the impure world is clearly defined, and one crosses into the community of the elect by a rite of initiation. Baptism served as the Christian rite of initiation. It was different from the Pharisees' immersion rite (*mikvah*) in that it constituted a one-time, permanent rite of passage; the Essenes likewise had an elaborate ceremony for entering the covenant, described in *The Rule of the Community* (1QS) and another document (CD) found among the Dead Sea Scrolls.[3] Besides a special initiation rite, the Christian sect practiced a ritual meal called the Lord's Supper, which bore similarities to other Jewish meals yet had its own distinct meanings. In addition, Christianity differed from other Jewish parties in its attitude toward the Sabbath, circumcision, kosher dietary laws, and tithing, which seemed to range from a more casual observance to outright abolition in the Christian assemblies that embraced Gentiles.[4]

Perhaps most significantly for future Jewish-Christian relationships, Christianity made no worldly territorial claims.[5] The very fact that Christians reached out intentionally to include the Gentiles (as opposed to simply receiving God-fearing Gentiles into Israel by circumcision and *mikvah*) also set apart Christianity from other Jewish parties. Eventually, Christianity would be dominated by Gentile congregations, and the Jewish congregations would be totally eclipsed. But as it emerged into the Greco-Roman world, Christianity was perceived as a Jewish messianic sect.

A Jewish Messianic Sect

Christianity may be regarded as a Jewish sect because it shared with other Jews a belief in one God, the God of Abraham, Isaac, and Jacob, the God who gave his Torah to Moses on Sinai. Christians shared with other Jews a body of sacred writings, which they read in their assemblies and studied. Christians believed that the God of Israel was also the Lord of the universe who guides human history and becomes involved in human affairs. This was the same God whom their teacher, Jesus, called *Abba*, "Father," and who designated Jesus as "Son" at his baptism by John.

Christians were not unique in believing that their teacher, Jesus, was a prophet, even the final prophet and, in fact, the Jewish Messiah, born of the house of David. Josephus, in his *Antiquities*, tells us there were many prophets and would-be messiahs who appeared in Galilee, Samaria, and Judea between the time of Herod the Great's death in 4 B.C.E. and the outbreak of the Roman-Jewish War in 66 C.E. These prophets and messiahs were routinely executed by Roman procurators as troublemakers, and their followers scattered. There is only one reason why the sect of the Nazarene stood out from the others that flourished briefly in the first century: it survived. It survived the execution of its teacher because God raised Jesus from the dead. As Luke reports Peter saying to the crowds on the Day of Pentecost, "This Jesus God raised up, and of that all of us are witnesses. . . . Therefore let the entire house of Israel know with certainty that God has made him both Lord and Messiah, this Jesus whom you crucified" (Acts 2:32, 36).

Jesus' career had begun as a prophet who typically called Israel to repentance. "Now after John [the Baptist] was arrested, Jesus came to Galilee, proclaiming the good news of God, and saying, 'The time is fulfilled, and the kingdom of God has come near'" (Mark 1:15). But Jesus identified the message of God's kingdom with himself: "Those who are ashamed of me and of my words in this adulterous and sinful generation, of them the Son of Man will also be ashamed when he comes in the glory of his Father with the holy angels" (Mark 8:38). For the disciples of Jesus, it was not enough to carry on his teachings; they also had to confess him as Messiah (Mark 8:27–29; Matthew 16:13–20; Luke 9:18–20). Jesus' death and resurrection brought about a crisis moment (*kairos*) to which his fellow Israelites had to respond. Nascent Christianity stood against the world not only in teaching the values of the kingdom of God, which reverse the conventional values of this world, but also against the Jewish world in calling people to faith in Jesus as Messiah. In whatever ways Christianity shared some of the apocalyptic "contempt for the world" characteristics of the Essenes, it differed from the Essenes in that it did not withdraw from the world but actively proselytized with a message of hope in the future that God would bring about, a future that was already inaugurated in the resurrection of Jesus. Christians shared with the Pharisees belief in the resurrection of the dead, but differed in that their Lord Jesus was already raised from the dead and therefore the future is beginning now.

Luke gives us in Acts 2–5 a picture of the worship of these Jewish Christians. The most striking point in Luke's account is the continuing participation of these sectarians in the worship of the Jerusalem Temple, although there is no mention of their participation in the sacrificial cult. At the same time, they gathered in homes for teaching and fellowship, to celebrate "the breaking of bread," the Eucharistic meal instituted by Jesus in which they continued to experience the presence of the risen Lord among them, and for prayer. But in the same community of Aramaic-speaking Jewish Christians were Greek-speaking Jewish Christians, who, if the example of Stephen is typical, were hostile to the temple (Acts 6–8). Stephen, at his trial, indicates a critical attitude toward the law, while we see in the Jewish Christian communities of Palestine a continuing commitment to fasting, observance of the Sabbath, circumcision, and ritual purity.[6]

Jewish Christianity was centered in Jerusalem, where it was headed by James, the brother of the Lord. The family of Jesus ruled the Jerusalem church. James's successor was Simeon, the son of Cleopas, a cousin of the Lord. On the whole, relations between the Christians and their fellow Jews in Jerusalem were amicable. But things came to an impasse over the response of the Christians to the defense of Jerusalem in the Roman-Jewish War (66–70). Because of the example of Jesus in advancing God's reign in signs and wonders among Gentiles as well as Jews in Galilee, Christians could not share with their fellow Jews a nationalistic zeal for the defense of Jerusalem when zealotry provoked a war with the Romans. The Gospel of Mark, written around the time of the Roman-Jewish War, has Jesus warn his followers, "When you see the desolating sacrilege set up where it ought not to be (let the reader understand), then those in Judea must flee to the mountains" (Mark 13:14). Many Jews in Palestine had no interest in fighting a war against the Romans, which they did not believe could be won. Flavius Josephus, most famously, defected to the Roman side. But when the Jewish population of Jerusalem banded together to defend the city, Simeon led the Christians of Jerusalem to Pella in Trans-Jordan. Jewish Christian refugees from Judea also headed to Galilee, to Antioch in Syria, and to Alexandria in Egypt, where there were already large Jewish communities. It needs to be stressed that the Christians who emigrated to these Jewish centers were also Jews.

It was for these Christian Jews that the Gospel of Matthew was written.[7] This Gospel could have originated in any of these locations because it reflects a rivalry with the religion of the scribes and Pharisees who were engaged in reconstituting Jewish religious life after the destruction of the temple by the Romans in 70 C.E. (see also the teachings of Jesus in Matthew 5:17–6:16). The rivalry between the Christian scribes and those who "love . . . being called rabbis" (23:6–7) became especially hostile between 70 and 90 and is reflected in Matthew 23, which has no counterpart in any other Gospel. The separation of Christians from the synagogue was made official by the inclusion of a malediction against "Christians and heretics" in the great prayer (*Tefillah*) of the synagogue, variously called Eighteen Benedictions (*Shemoneh 'esreh*) or Standing (*'Amidah*).[8] The intensity of polemic in this Gospel against the Sadducees as well as the Pharisees (22:23–32) argues strongly for its provenance in northern Palestine, where some of the priestly aristocracy settled in Tiberias and Sepphoris after the destruction of Jerusalem and struggled with the scribes over the future of the Jewish liturgy, although the more common scholarly opinion places the provenance of the Gospel of Matthew in Antioch. The priests promoted *Tefillah*, and the scribes promoted *Shema* with its blessings (*berakoth*).[9] The criticism of the hypocrites who "love to stand and pray in the synagogues and at the street corners" (6:7) may be a reference to *Tefillah 'Amidah* ("standing"). Against this and the orations of the pagan Gentiles (6:7), Jesus teaches his disciples how to pray (6:9–13). It is from the Gospel of Matthew that we have the text of the Lord's Prayer with its balanced parallelism as it came to be used in Christian worship and devotion. The emphasis on "making disciples" in the Gospel of Matthew reflects an intense instructional program, seen especially in chapters 5–7 (the "Sermon on the Mount"). Matthew 18 also reflects a disciplinary process typical of a tightly controlled sect.

The text of the Lord's Prayer with its concluding doxology is also found in another document that originated in a Jewish Christian community: the *Didache*, or *Teaching of the Twelve* (see 8:2).[10] This early church order was probably written around the end of the first century and either draws on material in Matthew or utilizes material that was also used in Matthew (especially in chapters 1–6).[11] It also tries to distinguish Christian practice from Jewish, even though the practices are similar; for example, Christians should fast on Wednesdays and Fridays because "the hypocrites" fast on Mondays and Thursdays (8:1). The *Didache* is a priceless treasure trove of Jewish Christian practices of catechesis, baptism, and the Eucharist. The eucharistic prayers in chapters 9–10 are so typical of the Jewish prayers before and after meals that they have been studied by Jewish scholars interested in establishing the forms of these prayers before the compilations of the Mishnah.[12]

The outflow of Christian leaders from Judea led to a tradition of traveling apostles, prophets, and teachers. Itinerant Christian prophets and teachers (who should be distinguished from the apostles and evangelists sent out by churches to found other churches, such as Paul, Barnabas, and Silas) went from being honored to being tolerated to being regarded as nuisances or worse; hence the warnings against "false prophets and apostles" in the Gospels. *Didache* 11 and 15 admonishes the Christian community to welcome apostles and prophets with proper hospitality and even give them the privilege of presiding at the Eucharist, but to put a time limit on their stay (three days) and not to despise the residential bishops and deacons elected by the community, who should enjoy a place of honor along with the itinerant prophets and teachers.

It is uncertain how long Jewish Christianity flourished. Jewish Christian congregations flourished in Bethlehem, Hebron, and Nazareth, in Pella in Trans-Jordan, and in Syria and Egypt. Elsewhere, their influence was eclipsed by the growth of Gentile Christianity. Jewish Christians living in Trans-Jordan and in eastern Syria lost touch with the mainline church and often by default embraced "heretical" positions. For example, the Ebionites took daily baths for purification, used unleavened bread and water in the Eucharist (rejecting wine), held a dualistic view of spirit and matter, and regarded Christ as the true prophet assisted by an archangel.[13] It may be that the Letters of Ignatius of Antioch (c. 110) reflect the concern of the Gentile church, emerging into dominance, about these teachings of Jewish Christianity, now considered aberrant.

In Syria a flourishing literature in Syriac (a language related to Aramaic) had a Gnostic cast; these works include the *Gospel of Thomas*, the *Acts of Thomas*, and the *Odes of Solomon*. Also in Syria, the ascetic features of sectarian Christianity emerged in the tradition of hermits, who practiced separation from the world. In the *Gospel of Thomas*, this meant separation from normal social functions, such as sex, family, commerce and money, and even the conventions of honor and shame (see saying 37). To "enter the kingdom of God," one must be "solitary" (see sayings 16, 23, 30, and 76). An ethos that had defined apocalyptic sectarianism became a means of personal salvation. Ascetic Christian solitaries flourished in eastern Syria already in the second century.[14] The aim of the first holy men was to be perfect, to live in "the ranks of angels." At first they lived on the edges of towns, but as more people visited their hermitages to seek advice, inspiration, arbitration, and healing, they began to move farther out. The object of the hermits was to escape the world. By the fourth century, they moved into the desert to escape the world in the church.

Some Christians returned to Jerusalem after the Roman-Jewish War, but they were expelled from Jerusalem along with all Jews after the Bar Kochba rebellion in 135. Emperor Hadrian had a new city built on the site of Jerusalem, Aelia Capitolina, which was dedicated to the Roman gods and goddesses. Christians from elsewhere came to Aelia as tradespeople to work on the construction site, but these were Gentiles. These Gentile Christians developed an interest in the site of Jesus' Last Supper on Mount Sion. They referred to the house of the Upper Room as the "Mother of the churches" and were allowed to assemble there because it was outside the city walls.[15] These new Christian settlers of Aelia also ventured to other sites connected with the life of Jesus, such as the site of his birth in Bethlehem and the cave of his burial and resurrection on the Mount of Olives. The development of a Christian interest in Jerusalem and the Holy Land came from Greco-Roman Christians, including the learned third-century Christian exegete and teacher Origen, who still referred to the heavenly Jerusalem as "the mother of us all."[16]

A Greco-Roman Household

Christianity, from its beginnings, was an urban religion. Jesus himself was from the village of Nazareth, located on the trade route from Damascus to the Mediterranean coast. Nazareth was a satellite village of Sepphoris, a splendid "model city" about one hour's walk away, built by Herod Antipas. It is possible that as carpenters, Joseph and Jesus worked at construction sites in Sepphoris, since the project was enormous and would have required all the skilled labor the region could supply.[17] There is no evidence that Jesus was affected by the Greco-Roman culture, except to contrast the lifestyle of a Herodian ruler with that of John the Baptist (Luke 7:25; see also Matthew 11:8). In spite of agrarian and nomadic images in his parables and sayings, Jesus himself was not a peasant, nor is it likely that Jesus attracted much of a peasant or "proletarian" following.[18] Jesus' trade (it was not uncommon for rabbis to have a trade) gave him some mobility, since tradesmen went where their skills were needed, as we see also in the example of the Apostle Paul, who was a tentmaker. Not many Galilean farmers or Judean shepherds were able to follow him because their livelihood depended on working the land and herding their flocks. The same was true of the fishermen Jesus called as his disciples; they had to leave their nets and boats in order to follow Jesus (although the Gospel records indicate that family members were left to carry on this lucrative industry, and these disciples returned to this business after the resurrection). Jesus' travels took him from town to town in Galilee. The Gospel of John reports three journeys to Jerusalem during Jesus' three-year ministry, not just the final journey reported in the Synoptic Gospels. The post-resurrection church used Jerusalem as a headquarters until the Roman-Jewish War. When Christianity spread, it was to other cities, including Damascus and Antioch in West Syria.

What was true about Jesus was even more true of Saul of Tarsus, who became Paul the apostle. Wayne Meeks has mapped the social world of Apostle Paul.[19] Paul hailed from the port city of Tarsus and was familiar with the urban culture of the Greco-Roman world. He used the military highways built by Rome and the sea lanes to take the gospel from place to place. He founded congregations in major port cities like Ephesus (Asia Minor), military posts like Philippi (Macedonia), and commercial centers like Corinth (Greece). It has been estimated that there was more long-distance travel in the first several centuries of the Roman Empire than at any other time in history before the nineteenth century. People traveled for business. For example, Paul met Lydia, a dealer in purple goods, in Philippi (Macedonia), but she was from Thyratira (Asia Minor) (Acts 16:14).

Something of the social mobility of the period is indicated in the fact that Lydia was a woman running her own business. Admittedly, it was a textile business. Women could operate such a business out of their own homes. Greek women did not usually play a public role in civil life (the Ptolemaic queens of Egypt being a notable exception). Nevertheless, women in Greco-Roman society did acquire business skills by managing the affairs of their household, which might include supervising slaves and keeping accounts. The primary outlet for women outside the home in both Greek and Roman society was participating in religious festivals and serving as priestesses in the cults of gods and goddesses, the most famous of whom were the Vestal Virgins in Rome. But Michael Grant showed that women were progressively liberated in Roman society so that they could even enter the civil arena to study law and politics in spite of the conservative social attitudes of prominent figures like Augustus and Virgil. In fact, women would not again achieve the emancipation they enjoyed in Roman society until modern times.[20]

The House Church

The primary social unit of Greco-Roman society was the household. The book of Acts indicates that when Paul and his missionary companions encountered hostility in synagogues, and even when they didn't, they often took up residence in the households of individuals: Lydia in Philippi (16:15), Jason in Thessalonica (17:5–9), and Prisca and Aquila in Corinth (18:2–4). The meeting places of Pauline congregations, as of other congregations, were in private houses. House churches mentioned include those in the homes of Gaius (Romans 16:23; 1 Corinthians 1:14), Crispus or Stephanus (1 Corinthians 1:14, 16), Prisca and Aquila with homes in Corinth and Rome (1 Corinthians 16:19; Romans 16:5), and Philemon, Apphia, and Archippus (Philemon 2). Four times in Paul's letters, he refers to "the church (*ekklesia* = assembly) at so-and-so's house" (*he kat' oikon*). It may be that the nucleus of a church was a household. But households in Greco-Roman society could be quite extensive, including immediate relatives, slaves, freedmen clients, hired workers, and sometimes tenants or partners in a trade or craft. It was not always the case that everyone in a household would convert to Christianity; sometimes one's spouse, a slave's master, or a master's slave remained pagan. But often the sense of social solidarity prompted all or most members of the household to embrace the cult of the head of the household. We read in Acts of a whole household receiving baptism (16:25–34). In such situations, not everyone held Christian convictions to the same degree, which probably explains why Paul's letters are so full of admonitions and exhortations.

We might wonder how large the congregations assembled in private homes could be. The number of people living in a Roman household of even moderate means could be large. Dinner parties of thirty to forty guests were not uncommon. If all the guests did not fit in the typical Roman dining room (called the *triclinium*, with reference to three couches, on each of which three guests could recline), the extra seating (or reclining) could spill into the peristyle or into open gardens. Larger homes of patrician families with spacious open gardens could accommodate as many as the two thousand guests that Cicero testifies he once fed.[21]

Determining the social background of the early generations of Christians has not been an exact science, but it is apparent that Christianity appealed to all social classes—many *humiliores* (the poor), some *potentiores* (the politically-connected), and even a few *honestiores* (respectable citizens)[22]—since Apostle Paul testifies to the clashes between social classes in the celebration of the Lord's Supper at Corinth. There must have been some *honestiores* among Christians with sufficient means to serve as patrons of the church and whose homes could accommodate congregations of considerable size. Prisca and Aquila, who owned houses in Asia and in Rome, may have been among them.

The greater freedom of women to participate in religious cults in Greco-Roman society contrasts with the more restricted role of women in the Jewish synagogue. Paul, as a Greek-speaking Jew with a Pharisaic education who held Roman citizenship, might have been conflicted about this, and it shows in the First Letter to the Corinthians. In 1 Corinthians 11:2–16, a passage devoted to the veiling of women, Paul mentions that women are not forbidden to pray or to prophesy in the public assembly (11:5). Prisca (Priscilla) was accorded a role in the assembly on the basis of her gifts (1 Corinthians 16:19; Romans 16:3; Acts 18:2, 18, 26), even taking precedence over her husband Aquila (Romans 16:3; Acts 18:18, 26). This license to pray and preach publicly does not remove creaturely differences, since Paul still requires that women wear a veil. On the other hand, in 1 Corinthians 14:34–35, Paul states that women are not allowed to speak in the churches but are to be subordinate and may ask questions of their husbands at home. This seems to represent a Judaizing tendency out of sync with the charismatic Greek assembly at Corinth, and one may wonder if this passage is authentically Paul.

One possible reason for the diminishing leadership role of women in the Gentile church by the second century may be not only a re-Judaizing but the prominence of women in Gnostic circles. Among Gnostic groups such as the Valentinians, as well as among the Marcionites and Montanists, women were equal with men and could hold all offices in the Gnostic conventicles, perhaps even that of bishop.[23] Orthodox Christians reacted as we see in 1 Timothy 2:11–15.

In 1 Corinthians 14, Paul dwells on "order" in worship, even to the point of curtailing speaking in tongues if no one is present to interpret the message. Paul assigns more importance to prophesying than to glossalalia and to lucid speech than to ecstatic. Here we might remember the social context. Even large cities tended to squeeze their populations into a small area. Ramsey MacMullen estimates that the average population density in cities of the Roman Empire was two hundred per acre. He further calculates that about one-fourth of the area of typical cities was given over to public facilities.[24] Life was crowded, and not much happened that escaped the notice of the neighbors. This situation undoubtedly influenced Paul's concerns in 1 Corinthians 14 that things be done "decently and in order," not only to avoid scandal, but also to appeal to potential converts with the gospel.

A Cultic Association

Another possible sociological model for the early church was the cultic association or club that flourished in Greco-Roman cities. Clubs and associations abounded in the Greco-Roman world.[25] These clubs existed as religious guilds, trade guilds, dining clubs, and funerary associations. In Rome they were often called *collegia* and could be public or private clubs.

Wayne Meeks analyzes similarities and differences between the voluntary club and the Christian assembly.[26] Both the clubs and the church were voluntary groups that gathered around a particular purpose rather than a social relationship. Burial associations, for example, were popular among slaves and the lower classes, because monthly dues provided a way of arranging for decent burials of association members. Some of the Greek clubs seem to have originated as means for sharing the costs of a sacrifice, especially if the deity being honored was not included in state sacrifices and festivals.[27] The banquet was a feature of all clubs and associations. Thus, both the church and the clubs could be devoted to the worship of a deity. Many clubs, like the churches, depended on the benefactions of a patron (or patroness). In contrast, membership in the church was by a process of initiation that entailed a resocialization and reorientation.[28]

The Christian assemblies were stricter in their membership requirements but also broader in their membership in terms of including people from all social classes. Also, many of the terms of officeholders and functions in the clubs are missing in Pauline terminology, except for the positions of *episkopos* (overseer) and *diakonos* (waiter) (Philippians 1:1; Romans 16:1). In the case of *diakonos*, the office of deacon, as it developed in the church, was broader than its use in the meal clubs. Where Roman influence was strong, as in Corinth and its port city of Cenchreae, *diakonos* may have meant *patronus*. This may be the sense in which the term is applied to Phoebe in the masculine form (Romans 16:2) because women could also be patrons of clubs or associations.

The club or cultic association was a model that could be used by Gentile Christians. It was not unrelated to a household, but it transcended family relationships. The Christian assembly did not offer sacrifices, as did some cultic associations, but it did have the eucharistic meal. It did not engage in public processions or sponsor public festivals, as some clubs did, but by the second century, Christians had learned because of intermittent persecution not to call undue attention to themselves. The Christian assembly did not practice esoteric initiation rites like those of the mystery cults, but it did have a rite of initiation in baptism. Whether or not Christians saw themselves as forming a club, it is clear that some Roman officials saw Christians as forming such a group. From time to time, Roman officials banned the meetings of clubs and associations because of the riotous behavior that often followed drinking parties or their potentially subversive character. In a letter to Emperor Trajan (c. 112), Pliny the Younger, the Roman governor of Asia, relates that the Christians he had interrogated reported that they gathered before daybreak "to recite a hymn antiphonally to Christ, as to a god," and again later in the day to partake of "ordinary and harmless food," but "they had ceased this practice after my edict in which, in accordance with your orders, I had forbidden secret societies."[29] There is evidence of other bans or restrictions on clubs.[30]

The fact that the banning of supper clubs affected Christian practice, perhaps relocating the Eucharist from the evening to the morning, suggests that some Christians were meeting as a cultic association. Dinner parties in private houses would not have been banned. Yet not all houses would have been large enough to accommodate growing assemblies. Coming together as a club or association and renting a dining hall provided one possibility. Public dining facilities would have been available to clubs and associations in taverns, inns, and outdoor gardens, as well as in temple complexes in which cultic associations met to eat. According to 1 Corinthians 8:10, Christians were invited to join dinner parties in pagan temples, where the participants would eat the meat sacrificed to idols, a practice Paul discouraged because it would have put the weak in bad faith. "Secular" dining facilities also were available, but it is uncertain whether Christians would have rented such facilities as inns and taverns, especially during a time of persecution or out of concern to protect a reputation for sobriety. Some clubs had their own facilities.

In contrast, Christians were not likely to be molested in cemeteries, since Romans respected burial and funeral customs. A Christian Eucharist celebrated on the grave of a deceased Christian would look to the Romans like the *refrigerium* (meal for the dead), and the church would look like a burial society. In fact, Christians could constitute a burial society and even take over certain cemeteries. The famous catacombs, or burial chambers, in Rome were acquired by Christians from previous pagan owners some time in the third century, reflecting a fashionable shift to Christianity among the middle classes as well as a place of refuge in times of persecution.

A Synagogue or School

Both in Palestine and in the Greco-Roman cities, it would be natural for Christianity, as an offshoot of Judaism, to organize itself as a synagogue. Synagogues flourished in the Jewish Diaspora. According to the book of Acts, Paul often went to the local synagogue first when he arrived in a new city. Yet, ironically, the term *synagogue* is not used in Paul's letters. In fact, it is used only in James 2:2 and Hebrews 10:25 to designate a Christian gathering for worship, and both letters are addressed to Jewish Christians. Some have questioned whether Acts is accurate, since the mission of Paul was to the Gentiles and not to the Jews. Yet he found many of his converts (like Lydia) among the God-fearing Gentiles who attended worship in Jewish synagogues. One may also wonder if the Diaspora synagogues of the early centuries C.E. were quite the imposing institutions we see today in contemporary Judaism. Diaspora Jews probably also gathered initially in private homes, to judge from the synagogues unearthed in Dura-Europas, Stobi, Delos, and elsewhere that were converted from private houses. Christian communities also received private houses that were donated to the congregation as the place of meeting for the *ekklesia*, including the house church discovered in 232 at Dura-Europas on the Roman-Persian frontier where a Roman garrison was stationed. In the plan of this house church, a wall was knocked down to make a room for a gathering of about sixty people. The bathroom had been converted into a baptistery with the walls decorated by mosaics of the three myrrh-bearing women. One room connecting the baptistery and the assembly hall could have been used for teaching catechumens; another room adjoining the assembly hall could have been used as a sacristy.[31] The title churches in the city of Rome (*tituli*) also go back to the time when titles to private houses were turned over to the church.

Christians did not call their places of assembly synagogues, but the name *synaxis* (gathering) was attached to their order of worship by the fourth century, especially for the service of readings, preaching, and prayer, which would have corresponded liturgically to the Jewish Sabbath service. The second-century Mishnah lists five liturgical elements that could not be performed without the presence of a quorum of ten adult males: the recitation of the Shema with its blessings, the recitation of the *Tefillah*, the priestly blessing, the reading of the Torah, and the reading of the Prophets (Megillah 4:3). Scholars have assumed that these constituted the main elements of the Sabbath service. In the churches in the East (especially Syria), the architecture of the church building also reflected that of the synagogue, with a central *bema* on which were seated the bishop and presbyters instead of the rabbi and rulers of the synagogues. But in the apse, which was empty in the synagogue, the Christian churches located the table for the Lord's Supper.[32]

Synagogues were places of study as well as places of prayer. They related to another model of the Christian assembly in Greco-Roman cities: the philosophic school.[33] The Christian assembly was certainly something more than a philosophic school such as those of the Pythagoreans and Epicureans. It is possible that Christian leaders, like philosophers, attracted disciples who kept their work going after their death; New Testament scholars have spoken of a Pauline school as well as a Matthean school and a Johannine school. But there was also a teaching component to the assembly associated especially in catechetical work with converts, which emerges in detail for the first time in *The Apostolic Tradition* attributed to Hippolytus of Rome (c. 215). Robert Wilken suggested that already by the middle of the second century, some Christians gravitated toward the model of the philosophical school as a way of countering the more negative image of Christianity as a new cultic association that would arouse the suspicions of imperial officers.[34] Apologists such as Justin Martyr, Clement of Alexandria, and Origen presented themselves as Christian philosophers. Clement, as head of the catechetical school of Alexandria, turned it into a center of Christian philosophy. Origen made it also a place of biblical scholarship and uncommon exegesis.

A Shadow Empire

Finally, we need to inquire how Christians, who developed a cohesive structure and group identity at the local level, were also conscious of belonging to a global movement "with all who invoke the name of Jesus Christ in every place" (1 Corinthians 1:2). Paul referred to each of his congregations as an *ekklesia*. This term is usually translated as "church," but *church* carries a lot of subsequent baggage that *assembly* lacks. When Paul appropriated the term, its most common use was to refer to the public meeting of the free male citizens of Greco-Roman cities. These assemblies met to acclaim candidates for office and to approve the proposals of city councils, although by the third century, actual elections were rare outside of North Africa.[35] But the term *ekklesia* had also been used in the Greek translation of the Hebrew Bible to render *Qahal Yahweh* ("the assembly of the Lord"), which referred to the gathering of all the tribes of Israel or their representatives. In either case, the term *ekklesia* transcended all the models of Christian community we have discussed: the sect, the household, the cultic association, and the school.

The work of the people that was done in the civic *ekklesia* was called *leitourgia*. The "liturgy" was a public work performed by representatives of the people. It was in this sense that Paul called his work of collecting charitable gifts from the assemblies in Macedonia and Greece for the assembly in Jerusalem a *leitourgia* (2 Corinthians 9:22). Paul also regarded his apostolic service as a *leitourgia* (Romans 15:16; Philippians 2:17). Yet this concept is not devoid of the connotation of the Old

Testament priesthood, since this term is used to describe the sacrificial ministry. The sacrificial gift rendered by Paul to God is the faith of the assembly (Philemon 2:17). Yet the liturgical aspect of the assembly is indicated by the fact that each person contributes his or her gift "for the common good" (1 Corinthians 12:7). In 1 Corinthians 14:26–31, Paul insists on some order in the use of these gifts. Interestingly, in a later letter to the Corinthians from Clement of Rome (c. 96), the word *leitourgia* was applied for the first time to the order of worship: "the sacrifices and services . . . that the Master has bidden us to do at the proper times he set."[36]

The Pauline mission was not just to found local churches; it was also to form a network of local churches that were kept in a conscious relationship with one another. Paul and his delegates visited the churches and sent them letters, which were read aloud in the assembly and were possibly shared from one local *ekklesia* to another. If the opening words of 1 Corinthians refer to "all who invoke the name of our Lord Jesus Christ in every place," the close of the letter also invokes a consciousness of the wider Christian fellowship: "The *ekklesiai* [plural] of Asia greet you; Aquila and Prisca and the *ekklesia* at their house greet you much in the Lord. All the brothers (and sisters) greet you. Greet one another with a holy kiss. I, Paul, greet you in my own hand" (1 Corinthians 16:19–21). This network made it possible for Christians to travel throughout the Roman Empire, equipped with letters of introduction from recognized leaders (such as Paul provided for Phoebe in Romans 16:1-2), and receive hospitality and fellowship in the Christian assembly at that place.

But by the end of the first century, the global fellowship could no longer depend on known leaders in a local assembly who would be recognized by other local assemblies. An office of local leadership was needed. This was provided in the office of overseer or bishop (*episkopos*) that had emerged in Christian associations. The Greco-Roman offices of bishop and servant or deacon (*diakonos*) were merged with the council of elders (*presbyteroi*) who governed the Jewish-Christian congregations. Ignatius, bishop of Antioch, wrote letters to the local assemblies in Asia even as he was being transported to Rome for trial and certain death in the arena, pleading for the recognition of the authority of a single bishop in each place along with the college of presbyters. To the Magnesians, he wrote that they should respect their youthful bishop, Damas. To the Trallians, he wrote, "Everyone must show the deacons respect. They represent Jesus Christ, just as the bishop has the role of the Father, and the presbyters are like God's council and an apostolic band. You cannot have a church without these. I am sure that you agree with me in this."[37] To the Smyrnaeans, he wrote that they could avoid schism if they would

> all follow the bishop as Jesus Christ did the Father. Follow, too, the presbytery as you would the apostles; and respect the deacons as you would God's law. Nobody must do anything that has to do with the Church without the bishop's approval. You should regard that Eucharist as valid which is celebrated either by the bishop or by someone he authorizes. Where the bishop is present, there let the congregation gather, just as where Jesus Christ is, there is the Catholic Church. Without the bishop's supervision, no baptisms or love feasts are permitted. On the other hand, whatever he approves pleases God as well. . . . He who pays the bishop honor has been honored by God. But he who acts without the bishop's knowledge is in the devil's service.[38]

The diversity of Christians within local assemblies throughout the cities of the Roman world required strong leadership that all Christians would recognize and respect. Bishops did not gain this recognition easily. They had to compete for respect with charismatic prophets, visionary Gnostic teachers, holy ascetics living in the deserts, and courageous confessors who were entitled to a seat in the presbyterate by virtue of their public witness to the faith. There was no comparable model of leadership in the Jewish world at the time of the emergence of the monepiscopate. "Rulers of the synagogue" were responsible for the orderly conduct of public worship, but they lacked the teaching authority that accrued to the Christian bishop, and their job was not necessarily lifelong. Lifelong rule by a single leader was also unknown in the cultic associations of Greco-Roman world. It is interesting that titles of rank were also developing in the Jewish synagogues of the second and third century; we hear of "principals," "fathers," and even "mothers." But these offices applied to local synagogues.

In contrast, in Roman Palestine in the second century, the office of "patriarch" developed in place of the high priest as the recognized leader of the Jews in Palestine. The patriarch was the head of the rabbinic academy, the chair of the rabbinic Sanhedrin, and the regulator of the calendar. The Romans also recognized in the Jewish patriarch a civic authority to collect taxes and appoint judges.[39] By the third century, the patriarch was exerting spiritual authority over all Jews in the empire. In the same way, by the third century, all the Christian assemblies of a city looked to one single or "monarchical" bishop, and some bishops of great metropolitan centers were exerting a spiritual authority over other churches in the province.[40]

Christian bishops appealed to other authorities to prop up their own authority. When Clement, a leader of the church in Rome in the 90s (though probably not a bishop), wrote to the church in Corinth to chastise them for ejecting their leaders from office, he explained how the apostles had appointed "bishops" from their first converts. Irenaeus of Lyons (c. 185) argued against the Gnostic claim of having secret knowledge from the apostles by pointing to bishops who were the "successors of the apostles," and he confounded the heretics by providing a list of twelve successive bishops in Rome beginning with Linus. By 250 Cyprian of Carthage was assuming that the apostles themselves had been bishops, and, for added measure, he argued that Christian bishops replaced the Old Testament priesthood. Moreover, bishops were not imposed from the outside or from above; they were elected by the local assembly. The authority of the people of God stood behind the selection of a bishop. As teachers who expounded on the scriptures read in the assembly, the bishops became authoritative interpreters of the authority that stood over both the bishop and the people: the Holy Scriptures.

Within a council of elders, there could be disputes and disagreements, not least when heretical ideas were promulgated in the assembly. As the number of Christians increased, the one Christian community of a city divided into several assemblies. Christians were supposed to be one body formed by sharing in the one bread and the one cup. The bishop could promote this unity by making the rounds from one assembly to another, presiding at the Eucharist in each place of assembly, or he could delegate a presbyter to preside in his place. The bishop became the badly needed focus in the Christian community of each city when heresy or persecution threatened to tear the Christian community apart.[41] The bishop became the Christians' civic leader. The bishops also provided a focal point for the network of local churches. They were elected by their local Christian assemblies. But as we see already in *The Apostolic Tradition*, bishops were ordained by other bishops from other local churches. This brought the recognition of the whole church to the election of the local church and extended the "catholic" dimension of Christianity.

CHAPTER 2

Sacraments and Cult

Whereas the first chapter discussed the sense in which Christianity could and could not be considered a sect, this chapter considers whether Christianity can be considered a cult. According to the sociological analysis of Rodney Stark and William Bainbridge, cults emerge independent of other religious groups; they are not schismatic, like sects.[1] Hence, they tend to see themselves in opposition not to a main religious group, but to society as a whole. Peter Berger defined sects also as opposed to the world.[2] In this sense, early Christianity can be regarded as a sect. It can therefore also be seen as a cult. Christianity embraced an apocalyptic worldview, regarding the world as being in the throes of a conflict between good and evil. Since apocalyptic cults regard the time as short, they are not interested in building permanent structures; they are concerned with making preparations for what is to come. Sources of revelation and leaders who interpret the revelations are indispensable to cults, but they have little interest in developing rituals beyond those that are essential to maintaining their community life. Their rites of initiation tend to be very important.

Early Christianity certainly met these basic conditions of being a cult. Paul, for example, saw the church being in continuity with Israel with the Gentiles grafted onto it (Romans 9–11). He did not regard Christianity as a Jewish sect, but he did exhort Christians not to be conformed to the world (Romans 12:1–2). He traveled extensively throughout the eastern Mediterranean world, establishing congregations of Gentile Christians, but he expected Christ to return soon and therefore kept organization to a minimum. He expected his congregations to be faithful to the gospel he preached and loyal to him personally. Baptism, in Paul's letters, is supposed to produce a morally pure community.[3] The Lord's Supper is also to be celebrated in a condition of purity (1 Corinthians 11:27–32).

According to Stark and Bainbridge, cults are important for their influence on more conventional forms of religion, even though few of them develop into "full-blown religious movements."[4] Usually emerging on the margins of society, cults provide (in Victor Turner's terminology) liminal experiences of *communitas*, inversion, and experimentation that are needed to renew the structures of mainstream society.[5] Of course, Christianity, which did emerge on the margins of Jewish and Greco-Roman societies (although it included a fair number of middle-class members), grew into a full-blown religion. It did so as Christians, realizing that Christ was not going to return as quickly as the first generation had expected, settled into the long haul through history. Part of becoming a full-fledged religion was to develop cultic rites that related the whole of life in all its particulars to the new life in Christ, lived "in, but not of the world" (see John 17:6–19).

It is noteworthy, in this connection, that the term *cultus* was avoided in the New Testament as regards distinctively Christian rites (even in the Latin Vulgate). The Old Testament sacrificial worship is called *cultura* in Hebrews 9:1, and those who perform it are called *cultores* (Hebrews 10:2). *Cultus* refers to the care directed to cultivating the fields, nourishing the body, furnishing the needs of life, instructing the mind, and attending to a relationship with the gods through sacrifices and prayers and the observances of fasts and feasts. To the extent that these rites and ceremonies served to bridge the gap between the sacred and the profane, Christianity had no need of a cultic apparatus. God himself has bridged the gap between sacred and profane, between heaven and earth, in the incarnation of the Word. By his death outside the city walls, Jesus the Christ has reconciled the world to God, making peace by the blood of the cross. Both the Lutheran theologian Peter Brunner and the Orthodox theologian Alexander Schmemann have pointed out that Christians used the term *leitourgia* instead of *cultus* precisely because it lacks cultic connotations.[6] Therefore, this word, which refers to the representative work of the people, was applied to Christian activities, including the gathering of gifts for Jerusalem (2 Corinthians 9:22), Paul's apostolic service (Romans 15:16; Philippians 2:17), and the exercise of roles in the assembly (1 Clement 42).

Yet the church that is "in" the world cannot avoid using the ritual repertoire of human societies and therefore also the cultic acts by which human societies initiate new members, rehearse their sacred stories, offer their gifts and prayers, celebrate their sacred meal, observe special times and occasions, consecrate leaders, marry their members, tend to their sick, and bury their dead. Moreover, as Schmemann points out, the eschatological reality the church celebrates has not yet come in its fullness. "In this world," he wrote, "the *eschaton*—the holy, the sacred, the 'otherness'—can be expressed and manifested only as 'cult.'"[7] The kingdom of God, inaugurated in the death and resurrection of Jesus Christ, is perceived in this world only by faith, not yet by sight. Eschatological reality can only be expressed and manifested through cultic forms. "Not only in relation to the world, but in relation to itself as dwelling in the world, the Church must use the forms and language of cult, in order eternally to transcend the cult, 'to become what it is'"[8]—the body of Christ. This is why Schmemann says the journey into the dimension of the kingdom of God begins by leaving earthly homes to convene in an earthly assembly in which the risen and ascended Christ is present in the gospel and the sacraments.[9] In the Orthodox conception, the Divine Liturgy is an ascension or anaphora into heaven without leaving this world behind.

The Sacraments in the New Testament

The Word and Sacraments constitute an economy of salvation. "Economy" means that each act is related to the others; they do not stand as independent rites. Christians broadly agree that the proclamation of the word convenes the church and that the primary sacraments of baptism and the Eucharist constitute the church. One is brought to faith by the preaching of the gospel. One becomes a member of the church by being baptized. The Eucharist defines the fellowship of the church. The goal of initiation is inclusion in the meal fellowship. Christians and churches are "in communion" who can eat and drink together at the Lord's table. As means of grace that bring the believer into a saving relationship with God in Christ, the sacraments are more than social rites. But they are also rituals practiced by a social group. They serve the social purpose of establishing the boundaries of church membership.

Tertullian of Carthage famously said, "Christians are made, not born." Christians were "made" in the ancient church in the processes of the catechumenate that led to baptism and first communion at Easter. Easter was a logical time to perform baptisms because, as Paul noted, baptism is a way of participating in the death and resurrection of Jesus (Romans 6:1–11). This Pauline conviction is repeated in the Letter to the Colossians, in which Paul speaks of the resurrection to new life already happening in baptism (Colossians 3:1). It is not possible to discuss baptism theologically without referring to Christology and soteriology.

However, baptism also served as the church's rite of initiation. It marked the boundary between being an "outsider" and belonging to the Christian community.[10] A consequence of baptism is not only being identified with Jesus Christ in his death and resurrection, but also being identified with the community of Christ. The church was differentiated from all other societies. This may explain Paul's hostility to circumcision (Galatians 5:1–11). Circumcision was initiation into Judaism. The continuing practice of circumcision might compromise baptism as the identifying rite of the church by suggesting that there was still another society that claimed the allegiance of Christians. Exclusive allegiance to the Christian community was important because baptism brought one into a new relationship with God, a relationship based on faith in Christ rather than on adherence to the law of Moses. This actually constituted a new social identity. Old social identities based on ethnicity (Jew or Greek), social status (slave or free), or biological chance (male or female) no longer applied to the Christian community, "for you are all one in Christ" (Galatians 3:28–29). The church constitutes a new society. It is precisely because the eucharistic meal (Holy Communion, the Lord's Supper) keeps the participants in union with their Lord and in fellowship with one another that only the baptized have been admitted to the fellowship of the Lord's table.

Since the sacraments served social purposes of initiation and incorporation, it is not surprising that the practice of the sacraments reflects the social reality of the world in which Christians live, even when they are called to live "not of the world." The dynamics of sacramental practice are not so much determined by theology as by social reality. The practices, in turn, provide grist for theological reflection. As the church fathers used to say in various ways, the rule of prayer (*lex orandi*) establishes the rule of belief (*lex credendi*). This is not a matter that practice influences belief, although that certainly happens, or that beliefs can have an influence on practice, although that happens too. Rather, it is the case that the "primary theology" of the encounter with God in Word and Sacrament is the basis for the "secondary theology" of reflection and analysis.[11] We will analyze this more extensively in Chapter 14.[12]

The task of this chapter is to demonstrate how the practice or performance of the sacraments has been shaped from the very beginning of Christian history by the church's appropriation of the cultural material of the social world in which Christians live[13] and how the practice of the sacraments, in turn, formed the culture of the church itself—the way of life that is passed on from one generation to the next.[14] The purpose of this historical survey of early Christian centuries is to demonstrate, in broad strokes, the profound influence of cult and culture on sacramental practices of the church. The last two chapters will return to the complex relationship between liturgy and culture in a more analytical way.

Christianity entered the world with a bath and a meal as its most constitutive cultic acts. Both baptism and the Eucharist were mandated by Jesus the Christ and have been performed in expectation of certain promised benefits, specifically the forgiveness of sins, new life, and salvation. But these rites were not instituted by Jesus *ex nihilo*. Even according to the Gospels, there are similarities and contrasts between the baptism practiced by John the Baptist and the baptism commanded by Jesus (Matthew 3:11; Mark 1:7–8; Luke 3:16; 7:18–30; John 1:25–26, 31, 33; 3:22, 26). According to the Synoptic Gospels, the Passover meal provided the context for the institution of the Lord's Supper (Matthew 26:17–30; Mark 14:12–26; Luke 22:7–23). What is only partially discernible in the New Testament is that these sacraments instituted by Jesus were practiced by Christians using the cultural practices of bathing and dining in the societies from which Christians were drawn, such as the "stone water jars for the Jewish rites of purification" in John 2:6, Jewish meal liturgies, and the Greco-Roman meal practices (e.g., 1 Corinthians 11) that provide the context for the celebration of the Lord's Supper. We will look at social practices and cultic patterns that influenced Christian celebrations of the sacraments.

Baptism in the Beginning

Why water purification rites were so pervasive in first-century C.E. Palestine remains a matter of social interpretation. Perhaps it had to do with foreign occupation of the Jewish land. But water purification rites played a major role in Jewish sectarian movements, especially among the Pharisees and the Essenes. Such baths were performed as full-body washings, in cold water or in catch-basin rainwater, in flowing water or in stone-held water, wearing white clothing during or after the bath, and in often-repeated performances.[15] Indeed, the ritual uniqueness of Christian baptism among the variety of lustration rites in the first century may have been its once-for-all character. The availability of Roman bathing technology in a dry land cannot be discounted as a matter of importance. Not only can the archaeological remains of swimming pools and private baths be found at such sites as Masada, Herodium, Qumran, and Jericho,[16] but Greco-Roman houses such as the one in Dura-Europas in which communities of Christians gathered for worship had private baths and fountains that could be used for performing baptisms.

The legacy of Roman bathing technology on the practice of Christian baptism is profound. Even after the abandonment of house churches in the Age of Constantine, baptisteries with pools were built adjacent to basilicas used for Christian worship.[17] Roman baths were public facilities, although they were segregated by sex. The so-called *Apostolic Tradition*, attributed to Hippolytus, specified that the men and women were baptized separately due to their nudity. The *Didascalia*, a fourth-century Syrian church order, directs presbyters or deacons to go into the water with the men and deaconesses to baptize the women. The point is that Christians used "bath rooms" (baptisteries) built in the church buildings. Contrary to what might be imagined, Christians did not gather at the river in imitation of the baptism of Jesus in the Jordan.

The Social Background of the Laying on of Hands

While the Greek word *baptizein* means "to bathe," the actual rite of baptism in the ancient church involved more than the water bath. The water bath was part of a larger cluster of rites involving the initiation of new Christians into the church. We can no longer think in terms of a straight linear development of the rites of Christian initiation. But certain elements were included in most of the rites by the third century. Rites of exorcism and renunciation of the devil, his *pompae* or honors, and his angels preceded the water bath. Prayers of thanksgiving blessing the water were common, as was the triple confession of faith in interrogative form and the triple immersion in the water. Following the baptism, there was an anointing with oil, a laying on of hands, and a gesture of welcome into the eucharistic assembly such as the kiss of peace. Various local rites differed primarily in how many exorcisms, renunciations, anointings, and imposition of hands there were before the actual water bath, and these were contingent upon the duration of the evolving period and structure of the catechumenate.[18]

It is clear from the writings of Tertullian and *The Apostolic Tradition* that the catechumenate with its exorcisms, renunciations, scrutinies, and laying on of hands involved a process of separating would-be Christians from the concrete manifestations of the demonic in daily life. Alistair Stewart-Sykes sees in this fact the meaning of the postbaptismal laying on of hands, usually by the bishop.[19] Baptism may be construed as liberation from slavery to sin, death, and the power of the devil. The laying on of hands is a symbol of this freedom and new relationship. In Roman society the ritual gesture of manumission was used before a magistrate such as a proconsul to effect officially the freeing of a slave from bondage to the master. But not all ties with the master were severed, and this affects the interpretation of the postbaptismal laying on of hands. The freed slave was now a client of the former master, who became his or her patron. In the client-patron relationship, the freed slave could expect to receive economic support from the patron, and the patron could expect to receive social or political support from the client. So close was the client-patron relationship that the client was regarded as a part of the patron's extended family and could even be buried in the patron's burial plot; the client, for his part, was expected to render *obsequium* (the giving of servile flattery) to the patron.

So pervasive was this social relationship in Roman or romanized societies, such as that of North Africa, that it is impossible to imagine that manumission was practiced in Christian initiation without this implying some form of patron-client relationship, if not to the bishop himself (as Stewart-Sykes suggests), since monepiscopacy was not established everywhere by the beginning of the third century, then to the bishop or presbyter as the representative of Christ who has freed the newly baptized from their former enslavement to the demonic powers. Certainly, the bishop was in a position to provide *beneficia* to the members of the congregation by holding the church's funds, dispensing charity to the needy, and taking care of the families of those imprisoned for the faith. The members of the church, for their part, were in fellowship with those churches whose bishops were in communion with their bishop and not in fellowship with those churches whose bishops were not in communion with their bishop. This seems very much like the client-patron relationship in terms of the relationship of financial and political support.[20] The concept of "family" (*familia*) in its extended form was very important in Roman society. The church itself, meeting in a house, could be understood as *familia Dei*, and the bishop, presiding at the table, as the *paterfamilias*. The church, based on social relationships, could be seen as a family of *clientele*, and its chief minister as a *senior*.

The Eucharist in the Beginning

Domestic settings also influenced the practice of the Christian Eucharist. Christians gathered around a dining table from which the meal was served. We see this not only in the Passover meal context of the Last Supper of Jesus and his disciples at which, according to the Synoptic Gospels, the Lord's Supper was instituted, but also in the description of the Lord's Supper given by Paul in 1 Corinthians 11, which took place in the context of a Greek banquet.

There has been much research into the Jewish background of the Christian Eucharist. Debates over whether the Last Supper of Jesus was a Passover meal,[21] occasioned by different chronologies in the Synoptic and Johannine Gospels, do not shed much light on the character of the Christian Eucharist because the main menu of the Passover meal was not continued in the Christian Eucharist; only the bread and wine, common to any Sabbath or festival meal, were used. The form and content of the prayer of blessing, or eucharistic prayer, was certainly influenced by Jewish prayers of blessing and thanksgiving.[22] The meal prayers in *Didache* 9 and 10 have even been studied by Jewish scholars because of their obvious Semitic character and the fact that they antedate the meal prayers described in the Mishnah.[23] To account for the structure and themes of the more developed eucharistic prayers of the third to fourth centuries (e.g., *The Apostolic Tradition*, Addai and Mari, Syrian and Egyptian anaphoras), Louis Bouyer suggested that there was a fusion of the synagogue and meal liturgies, a Christian blending of the meal *berakoth* with the *berakoth* preceding the Shema and the *Tefillah* of the synagogue liturgy. This was an ingenious theory, but it is too cumbersome to be acceptable.

More recently, liturgical scholars have sought to find a closer antecedent to the Christian eucharistic prayer in the Old Testament meal tradition known as *Todah* (the thank offering), especially because of the connection between suffering (e.g., illness, near-death, persecution, the threat of death) and salvation.[24] This theory is able to appeal to the many psalms of lament that end as expressions of praise and thanksgiving, a structure that is inverted in Christian eucharistic prayers that begin with praise and thanksgiving and end with supplication and even expressions of confession of sins or unworthiness.[25] The value of exploring the connection between the thank offering and the Christian Eucharist is that the thank offering made use of leavened bread and was celebrated for personal reasons but in groups gathered for the particular celebration. By the first century C.E., the bread of the thank offering was no longer presented in the temple; only the killing of the sacrificial animal took place in the temple precincts. This development within Judaism paved the way for the celebration of a sacrifice sealing a new covenant and lacking a connection to the temple such as even the Passover had in the first century—the Christian Eucharist. Not only did Christians offer a "spiritual sacrifice" of praise and thanksgiving, they also had no priesthood corresponding to the temple priesthood. In fact, the Christian Eucharist, as practiced at least in the first century, resembled no cult such as the ancient world would recognize. Christianity had no temples, no sacrificial cult, and no sacrificing priesthood. We don't even know who presided over the eucharistic meals of the first century.

The Symposium and the Eucharist

There is no doubt that the Lord's Supper was celebrated in the context of an actual meal throughout the first century, as we see in the witness of the *Didache* 9–10. Yet the sacramental meal was separated from an ordinary meal at some point early in the second century, because Justin Martyr, in *The Apology* 65, 67 (c. 150), gives no indication that the Eucharist was an ordinary meal in which regular food would be consumed. In *The Apostolic Tradition* (early third century), there is an agape meal that is separate from the Eucharist. The most likely reason for the separation of the sacramental meal from the ordinary meal was an imperial ban on meal clubs early in the second century, which caused the sacramental meal to be rescheduled in the morning. Pliny the Younger, the Roman Governor of Bithynia and Pontus, wrote in a letter to Emperor Trajan (c. 112) that it had been the custom of the Christians in his province to meet before daybreak to recite a hymn to Christ and then later in the day to partake of a meal of "ordinary and harmless food," but that "they had ceased this practice after my edict in which, in accordance with your orders, I had forbidden secret societies."[26] We don't know how long the ban lasted.

It might be assumed that it was at this point that the liturgy of the eucharistic meal was joined to the liturgy of the word and prayer, which was clearly influenced by the role of prayer, scripture readings, and commentary in the Sabbath service in the synagogue. The unity of word and meal is certainly seen in the description of Sunday worship given by Justin Martyr in his *Apology*, 67. However, the character of the eucharistic rite as a unified liturgy of word and meal may have been shaped by more profound cultural influences. One such influence may be the Greco-Roman meal ritual known as the symposium. Indeed, the symposium as a drinking party with food at which discourse was a main ingredient may have shaped the Jewish Passover meal as much as the Christian Eucharist.[27] We cannot discount the pervasive influence of the Greco-Roman culture even in first-century Palestine.

The symposium itself partook of the general characteristics of the banquet in the Greco-Roman world. All banquets—including everyday meals, symposia, funeral meals, sacrificial meals, mystery cult meals, as well as everyday Jewish meals, Jewish Sabbath meals, Jewish festival meals, and the Christian agape and eucharistic meals—had some common characteristics.[28] These characteristics included guests reclining on couches to eat; the order of the meal, with bread and food course first (the *deipnon* or *cena)* and cups of wine mixed with water after supper (the *symposion*); the care taken in the invitation, arrangement, and ranking of guests; leadership at the banquet (the host who invited and arranged the guests, the president of the symposium); entertainment at the banquet, ranging from music to games to philosophical conversation; and prayers, libation offerings, and songs to the deity at the banquet. We today might distinguish between sacred and secular meals, but this distinction would have been foreign to ancient Greco-Roman meals. Rather, the banquets would have been a continuum in which some were more sacred and some more secular, as we use those terms today; but sacred elements were a part of all banquets.

Banquets established social bonding among the invited guests. In some cases, but not all, class distinctions were maintained. However, the symposium was one form of banquet that ignored general social status because it was a gathering of friends who shared philosophic interests rather than of family members or guests of the same social rank.[29] Even so, the social bonds of the friends gathered for the symposium were so strong that the language of kinship was often used to describe their bondedness. While there was usually entertainment during dinner, symposia were as much about learning—using conversation, teaching, recitation, drama, initiation—as they were about drinking and merrymaking. Women could participate in the meal and may have contributed to the entertainment, but usually left before the discussion began. The literary symposia also anticipate the death of the main character (e.g., Socrates in Xenophon's *Symposion*, Ulpian in Athenaeus's *Deipnosophistae*, the Lapiths in Lucian's *Symposium*, Praetextatus in Macrobius's *Saturnalia*, Thecla in Methodius's *Symposium*, even the buffoonish Trimalchio in Petronius's *Satyricon*).[30] Before the drinking could commence, a libation offering was made to the patron deity, to the Olympian deities, to the heroes, or (after 30 B.C.E.) to Emperor Augustus. Prayer formulas do not exist, but if Petronius's parody reflects this custom ("Blessed be Augustus, father of our country"), they may have been short and formulaic and move from blessing to petition (e.g., "For this [offering] grant us safety, health, and many blessings; for all of us here, enjoyment in the good things before us"). In addition to blessings, there were hymns to the deities, especially to Dionysius, the god of wine.

While the Synoptic Gospels are clear that the Lord's Supper was instituted at a Passover meal, we do not know much about the Passover Seder at the time of Jesus.[31] It is certainly the case that the Passover meal did not become a true family-oriented observance until it ceased to be a pilgrimage festival after the destruction of the Jerusalem Temple in 70 C.E.[32] Many of the elements of the Passover Seder as we now know it did not come into Jewish practice until the Middle Ages. But the form of the symposium undoubtedly influenced the Jewish Passover Seder, both in the Jewish Diaspora and in Palestine. There can also be little question that elements of the symposium are present in the Last Supper of Jesus, especially in the Gospel of John 13–17, which includes the dramatic action of the foot washing, Jesus' long discourse following from that action, and prayer at table. The actual meal of the "Last Supper" is not described in the Fourth Gospel, other than a piece of bread dipped in a dish given by Jesus to Judas, his betrayer; there is no mention of a cup of wine. But Jesus had already identified himself as the "bread of life from heaven" in chapter 6, so this could also be a symbolic action of Jesus handing himself over to his betrayer, just as he would take charge of his execution in the Passion Narrative. In chapter 15, Jesus speaks of himself as a vine and the disciples as the branches who bear fruit.

Thus, while we cannot discount the influence of Jewish meals on the Christian Eucharist, especially in Jewish Christianity, we need to recognize that both Jewish meals and Christian meals flourished in a social milieu in which banquets were the common expressions of many cults and of ordinary life. This kind of banquet is clearly described by Paul in 1 Corinthians 11, which he calls "the Lord's Supper" (*kyriakon deipnon*). The function of the symposium to define but also to expand social boundaries was clearly at the heart of Paul's quarrel with the behavior of the Corinthian Christians at the Lord's Supper, and the need to include patrons, clients, and slaves in one meal fellowship certainly expanded even the egalitarianism of the Greek symposium.

The Sacraments and the Mystery Cults

It has long been thought that the ritual patterns of the mystery cults in the ancient world played a role in shaping the practice of the Christian sacraments.[33] It is preferable to refer to the mysteries as cults rather than as religions, because they were not independent systems, and they tended to be syncretistic. In fact, the mystery cults of Isis and Osiris and Serapis that emerged in Alexandria may have been a Ptolemaic effort to amalgamate the myths and rituals of ancient Egypt into a system that would have been familiar to the Greeks. Other mystery cults, such as the Iranian Mithra, the Syrian Adonis, the Asian Attis, the Thracian Dionysius, and the Greek Eleusis, are identified with particular places, and they may have originated as agrarian rites and later received philosophical interpretations.[34]

Information about these cults is not extensive precisely because they were secret. But unlike the waning civil cults of the era, they were voluntary associations; joining a mystery cult was a voluntary and personal matter. A common ritual pattern seems to have included a period of purification and probation, which may have included lustration rites and sacrifices, a moment of initiation or a series of initiations into different grades, and a crowning *epopteia* or mystical vision that may have been marked by an outward ceremony.[35]

There is a certain outward ritual correspondence with the patterns of Christian initiation that developed in the ancient world. The secretive character of the mystery cults may be manifested in the *disciplina arcani*, or "secret discipline," that was practiced in the fourth and fifth centuries (but not before): certain texts were delivered to the catechumens after they became *competentes* but were not to be otherwise revealed, and catechumens were dismissed after the liturgy of the word and before the liturgy of the eucharistic meal began. It is possible that this appeal to mystery cult practice was simply an attempt to arouse the interest of catechumens, since this secret discipline was practiced at a time when the church was increasingly a public institution and the mystery cults themselves were waning in popularity.[36] It is also possible that the "awesome" character of the rites of Christian initiation was part of a pastoral effort to engender a kind of conversion experience that was less possible in the public Christianity of the fourth and fifth centuries than it had been in the more subversive role of Christianity during the age of persecution.

The Eucharist and the Roman *Refrigerium*

We are on firmer ground when we explore the influence of Greek and Roman funeral practice on the Christian celebration of the Eucharist. A meal, called *refrigerium*, was held at certain times at the grave of the dead. Originally, the purpose of the meal was to refresh the dead. Food and drink was spread on the *mensa*, or tabletop of the sarcophagus. A pipe led from the *mensa* into the vault or tomb into which food and wine could be poured. The meal was a festival affair that included communal eating and drinking, music making and dancing, and decorating the graves with a wreath. A Greek relief from the fifth century B.C.E, now in the Museo Baracco in Rome, shows a meal of the dead at which a husband and wife recline at table while a lyrist entertains them with his playing. Banquets with musical entertainment are portrayed on Etruscan sepulchral monuments. Roman sarcophagi also show scenes of meals of the dead with the deceased reclining at table while food is brought to them and musicians entertain them.[37]

Thoughtful pagans voiced criticism of the excessive displays of grief and musical extravagance in Greco-Roman funeral practices. Critics made fun of meals for the dead in which the participants ate and drank everything and left the deceased only with a decorated gravestone. Not surprisingly, Christian leaders also felt the need to reject many of the Greco-Roman funeral practices. Christians were not to mourn their dead but were to rejoice over their entrance into eternal life. White rather than dark garments were to be worn. Psalms rather than dirges were to be sung. Musical instruments were not to be used, because they were associated with pagan cults. The Eucharist celebrated on the graves was to replace the *refrigeria*.

Understandably, church leaders were fighting a losing battle to suppress such long-established social customs. Christians continued to attend funerals of pagan family members and friends, at which the traditional customs were observed, including the riotous and drunken behavior that bishops often railed against. Only Ambrose of Milan successfully banned Christian *refrigeria* altogether. Augustine of Hippo only managed a moderation in the gifts brought to the tombs, and emphasized that the "refreshment" of the faithful departed consisted in the relief to the poor provided by their remaining Christian brothers and sisters.[38] Peter Brown has suggested that the real issue was not so much to wean half-converted Christians away from old pagan practices as to reduce the emphasis on the natural family in favor of the universal household of faith.[39]

One of the advantages of Christian celebrations in cemeteries was that Roman authorities respected the veneration of the dead and would not molest or intrude upon Christians gathered in a cemetery to honor their dead. So Christians continued to follow the custom of gathering at tombs to remember their dead on the third and thirtieth days after their deaths and on the anniversaries of their deaths. The Eucharist celebrated on the *mensae* were agape feasts that included the dead. The series of masses for the dead in later Christian practice reflect this custom.

The anniversaries of martyrs became occasions at which Christians could gather for all-night vigils in the cemeteries as pagans did. In fact, the Greek mystery cults made nocturnal vigils popular. These vigils were held in honor of the gods worshiped by the devotees of the cults. They were also occasions for which women could be out all night, and women were known to attend both pagan and Christian nocturnal vigils in large numbers. Christian bishops did not suppress the vigils but used them to curtail excesses and to promote Christian devotion through Scripture reading, psalm singing, and celebration of the Eucharist. The paschal vigil acquired the character of a more splendid version of the vigils held at the anniversaries of martyrs.[40]

The influence of these practices on the Eucharist is seen in the development of the altar. As Christianity became a legal cult in the Roman Empire, the church moved into basilicas to accommodate larger liturgical assemblies. Because of the popularity of the cult of the martyrs, church buildings were sometimes built over the graves of martyrs in cemeteries, with the communion table or altar located directly over the martyr's grave. Probably the most famous is Saint Peter's Basilica on the Vatican Hill, which was outside the city of Rome when it was first built. This also served the purpose of linking the martyr's grave with the bishop's Eucharist and making the bishop the patron of the martyr's cult rather than the martyr's family.[41]

If it proved impractical to build a church building over the grave of the martyr, relics of martyrs were transferred from their original resting place to the new churches, where they were placed in receptacles beneath or within the altar. The space between the altar legs was walled in, giving the altar a chestlike form. To allow worshipers to see the relic, an opening called a *fenestrella*, covered with a lattice or door, was left in front of the altar. By the sixth century, wooden altars in the West had generally been replaced by stone altars that looked like sarcophagi.[42]

Results

In this brief overview, we see that Christians appropriated cultic forms and social practices with which they were familiar in order to perform the sign-acts that Christ commanded his disciples to perform and to do the things that any human society must do to maintain communal life. Sacramental practice in particular and liturgical practice in general continued to be influenced by the cultural materials of the societies in which Christianity flourished. These ancient cultic forms, which gave foundational shape and meaning to Christians sacramental practices, continue to inform the cultic life of the church and may also serve as sources of renewal today.

Whereas a cult lives at the margins of society and is critical of society, religions, such as the state churches of Christendom, tend to support the values of the larger society in which they exist. Even after the Edict of Milan, it would take several centuries before Christianity completely supplanted paganism and evolved into Christendom. The leaders of the church in the fourth century realized that the church had to transform the values of Roman society. Liturgy was one of the means by which the values of the kingdom of God would be proclaimed and expressed in preaching and sacramental celebration.

CHAPTER 3

Apocalypse and Christian Liturgy

Christianity began as a sectarian movement among the Jewish people but spread quickly throughout the Greco-Roman world as a movement embracing Gentiles who also stood over against pagan cults, including emperor worship. It did so by developing an alternative cult devoted to Jesus as Christ (Messiah) and Lord (*kyrios*). The dynamics of Christianity as a sect with its own cult standing against the world are rooted in the tensions in which the Jews lived vis-à-vis the dominant Hellenistic culture in the three centuries before the rise of Christianity.

For roughly a thousand years, from the time of the Babylonian exile in the sixth century B.C.E. until the beginning of the Byzantine Empire, Jewish life was stamped by the polarity of living in the Diaspora versus living in the homeland. Jews were not alone in this, because the time of Greco-Roman domination of the Mediterranean world was characterized by population mobility created by opportunities for trade and commerce. For the Jews, however, the tension between homeland and Diaspora was particularly acute because the promise of God to be in covenant with Israel included an attached land. Certainly the Jews living in the Diaspora tried their best to maintain the marks of Jewish identity, even though this sometimes put them at odds with their neighbors. But the tensions between Jewish parties in the homeland and the world powers that occupied the land of Israel after the Babylonian exile became acute after the defeat of the Persians by Alexander the Great.

The Persians who conquered Babylon ended the Jews' Babylonian captivity. Jews were free to return to their homeland and pursue their common life with a degree of self-regulation. A Jewish prophet even hailed Cyrus the Persian as God's anointed or messiah (Isaiah 45:1). But Alexander, tutored by Aristotle and exposed to the best of Greek culture, was concerned to spread Greek culture as well as conquer the world militarily. Jewish relationships with the Seleucid rulers of the Middle Eastern portion of Alexander the Great's empire, with its capital at Antioch in Syria, were especially tense since Jews faced the challenge of forced conformity to pagan culture.[1] The Romans were generally more tolerant of local cultures. But under both empires, the Hellenistic culture clashed with revivals of Hebraism.

In times of peace, when the status quo was maintained, Greek language and thought penetrated Jewish thought and are reflected especially in the wisdom literature of the Bible and the Apocrypha. But in times of oppression when foreign occupiers of the land of Israel pressed their own culture and cults on the Jews, Jews reacted defensively. This sometimes led to violent confrontations, most famously in the Maccabean revolt against the Seleucids in 166 B.C.E., the Roman-Jewish War in 66–73 C.E., and the Bar Kochba rebellion in 132–135 C.E. During the time of persecution under the Seleucids, Jews communicated within their own circles through a genre of literature known as apocalyptic.

Apocalyptic Literature

Apocalyptic literature flourished in Judaism and then in early Christianity between the years 200 B.C.E. and 150 C.E. This was a period of time when Jews and then Christians suffered intermittent persecution, the Jews for their cultural intransigence under the Seleucid ideology of Hellenization and political resistance to Rome, and Christians because of their faith in Jesus as Messiah and *Kyrios*, which generated hostility from both Jews and Romans. Examples of Jewish apocalyptic literature include the book of Daniel in the Old Testament, a number of books in the Apocrypha, and some of the Dead Sea Scrolls.

This literature reflects disillusionment with the Jewish priesthood and national leaders, whose collaboration, first with the Greeks and then with the Romans, was perceived as compromising Jewish distinctiveness. Some Jews withdrew into small private groups in which they studied the Scriptures and refused to adopt the way of life their foreign rulers sought to force on them. In the book of Daniel, for example, the obedient community sees itself as the "saints of the Most High God" through whom God will establish his rule on earth (Daniel 7:11–18) and destroy the evil powers, which are depicted as horrible beasts. God will vindicate his saints who remain pure and faithful.

A similar perspective is seen in a group that emerged in the late second century B.C.E., whose life and discipline have come to light only in the discovery of the Dead Sea Scrolls. This community has been called Qumran, after the place where the scrolls were discovered. This group is sometimes identified with the Jewish sect known as the Essenes, who are known to us from the writings of Josephus and Philo. The scroll known as *The Manual of Discipline* was thought to correspond with the ancient description of the Essenes and reflect their concern to be a pure, gathered community untainted by the corrupt and misguided priests at Jerusalem. Norman Golb has questioned, against the majority of Dead Sea Scroll scholars, whether archaeological finds at Qumran support the assumption that Qumran was an Essenes community when compared with what is known about this sect from first-century Jewish authorities. He has also argued that the scrolls found in the caves at Qumran may more likely represent a depository of libraries from Jerusalem that were rescued from the ravages of the Roman assault on the city in 70 C.E.[2] There is no question, however, that some of the scrolls reflect an apocalyptic view that God will defeat the enemies of his people through a miraculous intervention in history.

Apocalyptic elements pervade the Gospels in bits and pieces, though they cannot be said to represent pure examples of apocalyptic literature. Mark 13 (which has parallels in Matthew 24 and Luke 21) has been called the "little apocalypse" because of its reference to "the desolating sacrilege" erected in the temple as a sign of the end time. Some portions of the letters of Paul, such as 1 Corinthians 15, also have characteristics of apocalyptic literature because of their emphasis on Christ subduing the powers of evil in his return as judge when "the dead shall be raised incorruptible." The Apocalypse itself (the Revelation to Saint John the Seer) is the most clearly apocalyptic writing in the New Testament and even draws on references from the book of Daniel. Some early Christian writings not included in the New Testament canon, such as the *Apocalypse of Peter* and *The Shepherd of Hermas*, also are examples of the literary genre.

The premise of this literature is that those oppressed for their faith see no hope for salvation on the plane of human history. Indeed, the battle being fought is not to be understood just in terms of politics and economics, but in terms of "spiritual powers in high places." So the apocalyptic writers looked beyond current history to the dramatic and miraculous intervention of God, who would set right the injustices inflicted on his people. They offer words of hope and encouragement to the persecuted faithful by envisioning the vindication of the elect in the resurrection of the dead and the blessing of heavenly life, the coming judgment of the world, and the creation of a new Jerusalem.[3]

The Christian writings differ from the Jewish writings in the place they give to Jesus the Messiah as the meaning and end of human history. Otherwise, familiar features of Jewish apocalyptic are evident in the Christian writings, especially in the book of Revelation: symbolic language, an allegorical use of numbers, fantastic imagery, angelic powers of good and evil, resurrection and judgment, the messianic kingdom, and the world to come. Since they were writing and circulating their books in situations of oppression and persecution, the writers used symbolic language that would be understood by those within their community but not understood by outsiders. The message is often a vision disclosed or revealed to the human writer by an otherworldly mediator; hence the origin of the term *apokalypsis*. The first attested use of this term is actually in the first line of the book of Revelation: "The *apokalypsis* of Jesus Christ."

The Apocalypse of John

The Apocalypse of John shares with other pieces of apocalyptic literature an emphasis on the admonition to remain faithful under persecution and hardship. But the unique form that the book of Revelation takes is epistolary. The book begins and ends as a letter. Literally, it is addressed "to the seven churches of Asia" (1:4a). Asia Minor was a Roman province, but seven symbolizes totality, so John may be speaking to all the churches in Asia or to all churches everywhere. The salutation is from the Holy Trinity: the eternal God, "the seven spirits who are before his throne" (perhaps meaning the Spirit of God, since in Isaiah 11:2 the Spirit operates in seven ways, again suggesting fullness), and Jesus Christ (v. 5), who is described in terms of his passion, resurrection, and ascension:

1. "The faithful witness" who crowned his perfect obedience to the Father by the sacrifice of his life;

2. "The firstborn of the dead" who by his resurrection inaugurated a new era; and

3. "The ruler of the kings of the earth" who is now exalted to a position of power over all creation. This is a political statement that represents an act of defiance on the part of the early church; Caesar is not ultimately in charge.

In this chapter, I consider the liturgical implications of the Apocalypse of John for the earthly *ekklesia* and its liturgy. I do this by looking at some of the specific liturgical allusions and material, especially in chapters 4–5, and then by reflecting on the implications of the vision of the heavenly liturgy for the earthly liturgy as it came to be practiced by the ancient Christians. The influence of apocalyptic literature is less on liturgical structures as they evolved than on the mind-set of worshipers. Some liturgical texts and practices may actually be mirrored in apocalyptic material, especially in the Apocalypse of John.

Liturgical Material in the Apocalypse

John, exiled to the island of Patmos during a time of persecution, relates that he received the visions he describes when he was "in the spirit on the Lord's Day" (1:10). This is one of only three texts in the New Testament that allude to the Christian observance of Sunday, the first day of the week, as "the Lord's Day" (the other two being Acts 20:7–12 and 1 Corinthians 16:2). It was believed that the first Christians chose Sunday as a day of assembly in order to differentiate themselves from the Jews, who observed the seventh day of the week as a Sabbath and as a day of worship. Some scholars, including Willy Rordorf, have argued that Jesus challenged the very idea of observing the Sabbath day and that Gentile Christians who adhered to Paul's view of the law would have had no reason to do so. Picking up an idea proposed by Oscar Cullmann, Rordorf suggested that the observance of Sunday grew out of the post-resurrection appearances of Jesus to his disciples (John 20:19, 26) and the meal fellowship between the risen Christ and his disciples (Luke 24:28–35, 36–43).[4] In other words, Sunday became a day of worship for the first Christians because it was a celebration of the resurrection of Jesus on the first day of the week, and the form of worship was the Eucharist.

As a celebration of the resurrection, Sunday was already an eschatological day for Christians. But already in the second century, first of all in the *Epistle of Barnabas*, Sunday was being called "the eighth day." Rordorf believes that Sunday came to be associated with the number eight in conjunction with baptism, which was also administered on Sunday. Certainly baptism was considered a Christian equivalent of circumcision, which was performed on the eighth day after birth.[5] But it was also the case that Jewish apocalyptic thought divided history into seven ages of a thousand years each, corresponding to the seven days of the week, the seventh of which was supposed to represent paradise on earth. At the end of the seventh age, a new age would be ushered in, and a new creation inaugurated. By the second century, Christians who called Sunday "the eighth day" were regarding it as the day that goes beyond the time of this world, beyond the Sabbath, because it celebrates the inauguration of the new creation in the resurrection of Jesus Christ.

We might note that John the Seer was "in the spirit on the Lord's Day," and the Holy Spirit was also associated with eighth-day symbolism with regard to the Feasts of Tabernacles and Pentecost. In John 7:37–39, Jesus says, on the last and great day of the Feast of Tabernacles, in connection with the ritual of water ablutions on this day, "Let anyone who is thirsty come to me, and let the one who believes in me drink. As the scripture has said, 'Out of the believer's heart shall flow rivers of living water.' Now he said this about the Spirit, which believers in him were to receive." Acts 2 describes the outpouring of the Holy Spirit on the disciples of Jesus on the Fiftieth Day (Pentecost, the Jewish Feast of Weeks). Liturgically, Pentecost was the octave of Passover: a week of weeks plus an eighth day. This same eschatological symbolism applies to the Christian observance of the Fifty Days of Pascha culminating on the Day of Pentecost.[6]

In chapters 4–5 of Revelation, John is summoned to become a spectator at the heavenly court. What he sees is not a vision of the future— that comes later, especially in chapters 21–22. Here "in the Spirit" he is given a glimpse of heavenly worship that is eternally rendered to God. He describes the glory of God in terms of precious gems (4:3). Around God's throne are "twenty-four elders" (perhaps the twelve Old Testament patriarchs and the twelve apostles), who represent the ideal church. As in a Roman court, God's counselors are "seated" (4:4); they share in the privilege and responsibility of ruling and judging.[7] Adopting this same idea, when Christians began meeting in basilicas in the fourth century, the bishop was seated on a throne in the apse, surrounded by his presbyters or elders seated on benches, with deacons standing around. "Flashes of lightning" and "thunder" express God's majesty (4:5). Again, "the seven spirits" before the throne are probably the sevenfold energies of God in Isaiah 11:2: wisdom, understanding, counsel, might, knowledge, and fear (awe) of God. The phrase "something like a sea of glass" in 4:6 indicates the inadequacy of description, but glass was a valuable commodity, and it suggests also the distance between God and the rest of the creation. Similarly, *1 Enoch* 14 also describes a great house or palace in heaven as having a floor of crystal. The "four living creatures" around the throne are angelic beings representing the creation. They are God's agents in unceasingly watching over all of nature (see Ezekiel 1:5, 10, 18; 10:12).[8] They symbolize what is most splendid about animals: the lion, nobility; the ox, strength; the human, wisdom; the eagle, oversight. About a century after this book was written, these creatures were equated with the four evangelists: the lion, Mark; the ox, Luke; the human, Matthew; the eagle, John. These symbols later achieved nearly universal usage in the decoration of Christian churches. Perhaps their "six wings" (4:8) express their swiftness in executing God's will. These living creatures continually praise God as the ruler of history (or time) who will restore (or liberate) creation, singing the same antiphons sung by the seraphim in Isaiah 6. The living creatures are joined by the elders representing heavenly beings, who acknowledge God's superior power by placing their crowns "before the throne" (4:10)—indicating that all power comes from God and acknowledging his worthiness. (It is from the sense of worthiness that we derive the English word *worship*.)

The "scroll" (5:1) is a record of God's plans for the end time (see also Daniel 10:21). Official documents were written "on the inside and on the back"; this scroll was such a document. It is perfectly sealed ("seven seals") so that it is unalterable. Its content is known only to its author, God. Verse 2 asks, in effect, who can initiate the events of the end time? No one in all creation ("in heaven or earth," v. 3) can be found to do it. The dilemma causes John to "weep" (v. 4), because the faithful wish to know the events planned for the end of the current era, and to see them put into effect—thus giving meaning to their suffering.

But there is one in heaven who can "open the scroll" (v. 5). As the titles "Lion of the tribe of Judah" and "Root of David" indicate, he is the Messiah. He is "worthy to open the scroll" because he has conquered death. He is "a Lamb . . . as if . . . slaughtered"; he holds the fullness of power and insight ("seven horns and seven eyes," v. 6) which are the marks of the "seven spirits of God sent out into all the earth" (which Jesus the Christ received at his baptism). He stands between the throne and the living creatures—the place of the mediator. When he had taken the scroll, the four living creatures and twenty-four elders fell prostrate before the Lamb. Each held a harp, by which the psalms are sung, and a bowl of incense, which is the prayers of the saints (the faithful on earth). They sing a "new song" (v. 9) because Christ has inaugurated a new era: he is "worthy" (v. 9) because he has rescued all the faithful everywhere. God made Israel a "kingdom of priests" (v. 10); now all the faithful are included in this royal priesthood by virtue of their baptism into Christ.

In a scene reminiscent of the honors given to a Roman emperor, large numbers of heavenly beings sing of Christ's worthiness to disclose God's plans. There are seven honors he is worthy to receive (v. 12). The first four concern his dominion: power, wealth, wisdom, might; the others express the adoration of those present: honor, glory, blessing. The "Lamb" and the Creator ("the one seated on the throne") are equal in majesty and are equally worthy to receive "blessing and honor and glory and might forever and ever" (v. 13). All creatures in heaven and on earth affirm this to be true by saying, "Amen" (v. 14).

What is most noteworthy here is that God and the Lamb are worshiped together. Within a setting that is loyal to the whole tradition of Jewish monotheism and opposed to pagan dualism, the author of the Apocalypse insists on placing Jesus next to God as the proper object of worship. As the book of Revelation wends its way toward its great apocalyptic climax, through one act of worship after another, this point is constantly underscored: heaven and earth—all creation—celebrate the victory of God the Creator and the Lamb over the forces of evil, of darkness, of deceit, and of destruction. Concomitant with this celebration of victory is the fact that the creation itself is reclaimed by the Creator. The Apocalypse is not finally world denying.[9] In the grand climax in chapters 21–22, the faithful do not escape from this world and go off to heaven. Rather, the new city, the heavenly Jerusalem, comes down from heaven to earth, and the saints reign on earth with

Christ. All creation will be renewed, as prophesied by Isaiah (65, 66), freed from imperfection and transformed to the glory of God (see also Romans 8:19–21). There is a marvelous description of the life-giving blessings of this heavenly city on earth ("the river" [22:1-2] and "the tree of life" [v. 21]) in whose midst God dwells, final exhortations to remain faithful, and an urgent plea, "Amen. Come, Lord Jesus."

The Implications of the Apocalypse for the Worship of the Earthly Church

While Revelation is a book of prophecy, it is full of liturgical elements. There are no less than three canticles in chapters 4 and 5—"Holy, holy, holy," "You are worthy to take the scroll," and "Worthy is the Lamb who was slain" (memorably set to music in Handel's *Messiah*)—two acclamations in chapter 7, and four hallelujah choruses in chapter 19. The work is studded with references to Old Testament and apocryphal texts, yet it undoubtedly reflects also the worship of the Christian communities to which it was addressed. After all, they would be expected to understand the symbolic references and could perhaps envision in Revelation's pictures of heavenly worship their own liturgical assemblies on "the Lord's Day." It was on "the Lord's Day" that John received this revelation on the island of Patmos (1:10).

The liturgical materials in Revelation have long been recognized. The idea that the hymns and anthems in chapters 4–5 reflect the worship of the church has been acknowledged. But Massey H. Shepherd Jr. pushed the liturgical data a little further in his study of *The Paschal Liturgy and the Apocalypse*.[10] He proposed that the very structure of the book of Revelation was influenced by the church's paschal liturgy, or what we would today call the Easter Vigil. We need to make a careful distinction here. Shepherd did not suggest that the Apocalypse is the paschal liturgy, only that it was influenced by it. Even so, an important caveat needs to be entered: we do not have any full description of the paschal liturgy before the third century. In fact, we are only assuming that the vigil with baptism and first communion described in *The Apostolic Tradition* attributed to Hippolytus of Rome (c. 215) was the paschal vigil; *The Apostolic Tradition* does not specifically give us the liturgical date for Christian initiation. Also, there is so much revisionist thinking about this document that it should now be referred to as "the (so-called) *Apostolic Tradition*, attributed to Hippolytus of Rome."[11] Paul Bradshaw also disputes that a standard or normative pattern of Christian initiation in early Christianity can be identified.[12]

Still, we know that a paschal vigil was observed in Asia Minor in the second century, because we have the famous homily *Concerning the Pascha* from Melito of Sardis (c. 165). We know that the Asians were called Quartodecimans ("Fourteenthers") because they always celebrated the Pascha of Christ in conjunction with the Pesach of the Jews on the 14th–15th of Nisan, and clung to this tradition tenaciously against the pressure of the Roman Church, which always celebrated the resurrection of Christ on a Sunday after Passover. But it was precisely the Quartodeciman practice that gave us the paschal vigil. The Christians assembled on the night of the 14th of Nisan and fasted and read from the Old Testament while the Jews feasted at the Passover meal. Then, after midnight, when the Jewish feast was over, the Christians proclaimed the resurrection of Christ and celebrated the Eucharist. By this ritual action, they proclaimed that the Passover of Christ from death to life fulfills the Passover of the Jews. The references in Melito suggest that this paschal vigil was a well-established custom by the time he wrote. If we accept the view that the book of Revelation was written toward the end of the reign of Emperor Domitian (81–96) (perhaps the beast who is "an eighth but belongs to the seven" in a line of Roman emperors [17:11]), as opposed to during the persecution that took place under Nero in 64 C.E., we are closer to the time when this tradition of paschal celebration was developing in Asia.

The basic pattern we see in Revelation is a simple one. Its prophecies unfold in a series of sevens: the seven letters to the seven churches, the seven seals, the seven trumpets, the seven bowls. At certain points there seem to be interludes: Chapters 4–5 are a preparation for opening the scroll, and chapter 7 is inserted between the opening of the sixth and seventh seals. Chapters 10–11:13 are placed between the sixth and seventh trumpets, but this interlude is prolonged after the seventh trumpet blast to the end of chapter 15, and it is again filled with liturgical materials. With the conclusion of the seventh bowl, the Apocalypse ends with paeans of victory: the song of triumph over the fall of Babylon (Rome) in chapter 18, the Hallel psalmody and marriage feast of the Lamb in chapter 19, and the vision of the world to come in chapters 20–22.

We should note that while the millenarian view of the Apocalypse (the thousand-year reign of Christ and his saints before Satan is loosed on the earth and the final battle is waged) is not popular today in the mainline churches, it was a very popular view in early Christianity and was shared by Papias, Irenaeus, and Tertullian. In this light it has been suggested that "the Lord's Day" in 1:10, in which John was "in the Spirit," is really a reference to the *Parousia*, the eschatological day of the Lord, not to Sunday. But this would have been a false dichotomy in the early church, when, as we have seen, Sunday was coming to be regarded as "the eighth day."

The outline of the paschal liturgy in the structure of the book of Revelation is, according to Shepherd,[13] as follows:

Chapters 1–3	The seven letters	Scrutinies of the elect
Chapters 4–5	The assembly before the throne	The vigil
Chapter 6	Seals I–VI	The readings
Chapter 7	The sealing of the white-robed martyrs	Initiation/baptism
Chapter 8	Seal VII and censing	Prayers
Chapters 8–9	Trumpets I–VI	The law
Chapters 10–11	The little scroll, two witnesses	The prophets
Chapters 12–15	Trumpet VII	The struggle between Christ and antichrist
Chapters 16–18	Bowls I–VII	Gospel
Chapter 19	The Hallelujah	Psalmody
Chapter 19	The Marriage Supper of the Lamb	Eucharist
Chapters 20–22	The Consummation	

Again, we should emphasize that John the Seer has not reproduced the paschal liturgy; Revelation may not even be a commentary on it. Shepherd is only suggesting that the structure of the paschal liturgy provided a (perhaps unconscious) structure for the book of Revelation. Moreover, John has not slavishly followed the liturgy. Some sections are difficult to assign to a particular part of the liturgy, especially the woes and plagues in chapters 8–18, which Shepherd assigns to the liturgy of the word. We must remember that Revelation was composed before there was a New Testament canon and possibly before all Christian communities knew all of the writings that came to constitute the New Testament.[14] There is no hard data to indicate that Christians read from both the law and the prophets as the Jews did in their synagogues; Justin Martyr (c. 150) mentions only "the writings of the prophets" and "the memoirs of the apostles." But it was the case that the Old Testament scriptures, the Epistles, and the Gospels were being read in the churches long before a canon of Scripture was received by the whole church; in fact, the liturgical use of certain writings led to their inclusion in the canon (e.g., four Gospels rather than one or the popular *Gospel Harmony* of Tatian). On the whole, then, it may be affirmed that the emerging liturgical, initiatory, and sacramental practices of the church are reflected in the Apocalypse, especially as they came together in the paschal vigil that celebrated the Passover of Christ from death to life.

What we may say with greater certainty about the book of Revelation and the worship of the early church is that in a time of struggle, the Apocalypse viewed the worship of the earthly church as a replication of the heavenly worship. A little detail that I passed over in commenting on chapters 4–5 occurs at the beginning of chapter 4: "After this I looked, and there in heaven a door stood open!" How intriguing to find this little detail at the beginning of a description of the heavenly worship: there is an open door in heaven for the human being to enter. The ancient view of the purpose of cult was to build a bridge between earth and heaven, between time and eternity. That's why the Roman high priest was the *pontifex maximus*—the great bridge builder, a title that accrued to the emperor and later to the pope. But by virtue of Christ's ascension into heaven and our union with Christ in the Spirit given at baptism, we too may participate in the worship of the heavenly beings before the throne of God. John the Seer says there is an open door in heaven, and Jesus himself says in John 10:9, "I am the door; whoever enters by me will be saved, and will come in and go out and find pasture." We are invited to enter heaven through the door that is Christ. Christ himself is the high priest, the *pontifex maximus*, who builds bridges between heaven and earth. What we see through the open door to heaven is a vision of unadulterated worship of God on the throne and of the Lamb. The worship of God is the purpose for which other things are done in and by the church. The mission of the church is to enlist worshipers who shall perform the true worship of the true God (*orthodoxia*). The purpose of proclaiming the word and celebrating baptism and the Lord's Supper is to form a community of priests who will offer a sacrifice of praise and prayer for the life of the world.

The Church as *Civitas*

The church itself is to replicate on earth the new Jerusalem that the Seer in his revelation saw coming down out of heaven from God (Revelation 21:10). Here in the Apocalypse we see a sectarian faith that stands against the world and moves toward the most catholic model of Christianity—that of the *polis* of a world empire whose *Kyrios* or *Dominus* is Christ Jesus. In the social world of the Greco-Roman cities, the city was hardly a secular place in the modern understanding of the city (*civitas*) as religiously neutral. Each city had a civic cult devoted to one or more gods and goddesses, under whose benefaction the city received protection and prosperity. It was a civic responsibility to participate in this cult. The civic cult did not claim exclusive devotion; other cults could exist alongside of it. But everyone was expected to participate in the civic cult as well as in their own cult. Those who would not participate in the civic cult were regarded as "atheists." This included Jews and Christians, whose "jealous" God allowed no competition. The Jews had long since been granted an exemption from participating in the civil cult, and it was more or less respected throughout the Roman Empire most of the time (with occasional exceptions). This was because the Romans respected the antiquity of the Jewish religion. But Christianity was granted no such exemption, because it was regarded as an offshoot of Judaism and a novel cult. This was the most frequent reason for the persecution of Christians and also why most persecutions before the middle of the third century were local. Christians were accused of being atheists who would not exercise civic responsibility by participating in the civic cult and offering incense to the emperor. In other words, they were not reliable citizens.[15]

The Apocalypse presents a counterimage to the Roman Empire's earthly cities with their many temples and public forums in which the civic religion was conducted. There is no temple in the holy city because the Lord God dwells in the midst of the city, making the whole city a temple. The presence of the Lord God of the universe eclipses all the other deities. The holy city also is not a gated community but one into which all nations and people are welcomed into citizenship. As Robin Lane Fox observed, when Christianity made headway in the Roman cities, was licensed as a legal cult, and given public buildings in which to assemble, its assemblies for worship eventually distorted town plans and created new centers that showed hospitality to a broad clientele of people, including (especially) the poor.[16] But while everyone is welcome in the city of God, they must go through a process of purification (conversion and baptism), for "nothing accursed will be found there any more" (22:3); citizens of the city must be purified with the seal of God and the Lamb upon their foreheads.

As a city in its own right, the church's assembly needed a space that occupies a place. As described in chapters 5 and 6, Christians acquired and transformed the public Roman building known as the basilica, and one of the most significant features of the transformation of Roman *civitas* in the fourth and fifth centuries was that Christians claimed and then reoriented the public space and claimed public time. The classical city, with its agora, forum, temples, stadiums, and theaters, was rebuilt with a new urban plan that placed a church—a Christianized basilica—at its center.[17] In time, not only did churches displace the pagan temples, but even cemeteries were moved from outside the city walls into the cities themselves (and even under the churches, with the entombment of apostles and martyrs beneath the altar). The church's telling of the story of Jesus produced a new calendar of festivals and fasting seasons that either transformed or eclipsed pagan feasts and fasts. Passages in human life were interpreted in the light of the story of Jesus, particularly the paschal mystery of Christ's death and resurrection, transforming Roman funeral and marriage rites. With the sanctification of space, time, and life, Christianity laid the foundation for its own distinctive culture—the culture of Christendom that emerged in late antiquity.

This may seem like quite a historical extrapolation from a book that has the character of escapist literature opposed to the world. But the basic view of Revelation is that the holy city, the new Jerusalem, shall come down out of heaven from God and replace the world city, Rome, the "beast," controlled by the "ancient serpent," the primeval enemy of God. Since heaven is presented as a parody of Rome, Rome is revealed as a diabolical parody of heaven. Christians are to know that its pomp and power are a diabolical artifice concealing the city-empire's predestined destruction and replacement. Christians did not take matters into their own hands in terms of trying to topple the Roman Empire; they expected God to deal with it in God's own time. Yet it seemed to ordinary Christians that apocalyptic hope was being fulfilled when an emperor, consolidating his power, had the sign of the cross drawn on the shields of his army and went into battle with the cry, "In this sign, conquer."[18] When the time came, the church was quite prepared to take up its newly acquired public role in the Empire, almost as if it were expected.

The church did not became a "shadow empire" in its first three centuries by identifying with the culture of the Roman Empire, but by using cultural material from the Roman world to produce its own culture. The church had a message, but it was more than the bearer of a message. It was a society with its own way of life and worldview. While aspects of liturgy in the book of Revelation reflect the cultic practices of the Greco-Roman culture, Revelation reverses them in every respect. Its exhortations challenged its readers even to ignore common sense: God can alter historical reality; therefore, "hold fast." The great insight of the fourth-century church historian and bishop of Caesarea, Eusebius, was that apocalyptic hopes were being fulfilled as a Roman emperor staked the renovation of the empire on the vitality of the Christian church and convened the bishops from throughout the empire to his summer palace at Nicaea to get the church's act together.

Other insightful Christians, however, recognized that if the church were successful in the world, the world would be in the church. The church needed to be a society existing "in, but not of the world." How would the eschatological witness of the church to a new heaven and a new earth with a new Jerusalem coming down out of heaven from God survive the tendency of leaders like Eusebius to accept the second best of a Christian empire? The answer was monasticism.

The Rise of Monasticism

Monasticism may be regarded as one specific example of the general climate of asceticism in the ancient world. The hedonism popularly associated with the Roman Empire was balanced with world-denying religions and philosophies that swept the Roman world during the first through the fourth centuries, including Gnosticism, Manichaeanism, and Neoplatonism. We have seen that the Essenes were one Jewish ascetic group; the Theraputae of Lower Egypt were another. It is not surprising that *ascesis* played a role in early Christianity spirituality. In 1 Corinthians 9:24–27, Paul compares the Christian life to running a race to receive the crown of victory, with all the bodily disciplines required to achieve this. By the third century, hermits were taking off into the deserts of Syria and Egypt to practice an extreme form of asceticism while doing combat with the demons. The new development in the early fourth century was the emergence of communities of ascetics or monks, gathered around star hermits like Anthony (c. 250–356), who attracted a celebrated biographer in Athanasius of Alexandria.

Anthony's own example and Athanasius's influential *Life of Anthony* attracted many converts and imitators. The austere sanctity of men like Anthony and Symeon the Stylite (389–459) in Syria, who lived for forty years on top of a narrow pillar sixty feet high, dazzled the world of late antiquity. Ordinary Christians sought them out rather than clergy for spiritual counsel, since these hermits were literally following biblical injunctions compatible with the kind of messianic, apocalyptic community the church had been called to be, while the bishops were busy organizing the Christian community for life within the world. Hermits like Anthony or Symeon claimed direct mystical experience of God without the mediation of clergy or the means of grace. Many were following the injunctions of scripture that they could not even read.[19]

As many followers clustered in huts near the caves of hermits, it became necessary to organize their lives for a productive ascetic life under the supervision of a father figure or abbot. Anthony himself organized hermit colonies into quasi-monastic communities. But another Egyptian hermit, the former soldier Pachomius (c. 292–346), became the true founder of monasticism by bringing to these communities a military-like discipline and strict obedience to the abbot.

This development began at the same time as the promulgation of the Edict of Milan, which in 313 granted legal status to Christianity in the Roman Empire. Throughout the fourth century, hundreds and thousands of earnest Christians joined the hermits in the deserts. Athanasius reported in his *Life of Anthony* that there were monasteries in the mountains and "the desert was made a city by the monks."[20] There are reports of more than five thousand monks living in the Nitrian Valley alone. A whole alternative society was being created in the deserts of Egypt, Palestine, and Syria.

Later, when monasticism was introduced to the West through Jerome's Latin translation of the *Rule of Pachomius* and Cassian's introduction of Eastern monastic life in his *Conferences* and *Institutes*, the same thing happened. Monks built towns on the slopes of the Alps, in the swamps of Burgundy, in the forests of Thuringia, and on craggy promontories off the coasts of Ireland and Scotland. The monks civilized western Europe by building cities of prayer and work (*ora et labora*, in the Benedictine slogan) where there were no cities and by transmitting the learning of the Roman world to barbarian peoples in the monastic schools and scriptoria.

The development of monasticism can be seen as both an escape from the world and a form of protest against the world coming into the church. But primarily it was a way of continuing the eschatological spirit of early Christianity by living in a pure, gathered community as monks awaited the arrival of the city of God, meanwhile erecting signs of the kingdom of God in their own works. Or, as Augustine of Hippo later taught, all Christians are "aliens and exiles" (1 Peter 2:11) who wend their way through this world toward the city of God. But these "sojourners" who took up temporary residence in the wilderness of this world managed to build up earthly cities in which every civic function was performed by the members of the community for the common good while they tried to keep themselves unstained by the influence of the world.

The primary function of the monastery, however, as it had been for the desert hermits, was prayer—"prayer without ceasing" (1 Thessalonians 5:17). In its "ceaseless prayer," monasticism made a significant contribution to the history of Christian worship but at the same time departed from the type of liturgy that was suitable as the public work of ordinary Christian assemblies. This is seen especially in the development of the prayer offices. Early monasticism was a lay movement and had no liturgical life of its own.[21] It continued but transformed early Christian practices. Christians in the early centuries certainly had been taught to pray unceasingly. In his treatise *On Prayer*, Tertullian held that morning and evening prayers are obligatory; Christians pray also at the third, sixth, and ninth hours when the forum bell rings; Christians pray before meals and before going to the baths; Christians may also rise at night and pray.[22] These were prayers of the household or of the individual during the day. The daytime prayers may have consisted of no more than reciting the Lord's Prayer, as the *Didache* 8 specifies.

Prayer practices learned in the household were undoubtedly continued by monks and taken over into the monasteries to be prayed communally. In the meantime, daily public prayer offices in the morning and evening (Lauds and Vespers) developed in the basilicas (cathedrals) of the fourth century. The content of the cathedral offices was determined by the time of the day at which they were prayed (e.g., Psalms 63 and 148–150 in the morning and Psalm 141 in the evening). Their purpose was to sanctify the pivotal times of the day (for example, at the beginning and end of the workday). But in the monasteries, the old concept of "ceaseless prayer" developed into a continuous recitation of the Psalter and meditation on the Word of God without regard to time of day.[23]

Monks who had left the world behind had no need to sanctify time; their goal was to practice the ascetic life in the pursuit of holiness. The concern of monks was to recite as many psalms as possible and to hear as much scripture as possible during the course of the day as forms of ascetic discipline. Instead of the selected psalms and scripture readings of the cathedral offices, there was continuous recitation of the psalms (*recitation continua*) and continuous reading of biblical books (*lectio continua*). Ceremonies like lamp lighting and incensations, practiced in the cathedral offices, were deemed distracting to meditation and were kept to a minimum. But bowings and repetitions of formularies were conducive to meditation.[24]

Fasting also received a different emphasis in the monasteries. Since the end of the first century, Christians had fasted on Wednesdays and Fridays. Fasting in the church is done in commemoration of the passion of Christ and in anticipation of Christ's coming as the church's bridegroom to begin the marriage feast. One would not fast in the presence of the Bridegroom, that is, on the day of the Eucharist. Hence, Sundays (and in the East, also the Sabbath) were never fast days. The fasting of monks, however, served an ascetic purpose: it was done to subdue the flesh. Fasting in the monasteries is related to the devotional rule, not to the round of liturgical life. The monastic life entailed a perpetual meatless fast, which let up only slightly on Sundays with a cooked meal.[25]

The act of receiving communion also received a different twist when it was placed in the service of monastic devotion. The Eucharist was celebrated in the church as the means of communion with the crucified and risen Christ. It was the liturgy of the Lord's Day and festivals of Christ. Receiving communion was an ecclesial act that established the fellowship (*koinonia, communio*) of the church. In the monasteries, the act of receiving communion was separated from the rhythm of the church's life and entered the rhythm of individual devotion. Whether or not one received the sacrament of the body and blood of Christ had less to do with church fellowship than with individual need determined by the private state of one's soul. Because monks might need to receive communion at any time according to their spiritual need, daily celebrations of the Eucharist became the norm in the monasteries (although most monks certainly did not receive communion daily).

At first the hermits and monks went into the towns and cities to celebrate the Eucharist with their bishop or local presbyter. Monks who lived at some distance from urban churches might take the consecrated elements back to their cells and commune when ready. This was a continuation of earlier practice. Christians in the early centuries took the consecrated elements home with them for self-communion at the end of a period of fasting or during times of persecution when it was not safe for the church to assemble. But this practice was being discouraged by bishops during the fourth century. Eventually some monks were ordained so that the Eucharist could be celebrated in their own communities. The Eucharist was thus built into the round of daily offices in the monastery as one office among others, rather than serving as the summit toward which all the church's liturgies pointed and from which they flowed.[26] Whereas receiving communion had been a communal act, receiving communion in the monastery became an act of individual piety. As Alexander Schmemann wrote, "Without being noticed the receiving of Communion was subordinated to individual piety, so that piety was no longer determined by the Eucharist (as in the early Church). Instead, the Eucharist became an 'instrument' of piety, an element of asceticism, an aid in the struggle against demons, etc."[27]

In these ways communities emerged on the margins of the institutional life of the church and maintained the eschatological vigilance of early Christianity by practicing the ascetic disciplines of prayer and fasting. Ordinary lay Christians (and sometimes clergy) sought out monks as advisers. Monks provided them with personal access to spiritual authority at a time when bishops' enlarged areas of jurisdiction and responsibility made them less accessible to ordinary Christians. This could be construed as a continuation of the patron-client relationship that also influenced the role of the bishop in Christian initiation and ordination. As this happened, bishops of the church acted to absorb monasticism into the ordinary life of the church by inviting monasteries into the cities. We will take up this story in chapter 6.

CHAPTER 4

Times, Occasions, and the Communion of Saints

As the church settled into its new historical role during the fourth century, there was interest in the sanctification of time not only in terms of the times of the day at which the daily prayer offices in the cathedrals and urban monasteries were celebrated, but also in terms of the development of the church year calendar as we know it today. During this period, when persecution was over and the church was moving toward an established position in the Roman Empire, interest developed in the historical Jesus and the events associated with his life.

Before the fourth century, we have no evidence of Christmas, Transfiguration, the individual events of Holy Week, Ascension, or the celebration of the outpouring of the Holy Spirit on the Day of Pentecost. Christians did observe Sunday as their fixed day of assembly, as Acts 20:7 and Revelation 1:10 already indicate. The annual paschal celebration was being observed by the middle of the second century, as we see from the example of the Quartodecimans in Asia Minor. There is evidence of an Epiphany celebration as early as the third century in Egypt, as attested in the writings of Clement of Alexandria. This celebration focused on the baptism of Jesus, rather than his nativity, because the Egyptian church read through the Gospel of Mark, starting at the beginning of the year, and the Gospel of Mark begins with Jesus' baptism.[1] There is also evidence of a forty-day fast in Egypt after the Epiphany in imitation of Jesus' forty days of fasting in the wilderness after his baptism. This was not yet Lent as we know the pre-paschal fast, but it certainly established the idea of a forty-day time of fasting. Moreover, this fast seemed to have ended with the celebration of baptism, as the later Lenten fast did. It may also have been used as the time for reconciling penitent apostates.[2] While initiation and penitential practices varied from place to place and changed in the fourth century, certain features remained stable. Both practices involved enrollment into an order of catechumens or penitents; both involved practices of almsgiving, fasting, and prayer. Commemorations of the martyrs at their graves on the anniversary of their deaths was already practiced in the second century, as we see in the ancient text of *The Martyrdom of Polycarp*, which describes an event that took place in 155 and testifies to the assembling of the faithful at the old bishop's grave "as occasion allows" to "celebrate the birthday of his martyrdom." Thus, the basic features of the liturgical calendar were set in place before the Age of Constantine: the Sunday assembly, two annual festivals, times of fasting, and days commemorating the saints.

But a tremendous superstructure was imposed on these basic units of time during the fourth and fifth centuries. This is attributable to a number of factors that are not totally explained by the theory of the loss of eschatological consciousness.[3] First of all, there was an interest in historical commemorations before the Council of Nicaea. By an exceedingly complex process, festivals based on the Jewish lunar calendar were superimposed on the Roman solar calendar. We see this in the attempts to calculate the date of Easter and possibly also the date of Christmas. Interest in the life of Jesus brought pilgrims to the Holy Land, where pilgrimage rites were developed on the dates and at the places associated with events in the life of Jesus. To this development of pilgrim sites we owe the origins of Holy Week (including the triumphal procession into Jerusalem on Palm Sunday, the anniversary of the Lord's Supper on Maundy Thursday, the commemoration of the crucifixion of Jesus on Good Friday), as well as distinct celebrations of the Ascension of Our Lord, the Day of Pentecost, and even the Commemoration of the Holy Innocents. Pilgrims like the Spanish nun Egeria were impressed with these commemorative rites and took them home to their churches. The influence of the Jerusalem church on the development of the church year calendar and lectionary was tremendous.

Second, during and after the reign of Constantine, the public church's need to compete with lingering pagan practices prompted the development of fasts and feasts. For example, bishops at first countered the excesses of pagan feasting on January 1 with a fast, but later with the development of a feast in honor of the Virgin Mary. The baptism of new members celebrated with "awesome" rites of initiation became identified with the forty-day season of Lent. The erection of basilicas over the graves of the martyrs and the transfer of relics of the martyrs and saints to new sites promoted the development of anniversary feasts of the deaths of the saints.

Sunday as a Day of Rest and Worship

We have seen that Christians observed Sunday as a fixed day of worship already in the first century. But there is no evidence before Tertullian at the beginning of the third century that Christians observed Sunday as a day of rest, a sabbath. Indeed, the theology of Sunday as the eighth day, which developed before the third century, requires that the Lord's Day be regarded as the day beyond the Sabbath. In *De oratione* (*About Prayer*) 23, the Christian lawyer Tertullian speaks of the solemnity of the Lord's Day, and also that it should be freed of business affairs:

> In accordance with the tradition, we must only on the day of the Lord's resurrection guard not only against kneeling, but every posture expressing anxious care, deferring even our business affairs lest we give any place to the devil. Similarly, too, in the period of Pentecost; which period we distinguish by the same solemnity of exultation.

The comparison of Sunday with the fifty days of Easter suggests that Tertullian is not advocating a complete day of rest, only that one arrange one's schedule so that one's business affairs do not interfere with worship. The Syriac *Didascalia* (c. 250) also stresses that Christians should not make worldly affairs more important than assembling on the Lord's Day for the word of God.[4] The fact that Sunday was not a day of rest in the Roman Empire in the early centuries of Christianity meant that Christians had to make a special effort to attend the assembly.

The first laws making Sunday a day of rest for the whole society were enacted by Constantine on March 3, 321, less than ten years after legalizing the Christian cult in the Edict of Milan. This decree ordered that "all judges, townspeople, and all occupations should rest on the most honorable day of the Sun." The fact that Constantine used the Roman civil terminology, "day of the Sun," instead of the Christian terminology, "the Lord's Day," suggests that the day of rest might appeal to sun worshipers in the empire as well as Christians. Interestingly, Constantine's legislation exempted agricultural work, whereas Old Testament Jewish Sabbath legislation emphasized agricultural rest above all. Further legislation stipulated that slaves could be manumitted (emancipated) on Sunday and that a recording of this legal transaction could be made. It is unlikely that this Sunday rest was legislated only to show favoritism toward Christians. It was considered a good idea to have a uniform day of rest throughout the Roman Empire, and Sunday would appeal to many pagans as well as promote the Christian cult.

The church did not ask for this legislation; none of the church fathers appeal to the imperial legislation in their own theological reflections on the Lord's Day. They continued to stress the need to assemble for worship on the Lord's Day. But the new idleness on Sunday meant that Christians had to be occupied in edifying ways so they would not succumb to vice.

In particular, Christians had to be urged to assemble for worship and not to assemble with the crowds that attended the circuses, theater, and games that were held on Sundays. As Christianity gained in influence during the course of the fourth century, we find further legislation under Emperor Theodosius in 386 that prohibited circuses and theatrical performances on Sunday. Plays in the theaters were usually based on pagan mythology, and the bishops portrayed them as schools of vice, although people continued to attend in droves. Major sports events, in the form of contests between men and beasts, gladiatorial combat, and chariot races, also were condemned by the bishops. They remained a problem for Sunday worship attendance in the fourth century.[5]

As the church assumed more responsibilities as an established religion for the morals of society, church fathers like Jerome and Ephraim appealed more frequently to the Old Testament Sabbath commandment to back up their moral exhortations not only to cease from work and immoral forms of pleasure, but also to assemble for worship on Sunday. The Lord's Day came to be interpreted as a sabbath, but a more excellent one than the Jewish Sabbath, since it is filled with the worship of Christ. Not only were Christians expected to attend the eucharistic liturgy, but they also were encouraged to attend morning and evening prayer. Lauds and Vespers were given greater attention on Sunday than on the other days of the week because ordinary Christians could attend public services on this day of rest.[6]

The Paschal Celebration

There is no question that the annual celebration of the Pascha of Christ in connection with the Jewish Passover on 14/15 Nisan was established in Asia Minor by the middle of the second century. It is attested by the *Paschal Homily* of Melito of Sardis. Some scholars, such as Joachim Jeremias, argued that the Quartodeciman (Fourteenther) practice was already established in Palestine in the first century.[7] The theme of Christ as the Paschal Lamb was important to the Quartodecimans. Drawing on the chronology and theology of the Gospel of John, they celebrated the death and resurrection of Jesus on the night of the Jewish Passover, even claiming that the name of their feast, *Pascha*, derived from the Greek verb *paschein*, "to suffer." Nevertheless, the *Paschal Homily* of Melito makes clear that the passion of Christ was observed in the context of his whole redemptive act, from the incarnation to his glorification. Later on, the commemoration of Christ's incarnation on the day of his death (the annunciation) would lead to the calculation of his nativity nine months later. This paschal commemoration took the form of a nocturnal vigil of fasting and readings during the time the Jews were celebrating the Passover; after the Jewish feast was over at midnight, these Asian Christians broke their fast by celebrating the Eucharist.

We have no doubt about the Asian Quartodeciman practice. The real question is when the Sunday observance of Easter began. Thomas J. Talley suggests that it may have begun early in the second century in Alexandria but was not established in Rome until after 165.[8] In the year 165, Bishop Polycarp of Smyrna visited Bishop (Pope) Anicetus to urge the Roman church to adopt the Asian celebration of the paschal feast on 14/15 Nisan. Anicetus refused; he argued that every Sunday was a celebration of the Lord's resurrection. The two bishops celebrated the Eucharist together, with Anicetus deferring to Polycarp to preside, and they parted company amicably.

It appears that the Roman church then settled on the Sunday after the first full moon of spring as the date for the annual paschal feast, and Pope Victor I (189–198) tried to convince the rest of the ecumenical church from Gaul to Mesopotamia to hold synods in which to enact this practice. Most of the rest of the church sided with Rome, but the Asians refused to give up their practice. As a result, Victor excommunicated or broke fellowship with Bishop Polycrates of Ephesus and the churches of Asia that maintained the Quartodeciman practice.[9] Even bishops who agreed with Rome's resolution of the calendar issue felt that this was too harsh. Irenaeus of Lyons pointed out that all previous bishops of Rome up until Pope Soter had tolerated the Quartodeciman practice and that the issue was not of the essence of the Christian faith. The fact that the Asian churches remained in communion with Rome suggests that Victor withdrew his excommunication under this widespread pressure. Nevertheless, at the Council of Nicaea in 325, the issue was resolved once and for all in favor of Rome and against the Asians. Easter would be on the Sunday after the first full moon of spring. In a bow to the Quartodecimans, however, the Eastern churches continued to celebrate Pascha after the Jewish Passover, a custom that was not observed in the West. Moreover, variations in calendars used in the Roman Empire (e.g., Roman and Egyptian) and different ways of treating the situation when the full moon fell on a Sunday resulted in Easter being celebrated on different dates in different places. Thus, in 387 Easter was observed on March 21 in Gaul, on April 18 in Rome, and on April 25 in North Italy and Alexandria.[10]

On whatever date Easter fell, the principal celebration in the fourth century was still observed as a nocturnal vigil (what we today call the Easter Vigil), reflecting the earlier Quartodeciman practice. While there are variations in the content of the all-night vigil from one church to another, we can discern a common shape to this liturgy from the sermons of Gregory of Nazianzus and John Chrysostom in Constantinople, the catechetical homilies of Cyril of Jerusalem, the *Diary* of Egeria, and the sermons and writings of Augustine of Hippo in North Africa. The vigil began with a light service (*lucernarium*), an elaboration of the lamp lighting at the beginning of Vespers that became common in the fourth century. It was followed by a long series of readings and psalms from the Old Testament. The vigil culminated in celebration of baptism and the Eucharist, which was never before midnight. The time of the Eucharist had to do with principles of fasting. As we shall see, the Friday and Saturday before Easter became days of full fasting, but there was reluctance to extend the fast too long into the Lord's Day, the day of resurrection.

The Alexandrians contributed an understanding of the Pascha that disagreed with the Asian interpretation. Origen held that *Pascha* does not derive from *paschein* but was a Greek transliteration of the Hebrew *Pesach*, Passover. The Pascha was a commemoration of the Lord's passover from death to life.[11] This interpretation undoubtedly contributed to (or perhaps reflected) the tendency in Alexandria and

Rome to distinguish between Christ's death on Friday and his resurrection on Sunday, with Saturday as the day of the Lord's Sabbath rest in the tomb. Fridays had been a fast day for Christians anyway, in commemoration of the Lord's passion, and this fast was extended to Saturday before Easter. The Syriac *Didascalia* (c. 250) prescribes a six-day fast beginning on the second day of the week before Pascha. This fast is also testified in Egypt in the pastoral letters of Bishops Dionysius and Athanasius of Alexandria (247 and 329, respectively). This fast demarcated Holy Week. But the fast of Friday and Saturday was still considered more important. The Holy Week fast terminated on Holy Thursday with the celebration of the evening Eucharist in commemoration of the institution of the Lord's Supper. The paschal fast of the Three Days (Triduum) ended with the Easter Eucharist.

Before the fourth century, we cannot say with certainty that Easter was the preferred time for baptism. In fact, Epiphany could make more of such a claim in the East; only in North Africa and Rome can we say that Easter was the primary time of Christian initiation. The so-called *Apostolic Tradition* attributed to Hippolytus of Rome (c. 215) specified that, following enrollment, catechumens spent three years in the catechumenate, although it was the behavior that was judged rather than the time. Once Christianity was legalized, many catechumens were in no hurry to complete the process of Christian initiation, since it would curtail the activities of their lifestyle or vocations. Many parents presented their children for enrollment as catechumens early in life, but these candidates waited until the passions of youth had burned down before being baptized (Augustine is an example). Many public officials delayed baptism until they were on their deathbed, since the demands of the gospel would conflict with their public responsibilities, especially as regards capital punishment (Constantine is an example). We know that Augustine of Hippo was baptized in his thirtieth year after a conversion experience that was a culmination of a growing period of uncertainty probably prompted by the preaching of Ambrose of Milan. It is possible that the bishops developed a period of preparation for baptism before Easter (the forty days of fasting, *Quadragesima*)[12] in order to provide a definitive date by which to corral those who could be declared "competent" (*competentes*) to receive baptism: the chosen ones (*electi*). Thus, throughout the Catholic church during the fourth and fifth centuries, practices developed of "handing over" (*traditio*) to the catechumens the essential texts of the faith by "sounding down" to them the introductions to the four Gospels, the creed, and the Our Father; in the rites of the scrutinies, they had to repeat what they had learned. We know from Augustine's *Confessions* that this was a nerve-racking experience, even for one trained in rhetoric.

According to what we learn from Augustine's sermons and other writings, the catechumens in Hippo were permitted to break their forty-day fast on Holy Thursday and take a bath in the public baths of the town so that their bodies would not stink when they went into the baptismal pool. In some churches, including that of Hippo (perhaps in imitation of what Bishop Augustine had learned in Milan from Bishop Ambrose), the bishop washed their feet in memory of the Lord's example and command—the *Mandatum* from which Maundy Thursday received its name. Distinct observances in Rome on Maundy Thursday included the blessing of oils by the bishop to be used in Christian initiation and the reconciliation of public penitents so they could be restored to Holy Communion on the day of its anniversary.

On Good Friday in Hippo, everyone attended the basilica, sang Psalm 22, and listened to the Passion of our Lord (from Matthew in Hippo, but John in Jerusalem) and also a sermon, which sometimes took the form of a commentary on the Psalm of the Passion. We know that before the end of the fifth century, the Roman Good Friday liturgy included a series of bidding prayers (*orationes sollemnes*), which included bids and collects for unbelievers, idolaters, Jews, heretics, schismatics, lapsed Christians, and catechumens.[13] From Jerusalem, practices associated with the veneration of the cross spread everywhere. This was the consequence of the supposed discovery of the true cross of Christ by Empress Helena during excavations on Golgotha for the erection of the Basilica of the Holy Sepulcher, an event that electrified the Christian world.

After a quiet day on Holy Saturday, innumerable lamps were lit at sundown, and the greatest *lucernarium* of the year commenced; the whole Christian population thronged to the basilica for the nocturnal vigil. In Jerusalem the bishop emerged from the tomb of Christ with lighted tapers, proclaiming the resurrection of Christ. From this practice, the ceremony of lighting and blessing the paschal candle developed in the West between the fifth and seventh centuries. The text of the Easter proclamation known as the *Exsultet* draws on the thought of Ambrose and Augustine. In *The City of God* 15.22, Augustine quotes from the text of a *laus cerei* (praise of the candle) that he had composed three years before. The text of the *Exsultet* with which we are most familiar comes from Gaul in the seventh century.[14] The long series of readings from the Old Testament followed, always including in the various lectionaries the stories of the creation in Genesis 1, the binding of Isaac in Genesis 22, the Passover and passage through the Red Sea in Exodus 14, and Jonah, as well as the canticles of Miriam and of Isaiah, and the canticle of the three young men in the fiery furnace. These are included in the twelve readings assigned to this vigil in the fifth-century Armenian Lectionary.

The catechumenal process culminated at the Easter Vigil. Again, while there are variations in the order of baptism from one local church to another, certain features emerged as common to all of the churches. Following the readings and a discourse that Augustine and other bishops provided on them, the candidates for baptism removed all their clothing and jewelry and loosed their hair before going into the water. There was no embarrassment about this, because people were used to being naked in the public baths. But women and men were baptized separately, deacons and presbyters going down into the pool with the men and deaconesses going down into the pool with the women. The candidates renounced Satan and all his pomps and works and confessed their faith three times in God the Father, the Son, and the Holy Spirit in the Holy Church. A triple immersion corresponded to the triple profession of faith, although immersion usually meant having water poured over the head of the candidate while he or she stood in the waist-high water. Upon emerging from the water, the newly baptized (called neophytes) were anointed with oil, clothed in a clean white garment (alb), and led into the assembly before the bishop. The bishop in the assembly laid on hands, invoked the Holy Spirit, extended the greeting of peace, and welcomed the neophytes into the eucharistic assembly. This was the first time they attended the Eucharist or even made an offering.[15]

During the week after Easter Day, the neophytes attended the liturgy daily, wearing their white robes, while the bishops instructed them in the mysteries (sacraments) they had just experienced. We have the "mystagogical homilies" of many of the great bishops of the ancient church: Cyril of Jerusalem and Theodore of Mopsuestia, John Chrysostom and Proclus of Constantinople, Ambrose of Milan and Augustine of Hippo, and many others. These homilies provide the sacramental theologies of the fathers as well as information about the actual liturgical orders used in their churches. Ferdinand van der Meer relates that the faithful were also permitted to attend these sessions during the "week of white robes" and to ask questions of the bishop as he sat in his chair (*cathedra*) and expounded upon the mysteries of the faith. Augustine's answers to these questions aroused so much interest that in 413 he committed in advance to write down his addresses on the First Letter of John, which incorporated his ideas on the love (*caritas*) of God and the eucharistic fellowship.[16] On the eighth day after their baptism, the neophytes were able to remove their white robes, leave the chancel, and mingle with the faithful—but not without a final exhortation to choose the narrow way of life into which they had been initiated rather than the broad way of death they had left behind.

This was not the end of the paschal season. Like the Jewish Passover, it extended for fifty days until the Feast of Weeks (Pentecost)—an octave of octaves (seven times seven weeks plus an eighth day). Robert Cabié has shown the tenacity of the ancient Pentecost in Egypt.[17] Milan seems to have been influenced by Alexandria in many areas of ritual, so it is not surprising that Ambrose maintained a full fifty days of rejoicing. But John Chrysostom also said of the great Fifty Days, "We have unending holiday."

The Christmas Cycle

The origins of Christmas are wrapped in obscurity and controversy. It used to be a stock opinion that both Christmas, celebrated in Rome on December 25 according to the Julian calendar, and Epiphany, celebrated on January 6 in the East according to the Egyptian calendar, were developed by bishops as counter-festivals to the Roman solstice festival, which since the time of Emperor Aurelian in 274 was observed as the Nativity of the Invincible Sun (*dies natalis solis invicti*). Western Europe (Gaul and Spain) was more influenced by the East than by Rome in this regard and also observed the Epiphany on January 6. This theory held that Christians were gathered in their basilicas away from pagan celebrations to celebrate the Nativity of the Sun of Righteousness.

There is no doubt that the sermons of church fathers, such as Pope Leo the Great, contrast the Christian celebration with the pagan one. In his *Seventh Sermon on the Nativity*, Leo rails against "the ungodly practice of certain foolish folk who worship the sun as it rises at the beginning of daylight from elevated positions" and castigates ignorant

Christians who continue these pagan pieties even on the steps of Saint Peter's Basilica: "When they have mounted the steps which lead to the raised platform, they turn round and bow themselves towards the rising sun and with bent neck do homage to its brilliant orb."[18] Talley wonders if Pope Leo may have been unaware of the older Christian custom of facing the east for prayer, which may have continued to be practiced by Eastern Christians visiting in Rome.[19] In any event, sermons like this lend credence to the "history of religions" theory of the origins of Christmas.

However, as long ago as 1903, Louis Duchesne attributed the emergence of Christmas and Epiphany to efforts to calculate the exact date on which Jesus had been born.[20] More recently, Thomas Talley has revived and championed Duchesne's "computation" theory of the origins of Christmas and Epiphany.[21] Briefly, this theory holds that Christians in the third century appealed to the Jewish view that the creation of the world occurred at Passover time in the spring, and reasoned that the new creation must also occur at that time. Since Passover time was the time in which Christians celebrated the passover of Christ from death to life, they believed that Jesus was conceived on the same date on which he died. When Christians were cut off from the synagogues and the computations of the rabbis, they had to find an equivalent date in the solar calendars for 14/15 Nisan. Once the dates of Christ's pascha had been fixed as March 25 in the Roman Julian calendar and April 6 in the Egyptian calendar, it was a simple matter of counting nine months from conception to birth; hence December 25 as the Roman Christmas and January 6 as the Epiphany in the East as well as in Gaul and Spain.

Further exploration of calendars shows that this hypothesis works. The Egyptian calendar consisted of twelve months of thirty days, plus five epagomenal days to complete the solar year of 365 days. The Roman calendar, which is more familiar to us, does not have months with an equal number of days. The first spring month in the Egyptian calendar was Teireix, which was about March 11 or 12 in the Roman calendar. The fourteenth day of the first spring month (the equivalent of 14 Nisan) was 14 Teireix in Egypt and apparently also in Cappadocia, which followed the Egyptian calendar, and 14 Artemisios in Asia, which was March 25 in Rome. Nine months after March 25 brings us to December 25.

Calculating the time of Jesus' birth does not mean it was celebrated as a festival. As we have seen, the East celebrated the baptism of Jesus, not his nativity, on January 6, even though already in the third century, Clement of Alexandria calculated that Jesus had been born on January 6. The earliest evidence from Rome of the date of December 25 as Jesus' birth is in the *deposition martyrum*, part of the Roman Chronograph of the year 354, with indications that the dates in this calendar were assembled in 336. But there is no evidence of an actual liturgical celebration. Because of references in Augustine's *De Solstitiis*, Thomas Talley tentatively proposed that the celebration of Christmas may have begun in North Africa before it began in Rome.[22] We know that when Gregory of Nazianzus was elected bishop of Constantinople in 379, he instituted an observance of the nativity of Christ on December 25 separate from the celebration of the baptism of Christ on January 6. It should be noted that this was also the year of the accession of the orthodox emperor Theodosius I and the political defeat of Arianism. There had been an effort to counter Arianism by emphasizing the incarnation of the Word. Egeria, in her *Diary*, indicates that the nativity had been the content of the January 6 celebration in Palestine when she visited there in the late fourth century. Thus, it is possible that the celebration of the birthday of Jesus may owe more to theological concerns and historicizing interests than as a way to counter the pagan solstice festival.

Holding to the "computation" hypothesis of the origins of Christmas does not require that we ignore the countercultural aspects of this festival in the Mediterranean world. The celebration of Christ's nativity, calculated from the incarnation of the divine Word in the womb of the virgin Mary on the same day as Christ's passover from death to life, certainly, if unintentionally, bumped into the solstice festivals. Bishops would naturally use the occasion of Christian worship to draw contrasts between the Christian celebration and the pagan celebrations. Like Pope Leo, they would try to wean Christians away from lingering pagan practices (like standing on an elevated place and bowing toward the rising sun). However, we should note that there was no need to counter paganism in Constantinople, which was founded as a Christian city (even though there was a need to counter heresy). In conservative Rome, on the other hand, paganism lingered on among the senatorial families and their clients. The sermons of Leo I were preached a full century after the Chronograph of 354 lists December 25 as the date of Christ's nativity.

The pre-Christmas season seems to have several possible precursors. The season of Advent as we know it originated in Gaul and Spain as a forty-day fast comparable to Lent, although clear references to this do not exist prior to the Synod of Tours (567). The fast began near the Feast Day of Saint Martin (November 11) and was known as "Saint Martin's Lent" (*Quadragesima Sancti Martini*).[23] Gospel readings in Gallican lectionaries proclaim the ministry of John the Baptist and thus could relate to themes of baptism and repentance.[24] If this time frame between November 11 and January 5 had been a time of preparation for baptism on Epiphany, it would have allowed forty days of fasting (excluding Saturdays and Sundays as nonfast days). The problem with this scenario is that the adoption of the Roman Christmas in Carolingian Gaul (the period in which we have liturgical material for Advent), with twelve days of feasting between December 25 and January 6, would have curtailed a period of fasting in preparation for an Epiphany baptism. But by this time, the ancient baptismal schedule would have been irrelevant in the prevailing situation of infant baptism.

This forty-day fast was unknown in Rome, and a clearly demarcated pre-Christmas season was never adopted in the East. But Talley notes that Filastrius, bishop of Brescia (d. 397), mentions a pre-Christmas fast observed before Saint Lucia's Day on December 13, along with three other fasts that precede Easter in the spring, Pentecost in the summer, and the Triumph of the Cross on September 14.[25] This may have been the origin of the ember seasons, and these quarterly fasts may have had a pre-Christian history in Rome. The pre-Christmas fast in Rome was not forty days, like the Gallican fast. Since Epiphany was not a day for solemn public baptisms in Rome, a time of fasting comparable to Lent was not needed.

On the other hand, fasting need not always be related to initiation or penitence. The Gospel reading for the December Ember Wednesday in Rome was the annunciation, whose theme is certainly not penitential but rather is one of joyful anticipation. There could be another explanation for the pre-Christmas fast, one that also explains the lack of an Advent season in the East. It could be related to the completion of the harvest and the closing of the pastures during winter in the agricultural regions of Italy, Gaul, and Spain. Winter herds could not be as large as the summer herds since feed was limited, so December was a time when some of the livestock was slaughtered. The harvest and slaughter naturally provided food for feasting at the end of the old year and the beginning of the new. The origins of the fasts in western Europe during November and December could simply have been a way of anticipating the feasts of harvest time. This mundane fact could explain similarities in practices between the German Yuletide and the Roman Saturnalia and Kalends.[26]

A season of harvest festivals was held in Rome between December 15 (Consualia) and December 23 (Laurentalia). Themes of thanksgiving for harvest and eschatological fulfillment dominate the nine sermons of Pope Leo the Great on the fasts and feasts of the Tenth Month (December). In *Sermon XVII* he notes that God's work precedes the church, as we see in the Old Covenant:

> The teaching of the Law, dearly beloved, imparts great authority to the precepts of the Gospel, seeing that certain things are transferred from the old ordinances to the new and by the very devotions of the Church it is shown that the Lord Jesus Christ "came not to destroy but to fulfill the Law." For since the cessations of the signs by which our Savior's coming (*adventus*) was announced, and the abolition of types in the presence of the Very Truth, those things which our religion instituted, whether for the regulation of customs or for the simple worship of God, continue with us in the same form in which they were at the beginning, and what was in harmony with both Testaments has been modified by no change. Among these there is also the solemn fast of the tenth month, which is now kept by us according to yearly custom, because it is altogether just and godly to give thanks to the Divine bounty for the crops which the earth has produced for the use of men under the guiding hand of Providence. And to show that we do this with ready mind, we must exercise not only the self-restraint of fasting, but also diligence in almsgiving, that from the ground of our heart also may spring up the germ of righteousness and the fruit of love, and that we may deserve God's mercy showing mercy to the poor.[27]

Here Leo does not distance the church from the Roman harvest festival, but emphasizes the sense of gratitude and fulfillment that it should engender. He does not denigrate the old Roman customs of gift giving at the beginning of the new year, but sees it as a way to live the gospel rather than just to assure abundance for oneself in the coming year. Yet in *Sermon XXIX* he issues an eschatological warning that is clearly related to the feasting of this time of harvest and thanksgiving:

> When the Savior would instruct his disciples about the advent of God's Kingdom and the end of the world's times, and teach his whole church, in the person of the apostles, he said, "Take heed lest haply your hearts be overcharged with surfeiting and drunkenness, and care of this life." And assuredly, dearly beloved, we acknowledge that this precept applies

more especially to us, to whom undoubtedly the day announced is near, even though hidden, for the advent of which it behooves every man to prepare himself lest it find him given over to gluttony, or entangled in cares of this life.[28]

What is remarkable in these sermons is that the advent of Christ has nothing to do with the coming festival of the nativity of Christ, even though it is almost Christmas Eve. But the church's ritual system has always been strengthened by relating it to the agrarian calendar.

Advent as a time of eschatological fulfillment clearly precedes ideas about Advent as a preparation for either baptism or Christmas. The idea that the harvest rather than baptism underlies the origins of Advent is given further support by the prayers in the ancient Roman, Gallican, and Mozarabic sacramentaries, which appeal to the eschatological coming of Christ using the terms *venire, veniens, venturus* (to come, coming, will come).[29] In fact, we know that the classical Advent prayers come primarily from Gallican sources because they are addressed to Christ rather than to God the Father, as Roman prayers would be, and several of the collects petition Christ to "stir up your power, O Lord, and come." Christ's coming in power belongs to his second *parousia*, not to the incarnation of the Word. These prayers are not related to baptism or Christmas. This could also be another way of understanding the Gospel readings concerning the ministry of John the Baptist in the Gallican lectionaries: John pointed not to his baptism as a sign of repentance but to the coming of the Greater One who will bring God's eschatological judgment.

The Cult of the Saints

As mentioned in chapter two, several popular practices were associated with the cult of the saints. Christians assembled at the tombs of their martyrs as other Romans assembled at the tombs of their heroes for all-night vigils and *refrigeria*, although the meals with the dead were transformed into celebrations of the Eucharist on the *mensae* of the tombs. The main developments of the fourth and fifth centuries were the building of basilicas over the graves of the martyrs, which we shall discuss in the next chapter, and rituals involving the transfer of remains or relics of the saints.[30]

The relics of the saints were transferred when it was necessary to move their bodies from one cemetery to another, or from a cemetery to a church building. Sometimes relics of the saints were transferred from one country to another. The relics of Saint Stephen the proto-martyr were found in Gaza in 415, as a result of a vision seen in a dream, together with the relics of Nicodemus, Gamaliel, and his son Habib. A small quantity of the relics of Stephen were brought to the West and occasioned much excitement in North Africa, including a sermon by Augustine. A shrine was erected over this handful of dust near the cathedral in Hippo in 424.

An aura of sanctity accrued to the body of the saint, the physical presence of the holy (*praesentia*).[31] The idea of dismembering the body of a saint to send relics to different places was repugnant to church leaders of late antiquity, although it was practiced in the Middle Ages. However, the holiness of the saints even extended to objects that had come into contact with their bodies, such as cloths (*brandea*) that pilgrims lowered to touch the body of the saint. When Byzantine empresses or the young Justinian asked for pieces of saints interred in the West, *brandea* were sent to them instead.

When pilgrims visited the shrines of the saints, they were visiting the person. As the prayers of the martyrs, confessors, and ascetics were considered especially efficacious because of the sanctity of their lives, so it was believed that the intercessions of the saints continued to be efficacious even after their deaths. Many experiences of healing attributed to intercessions of saints at their shrines, such as at the shrine of Saint Martin of Tours in southern Gaul, contributed to the popularity of these shrines as places of pilgrimage. As Peter Brown notes, this cult was supported by the most intellectual of scholars and bishops (Jerome and Augustine among many), as well as ordinary believers.[32] While the cult was a feature of popular religion, in no way was there a tension between leaders and people in its promotion. Local communities adopted certain saints as their patrons, just as the old cities of the Greco-Roman world had their patron gods and goddesses or heroes. Rome adopted Peter and Paul, both of whom had been martyred in the city, as double patron saints. Great basilicas were built over the tombs of Saint Peter on the Vatican Hill and Saint Paul outside the walls. Peter and Paul replaced Romulus and Remus as the patrons of Rome, and the date on which the founding of Rome had been celebrated, June 29, became the Feast Day of Saints Peter and Paul. Patron saints thus served as symbols of civic pride and concord.

The double preoccupation of the spiritual power associated with the saint and the concord that accrued to the saint's city made a saint's coming (*adventus*) into a city a state occasion. The relics of the saints were brought into the city with all the pomp and ceremony that befitted the arrival of an emperor. The panegyric read on the arrival of the emperor was replaced with the *passio* of the saint read on the anniversary of his or her death or *adventus* to the new resting place. A whole hagiographic literature developed in such genres as acts of the martyrs or lives of the saints, which could be read on these occasions. The injustice with which the saints had often been treated in their lives and in the circumstances of their deaths, combined with their triumphs over physical pain, became sources of inspiration and encouragement. As Brown writes, "We should not underestimate the gusto with which the Christian communities of the western Mediterranean turned the celebration of the memory of the martyrs into a reassuring scenario by which the unambiguously good power, associated with the amnesty of God and the *praesentia* of the martyr, overcame the ever-lurking presence of evil power."[33]

The feasts of the martyrs and the reading of their *passiones* brought not only comfort and hope to those afflicted with illness and physical pain, but also a reminder to the local community that God's justice trumps human injustice. Daily life at the shrine of a saint in late antiquity could be a frightening experience, since there was a constant confrontation between "clean" power and "unclean" power. The shrine was visited by the sick crying to be healed, and by the demon-possessed—shrieking, bellowing, or writhing. As Jerome's letter to the Roman pilgrim Paula suggests, she of more refined sensitivities blanched at the exorcisms she encountered in the tombs of the prophets in the Holy Land. The shrine of Saint Martin of Tours was overrun with beggars as well as the demon-possessed, who were fed and given odd jobs like scrubbing the floors of the basilica and picking up sticks and stones to the honor of their patron saint.

The power of the saints in light existed to protect the faithful on earth from the powers of darkness. As the cult of the saints developed from the forms of veneration associated with the Greco-Roman cult of the dead, so the Christian cult of the saints was used to transform the cult of the dead in the lands of western Europe being evangelized. James Frazer documented the widespread belief among primitive peoples, including the peoples of western Europe, that the dead in general, and ancestors in particular, could "steal the souls" of the living, or at least haunt or play tricks on the living. He notes that concern to ward off or pacify the dead were especially acute during Yuletide or the late autumn harvest, when they came in from the cold, as we see surviving in the custom of Halloween jack-o'-lanterns or leaving food for the dead.[34]

The emergence of the Christian Feast of All Saints on November 1, which spread from Celtic Britain and Ireland to the continent in the eighth century, was a way of assuaging the fears associated with the dead by drawing them into the paschal mystery of Christ. There had been a feast of all the martyrs in the East as early as the fourth century, although the date varied, and a similar observance was held in Rome at the dedication of the Pantheon on May 13, 609 (or 610). But the Celtic All Saints' Day on November 1 quickly caught on precisely because of a fixation on the needs of the dead, which were particularly acute at this time of the year. All Souls' Day on November 2 spread throughout Europe after the tenth century for the same reason. Thus, a more beneficial relationship was established between the faithful on earth, the saints in heaven, and the souls in purgatory. In one communion between the living and the dead, the faithful on earth could pray to the saints in heaven and ask for their prayers in turn, and by their prayers and good works extend charity toward their own dead by providing for their relief in the afterlife.

CHAPTER 5

Sacred Places and Liturgical Art in Late Antique Culture

The landscape of Greco-Roman antiquity was dotted with sacred places. Religious buildings attested to the vitality of the community or group that maintained them. The ubiquitous presence of shrines, temples, and altars in the cities and country places of the Roman Empire attested to the economic vitality of the empire that maintained the public sacred places; the prosperity of the private groups that erected shrines, temples, or altars to their own patron deities; and the wealth of landed patrons, who maintained sacred structures on their estates.

Some distinctions were made between public and private shrines. Public sacred places were dedicated to the gods in the name of the people (*populus*). Damage to public sacred places was considered a sacrilege, whereas damage to private shrines was not considered a sacrilege, even though all sacred places were respected. This was because publicly dedicated *res sacra* (holy things) were regarded as belonging to the deity, not to the city; private shrines remained private property.[1]

With the sheer number of shrines, temples, and altars, it was inevitable that some would fall into a state of disrepair if the city, cultic group, or patron could not afford to maintain them or if the cult no longer flourished. Some cults did lose their appeal and decline, and their religious buildings were also left to decay. As in our cities today some church buildings are sold by their congregations to other congregations or religious groups, so cultic buildings could be sold to other groups to be dedicated to another deity. In other situations, a process of desacralization would render the facility usable for "secular" purposes. Public shrines dedicated to patron deities could not be desacralized, since they belonged to the deity. Therefore, urban shrines were often left to decay until they could be revitalized by the city or by a benefactor.

Sacred space was a fluid concept in which sacralization and desacralization were constantly taking place. This can be seen especially in the mobility of the Roman legions. When Roman armies built a camp, they consecrated the place to the gods. While they brought their own gods with them, they did not want to anger the gods who were believed to have some power over the local place. So while they installed shrines to their own gods inside the camp, they also built or maintained temples to the local deities outside the camp. Sacralization of the land could be undone by desecrating religious spaces. So when a Roman legion left an area, the local inhabitants might destroy the shrines and cult statues left behind as a way of showing the weakness of the invaders' gods.

Sacralization involved the dedication of a space to a god. The holy place sets up a point of communication between the god and his or her devotees. This opening up of communication ensured the benevolence of that god over the camp, the city, or the region. Rites of dedication might include a public or a private offering and the use of incense. Desacralization was more complex because it was often less formalized. It included a return of sacred things to a profane use, such as a secularization of religious buildings or the desecration of a shrine. Desacralization was a process of closing down communication with that deity.[2]

Christian liturgical space did not fit in with the procedures of sacralizing space in the ancient world. The earliest places of Christian assembly were houses of members of the church or houses whose titles were given to the church and held in trust by the bishop. They were not temples or shrines in the pagan sense. There were no public rites to take possession of these places other than performing the sacramental rites within them. Buildings held by Christians were regarded as private and could be damaged without the penalties of sacrilege during persecution.

Moreover, Christians, unlike other citizens, refused to take part in the civic religion and did not honor other gods of the place. After the expulsion of the Christians from the Jewish synagogues toward the end of the first century C.E., Christians were no longer protected under the exemption from the civil rites accorded the Jews as a *religio licita* (licensed religion). Christians could be persecuted for their refusal to participate in the civil cult by capital punishment and the confiscation of their goods. Such persecution was often local or provincial. There were few empire-wide state-sponsored persecutions of Christians. The most systematic persecution of Christians occurred under the emperors Decius and Diocletian in 250 and 303, respectively, because these emperors had ordered a general sacrifice throughout the empire to preserve the *pax deorum* (peace of the gods) and to show loyalty to the rulers, and Christians refused to make such an offering. The result of this civil disobedience was the arrest and execution of Christian leaders, the confiscation of church property and sacred vessels, and the burning of Christians' sacred books.

The specific purpose of the Edict of Milan, issued by the emperors Constantine and Licinius in 313, was to secure for Christianity the privileges of a "licensed cult" (*religio licita*). It guaranteed the right of all people to profess the Christian faith, and removed any legal disabilities they might suffer for doing so. It restored the status of those who had been expelled from imperial service on religious grounds, particularly because of their conscientious objection to offering the required sacrifice in the pagan courts. It secured the right of Christian believers to follow their law and to assemble publicly for worship. It restored the buildings and property of Christians and the church that had been confiscated during the time of persecution, including the properties that had been subsequently sold. Finally, it recognized the church as a corporation with the right to hold property.[3]

The provisions of this edict went beyond the terms required for the licensing of a new cult. The freedom granted to Christians was broad and actually extended to adherents of all religions. This represented a change of policy on the part of the state; it would no longer attempt to control the religious life of its citizens. Tolerance was embraced as a principle of public law and was to remain on the books until the accession of Theodosius in 378. It was affirmed by Constantine's successors, including emperors with religious views as different as those of Julian the Apostate and the Christian Valentinian.[4]

We should understand what this edict meant for the church and its public building projects. Christianity was a legal religion and actually favored by Constantine and most of the rulers who followed him, but until Theodosius, it was not the official state religion. It continued to compete with other cults, including the classical civil cults established in the cities of the Roman Empire as well as new cults that entered the empire from outside its borders, particularly from Persia. The eastern regions of the empire became evangelized more quickly than the western regions. The city of Rome remained under the control of the Senate during the fourth century, and most of the senatorial families were pagans who supported the traditional civil religion of Rome. It was precisely because the ceremonial heart of the city of Rome, the Forum, was dominated by the old pagan shrines and temples that could not be violated that Constantine in 324 established Constantinople as a new capital in which Christian shrines and temples could dominate the ceremonial heart of the city. Interestingly, the new city was dedicated using traditional pagan rites for the dedication of a city to a god or goddess, although in this case, the city was dedicated to the Christian God. Even so, pagan shrines were allowed to be erected in the city.

Not until the end of the fourth century did Christian emperors make a more concerted effort to close down the pagan temples and halt the sacrifices with a strict interdiction.[5] Emperor Gratian set up his court in Milan, came under the influence of Bishop Ambrose, refused the title *Pontifex maximus*, and issued an interdict in 383 to remove the Altar of Victory in the Roman Senate. Senators offered incense and libations on this altar, and emperors took an oath of loyalty on it. This created a crisis of conscience for pagan senators in Rome, who were facing the perils of the invasion of the Goths. They believed that the gods would remove their protection of Rome if state-sponsored and state-funded sacrifices were no longer performed to their honor. In a compromise agreement, the statue of Victory remained in the Curia as a secular symbol of the state, but sacrifices were no longer offered to her.

Legislation closing the public pagan temples was the work of Christian emperors. As *Pontifex maximus*, only emperors had the authority either to consecrate or to deconsecrate a public temple. Constantine himself used that power sparingly, and usually only to remove temples that were on biblical sites in the Holy Land on which Christian shrines would be erected. Legislation left open-ended what was to become of the buildings. Some were desacralized by removing the image of the god or goddess from them and then left to decay. Others were desecrated as well as desacralized. Some were used as stone quarries, their *spolia* adorning other buildings, including churches. Others came back into use as secular buildings and, in a few instances, as Christian churches. But by and large, Christians did not take over pagan temples as churches because this would have been impractical. The temples were not places of assembly that could shelter a large congregation. Usually only the priests entered the temple; the devotees remained in the courtyard or precincts or held banquets in adjoining rooms.

Basilicas

The kind of building suitable for Christian liturgical assemblies was the Roman *basilica* ("royal portico"). The basilicas were large public buildings, usually situated next to the forum and used as a marketplace, a law court, or as a place for public gatherings. The architecture of basilicas varied from place to place, but most of them were longitudinal (longer than they were wide), with internal colonnades that either demarcated an open atrium or served as trusses supporting a roof. The colonnades of enclosed basilicas also divided the nave from the side aisles. Some basilicas had no colonnades or side aisles, but they were still longitudinal and included three distinct areas: a narthex vestibule, the nave itself, and the apse. One of the best preserved examples of this kind of basilica is the one Constantine built in Trier in 305 to 312 to be used as the audience hall of the imperial palace.

Basilicas were not sacred buildings in the same sense that temples were. But basilicas used as law courts contained a statue of the emperor, to whom an incense offering was made. Jews had already used the basilica plan for synagogues as early as the third century. But this was the type of building Constantine selected to meet the liturgical needs of growing Christian congregations. As a "royal" building, the basilica was also a suitable symbol of imperial patronage. The earliest basilica built for Christian use adjoined the Lateran Palace in Rome, which Constantine gave to the bishop of Rome as his residence. Later named Saint John Lateran, this first truly monumental Christian building, built circa 312/13–320, had four aisles, two on each side, separated by colonnades. Another significant basilica built by Constantine was the Church of the Holy Sepulcher in Jerusalem, erected in 325–336 over the reported site of Mount Calvary and the tomb of Christ. Its distinctive feature was a colonnaded atrium on the east end.[6]

As the church moved into basilicas, it began to approximate the layered strata of Roman society. New and old social divisions in the church (clergy and laity, faithful and catechumens, men and women, imperial dignitaries and common people) were coordinated with physical arrangements in the architectural design of the basilica (atrium, narthex, nave, apse, aisles, galleries). Generally the clergy were on the bema or in the apse, the faithful were in the nave for the liturgy of the word and gathered around the chancel for communion, the catechumens were in the aisles, and the seekers were in the narthex. The public penitents were in different parts of the building. Gregory Thaumaturgus distinguished four degrees of participation of penitents in the liturgy. These included "weepers," who remained outside the door and asked the prayers of the faithful who entered; "listeners," who remained in the narthex, listening to the scripture readings and preaching, but left before the prayers and before the catechumens had gone out; "those who fell down" within the doors of the church before leaving with the catechumens; and the "bystanders," who remained with the faithful throughout the liturgy but abstained from receiving communion.[7]

The bishops presiding over the liturgy from the bema or in the apse would have looked like the magistrates who presided over civil proceedings in civic basilicas, because they were dressed in the same way. This is because Emperor Constantine convinced the bishops to take over some functions of the state as his representatives. In legislation of the year 318, bishops were given the authority to adjudicate civil cases between Christians and non-Christians, as well as between Christians (which they had been doing before the reign of Constantine as part of their ministry of reconciliation). In 316 and 321, Constantine enlisted their aid in settling legal questions concerning the acts that granted manumission to Christian slaves and, in connection with this, the granting of citizenship to all freemen. As Theodore Klauser pointed out, within the highly bureaucratic Roman state, the granting of these privileges and responsibilities required assigning to the bishops and their assistants (presbyters and deacons) their correct status in the carefully graded social protocol of the imperial court.[8] This meant granting to the bishops the titles, insignia, and privileges that corresponded to their social rank. Since for the most part the bishops were given the highest social rank, that of *illustres*, they also received the insignia of that rank: the *pallium* (a kind of stole), the *mappula* (a ceremonial handkerchief), the *campagi* (a special kind of footwear), the *camalaucum* (a distinctive headgear), and probably a golden ring. They had the right to a throne (*cathedra*) of a specified design and height, the right to be accompanied by lights and incense, and the right to be greeted with a kiss on the hand. Since the bishop of Rome had a status almost equal to that of the emperor, his portrait could be hung in public places, and he could be greeted on his arrival for a liturgical event by a choir of singers.

Vestments that are familiar to us today in the historic Western rite, such as the alb, tunic, dalmatic, and chasuble, were not insignia as such in the fourth century, but the ordinary attire of Roman citizens. However, among the gifts given to the church by wealthy patrons was rich apparel to be worn by sacred ministers presiding at the liturgy and other sacramental rites. So when the clergy began wearing their "Sunday best" for the liturgies, their clothing was a cut above that of the ordinary worshipers.[9] As styles of clothing changed, these precious robes were kept in the closet for liturgical wear and so over the course of the years became "vestments." It was up to bishops, of course, to decide to receive and wear these insignia and vestments. Most of them did. The few who resisted were certainly among the best bishops of the time: Hilary of Poitiers, Martin of Tours, Fulgentius of Ruspe, and Augustine of Hippo.[10]

A new approach to liturgy took into account these new divisions within the assembly. The churches were populated by seekers as well as catechumens, penitents as well as communicants, and among the communicants, some received communion and some abstained. Except for penitents who were excommunicated, whether one received or abstained from communion became a matter of personal decision rather than an act of church fellowship as it had been in the more intimate eucharistic celebrations in house churches using the form of the symposium. According to Robert Taft, "Under such conditions the eucharist could no longer sustain its former ideology as a rite of koinonia, and Antiochene liturgical explanation begins to elaborate a symbolism of the presence of the saving work of Christ in the ritual itself, even apart from participation in the communion of the gifts."[11] This is evident in the allegorical interpretation of the liturgy practiced by the church fathers of late antiquity. As Hans-Joachim Schulz explains, allegory does not mean for theologians like John Chrysostom and Dionysius the Aeropagite what it means for us today. For us, allegory is a free-floating but arbitrary assignment of meaning to symbols and actions. But the interpretation of liturgy in the Antiochene school is kept within bounds by the fact that "in every case the meaning of the rite emerges from a 'higher' and never from 'another' irrelevant reality."[12] Taft explains, "All healthy liturgical interpretation depends on a ritual symbolism determined not arbitrarily, but by the testimony of tradition rooted in the Bible."[13] This kind of liturgical theology is seen in the mystagogia, or explanations of the mysteries (sacraments), practiced by the church fathers in late antiquity.

Theodore of Mopsuestia among them understood that Christians gather to celebrate the mystery or work of redemption in Christ. Therefore, in his mystagogical catecheses, everything in the liturgy was related to an event in the life of Christ.[14] So the whole liturgy became a kind of dramatic reenactment of the Christ event, especially of his passion. Everything done in the liturgy reminded the assembly of some aspect of the life of Christ. For example, the deacons spreading the linens on the altar remind us of the burial sheets of Christ. The offering procession reenacts Christ being led to his passion. The *epiclesis* (invocation of the Holy Spirit) in the anaphora of Great Thanksgiving represents the resurrection of Christ. In Theodore's symbolism, the deacons standing around the bishop are an image of the angels surrounding the throne of God. The Divine Liturgy is the intersection of heaven and earth. The "great entrance" at the offertory with its cherubic hymn, "Let All Mortal Flesh Keep Silence," reenacted Christ borne aloft on the shields of the angels in victory.

Needless to say, the size of the buildings in which Christians assembled; the need to develop a ceremony appropriate to such spaces; the acquisition of vestments for the bishops, presbyters, and deacons derived from imperial court ceremonial dress; and the use of a typological interpretation of the Bible as promise and fulfillment in Christ, as practiced especially by the Antiochene fathers—all these reinforced the view of liturgy as a sacred drama. Merely attending the liturgy was an act of sanctification, whether one received communion or not, because it was a way of participating in the saving mystery of Christ.

Cemeteries and Church Buildings

Not only were the Christians of late antiquity sanctified just by attending the liturgy, they also came into contact with sanctity by being in physical touch with the saints. A practice that began before the Age of Constantine but continued with gusto during and after his reign was the building of monumental buildings in cemeteries. Pagans, too, had erected shrines to family members and heroes in the cemeteries or necropolis, but Christians outdid their pagan friends and neighbors by erecting basilicas in the cemeteries.

The Church of the Holy Sepulcher is typical of this phenomenon of Christian church construction, which scandalized pagan society even though it was not in a cemetery, but only over the discovered tomb of Christ. That which defiled space in Roman eyes—the presence of the corruption of death within urban space—sanctified space in the Christian view. Far from being viewed as sources of pollution, the bodies of the martyrs were venerated by Christians. As Christ himself had risen from the dead, causing the tomb over which the Church of the Holy Sepulcher was built to be "empty," so the martyrs were deemed to be alive and in God's presence, their bodies awaiting the general resurrection of the dead.

Already in the second century, Christians had erected a chapel over the grave of Saint Peter in the cemetery on the Vatican Hill in the northwest corner of the City of Rome along the Tiber, where Nero had built the Circus next to the necropolis. In the fourth century, when Emperor Constantine decided to build a great basilica over Peter's grave, beginning in 324, it was erected on the site of that chapel, and the altar was placed over the tomb of the apostle. The basilica was so massive that it required leveling the top of the hill and moving the pagan cemetery. At the same time, Constantine began building the Basilica of Saint Paul Outside the Walls, where a similar cemetery chapel had been erected. These are two celebrated examples of a phenomenon that occurred throughout the Roman world.

The Romans respected cemeteries and left tombs and private chapels undisturbed. Therefore, the places where the saints and martyrs were buried were cared for by Christians. That is why we can be reasonably certain that they are authentic sites. Many of these new edifices attracted thousands of pilgrims to areas outside the city walls that the pagans had regarded as defiled. Tombs had been regarded as private property, but Christians made them public shrines. Emperor Julian the Apostate viewed with abhorrence the Christian cult of the saints: "You keep adding many corpses newly dead to the corpse [i.e. Jesus] of long ago. You have filled the whole world with tombs and sepulchers."[15] Pagans feared that Christians would do more than build basilicas over the graves of the saints. They feared that Christians would bring the remains of their saints into the cities. Even emperors as friendly toward the church as Gratian, Valentinian II, and Theodosius I tried to curb this development by decreeing, "All bodies that are contained in urns and sarcophagi and are kept above the ground shall be carried and placed outside the city, that they may present an example of humanity and leave the homes of the citizens in sanctity."[16]

A riot broke out in Gaza City in 396 when pagans thought Christians were carrying a dead body into the city. But even with imperial legislation, the pagans could not win this battle against the tide of Christian popular devotion. From the fifth century on, dead saints made triumphal processions into cities. At first it was the very special dead, the martyrs, whose remains were interred in churches located within the city walls. It continued with the remains of the privileged dead, such as bishops, clerics, and church patrons who wished to be buried close to the saints. Finally, the tombs of ordinary Christians appeared inside the cities. Eventually cemeteries were located adjacent to church buildings, although this development occurred more in the less urban areas of western Europe, since there was simply no space for new cemeteries in the old cities of the Mediterranean world. Nevertheless, in the span of a century, a revolution occurred in ideas of sanctity and defilement, making this development possible. Christians wanted to be surrounded by the dead and gloried in the faithful departed in a way that Peter Brown says "would have been profoundly disturbing to pagan and Jewish feeling."[17]

Christians performed their most sacred act, the Eucharist, on the *mensae* of graves of the saints. At first this was a way of curbing *refrigeria* among Christians. But eventually they placed their altars over the tombs of the saints, as the altar in Saint Peter's Basilica (the ancient edifice as well as the Renaissance edifice) was placed over the crypt in which lie the remains of the apostle. Finally, relics of the saints were embedded within the altar *mensa*. Bishops whose cities lacked the remains of saints gathered relics on their journeys to enshrine in their own churches, at least *brandea* if not actual pieces of the body of a saint. Thus, even a city as unfavored with its own local saints as Rouen could boast in 396, "Our habitation is now among a legion of Saints and the renowned powers of the Heavens."[18]

Liturgy Inside and Outside of Basilicas

The liturgy celebrated in a great basilica took on a character very different from the liturgy celebrated in a house church. The sheer size of these public buildings and of the throngs of people in attendance necessitated a series of processions that would not have been practiced in the house churches. In the house church the presiding minister could begin the liturgy with a simple greeting, and then the order moved directly to the readings. This also seemed to be the case in Augustine's smallish church in the North African city of Hippo, where the liturgy began with an abrupt entrance of the bishop, a simple greeting, and then proceeded to the readings. But in the basilicas of the great cities of the empire, it was necessary for the bishop and his entourage to enter and process down the center aisle. Like civil dignitaries, bishops were accompanied by lights and incense. The bishop of Rome was also greeted by a band of singers. While psalms, litanies, and canticles were sung, the bishop and his entourage made their way to the bema (in the Eastern basilicas it generally was located in the center of the nave) or the apse (in the West it usually was located at the east end of the basilica), where the bishop's throne was placed, surrounded by the benches of his presbyters. Elaborate entrance rites developed to cover this impressive entry of the clergy. In Rome and elsewhere, professional schools of singers (*scholae cantorum*) developed and could lead the singing of the people. The Introit, Kyrie Eleison, and Gloria in Excelsis in the Roman liturgy constituted a "praise medley" covering this grand entrance.

This was followed by the liturgy of the word, after which there was a lengthy series of dismissals of catechumens and penitents with prayer and blessing. As Aidan Kavanagh has suggested, from this solemn dismissal came the name given to the Latin liturgy: *missa* (Mass).[19] Then another procession was required as the people brought forward their offerings of bread and wine for the eucharistic meal. The bishop and his entourage moved to the altar table while deacons collected the gifts of the people. A third procession involved the movement of the people to the chancel area (the fenced-off area around the altar table) to receive Holy Communion. Paul Bradshaw suggests that the efforts of the bishop to encourage "worthy reception" of communion led to the unintended consequence of people declining to receive at all and leaving before the liturgy was completed. To facilitate a more orderly departure, the noncommunicants were dismissed with a blessing before communion, and the deacon announced the "station" for the next pontifical liturgy.[20]

This announcement of the next station was especially important in the city of Rome itself. Because the ceremonial heart of the city, the Forum, was filled with pagan temples, shrines, and altars, there was no space available for building Christian basilicas. The temples in the city of Rome were not secularized until 408, two years before the sack of the city by Alaric, which produced a great outcry among the pagans that the gods had forsaken the city, which in turn produced Augustine's response in *The City of God*. But Christian basilicas were located in the suburban regions of Rome and in the cemeteries outside the city, as in the case of the basilicas of Saint Peter and Saint Paul. There were, in fact, seven great basilicas in Rome, each one associated with one of the seven administrative units of the diocese.

Sometimes the main Sunday liturgy of the city was celebrated at the Lateran Basilica. At other times it was necessary for the pope to leave the Lateran in order to get to the station where the day's most public liturgy would be celebrated. This entailed a great procession with psalms and litanies as the papal entourage made its way through and across the city from one station to the next. Along the way, there were other liturgies, such as Lauds (morning praise) and Vespers (evening prayer), en route from the Lateran and back again. Aidan Kavanagh identified seven distinct services during the course of Sunday in Rome and commented, "The time-scale of this entire series of services was the whole of a Sunday. The space-scale of it was the whole city."[21] Whether it was intended or not, this massive liturgical scale constituted a veritable liturgical evangelization of the city. But civil religion has always been primarily an outdoor affair. John Baldovin has written about the processional boulevards constructed in the Christian city of Constantinople to facilitate liturgical processions from one station to another.[22]

Christian Attitudes toward Art

Not surprisingly, as Christianity became a favored and then the established religion of the Roman Empire, Christian leaders called for the destruction of pagan temples and idols. But the destruction of temples was a costly process, since they were so ubiquitous in the landscape of antiquity. Only where the army worked on razing these temples were they destroyed; most were left simply to decay. Christians sometimes took matters into their own hands. In his *Church History*, Theodoret reports instances of temple bashing and idol smashing. Bashing and smashing appealed to zealous monks or energetic young men. Such activities were even projected back onto the martyrs, who were portrayed in later *Acts* as engaging in idol smashing and book burning.

For pagans, the idols were representations of the presence of the deity. They believed that the gods and goddesses could act through these idols. For Christians, these idols were identified with demons and were still regarded as dangerous; their utter destruction was the only safe course of action. Sometimes the sign of the cross was chiseled onto the temple columns or remains of statues as an exorcistic act.

Even with this zealous iconoclasm, Christians in the curial class still were respectful toward statues of Greco-Roman heroes and Roman emperors (though the latter had been deified). Constantine himself demonstrated this ambivalence by ordering the destruction of idols but also collecting statues with which to adorn his new capital, Constantinople. Eusebius of Caesarea, in his *Life of Constantine*, noted this discrepancy in the emperor's actions and attributed the emperor's collection of statues to the purpose of ridicule. Yet for Constantine, as later for Constantius, collecting these statues of heroes and emperors served the purpose of proclaiming Rome's grandeur and continuity between the old and the new Rome.

But statues were not to have a place in Christian basilicas, even though they had adorned the civic basilicas of Roman cities, because of the commandment prohibiting idol worship and any pictorial image of God. Christians would have developed a negative attitude toward statues and images and toward art in general, even apart from the example of the Jews, because of the idolatry associated with works of art. The so-called *Apostolic Tradition* attributed to Hippolytus of Rome in the third century specified that sculptors or painters who applied to become catechumens had to be taught not to make idols or else be rejected.

However, Christians also had the example of the Jews in finding appropriate works of art with which to adorn their new buildings (and it has to be admitted that Jews of the Diaspora were not always rigorous in their observance). The third-century-C.E. synagogue in Dura-Europas and the basilican synagogues in Palestine from the fourth through the sixth centuries show examples of floral and geometric designs done in ceramic tiles and mosaics. Christians could add to these designs symbols such as loaves and fishes, grain and grapes, which evoked events in the life of Jesus and the sacramental life.[23]

Nevertheless, Christians with roots in the pagan culture were eager to have pictorial representations of Christ and the apostles. We don't know how early Christians were appropriating images (icons) in imitation of their pagan friends and neighbors who had images of their gods and heroes. Eusebius reported in his *Church History* (7:18) that on the stone gates of the house purportedly belonging to the Syro-Phoenician woman with a hemorrhage who had been healed by Jesus, there was on one side a bronze statue of a woman, kneeling and resembling a suppliant with arms outstretched, and on the other side was a figure of a man with a double cloak draped over his shoulders and his hand stretched out to the woman. This was believed to be a representation of Jesus and the Syro-Phoenician woman, which Eusebius said he had seen with his own eyes. He understood the desire of Gentiles to express their gratitude by making images, since the pagans used to honor their heroes in this way, even though he did not think it was appropriate. He also reported that he had seen pictures of Peter and Paul and Christ himself.

For the art historian, there is a gap of two hundred years between the time of Eusebius and the sixth century, the time from which the oldest Christian icons survive. This means we do not have a pictorial record of the development of Christian icons, nor do we know when they were first incorporated into public Christian buildings. We only know that icons were being painted in the fourth century and Eusebius was skeptical about their use by Christians, but that Basil the Great had high regard for their pedagogical value (especially paintings of martyrdoms), and Gregory of Nyssa was the first theologian to argue that Christ could be pictorially represented, since his human nature is not fused with his divine nature. But we do not have examples of icons incorporated into Christian basilicas before the sixth century, when they were adorning Emperor Justinian I's great Basilica of Holy Wisdom (*Hagia Sophia*) in Constantinople. This great church became the norm for church buildings throughout the Byzantine world. Two spheres, the earthly (the nave) and the heavenly (the sanctuary) were bridged, not separated, by the development of the icon screen (iconostasis), on which were placed the images of Christ, his Blessed Mother, and the saints. As Schulz wrote, "By reason of the images that adorn it, the church itself henceforth becomes a liturgy, as it were, because it depicts the liturgical-sacramental presence of Christ, the angels, and the saints, and by depicting it shares in bringing it about. The iconography of the church also shows it to be the place in which the mysteries of the life of Christ are made present."[24] The icons thus become "windows into eternity" but also windows into history, both of which are made present by the icon.

Even in the sixth century, the use of icons in Christian worship was being questioned. Pope Gregory the Great had to write a letter condemning not only image worship but also the iconoclasm set in motion by Bishop Serenus of Marseilles at the end of the sixth century. In the process, he established the view generally held in the West that images serve pedagogical purposes and put the faithful in touch with history.[25] But there was no image worship or iconoclasm in the West comparable to what was practiced in the Byzantine Empire in the eighth century.

The Iconoclastic Controversy

The popular development of the veneration of images without a sound theological rationale contributed to the great outburst of iconoclasm that threatened to tear apart the Byzantine Empire in the eighth century. The stage was already set for the coming crisis when the Trullian Synod of 692 validated the developing use of icons by prescribing, "From now on, in place of the lamb of old, Christ our God, the lamb of God who takes away the sins of the world, is to be portrayed in human form in the icons, so that in his state of abasement the majesty of God the Word may be seen and we may be reminded of his life in the body, his suffering, his saving death and the redemption of the world which his death accomplished."[26]

In 726 Emperor Leo III, who had risen in the ranks of the army from peasant stock to being elected to the purple, openly took a position against the veneration of icons. Why Leo took this position has been subject to various interpretations. Some have thought he was influenced by Islam, to which the very idea of pictorial representation was abhorrent. It is just as likely that his views were the result of Monophysite belief.[27] If we accept only a divine nature for Christ, there cannot be human portrayals of him. Leo insisted that Patriarch Germanus of Constantinople sign a decree to remove icons from churches.[28] Germanus categorically refused. He was the first to see that iconoclasm threatened the incarnation.[29] In a letter to John Synades, he used an argument that John of Damascus and Theodore of the Studios would use in defense of icons: "We make no icon or representation of the invisible divinity. . . . But since the only Son himself, Who is in the bosom of the Father, deigned to become man . . . we draw the image of His human aspect according to the flesh."[30] Against the Arians two centuries earlier, Byzantine theology had defended the full divinity of Christ; now it was necessary to defend his full humanity.

The controversy went through three stages. The first stage, during the reign of Leo III (717–741), was content with a relatively straightforward appeal to biblical prohibitions of idols, accompanied by the smashing of icons. Leo III himself instituted this iconoclastic campaign by preaching a series of sermons in 725 against flagrant excesses of the iconodules (as the image worshipers were called) and then destroying the great image of Christ above the gateway into the Imperial Palace. The popular reaction was immediate; the commander of the demolition crew was set upon by women and killed on the spot. Seeing the effect of his work, Leo might have been expected to call a halt to his campaign. Instead, in 730 he issued his one and only edict against icons, which were to be destroyed forthwith. The decree fell most heavily on the monasteries, which possessed vast quantities of icons and relics. Many monks fled to the West, and Pope Gregory II condemned iconoclasm and suggested that the emperor leave the task of defining Christian dogma to those who were qualified to do so. His successor, Pope Gregory III, threatened to excommunicate all who laid impious hands on sacred objects.

The second stage of iconoclasm commenced at the beginning of the reign of Leo III's son Constantine V (751–775), who seemed even more fiercely iconoclastic, and also more antimonastic, than his father. He convened the iconoclastic Council of Hiereia (754), taking care not to invite any representatives from Rome, Antioch, Alexandria, or Jerusalem. Constantine V repeated the Chalcedonian formula in a not-quite-correct way, saying that the unity of the person of the God-man was not "of two natures," but "out of two natures." The council affirmed that the two natures of Christ could not be separated or commingled. Therefore to paint a picture of Christ is to be a Nestorian, since one is emphasizing the human nature only.[31] Armed with this theological rationale, the emperor unleashed a violent persecution of iconophiles and, more generally, directed attacks against the monastic establishment and even relic worship. It is noteworthy that iconoclasm did not extend to the art in imperial palaces, in which mosaics depicting the life of Christ were replaced with landscapes or even pictures of the emperor and the imperial family. Moreover, while the image of Christ disappeared from imperial coins, the image of the emperor did not. The former coins had Christ sitting and the emperor standing; the new coins showed only the emperor sitting. A monk named Stephen, martyred in the cause of icons, threw the coin to the ground in order to demonstrate that if no human image of Christ could be on the coin, neither could the human image of the emperor.[32]

The third stage began when Empress Irene, the Athenian consort of Leo IV, had her son Constantine VI blinded and perhaps was even responsible for his murder and then ruled the Byzantine Empire as regent. As a Greek, she did not agree with the positions of Leo III or Constantine V and worked to convene a truly ecumenical council that would provide a theological rationale for icons. This council was convened in Constantinople in 786 but was disrupted by iconoclastic soldiers. Irene had the soldiers dispatched to Asia to fight the Saracens and then reconvened the council, including delegates from Pope Hadrian I of Rome plus three Eastern patriarchs, at Nicaea in 787. This Seventh Ecumenical Council, the Second Council of Nicaea, decreed that both "the figure of the sacred and life-giving cross" and "the venerated and holy images" were to be "placed suitably in the holy churches of God," but that the honor paid to them was to be "only relative for the sake of their prototype"; that is, they were to receive "veneration, not adoration." The council thus acted to discourage the excesses in image worship that had unleashed the iconoclastic reaction, while reaffirming the two natures of Christ against the Monophysite tendencies of iconoclasts.

Irene is revered in the Orthodox Church as a saint for her role in the restoration of icons. She also had grand political ambitions and took for herself the male title of the Byzantine emperor, *Basileus*. She became the first woman in Byzantine history to rule in her own right, not as a co-ruler or regent. She was deposed in 802 before she could accept the proposal of marriage from Charlemagne, the newly crowned emperor of the Romans in the West, by Byzantine military leaders who feared a consolidation of Western power over Constantinople. The pope's act of crowning an emperor in the West brought about a crisis of trust between the Byzantine Empire and the papacy that had not existed before. This may have contributed to a final resurgence of iconoclasm beginning in 815 under the emperors Leo V, Michael II, and Theophilus, although the treatment of iconodules was mild in comparison with former times and elicited the powerful theological defense of Theodore of the Studios. With the death of Emperor Theophilus, Empress Theodora became regent on behalf of her two-year-old son, and she determined to bring iconoclasm to an end by convening a council in 843, which affirmed the decisions of Nicaea II.

In terms of social history, it is noteworthy that the two persons most instrumental in the restoration of icons were women. Some scholars view iconoclasm as an act of imperial control over the powerful Byzantine church, and conversely attribute the restoration of icons during the reigns of women to weaker imperial control during times of regency. Others see women as more fervent venerators of images than men, and more prone to seek intercessions and mediation by appealing to Christ, the Virgin Mary, and the saints. There's no doubt that the iconoclastic controversy divided Byzantine society along social lines, pitting women and monks against the emperor and the army. The women and the monks finally prevailed. It is also noteworthy that the greatest theological minds of the Byzantine world (Maximus the Confessor, Germanus, John of Damascus, Theodore of the Studios, Nicephorus) sided with ordinary Christians and defended their piety even while placing it on a firmer theological basis.[33]

From the perspective of the history of ideas, the settlement of the iconoclastic controversy has been viewed as a victory of Greek thought over Arab and Semitic mentalities. Iconophiles hailed their victory as the triumph of Christianity over Judaism. Von Campenhausen asked "whether the victory of the Church over 'Judaism' was not bought, to a great extent, at the price of a victory of paganism over the genuine Christian heritage."[34] Sight was placed on the same level in Christian devotion as hearing; the picture became the equal of the word.

From the perspective of art history, the iconoclastic controversy set back Byzantine artistic development, even of icons, in comparison with the development of iconic art in places like Ravenna, which remained outside of Byzantine political control. Also, the techniques for sculpting statues disappeared from Byzantine culture forever. One of the compromises of the settlement of the iconoclastic controversy was that three-dimensional art was prohibited. This prohibition did not affect the development of church art in the West.

Finally, the iconoclastic controversy weakened the Byzantine Empire during the time of Arab advance and consolidation in the Middle East. Once the controversy was settled, there was a period of Byzantine resurgence between the reigns of Basil I (867–886) and Basil II (976–1025) as the empire spread east as far as the Euphrates, west to southern Italy, north to the Danube (destroying the Kingdom of the

Bulgars), and elicited the cooperation of the princes of Kiev, preparing the way for the introduction of Byzantine Christianity into Russia. Relics rescued from Palestine and Syria attracted Christian pilgrims to Constantinople, who were unwilling to risk the danger of visiting sites under Muslim domination.

CHAPTER 6

People and Places
for Different Liturgies

As described in the previous chapter, the basilica was the major
building for Christian liturgy in the Roman world. Except in
Constantinople, which was built as a city with a Christian ceremonial
center, Christian basilicas were built some distance from the city center
and often outside the city walls in cemeteries. Liturgical processions
were required to move the congregation from one station to another
for different liturgies. This was especially true of pontifical or episcopal liturgies, in which the whole church of the city assembled with its
bishop for celebrations of the Eucharist on Sundays, festivals, and days
of commemoration. Stational liturgies with processions existed in such
places as Ravenna, Vercelli, and Tours, as well as in Constantinople,
Jerusalem, and Rome, and continued well into the Middle Ages in
Metz, Strasbourg, Mainz, Cologne, Liège, and Paris.[1]

In this context, "local church" means the diocese, not the congregation or the parish. It is the church of the city and its surrounding suburbs and countryside. Parishes were subgroups within the local church
that met in specific locations with a presbyter appointed by the bishop
to serve that portion of his flock. Whenever possible, however, the
whole local church—or at least significant representatives of it if the
diocese was very large—gathered with its bishop at one place around
one altar and often received communion from his hand. The full rites
of Christian initiation also were celebrated at the bishop's church. But
other liturgies were held at other churches. In fact, unlike the typical
situation today, in which every liturgical rite is celebrated in every little

church building, in late antiquity different kinds of liturgies were celebrated in different kinds of buildings.

The Liturgical Leadership of the Bishop

We have no idea who presided at worship in the earliest Christian assemblies. But by the end of the first century, the church manual known as the *Didache* prescribed to the congregation, "You must elect yourselves bishops and deacons who are a credit to the Lord, men who are gentle, generous, faithful, and well tried. For their ministry to you is identical with that of the prophets and teachers. You must not, therefore, despise them, for along with the prophets and teachers they enjoy a place of honor among you" (15:1–2).[2] Since the *Didache* had already said that when prophets preside at the Eucharist, they could give thanks as they see fit (10:7), it seems reasonable to assume that bishops and deacons would fill this role in the absence of prophets.

The *Didache* was probably written at about the time when the ministries of itinerant charismatic prophets and teachers were waning and were being replaced with the local ministries of bishops and deacons. Only a few years later, and perhaps from the same area if we assume the provenance of the *Didache* to be Antioch, Bishop Ignatius of Antioch, on his way to martyrdom in Rome (c. 110), wrote to churches along the way to, among other things, rally them around their bishops. We cited in chapter 1 his appeal to the Smyrnaeans (8:1-2):

> You should all follow the bishop as Jesus Christ did the Father. . . . Nobody must do anything that has to do with the church without the bishop's approval. You should regard that Eucharist as valid which is celebrated either by the bishop or by someone he authorizes. Where the bishop is present, there let the congregation gather, just as where Jesus Christ is, there is the Catholic Church. Without the bishop's supervision, no baptisms or love feasts are permitted.[3]

For Ignatius, to be a member of the church meant to be with the bishop, especially to submit to his liturgical leadership. The fact that Ignatius had to make such strong claims for the role of the bishop suggests that, as in the *Didache*, the church's polity was in a situation of transition. The earlier "charismatic" ministries of apostles, prophets, and teachers were being replaced with "institutional" ministries of bishops, presbyters, and deacons.[4] Ignatius argued that the leadership of these ministers must be accepted in order for the church to be one in Christ:

> As . . . the Lord did nothing without the Father (either on his own or by the apostles) because he was at one with him, so you must not do anything without the bishop and the presbyters. Do not, moreover, try to convince yourselves that anything done on your own is commendable. Only what you do together is right. Hence you must have one prayer, one petition, one mind, one hope, dominated by love and unsullied joy—that means you must have Jesus Christ. You cannot have anything better than that.
>
> Run off—all of you—to one temple of God, as it were, to one altar, to one Jesus Christ, who came forth from one Father, while still remaining one with him, and returned to him.[5]

There is no evidence in the first century for the prominence of the role of the "monarchical" or single-ruling bishop such as we see beginning in the second century.[6] The Jewish sect described in the Dead Sea Scrolls had an "overseer" who taught the community and arbitrated disputes, but as far as we know, this overseer exercised none of the liturgical leadership invested in the Christian *episkopos* (overseer). Nor did any of the offices in the Jewish synagogue correspond to the office of bishop in the Christian church. In other respects, however, the Christian bishop exercised a role not unlike that of the Jewish patriarch in Palestine: he served as the Christian spokesman to the Roman state or the local municipality (especially during times of persecution, but also after the church became a licensed cult), looked after the needs of the members of the church (especially widows and orphans, but also the salaries of the clergy), and settled disputes (personal, but also theological). Thus, there were sociological reasons why the office of bishop emerged as a unique form of Christian leadership.[7]

It is now commonly thought that Christian bishops might have emerged out of a college of elders (presbyters). The *First Letter of Clement of Rome to the Corinthians* (c. 96), intervening in an internal dispute in the Corinthian church to criticize the ejection from the episcopate men who had offered the Eucharist, gives the impression that these officers were presbyter-bishops, since *episkopoi* are mentioned in the plural (*1 Clement* 42:4). Yet just a few years later, it seemed that the bishop mentioned by Ignatius in his *Letter to the Magnesians* was not a presbyter himself and may have been elected from outside the presbyterium.

Careful liturgical historians like Paul Bradshaw warn us against drawing any kind of straight line of development from one document to another, since they emerged in different places a few years apart from one another. Yet as the Christian population grew in the larger cities, it is obvious that several places of assembly were needed, since the usual meeting places were in domestic homes. Even if they were deeded over to the church ("titular churches") and rebuilt to hold a larger assembly (like the house church at Dura-Europas), there was a limit to how many people could be accommodated in a house church. The bishop provided unity in liturgical leadership and general church administration for a local church meeting in several locations. These dual responsibilities also ensured the bishop's close relationship with the people. While the people looked principally to the bishop and his presbyterial delegates for liturgical leadership and to meet their sacramental needs, the bishop in turn depended on the tithes and offerings of the people to maintain the church's charitable ministries and to provide stipends for the clergy. It is not surprising, therefore, that the bishop's role as liturgical leader actually increased with the move from house churches to basilicas in the early fourth century. The bishop assumed the responsibility of holding together liturgically and administratively a diverse flock sometimes gathered in different places at the same time around a common Eucharist over which he presided. In late antiquity, Ignatius's ideal of one church gathered around one bishop at one altar was realized through some striking liturgical practices, especially the practice of stational liturgies.

We will look at two important local churches whose practices were exported by pilgrims or visitors who carried these practices home with them: Jerusalem and Rome. We will see the breakdown of this collegial form of ministry in the non-urban places north of the Alps. And we will consider how the emergence of monasticism affected this whole system.

The Jerusalem Church: Pilgrimage Sites

Emperor Constantine's church-building program was nowhere more evident than in Palestine. While the Emperor himself never visited the sites in the Holy Land on which basilicas and shrines were built, he took a personal interest in their construction, sent architectural experts and materials to the sites, and authorized his mother, Helena, to serve as his personal representative at the dedication of the churches over the cave of Jesus' nativity in Bethlehem, at Mount Calvary and the cave of the holy sepulcher in Jerusalem, and on the Mount of Olives at the site of Jesus' ascension. It only remained for the leaders of the Jerusalem church to make effective use of these facilities to attract pilgrims from all over the Roman Empire, and they did!

Firsthand information about the liturgies done at these sites is provided by the Spanish nun Egeria in her *Diary*. She made her pilgrimage between 381 and 384 and was able to attend Holy Week, Easter, and Ascension services while in Jerusalem. We should note that pilgrims with religious vocations, such as Egeria, Cassian, and Palladius, visited the Holy Land not only to see the sites of salvation history but also to visit the famous ascetics and monks in the region in order to learn about the religious life from them. Their feats of endurance made these ascetics tourist attractions in their own right, and created problems of providing hospitality to so many visitors who found their caves and hermitages when the point of living in the desert was to be removed from the world. This means that the Jerusalem church had a large number of religious monks and nuns in attendance at Sunday and festival liturgies as well as at the daily prayer offices. Modern pastors can appreciate the advantage of having a number of enthusiastic religious professionals in the congregation when trying to introduce new practices. Certainly new practices were being developed during the fourth century in special rites at the sites of events in the life of Christ.

The special sites and shrines in and around Jerusalem affected both liturgy and church organization. As John Wilkerson has pointed out, there were regular pilgrimage offices at the holy places and special liturgies celebrated at particular shrines in order to commemorate the events that occurred at these sites.[8] Appropriate psalms and scripture readings were read as part of the rites observed at these sites, and this contributed to the development of the church year calendar and lectionary. Festivals such as the Presentation of Jesus in the Temple and the Ascension of Jesus entered the church year, along with special liturgical-dramatic ceremonies such as the Palm Sunday procession, Good Friday's veneration of the Holy Cross (which was believed to have been discovered by Empress Helena during excavations for the Church of the Holy Sepulcher), and the *lucernarium* (light ceremony) with fire and candles at the beginning of the Paschal Vigil. All of these practices duly impressed pilgrims, who tried to implement them in their home churches.

We know from Egeria's *Diary* that the bishop was in the midst of the people for these celebrations. He lit the paschal fire and candle in the cave of the sepulcher (in the Anastasis Church) and brought it out into the midst of the people to light their candles. He read the gospel of the resurrection on Sundays at the Anastasis. He gave solemn blessings at the end of the liturgy while the people bowed their heads. He allowed the people to kiss his hand after the solemn blessing, thus ensuring physical contact between the people and the bishop.

The presbyters collaborated with the bishop in liturgical leadership. They presided in his absence and shared preaching and teaching responsibilities with him. Egeria notes, "It is the practice here that as many of the priests who are present and are so inclined may preach; and last of all, the bishop preaches" (25:1). Given the number of services and the throngs of worshipers, it is not surprising that the bishop shared his role as *didaskalos* (teacher) with the presbyters. It is thought that Cyril of Jerusalem preached his catechetical homilies several years before his election as bishop.[9]

There were many deacons in Jerusalem. They took charge of the crowds at gatherings and assisted the bishop at the Eucharist with the distribution of the sacramental elements. Without printed bulletins or worship books, the deacons played an important role in giving oral directions and announcements. The duty of announcing the time and place of the next service fell to the archdeacon. The deacons served as the leaders of prayer in the liturgy of the hours by chanting the bids in the intercessory prayers, to which the people responded *Kyrie eleison*.

With the use of Scripture readings at the pilgrimage offices as well as in the liturgy of the word, the role of lector or reader was important in Jerusalem. With the use of psalmody in processions, at pilgrimage rites, and in the liturgy of the hours, the role of cantor also was important. Finally, the use of several languages by worshipers—primarily Greek, Latin, and Syriac—required the use of translators at liturgies.

As far as church organization is concerned, it is important to note that various liturgies were celebrated in different buildings in and around Jerusalem. The unique situation of Jerusalem is that we are not aware of other liturgies being celebrated simultaneously with the chief liturgy at which the bishop was presiding. But fourth-century Jerusalem was not a large place, and the size of the resident congregation was small, even though its ranks swelled with visitors, especially during the high seasons in the church year. It was possible for the bishop of Jerusalem to be front and center in all of the major liturgical celebrations. But there were strategies for maintaining the central liturgical role of the bishop even in large cities like Rome.

The Roman Church: Held Together in One Eucharistic Communion

In his *Apology*, Justin Martyr gives the impression that Christians in Rome circa 150 were still able to assemble in one place. The minister presiding over the Eucharist is not called "bishop" but "president," in the style of a Roman dining club. But during the third century, the Christian population of Rome grew considerably and was no longer able to meet in one place. Eusebius reports that during the time of the persecution under Emperor Decius, during the episcopate of Cornelius, there were under the one bishop "forty-six presbyters, seven deacons, seven sub-deacons, forty-two acolytes, fifty-two exorcists, readers, and doorkeepers, and more than fifteen hundred widows and distressed persons" who were supported by the charity of the church.[10] It has been estimated from these numbers that the Christian population of Rome in around 250 C.E. was between thirty thousand and fifty thousand.

Places of worship multiplied with the growth of the church of Rome. The catacombs were extended as places of assembly for worship as well as places in which to take refuge during times of persecution. The titles of many large houses were turned over to the bishop of Rome by their owners. These "title churches" (*tituli*) and the cemetery churches were served by presbyters. The bishop of Rome, or "Pope" (an affectionate title for father or patriarch), presided at the Eucharist in different places at different times. The place where the pope presided was called the station (*statio*). As we saw in the previous chapter, after the Edict of Milan, basilicas already were erected in Rome by Emperor Constantine for the use of the church.

The Roman church actually used four kinds of church buildings. First, there were the basilicas, which served as the cathedral churches of Rome. These included Saint John Lateran, Saint Mary Major, Holy Cross-in-Jerusalem, Saint Peter on the Vatican Hill, Saint Paul on the Ostian Way, Saint Lawrence over the tomb of this Roman martyr, the Holy Apostles, and Saint Sebastian by the catacombs. From the dedication of some of these churches, several lesser festivals came into the church calendar; these include Holy Cross Day, the Chair or Confession of Saint Peter, and All Martyrs' Day (which later was transferred to November 1 as All Saints' Day, under British influence). The pope's official church was Saint John Lateran; suffragan bishops resided at each of the other seven basilicas, which were located roughly in each of the seven political jurisdictions of the city of Rome. The second category of church buildings consisted of the title churches scattered throughout the various neighborhoods of Rome, each served by a single presbyter. Then there were the deaconries, each served by a deacon. Finally, on the outskirts of the city were the suburban cemetery churches, each served by a presbyter. Further on in this chapter, I will discuss the monastery churches that were established near the basilicas in the fifth century so that the monks could assist in the daily prayer offices.

It is important to realize that these different church buildings served different purposes. The basilicas became the primary places of eucharistic celebration on Sundays and festivals. While the Eucharist could also be celebrated at the title churches, it seems that their original liturgical purpose was for catechetical and penitential services. The deaconries were not liturgical centers at all, but administration buildings for the charitable work of the diocese; hence, one was located in each of the seven political districts of Rome. The cemetery churches were places where burial services were conducted.

The pope began the custom of presiding in different basilicas, as well as making visits to the title churches, on different Sundays and festivals. Most typically, the pope presided at Eucharist or the Mass (*Missa*, as the Romans called it) on the feast day of the saint whose relics were entombed or deposited in a particular church. As we said, this required elaborate processions through the city to get from one station to the next. As far as possible, the whole congregation of the diocese of Rome gathered with its bishop to celebrate the Eucharist. In actuality, this was not possible. Since the suffragan bishops in other districts and presbyters who served the title and cemetery churches could not be present at the pope's mass, he sent to each of them, by means of acolytes carrying a linen sack, a piece of bread he had consecrated at his Eucharist. Called *fermentum*, this piece of consecrated bread was added to the chalice (the commixture) by the celebrant at the words *Pax domini sit semper vobiscum* (The peace of the Lord be with you always). This may be a reason why the greeting of peace came to precede the communion in the Roman Mass, instead of preceding the offertory as it did in other liturgical traditions. But by this means the whole congregation of the church of Rome was gathered into the bishop's Eucharist, even though portions of the congregation were assembled at different places through the city and its suburbs. There is a discussion exactly of this idea in a letter of Pope Innocent I to Bishop Decentius of Gubbio (*Epistle* 25:8). What we see at work here is an adaptation of the ancient communion ecclesiology to the sociological requirements of a church that embraced much of the population of a great metropolis.

The papal masses at Saint John's Lateran or one of the other basilicas were the most solemn type of liturgy. The oldest document describing a papal station mass is *Ordo Roman Primus*, which is of late-seventh-century vintage.[11] At these liturgies, as many of the clergy as possible joined the pope, as well as the civil dignitaries of the city as they became Christian. This included the suffragan bishop, deacons, subdeacons, and acolytes of the district, as well as whatever presbyters were free of other responsibilities to be able to attend. The corporate character of the liturgy was maintained by observing a diversity of liturgical roles. The numerous deacons, subdeacons, and acolytes were used to carry tapers, fetch books, read the lessons, hold linen sacks and containers in which to receive the people's offerings of bread and wine, carry the *fermentum* to other churches, assist with communion, and announce the next station.

The diocese extended outside the city walls, and this part of its jurisdiction was called *parrochia*. The presbyters who served the churches outside the city were called "parish priests" (*presbyteri parrochiales*). Pope Innocent indicates in his *Letter to Bishop Decentius* that the *fermentum* is not sent to them (too far!). Accordingly, these presbyters had the right to celebrate mass as well as to administer baptism and penance.[12]

The worship of these rural parishes thus constituted a third type of liturgy. A pontifical liturgy was almost never celebrated in them, and they lacked the diversity of liturgical roles found in the urban churches. There may not have been any deacons serving these parishes, and undoubtedly there was no *schola cantorum* to sing the psalms and lead the singing of the congregation. At most there may have been a cantor and some acolytes in addition to the presbyter-in-charge. He was the real pastor to the people and obviously had a greater sense of autonomy than the presbyters who served in the urban churches.

The Gallican Church: Rural and Small Town Ministry

The basic problem with transplanting Roman or Mediterranean practices into trans-Alpine Europe was that the dioceses covered immense territories, which greatly limited the bishop's role as the liturgical leader of the diocese. This is seen especially in the bishop's role as the minister of Christian initiation. The Roman practice assigned to the bishop the role of laying on of hands and sealing to the newly baptized the gift of the Holy Spirit in the post-baptismal anointing. With the increase in the number of candidates for baptism, especially as the practice of infant baptism became more prevalent, children were baptized in their parish church at any time of the year (not just at the Easter Vigil). However, the post-baptismal ceremonies were delayed until the child could be taken to the bishop's church or the bishop could visit the parish to "confirm" the baptized.[13] It was often impossible even for a conscientious bishop to travel his entire diocese in the course of a normal episcopate. David R. Holeton notes, "It was not uncommon for bishops to confirm on horseback as they rode through their dioceses and for canons to require parents living within a particular distance from the bishop's projected route to bring their unconfirmed children to line the roadside so that they could be confirmed as the bishop passed."[14]

The territory of Gaul was marked by large basilicas and small *ecclesiae*.[15] There were three kinds of basilicas: urban (often the principal church of a town), monastic (forming an integral part of the monastery complexes), and rural (actually the village church). Basilicas were basically temples with tombs or relics of the saints. If a town was large enough to have several basilicas, the oldest or most important was the *basilica senior*; normally it served as the cathedral, or bishop's church. *Ecclesiae* were smaller and simpler places of worship that might be located in market towns and sometimes on feudal estates. These must be distinguished from *cellulae*, or oratories, which were also located on the feudal estates of great lay lords or bishops. *Ecclesiae* and *cellulae* existed only to increase the places of worship and administration of the sacrament, although often with the exception of the sacrament of baptism in the early Middle Ages. The solemn celebrations on great feast days, as well as the administration of baptism, at first took place only in the bishop's church.

The head clergy of basilicas, like the heads of monasteries, were called *abbas* (fathers), as were the chief clergy of cathedrals. These clergy were required to observe the canons regulating clerical life; hence they were called *canonici* (canons). The *clerici canonici* formed the presbytery of the bishop and were attached to his service in the exercise of pastoral care and in their liturgical leadership. But this attachment was largely in theory only, because the non-episcopal basilicas and even some of the *ecclesiae* were beginning to assert their independence as "parishes" with the right to celebrate all liturgical and sacramental rites. The *ecclesiae* and oratories on feudal estates often belonged to the lords, who could call and dismiss the priests who served them. Especially in German lands, this created a tension between secular and spiritual authority, because princes were exercising episcopal functions in the calling of pastors.

The multiplication of liturgical offices celebrated in non-episcopal churches—Eucharist, baptism, penance, the liturgy of the hours, and so on—required multiple clergy staffing. The clergy tended to be presbyters (increasingly called "priests") because of the need to have the Mass celebrated, especially as the practice of the votive mass (masses offered for special intentions) gained in popularity. Parish priests only loosely connected to a bishop, who might reside at considerable distance from the town or village church, necessarily began to acquire both episcopal and diaconal functions in the absence of bishops and deacons. Thus, the seeds of two characteristics of Western Christianity were planted in the early Middle Ages: presbyterianism and parochialism.

The office of presbyter became the dominant ordained office in the Western church. The diaconate became only the last rung up the ladder to priestly ordination rather than an office in its own right, and bishops came to be viewed as priests who had wider jurisdictions. A theology of orders eluded medieval theologians, even though they devoted a great deal of attention to it. Isidore of Seville argued that since priests were *consortes cum episcopis* (companions with the bishop), they could on occasion ordain other priests. The absence of bishops did not deter some abbots from ordaining their monks as deacons and presbyters, who could serve the monastic community in these functions.[16] Among those who held that priests could have such power by episcopal delegation were William Durandus and Pope Innocent III. Thomas Aquinas added to the confusion because his scheme of seven sacraments did not allow for two sacraments of orders. So he reasoned that power over the sacramental body of Christ was primary, and power over the ecclesial body of Christ was secondary. Hence, investiture with the chalice and paten in the rite of priestly ordination (a clearly feudal ritual) was the act that conferred priestly power, not the laying on of hands. The bishop, "though he is given spiritual powers with regard to some sacraments at his consecration, does not receive a sacramental character."[17] The sacrament of orders is conferred in the rite of ordination to the priesthood. The commonly accepted medieval sevenfold *cursus honorum* (course of honors)—acolyte, porter, lector, subdeacon, deacon, priest, bishop—are all expressions of the one sacrament of orders, which is fully granted in ordination to the priesthood.

As the priest became autonomous from the bishop, so the parish church became autonomous from the cathedral because it could offer Christians every means of grace they would need on their way through this life to the life of the world to come. This was, in part, a consequence of their financial independence. The feudal economy dealt primarily in the commodity of land. Lands were given to parishes as well as to cathedrals and monasteries in bequests. The produce and profits of the land would then accrue to the church or institution that held them. Some churches and monasteries became very wealthy. Also, in their concern to secure masses and prayer offices that would be said or sung for them in perpetuity, some people endowed clerical positions or chantries in their wills. In these ways, parishes even in smaller towns could become as well equipped as cathedrals to carry out a full round of liturgical offices. It apparently never occurred to church leaders to make these town and village churches cathedrals by multiplying the number of bishops so that bishops really could be the chief pastors of their people.

In these ways, presbyterianism and parochialism were well established in the Western medieval church long before the Reformation worked for church renewal by reviving the sense of the church as the local assembly for Word and Sacrament, and of ordained ministry as the office of the Word and the Sacrament—that is, congregationalism and the one office of pastor.[18]

The Monastic Church: Liturgy at the Margins

As chapter 3 already noted, another major development that began in late antiquity had an important bearing on people and places for different liturgies: the emergence of the monastic movement. The roots of monasticism are found in Christian asceticism, which existed long before the foundation of the first monasteries in the early fourth century.[19] The great contribution of Pachomius of Egypt was to organize ascetic solitaries into communities of hermits living under the discipline of a rule administered by a superior (abbot) for mutual support.

It is not surprising that anchoritism, the retreat into the desert, spread so rapidly at just about the time the Roman state made its peace with the church. A world in which Christians had been persecuted and suffered martyrdom gave way to a world that showed favoritism toward the church but was hardly changed at all. The most earnest Christians, still inspired by examples of virginity, asceticism, and martyrdom from previous generations, went into Middle Eastern deserts to escape from the very world that now tolerated Christians.[20] Ironically, even though the monasteries had no inclination to develop a liturgical life of their own that would differ from the liturgical life of the church, these solitaries had to escape from the ordinary life of the church in order to escape from the world, since the church was in the process of bringing the world into its assemblies. So whether as solitaries or cenobites (those who lived in community), monks took the worship of the church with them to their places of seclusion. The treatment of the liturgical offices in the monasteries was profoundly influenced by the very nature of monasticism. As I have said, the monastic principle was that of "ceaseless prayer." Prayer was the constant work of the monk, and the Eucharist the monk's daily food.

Had the monasteries remained far removed from the urban churches, these developments might not have had any impact on the liturgical life of the church. But by the fifth century, monasteries were being established in or near the cities. In fact, the majority of monasteries in Palestine were not far from Jerusalem, even if they were located in the Judean desert. Also in the fifth century, the Studite Monastery was located in Constantinople. Especially under the influence of the great Cappadocians, Basil the Great, Gregory of Nazianzus, Gregory of Nyssa, and Macrina, monasteries became places of learning, of biblical transcription and commentary, and of mystical writings.[21] Monks served as scholars and teachers to the whole church.

Many of the great bishops of the church, such as Augustine of Hippo, Basil the Great, and Gregory of Nyssa, would have preferred the contemplative life to the administrative life, so they promoted monasticism, invited monks into the cities, and even developed a kind of quasi-monastic life together with their fellow clergy. Monks in the urban monasteries were available to assist in the daily prayer offices of the local church to relieve the basilican presbyters for other pastoral work. Especially Pope Gregory the Great, who promoted Benedictine monasticism, found this a practical reason to have monasteries adjacent to the great basilicas of Rome. The result of locating monasteries adjacent to cathedrals was a hybridization of the cathedral and monastic offices by a blending of styles. The influences were mutual. Prayer offices in the basilicas took on more of the contemplative character of monastic prayer, and prayer in the monasteries, especially Vespers, took on more of the ceremonial character of cathedral prayer. The sheer increase in the number of psalms sung in the cathedral offices augmented the musical needs of the cathedrals, which the monks provided.[22] The Roman liturgy of the hours became almost indistinguishable from the Benedictine office, which Pope Gregory I championed.

A more subtle change occurred, however, as church leaders dipped into the monasteries to find clergy to serve secular churches. Those clergy formed in the monastic ideal brought that ideal to the cathedral and parish church. They also operated hospitals, orphanages, and schools. They provided an ideal of Christian discipleship that laity involved in the affairs of everyday life could not meet. The implication was that those who wanted to be serious Christians had to undertake a monastic profession over and above their baptism.

Monks, noted for their evangelical fervor, also showed missionary zeal. Pope Gregory dispatched Augustine and forty Benedictines to establish a beachhead for the evangelization of Britain at Canterbury. In Ireland, a land with no cities, monasteries became the centers of church life as well as of civic life; abbots were often more important figures than bishops or kings. Hardy Celtic monks took their monastic rule to the continent of Europe to establish houses in the Alps and in the forests of France and Germany. Monks were at the forefront of the evangelization of Europe. In all these ways, the monastic life came into contact with and had a profound influence on the ordinary life of the church, including the church's liturgical life.

In the Byzantine East, the triumph of the iconophiles at the conclusion of the iconoclastic controversy was also the triumph of monasticism, which had defended the iconodules, and the Studite liturgical ordo had as much influence on the Byzantine "liturgical synthesis" as the ordo of the Hagia Sophia.[23]

Also in the West the monasteries played an important role in transmitting and adapting the liturgical material during the Carolingian

Renaissance. We shall see in the next chapter the work done to import and make usable Roman liturgical books in the Frankish church. Charlemagne also promoted a solidly educated clergy leading lives of unquestioned moral example.

Monks were models of this, and their example was imposed upon the secular clergy. Both learning and morality could be promoted if the clergy lived together, worked together, and supported one another collegially as a presbytery under the supervision of a bishop. Even where a bishop was not present, clergy assigned to basilicas were required to live together under the supervision of the senior presbyter or pastor. While Charlemagne enforced this polity, it was already established by Merovingian synods such as the Council of Auvergne in 535, which took precautions against isolated clerics.[24] What we see in the polity of the Frankish church is both a replication of the urban polity of the church in the Roman Empire and also a growing organization of the clergy according to a monastic ideal, including the ideal of celibacy. Indeed, the canonical clergy of the cathedrals and basilicas lived together in a compound (called "the Close" in England).

Thus, as we move into the medieval period, the monasteries are ready to play a dominant role both in terms of their presence on the landscape and their influence on the ordinary life of the church both in the East and in the West. In addition to their influence on the lifestyles of the clergy, they provided an alternative place of worship to the cathedrals and parishes that attracted worshipers from outside the monasteries, and they often met the liturgical, sacramental, and other religious needs of lay people more fully than might be possible in, say, a village church.

The high regard for monastic communities is evident in the sheer number of bequests left in wills to monasteries to their enrichment. Fashionable Roman senators and aristocratic ladies converted villas and country estates into ascetic communities. Prominent Gothic and Frankish families donated income-producing land to the support of monasteries. Through these endowments, the monasteries increased in wealth, power, and prestige.

CHAPTER 7

Church Music through the Carolingian Renaissance

Ritual dancing and ritual music were well known to the church fathers, and most of them disapproved of it most of the time. Yet Christians danced and sang just as the pagans did.[1] Music and dancing have always been an important, even an essential, element in cultic rites and ceremonies. Christianity entered the world with no music of its own, but Christianity could not hope to embrace the Greco-Roman world if it didn't provide for ritual music and dancing, sometimes even against the wishes of the episcopal leadership.

The pagans of Greco-Roman antiquity regarded music as a gift from the gods and as something, like incense, that was pleasing to the gods. The task of cultic music was to please the gods or appease them. Flutes, tambourines, cymbals, and dancing accompanied the offering of sacrifices to the Greek gods. In music as in other areas of cultic practice, the Romans were more restrained, using at first only the flute. They were also at first as opposed to dancing as they were to gymnastics. Only under Greek influence in the early imperial era did other instruments and dancing come into Roman cultic ceremonies. Not surprisingly, the Romans liked trumpets in their civic ceremonies. They even had an annual ritual, called the *Tubilustrum*, for the cleansing of the trumpets used in the sacrifices.[2]

The apostolic church used music in its worship. Paul calls on the Ephesians to "address one another with psalms, hymns, and spiritual songs, singing and making melody to the Lord in your heart" (Ephesians

5:19). The Colossians letter also includes a reference to "psalms and hymns and spiritual songs" (Colossians 3:16). But the expression "singing and making melody to the Lord in your heart" expresses the conviction that music in worship has meaning only as an expression of inner devotion. This attitude reflects that of the pagan philosophers, who, beginning with Plato, rejected the use of instrumental music in cultic sacrifices, preferring only the vocal singing of texts. Odo Casel demonstrated the background of "spiritual sacrifice" (*logike thusia*) in pagan philosophy and how it was taken over into Christian liturgy.[3] The preference for "rational worship" (Romans 12:2) excluded the use of instrumental music, and the bishops were able to maintain this ban on instruments in worship throughout antiquity.

Psalms and Hymns and Spiritual Songs

In contrast, singing or chanting was an accepted element in Christian worship. Texts of readings and prayers would have been chanted to facilitate both hearing and memorization.[4] The Old Testament psalms came into Christian worship, although how early cannot be determined, and these were always sung, though exactly how, in the early centuries, we cannot say.

The book of Psalms is often described as the Hymnal of the Second Temple (520 B.C.E.–70 C.E.). Many of the psalms were composed during this time, although some in the collection were gathered from earlier times. They were sung by choirs of Levites accompanied by an actual orchestra, as described in 1 and 2 Chronicles, often with the people responding by singing refrains. Psalm 150 specifically mentions praising God with trumpets, lutes and harps, timbrel and dance, strings and pipes, and the clashing of cymbals.

Some of the use of the psalms in the temple liturgy is recalled by the Mishnah. For example, the Mishnah *Tamid* tractate 7:4 recalls that the Levites recited Psalm 24 on Sunday, Psalm 48 on Monday, Psalm 82 on Tuesday, Psalm 94 on Wednesday, Psalm 81 on Thursday, Psalm 93 on Friday, and Psalm 92 on Saturday.

The use of the psalms in the synagogue in the early Common Era is uncertain. The origins of the synagogue itself are uncertain. It did not originate as a place of worship but as a place of study and community gatherings. It may be that worship in the synagogue did not develop until just before the time of Jesus. We know from Luke 4:16–22 that

Sabbath worship in the synagogue included the reading of the scripture with commentary by the rabbis, since Jesus was invited to read from the scroll of Isaiah and comment on it in the synagogue at Nazareth. Evidence for the use of the psalms in Christian worship suggests that their use in the church actually antedates their use in the synagogue liturgy.

Eric Werner has noted several contrasts between the use of the psalms in the early church and synagogue and their previous use in the Temple:[5]

1. The psalms were sung by cantors, with the people singing refrains, not by choirs.

2. The psalms were sung unaccompanied, since the leaders of both church and synagogue in the Greco-Roman world associated musical instruments with pagan rites and generally forbade their use in worship.

3. The basic pattern of singing involved a monotone with inflections to convey the sense of the text, except for more melodious hallelujahs.

Werner also notes contrasts between the use of the psalms in the church and their use in the synagogue:

4. The Christian use of the psalms between lessons was unknown in the synagogue before the eighth century C.E.

5. The sequential use of the psalms in the Christian prayer offices as developed in the monasteries was unknown in Jewish worship, except for the Hallel Psalms (113–118) on great festivals.

Jewish liturgy has not used all of the psalms as Christian liturgy has done. Christian liturgy has also used other psalm-like canticles in the Old Testament (the Song of Moses and Miriam, Exodus 15; the Prayer of Moses, Deuteronomy 32: the Song of Hannah, 1 Samuel 2; the Song of Habakkuk, Habakkuk 3; the Song of the Vineyard, Isaiah 26; Hezekiah's prayer, Isaiah 38; the Prayer of Jonah, Jonah 3), the Apocrypha (the Song of the Three Children, Daniel 3; Azariah's prayer, Daniel 3; the Prayer of Manasseh), and the Gospels (the Song of Zechariah, Luke 1:68–79; the Song of Mary, Luke 1:46–55; the Song of Simeon, Luke 2:29–32; the Song of the Angels, Luke 2:14)—fourteen biblical canticles in all.

The New Testament itself is a testimony to the Christian use of the psalms. There are more quotations from Psalms than from any other book. The psalms were quoted by Jesus in his teaching and from the cross (Psalm 22:1 in Mark 15:34 and Matthew 27:46; Psalm 31:5 in Luke 23:46). Jesus is seen as the fulfillment of prophecies concerning the Christ in the psalms. Jesus' passion is regarded as prophesied in Psalms 22 and 69. The entire Epistle to the Hebrews has been seen as a midrash on Psalm 110, which the author believes supports belief in Christ's incarnation, ascension, and eternal priesthood.[6] Paul quoted Psalm 19:4 in Romans 10:18 as foretelling the universal mission of the church to the Gentiles. The psalms celebrating Jerusalem and its temple were reinterpreted as pointing to the "new Jerusalem, coming down out of heaven from God" (Revelation 21:2), and allusions to the Hallel Psalms are woven into John the Seer's paeans of praise surrounding the marriage supper of the Lamb (Revelation 19).

With this much use of the psalms in the Christian Scriptures, it is not surprising that the Psalter became the hymnal also of the church.[7] References to the specific uses of the psalms in Christian worship do not antedate the fourth century. But by then, Eusebius tells us, psalms were sung by the whole congregation, including the women, especially in the night vigils. Egeria, in her *Diary*, also mentioned singing psalms during the night "with responses and antiphons . . . sung alternately."[8] By the end of the fourth century, John Chrysostom was introducing antiphonal and responsorial methods of psalm singing in Constantinople, and Ambrose was doing the same in Milan.

Hymns (i.e., metrical poems) also came into Christian liturgy quite early. The New Testament itself is full of hymns or allusions to hymns, especially in praise and adoration of Christ (e.g., John 1:1–14, Philippians 2:6–11, Ephesians 1:3–14, Colossians 1:15–20, Revelation 4–5). Hymns were probably sung in private homes as well as in public assemblies. Yet hymns did not readily acquire a place in Christian liturgy, and there are few references to hymns of the type quoted or alluded to in the New Testament in second- to fourth-century "mainline" Christian sources. A possible explanation for this is that heretical groups such as the Gnostics, Donatists, and Arians made use of hymns to promote and teach their doctrines, and the reaction of the "orthodox" church was to avoid the singing of hymns. Particularly in Western, and especially Roman, liturgy, psalmody was preferred to hymnody.

While the ban on musical instruments in late antique Christian worship is clear, the use of instruments by Christians in their homes and even in the assemblies in the earlier centuries is ambiguous. It is possible that the lyre was used in private homes to accompany singing, since this instrument was uncompromised by use in idol worship. Clement of Alexandria makes reference to the use of lyres and cithars at the agape meal, so it cannot be categorically held that instrumental accompaniment was forbidden in early Christian worship. The increasingly strident denunciation of instrumental music in the writings of the church fathers of the fourth and fifth centuries suggests that instruments were, in fact, being used in public worship, or that there was popular pressure to use them, and that this had to be discouraged precisely at a time when a stark contrast was being drawn between Christian and pagan cults.

In Syria church leaders also had to discourage Christian interest in the synagogue. In his *Discourses against Judaizing Christians*, preached in Antioch from the fall of 386 into 387, John Chrysostom asked his congregation in Discourse IV, "What is it that you are rushing to see in the synagogue of the Jews who fight against God? Tell me, is it to hear trumpeters?"[9] In Discourse I he asked:

> Do you wish to see that God hates the worship paid with kettledrums, with the lyre, with harps, and other instruments? God said: "Take away from me the sound of your songs and I will not hear the canticle of your harps." If God said, "Take them away from me," do you run to listen to their trumpets? . . . Do you wish to learn that, together with the sacrifices and musical instruments and the festivals and the incense, God also rejects the temple because of those who enter it? He showed this mostly by deeds, when he gave it over to barbarian hands, and later when he utterly destroyed it.[10]

As Michael Peppard notes, this reference indicates that Christians were interested in the use of musical instruments and that the prosperous synagogue in Antioch had a whole orchestra.[11]

In contrast with the use of "lifeless" instruments in pagan rituals and whatever instruments Jews may have been using in their synagogue, the church fathers, like the rabbis of the Babylonian Talmud, preferred the "living" instrument of the human voice. Writers as diverse as Clement of Rome, Clement of Alexandria, Origen, Pachomius, John Chrysostom, and Augustine of Hippo extol unison singing as a powerful witness to unity.[12] The fact that the Old Testament makes reference to instruments in the temple was explained by John Chrysostom as God's concession to the weakness of the Jews.[13] The fathers also criticized the lewdness that accompanied pagan instrumental music and dancing. Thus, the condemnation of the use of musical instruments by the church fathers was not an aesthetic criticism, but a matter of staking out Christian identity and morality.

Johannes Quasten notes that in the first few centuries, women sang in the Christian liturgical assembly even though choirs of women were prominent in pagan cults and in Old Testament examples. Among the Gnostics in the third century, women enjoyed an exalted status as prophets, teachers, readers, and singers. This may have been a reason why church fathers inveighed against the public role of women in the church, including in the singing.[14]

Nevertheless, the ideal of communal singing involving everyone trumped both the example of heretics and Paul's admonition that women should be silent in church (1 Corinthians 14:34). As a counter to heretics, Ephraim (306–373) organized choirs of women and choirs of boys in Edessa to sing his hymns. Choirs of boys and female virgins were used by the Nestorians to spread their hymns and songs. The choirboys were also trained as lectors, who read the Scriptures in the services.[15] The choirs of boys took over the role of the cantor in leading the singing of psalms and canticles and, in Jerusalem, responding to the intercessory prayer petitions with *Kyrie eleison*, as Egeria reports. In Rome the cantor became the head of the choir school, or *schola cantorum*, which alone sang the entrance, offertory, and communion songs, according to *Ordo Romanus Primus*.[16] But this reflects usage circa 800, and there was undoubtedly more responsorial singing with the congregation in the earlier centuries. The move from house churches into basilicas necessitated a more elaborate liturgical music, which required more professionalism among the singers, which reduced the people's role in singing.

The Constantinian Age was also the time when hymnody, or spiritual songs, also flourished. The strophic hymn, which originated in Syria, countered the professionalization of recitative singing in larger assembly halls by making it possible for the people to sing. Ephraim is credited with developing a type of strophic hymn in which quantitative verse was replaced by isosyllabic verse, in which there was a regular pattern of accented syllables and the endings of lines often rhymed. This made possible singing all the stanzas to the same melody. According to Egon Wellesz, these Aramaic and Syriac hymns were translated into Greek, and sometimes Greek texts of pagan hymns, such as those from the cult of Aesculapius, were adapted for Christian (or Gnostic) use.[17] This made possible a rich use of hymnody in the Syro-Byzantine liturgy. A Latin hymnody also developed in the West, enabling congregational participation in the singing.

Frankish Christianity

At the time that liturgical music was developing to a high degree in the eastern Roman Empire and in Syrian Christianity beyond the eastern frontiers of the empire, the western Roman Empire was being infiltrated by barbarian peoples whose migrations could not be stopped. The name *Goth* embraced diverse Germanic and even non-Germanic peoples who have been subdivided into such groups as the East Goths (Ostrogoths), who settled in Italy; the West Goths (Visigoths), who settled in Spain; the Vandals, who moved into North Africa; the Burgundians, who settled in Gaul; and others as well.[18] Ostrogothic rule in Italy lasted from 493 until the death of Theodoric in 526. This provided the pretext for the Roman emperor of the East to invade Italy to reclaim it for the empire. But by the time Italy was reclaimed, it lay in ruins.

This political instability in western Europe lasted until one group of people, the Franks, could impose order. The Franks were a confederation of people who lived east of the northernmost part of the Rhine frontier of the Roman Empire and who spoke a Germanic language. Unified under a single king, Clovis (reigned c. 481–c. 511), they engaged in a series of military campaigns that made them one of the most powerful of the Germanic peoples. The Franks expanded their influence south, west, and east to finally cover all of present-day France, the Low Countries, northern Italy, and western Germany.[19] It should be noted that the Franks, like the Gothic tribes, had lived in proximity to the Roman Empire and were probably distinguishable from "Romans" only by their language and dress. The *Ten Books of Histories,* written by Bishop Gregory of Tours (d. 594), sometimes erroneously called *The History of the Franks*, is our primary source of information for sixth-century Gaul, and the only time he mentions the ethnic identity of a particular group of Germans is when he refers to people living outside the boundaries of the old empire—for example, the Saxons, Thuringians, or Burgundians. Otherwise, Gregory feels no need to point out that this person is a Gallo-Roman or that person is a Frank. They are all the people of Gaul.

We need to remember that sixth-century Gaul was a mostly Christian country. Christians had lived in Gaul at least since the second century, if not earlier, and their numbers increased dramatically in the fourth and fifth centuries, when Christianity became a legal cult and then the state religion of the Roman Empire. Moreover, the barbarian peoples who moved into western Europe were not pagans; they had been converted to Christianity by Arian missionaries from Constantinople. This is why the bishop of Rome was able to negotiate with barbarian invaders over the fate of the city. Nevertheless, from the Catholic perspective, the Goths, Vandals, and Burgundians were heretical Christians, and it took more than a century to convert them to orthodox Christianity. Many liturgical texts in the Western church developed as a way of combating Arian views and promoting orthodox trinitarian theology; examples include the termination of collects, the *Te Deum laudamus* (We praise you, O God), and *Quicunque vult* (Whoever wishes to be saved), the so-called Athanasian Creed.

The Franks were the first of the barbarian peoples to embrace Catholicism from the outset of their conversion to Christianity. When Clovis, the first Merovingian king of the Franks, was converted to Christianity, it was to Catholic Christianity. The story of his conversion is told by Gregory of Tours in his *Ten Books of Histories*.[20] Clovis's conversion was fortuitous for the Roman Catholic Church because the powerful Franks consistently sided with and defended the bishops of Rome. The Frankish ruler Charles Martel (c. 688–741) held the Muslim advance into Europe at the Pyrenees at the Battle of Poitiers in 732. His son Pippin III (714–768) defeated the Lombards in Italy when they threatened Rome. He turned over Ravenna and the Pentapolis, not to the Byzantine emperor, but to the pope. The popes returned the favor when Stephen II anointed Pippin III as king of the Franks in 754 and made his family "patricians of the Romans," and when Leo III crowned Charlemagne Holy Roman Emperor on Christmas Day 800 (an unexpected Christmas present).

Pope Stephen II's visit to France and to the Saint-Denis Monastery in 754 stimulated an interest in the Roman liturgy, which was promoted by the Frankish kings Pippin III the Short (751–768), Charlemagne (768–814), Louis the Pious (emperor 814–840), and Charles the Bald (emperor 843–877). Under these Frankish kings, learning was restored largely through the development of the palace school at Aachen (Aix-la-Chapelle) and in the monasteries at Tours, Metz, Saint-Denis, and Corbie near Reims. The flourishing of art, architecture, and learning during the eighth and ninth centuries has been called the Carolingian Renaissance.

This renaissance was primarily a liturgical renewal movement carried out under the guidance of the scholars imported to Aachen, especially the British monk Alcuin of York (c. 732–804),[21] who had been a student of the Venerable Bede in Northumbria, and Amalarius of Metz (c. 780–c. 850), who had been a student of Alcuin's when the master retired to Tours. This scholarly lineage reminds us that there had been a "Northumbrian renaissance" in the decades around 700, before the British monks helped to bring about the Carolingian renewal. Common features of these two centers of renewal were the writing of histories (Bede's *Ecclesiastical History of the English People*, c. 720, and Gregory of Tours's *Ten Books of Histories*, c. 590) and the copying and illuminating of gospel books. But the unique aspect of the Carolingian Renaissance was the liturgical renewal that took place in the Frankish lands through a blending of Roman and Gallican liturgical resources.

The scholarly lineage is important for its conceptual continuity. Bede's contemporaries attached great importance to his biblical commentaries, especially on the Old Testament books. There was a great revival of interest in the Old Testament. The Carolingian rulers applied to their reigns the examples of the kings of Israel in their understanding of the duty of the Christian ruler to promote justice and spread the gospel of God. Like the kings of Israel, they were anointed rulers, beginning with Pippin III in 754, and anointed by the pope, which gave them legitimacy in the eyes of the people, since they could not appeal to a royal lineage such as the previous Merovingian dynasty had possessed. But if they were anointed kings, they also looked to the clergy to serve as prophets who provided advice to the kings and taught the faith to the people. Charlemagne outlined the social authority of the clergy in his *Admonitio Generalis* (789), which had probably been drafted by Alcuin.[22] In this document, Charlemagne compared himself to Josiah, the king of Judah who attacked idolatry and reformed the worship of Israel.

Royal Patronage of Liturgy in the Kingdom of the Franks

It is not uncommon in the history of high culture for the arts to be supported by patrons or benefactors. Liturgy is somewhat different. It is promoted by bishops and archbishops because it is their pastoral responsibility to order and reform liturgy. Nevertheless, there was a lay patronage of liturgy from early times in the sense that wealthy Christians turned over their houses to the church to use for its liturgical assemblies. Emperor Constantine began the custom of rulers turning over public buildings to the church to use for its liturgies. In the Western medieval feudal society, noble landowners had chapels built on their estates and even hired priests to serve in them. But the royal patronage of the liturgy by the Carolingian kings, even in terms of overseeing the production of liturgical books, was unique.[23]

Appropriating or reviving Roman culture served the purpose of the Carolingian dynasty in bringing order into their unruly realm. The architecture of this period is noteworthy for the revival of the Roman basilica, often on a large scale. There was also a great interest in Roman liturgy and music, which required the importation of hard-to-acquire Roman books such as sacramentaries (prayers for the Mass) and antiphonaries (music for the Mass and prayer offices).[24] The Carolingian rulers were able to use Roman liturgy to promote unity within their vast realm. But Roman liturgy could not be used in a pure state in Gaul; it had to be inculturated by supplementing Roman material with Gallican material for propers that were lacking.

We also need to consider what Roman liturgy the Carolingian rulers were importing. According to Jeffrey Richards, there was during the early seventh century a "dramatic influx into Rome of Eastern monks and clerics, refugees from Arab invasion and Monothelete persecution."[25] The influence of these Christian refugees became so pervasive that they eventually came "to dominate the councils of the papacy and swamp the native element in the Roman clergy."[26] They brought with them not only the Greek language, liturgical pieces, and Byzantine customs, but also new fashions in ecclesiastical art and architecture. "A lavish programme of painting, ornamentation and elaboration, much of it undertaken by refugee Eastern artists, bid fair to turn the churches of Rome into Oriental sacred domes."[27] Even Latin was displaced, to some extent, by Greek. It found a permanent place in Latin liturgy in such pieces as the Kyrie Eleison and Trisagon. The solemn papal liturgy that evolved during the seventh and eighth centuries resulted largely from the increase in size of the papal household, which accompanied him in processions, and assimilation of the immigrant Greek culture. The kind of liturgical books being imported into the kingdom of the Franks reflected this ceremonial growth in the papal liturgy.

As described by S. J. P. van Dijk, the papal liturgy of the seventh century was the result of "the spectacular growth of the pontiff's household and the parallel evolution of the station services," all of which "were consequences of Byzantine culture. In its caesaropapism this had become a wonderland of unlimited treasure, an ideal of splendour centred at the imperial court which admitted no improvisation in its unapproachable and rigid etiquette. Centre of social and intellectual life, sovereignty found its expression and symbol in awe-inspiring magnificence."[28] Imported in the Latin West, such magnificence required a profound change. Increasingly, the papal liturgy—especially its music—required the services of skilled experts, specially trained singers, whose presence constituted "at once, a political and artistic event, symbolizing and ensuring the pontiff's supremacy in the West."[29] This musical professionalization reduced the people to spectators and listeners rather than participants, as they had been in the old urban liturgy. As Richards put it, "The new papal rite excluded the congregation and was built around the glorification of the pope."[30]

Roman Music Books in the Kingdom of the Franks

When dealing with kings, even music becomes politicized. When Pippin III suppressed the Lombards in Italy, he turned over the lands in central Italy that the Lombards had occupied to the pope rather than to the Byzantine emperor, and sent his brother, Chrodegang, bishop of Metz, as one of his envoys to Rome. While in Rome, Chrodegang developed an interest in the Roman liturgical music and took a Roman antiphonary back to Metz. This was, in part, because Chrodegang had instituted a quasi-monastic rule of life for the canons of the Metz cathedral. Within the limits of the canons' active pastoral ministry, Chrodegang stressed the performance of a communal liturgy. The kind of antiphonal singing that Chrodegang experienced in Rome, whose basilicas had been served by communities of urban monks since the time of Pope Gregory the Great, would serve the needs of Metz very well. When Pope Stephen II visited the Saint-Denis Monastery in 754, Roman ritual and music clashed with the local Gallican ritual and music. Whether because he was genuinely impressed with the Roman chants or because it was politically expedient to champion Roman styles, Pippin III encouraged a study and implementation of the Roman liturgy and music. Hearing of Pippin's musical interest, the Byzantine emperor Constantine V, perhaps in an effort to reassert imperial influence in the West, sent an organ to the king of the Franks in 757. This instrument had been forgotten in the West since earlier Roman times but was to achieve a greater technical development and liturgical use in the West than in the East. Not wanting to lose his edge in the "music competition" between Rome and Constantinople, the pope dispatched a singing teacher to Metz in about 760 to establish a *schola cantorum* and sent to Pippin an *Antiphonale* and a *Responsale*, which contained the chants of the prayer offices and the Mass, respectively.

Charlemagne also promoted the use of Roman liturgical music. Because those using the old Gallican chants resisted this, Charlemagne decreed in his *Admonitio generalis* that all clergy should learn and employ the *cantus romanus*. The Synod of Aix-la-Chapelle in 803 decreed further that all bishops would establish *scholae cantorum* in their dioceses. Perhaps as a way to impress on the Frankish clergy the value of the Roman music, the Roman system of chants was attributed to the highly regarded Pope Gregory the Great. But it is unlikely that Gregory, who did not regard music as a proper concern of the higher clergy, developed the system of music known as Gregorian chant.

As Roman books made their way north of the Alps and were compared with earlier Roman books, it was apparent that discrepancies existed. Some differences might be attributable to the fact that music continued to evolve in the Roman church and that the Franks were always a generation behind in the books they acquired. Amalarius of Metz was the first to discover the problem, as he relates in the preface to his *De ordine Antiphonarii*. Puzzled by discrepancies in the office books that had been deposited at Metz since Chrodegang's time, he went to Rome in 831–832 to study the sources and to request of Pope Gregory IV an authentic antiphonary that he might take home. The pope was unable to oblige but suggested that Amalarius consult the four office books that had been given to the abbot of Corbie a few years before. Amalarius did so and was astonished to discover that the order and words, as well as some chants for antiphons and responsories, differed from those in the books at Metz, and that this represented a revision of the Roman Rite under Pope Hadrian I (772–795). Realizing that there was no definitive Roman book or system of chants, Amalarius set about to compile a new antiphonary for use at Metz, drawing on the Metz books, the Corbie books, and things taught to him when he was a student of Alcuin. The result was a fusion of the old Roman system of chants with the newer Roman system. This fusion of chants can be regarded as the real origin of "Gregorian chant" as we have come to know it. It developed not in Rome during the time of Pope Gregory I but in the Frankish Empire during the ninth century (just as the blending of Roman and Gallican sacramentaries constituted the hybrid origin of the Western medieval Latin mass). The Metz books were taken as archetypal and, in the tenth century, were brought to Rome itself by the Germans under Emperor Otto I.[31]

Nor did the chants remain static: the northern spirit expanded the range of expression and modified the melodic line with the introduction of skips, especially the interval of a third. The tendency of northern music was toward organization by thirds; the ultimate consequence of this was the gravitation toward harmony in major and minor scales rather than the modes in which the chants were written. The eight modes on which the so-called Gregorian chants were based were not Roman at all, but Byzantine. Musical modes had developed already among the ancient Greeks, but Egon Wellesz held that the Byzantine chants were derived from the churches of Antioch and Jerusalem, which may reflect a Jewish foundation.[32] The modes were used to establish simple tones by which the psalms could be chanted.

The Use of the Psalms in Western Liturgy

We have seen that the Roman church was very slow to admit nonbiblical hymns into its liturgy; its primary liturgical text was the Bible. Christians made as much if not more use of the Psalter as the Jewish synagogue, especially when one considers the extensive use of the psalms made in the monastic prayer offices. The very structure of Hebrew poetry lends itself to communal recitation. Each verse is divided into two and sometimes three parts called stichs, each of which repeats or completes the thought of the first part of the verse. The parallelism of Hebrew poetry invites antiphonal and responsive recitation in which two groups or a leader and a group recite the two parts of each verse.

Psalms were included in the eucharistic liturgies as responsorial readings between the other lessons and to cover processions at the entrance (the introit), at the offertory (the offertory antiphon [anthem]), and during the Communion (the Communion antiphon [anthem]). The practice of terminating the psalms with a trinitarian doxology, the Gloria Patri, seems to have emerged first in the church of Antioch, which stressed the co-equality of the three persons of the Godhead by saying "Glory to the Father, and to the Son, and to the Holy Spirit." By the ninth century, the Old Testament reading had disappeared in both the East and the West, leaving the responsorial psalm or a portion of a psalm alone before the epistle. In the West this became known as the gradual, since it was sung on the steps to the altar (*gradus*). It was combined with the Alleluia or Lenten tract and sung between the Epistle and the Gospel.

The psalms received pride of place, however, in the daily prayer offices of the church that also emerged in the fourth century. At first, the daily public morning and evening prayer services, like the synagogue services, made a selective use of psalms: those psalms which were appropriate to the morning or the evening. Most commonly this meant Psalm 63 for morning prayer and Psalm 141 for evening prayer. New Testament canticles also were assigned to these prayer offices: the Benedictus (Song of Zechariah) for morning prayer and the Magnificat (Song of Mary) for evening prayer. But the monastic communities in Palestine and Egypt gathered for the "interval hours" at the third, sixth, and ninth hours of the day that ordinary Christians might observe privately, as well as for the pivotal times of morning praise (Lauds) and evensong (Vespers), and during the night also for the vigil offices of Matins and nocturns. Thus, a course of seven daily prayer offices developed in the monasteries, appealing to Psalm 119:164, "Seven times a day do I praise you, because of your righteous judgments." The heart of these prayer offices was the antiphonal singing of psalms: three each at the interval offices of Terce, Sext, and None and twelve at Matins/ Nocturns. Psalms 148–150 were always sung at morning prayer, from which it derived its name, Lauds.

Through the *Institutes* and *Conferences* of Cassian, information about Eastern monastic life was received in the West. It was replicated with gusto by the Celtic monks in the British Isles. This Eastern form of monasticism, as adapted by the Irish, was brought to the continent of Europe by Columbanus (c. 543–615) and his twelve companions about 590.[33] The Irish monks brought ascetic discipline to a wealthy, and therefore possibly lax, Gallican church. This strict regimen is evident in the structure of the prayer offices in the *Rule* of Columbanus. He varied the offices by having fewer psalms per day in the summer months and more in the winter, increasing or decreasing by three psalms per week during the autumn and the spring.[34] Thus, he imposed on his monks a range of 72 psalms at the minimum and 123 psalms at the maximum each day!

It is not surprising that the gentler *Rule* of Benedict of Nursia (d. c. 540), as implemented at Monte Cassino in Italy and adopted in Rome, found favor in Britain when Augustine of Canterbury took it there. It also found favor in the Frankish lands. Pope Gregory the Great's patronage of the Benedictines helped to ensure the success of the Benedictine order. For several centuries it was the only religious order in the Western church apart from the Celtic monasteries. But the genius of Benedict's *Rule* also commended the order.

Benedict reorganized the scheme of the Divine Office by adding Prime between Lauds and Terce and ending the day with Compline but singing Matins and Nocturns so that there were in actual practice seven hours, even though the liturgical books counted eight. (The vigil office was actually called first and second Nocturns, and Lauds was called Matins.) The psalms were redistributed so that all 150 were sung in a week. In the Benedictine office, the antiphon was sung after each verse of the psalm. The psalm could be sung antiphonally by two soloists, not just by two choirs, if the community were too small. Gloria Patri was sung at the conclusion of each block of psalmody, and not after each individual psalm. In the long night vigil, Benedict had the three or four lessons with their responsories follow the first six psalms, not all twelve as in the Eastern office. He also provided a proper hymn for each office, which had not been the custom previously in the Roman office.

The *Rule* of Benedict was noted for its moderation and balance. In a twenty-four-hour day, about eight hours were given to worship, eight hours to work, and eight hours to rest. As more monks became priests and more lay brothers who could do manual work joined monasteries, the priest-monks had more time for prayer. As priests offered masses and prayer offices for special intentions—for the monks, for the secular rulers, for the dead, for benefactors—special devotional uses of sets of psalms developed. These included the fifteen Psalms of Ascent (120–134) and the seven Penitential Psalms (6, 32, 38, 51, 102, 130, and 143). In the ninth century, an office for the dead began to be recited daily in the monasteries, and it had its own set of appointed psalms.

The singing of the psalms and canticles facilitated memorization. In a time before widespread literacy, it was necessary to learn texts by rote, even in the monasteries. The monks knew by heart a tremendous amount of biblical text. The text of the Bible was, for the most part, the text of the liturgy. The prayer offices in particular—with their psalms, readings, canticles, responsories, and suffrages based on Psalms and other biblical texts—were actually a way of praying the Bible. The Bible also formed the worldview of emerging Christendom. Between typological and allegorical methods of interpretation, there was no sense of historical distance between the biblical world and the contemporary world.

Latin Hymns

When hymns acquired a place in Western liturgy, it was in the prayer offices rather than in the Mass. It should also be noted that Latin hymnody did not originate or flourish in Rome but began in Western Europe. In fact, during the fourth and fifth centuries, southern Gaul experienced significant literary activity, which included the writing of Latin poetry and hymnody. The Syrian model of the strophic hymn was taken up in the Latin West, first by Hilary of Poitiers (d. 367), who was reported by Jerome to have written "a book of hymns and mysteries,"[35] and then more successfully by Ambrose of Milan (340–397). Augustine of Hippo was able to attribute four Latin hymns to his mentor Ambrose, and at least ten other hymns are from the pen of either the bishop of Milan or his imitators ("Ambrosiani"). Among the hymns of Ambrose still sung today are "Veni, Redemptor Gentium" (Savior of the nations, Come) and "Splendor Paternae" (O splendor of the Father's light).

Other Latin hymn writers of antiquity include Marcus Aurelius Clemens Prudentius (348–c. 413), a Spanish lawyer and poet from whose pen we have "Corde natus ex Parentis" (Of the Father's love begotten) and "O sola magnarum urbium" (O chief of cities, Bethlehem); Coelius Sedulius, a convert to Christianity in the early fifth century who has given us "A solis ortus cardine" (From east to west) and "When Christ's appearing was made known"; and Verantius Honorius Clementianus

Fortunatus (530–609), a Roman who became bishop of Poitiers in 599 and authored "Quem terra, pontus, aethera" (The God whom earth and sea and sky), "Vexilla Regis" (The royal banners forward go), "Pange, lingua, glosiosi" (Sing, My Tongue, the Glorious Battle), and "Salva festa dies" (Hail, thee, festival day). "Pange, lingua, gloriosi" was sung at Matins and Lauds during Holy Week from Palm Sunday through Maundy Thursday, although it later came to have a place in the devotions before the cross in the Good Friday liturgy. "Salve festa dies," originally a 110-line poem comparing the resurrection to spring and the renewal of nature, came to be used during the Middle Ages as a processional hymn. Its stanzas were broken down for particular use on Easter Day, Ascension Day, and Pentecost.

The Bangor Antiphonary shows that the Celtic church of Ireland utilized these Latin hymns from Ambrose, Prudentius, and Fortunatus as models for their own hymns. Ireland was the first place outside of the boundaries of the Roman Empire to adopt the Latin language, and Christian literature from the continent (including hymns) served as models for the development of a unique literature bearing the characteristics of "insular Latin."[36] Irish Latin hymns developed themes unique to the Celtic experience. For example, in "Hymnum dicat turba fratrum" (The brotherly throngs sing hymns), attributed to Hilary of Poitiers (c. 310–366), Christ is hailed as King and Christians as his loyal subjects. The theme of Christ's kingship was common in Irish religious poetry, since the island was ruled by many local kings and a few high kings. The oldest European writings on the just rule of kings come from southern Ireland circa 700, written in Old Irish.[37] Nature themes, which are also prevalent in Irish poetry, pervade "The Breastplate of Patrick," although this text is later than the saint to whom it is attributed.[38]

In Great Britain the Venerable Bede made his own contribution to Latin hymnody with "Hymnum canamus gloriae" (A Hymn of Glory Let Us Sing), which interprets Christ's ascension as an enthronement in heaven, "Where, seated on your Father's throne, / You reign as King of kings alone." In his *Ecclesiastical History*, he also told the story of the poet Caedmon, who had composed a poem in praise of God the Creator, which Bede paraphrased in Latin (the original was composed in Old English).

Most Latin hymns came into liturgical use through the Divine Office and were promoted by the Benedictines. That is how Latin hymnody came to Rome and was championed by Pope Gregory the Great, who had been abbot of the Benedictine Monastery of Saint Andrew. Hymns attributed to Pope Gregory include: "O Christ, Our King, Creator, Lord," "Ex more docti mystico" (Again we keep this solemn feast), "Clarum decus jejunii" (The glory of these forty days), and "Nocte Surgentes" (Father, we praise you now the night is over).

The Frankish church made its own contributions to Latin hymnody through Rhabanus Maurus (776–856) and Theodulph of Orléans (c. 750–821). The hymn "Veni, Creator Spiritus" (Come, Creator Spirit), sung at Pentecost Vespers, most surely came from the pen of Rhabanus Maurus, though it has been attributed to other possible authors, including Charlemagne. Rhabanus was born in Mainz, educated at Fulda, studied under Alcuin at Tours, was the principal of the school at Fulda, and ended his career as archbishop of Mainz. This particular hymn, however, was not restricted to the prayer offices; its use for ordination rites is recorded the first time at a synod in Reims in 1049, and it was used for the first time in the English coronation rites in 1307.

Theodulph was born in Spain of a noble Visigoth family, entered a monastery at Florence, and was brought to France by Charlemagne in 781, where he was made abbot of Fleury and then bishop of Orléans. One of the great Carolingian scholars, he wrote church statutes and a theological treatise, and he produced a Latin edition of the Bible that included variant readings. He also wrote poems, some of which were satirical views of Carolingian court life. Accused of conspiring against King Louis the Pious, he was removed from his bishopric and in 818 was imprisoned at Angers, where he died. It was probably while incarcerated that he wrote the hymn "Gloria, laus, et honor" (All glory, laud, and honor). This hymn was intended not for the Divine Office but for the Palm Sunday procession, which varied in detail from place to place but was everywhere arranged with a considerable degree of pomp, proceeding through stations and ending with Solemn High Mass.[39]

Thus, Latin hymnody flourished from just before 400 to a little later than 800, not so much in Rome as in western Europe, where it achieved the apex of its development in the Carolingian Renaissance. The Frankish church transmitted to the medieval church the Latin liturgy and its music of late antiquity. This was the period during which other peoples moved into the territory of the Western Roman Empire. Their own languages had not yet achieved literary form and, in any case, they desired, above all, to appropriate *Romanitas* (Romanness). Nevertheless, by the end of this period (the ascendancy of the Frankish Carolingian Empire), the issue of vernacular language had to be addressed.

CHAPTER 8

Vernacular Elements
in the Medieval Latin Mass

The evangelization of Europe north of the Mediterranean basin occupied the energy of the church for a thousand years, from roughly 400 (the conversion of Ireland) to 1400 (the conversion of the eastern Baltic lands).[1] The period of the most intense evangelization occurred during the Carolingian era. Without impugning the religious motives of either the Carolingian rulers or their missionaries, we note that evangelization met needs for military security and political competition with the Byzantine Empire.[2] In terms of security, the Franks could not hold the Rhineland until the Frisians at the lower end of it and the Saxons west of it were subdued and christianized. For this purpose, the Frankish kings supported the great British missionary monks, Willibrord, apostle to the Frisians, and Boniface, apostle to the Saxons. The same external threats from the Vikings to the north and the Magyars to the east spurred the next wave of evangelization. But in the East there was competition from the Byzantine Empire. In the centuries following the fall of Rome, the Byzantine emperors constantly tried to reassert their (Roman) authority over the West. It is not surprising that when Constantinople dispatched the Greek brothers Cyril and Methodius to convert the Slavs, German emperors encouraged their church to enter into evangelistic competition with the Greek missionaries. German bishops were able to wrest Moravia, Hungary, and Poland from the Greeks, but the Greeks were successful among the Bulgarians, Romanians, and Russians. We should also note that the

Bulgars and Slavs posed as much a security threat to the Byzantines as the Frisians, Saxons, and Magyars did to the Franks. In particular, Bulgarian kings, being south of the Danube, were within military striking distance of Constantinople.

The Continuing Use of Latin

One of the major disagreements between the German and the Greek missionaries was over the language of the liturgy. Cyril and Methodius translated not only the Bible but also the Byzantine liturgy into Slavonic, inventing a Slavonic alphabet using Greek (Cyrillic) characters to give the Slavic language a literary form. The Germans argued that there were only three permissible liturgical languages: Hebrew, Greek, and Latin. They appealed to the fact that the sign Pontius Pilate had fixed to the cross proclaimed "Jesus of Nazareth, King of the Jews" in three languages. This made Latin, as well as Hebrew and Greek, a sacred language because of its role in salvation history.[3] Interestingly, Cyril and Methodius were summoned to Rome by Pope Nicholas I (858–867) to debate the language issue and possibly also the missionary methods of the German clergy. Arriving in 867, the Greek brothers discovered that Pope Nicholas had just died, but they were received by Pope Hadrian II (867–872). They brought with them the supposed relics of the early Roman bishop and martyr Clement as a gift to the pope. Amid great rejoicing at the entombment of the relics, the pope approved the Slavonic liturgy and had it celebrated in Saint Peter's Basilica. He would have appointed Cyril a bishop to the Slavic churches independent of the German bishops, but Cyril fell ill and died in 869, leaving Methodius to carry on under Byzantine authorization.[4] The issue of using languages other than Greek and Latin in the liturgy continued. Pope John VIII (872–882) sided with Methodius and approved the use of Slavonic for the Roman liturgy, but this permission was withdrawn by Pope Stephen VI in 885.

In the West as well as in the East, missionaries had to learn the languages of those whom they were intent on converting. Presumably, Patrick learned Irish during his years of captivity in Ireland, which enabled him to preach to the Irish in their native language when he returned. In contrast, Columba used interpreters when he was in Pictland (Scotland), and Pope Gregory I advised the Benedictine monk Augustine to pick up some interpreters on his way to England. The difficulty was compounded by the nonexistence of written literature in these languages. It became the task of Christians to apply the letters of the Latin alphabet to the sounds of "barbarian" languages and develop a grammar and sometimes even a vocabulary for expressing Christian concepts in the Celtic, English, Romance, and German languages. In the process, Christian scholars wrote down native poems and epics, including *The Dream of the Rood* and *Beowulf* in Old English and the *Heliand* (a Saxon epic treatment of the life of Christ) in Old German. They also provided translations of catechetical texts and some biblical material.[5] Bede was translating the early chapters of the Gospel of John into Old English as he was dying. The previous year, he had urged Archbishop Egbert of York to encourage the people to learn the Creed and Lord's Prayer in their native tongue. The monks of Fulda produced a German translation of the *Diatessaron*, the gospel harmony of Tatian the Syrian, under the supervision of the master of the monastic school, Rabanus Maurus, a student of Alcuin's. But the liturgy remained in Latin in the West, as Latin remained the language of theology and of the schools and courts. To a great extent, this was because of the multitude of Germanic and Slavic dialects that lacked a literature.

We must remember, however, that Latin never ceased to be a living language in the medieval West. It certainly did not immediately die out among the populations of the old Roman Empire in the West, although Gregory of Tours complained that the written Latin of his era was marred by glaring errors in syntax and grammar. But such "corruptions" are a sign of a living language, a language still being spoken and used. Indeed, Christian preachers had corrupted classical Latin in their effort to communicate with a wide audience. For example, Augustine, a master of Latin rhetoric, had infused classical Latin with "Africanisms," neologisms, and loanwords from other languages when he preached to his mixed congregation in the port city of Hippo. Jerome translated the Bible into a "vulgar" form of Latin (hence the name Vulgate). Even after the collapse of Roman civilization in the West, Latin continued to be used in the monasteries, schools, and courts. The flourishing of Latin hymnody from approximately 400 to 800 means Latin poetry continued to be written for centuries after the so-called fall of Rome in the West. There was actually a resurgence of Latin poetry in the twelfth century, although Latin functioned more like a vernacular language in vocabulary and syntax than did the classical Latin of antiquity. But the Goliardic poets of the twelfth century could make Latin sing in an incomparable way. Their good-humored begging songs, satires against luxury-loving prelates, rhymes for drinking bouts, and love songs were collected by Symonds in *Wine, Women, and Song*. The Goliards flourished alongside the first great vernacular poetry, the *chansons de geste* (songs of exploits), including "The Song of Roland." In fact, one wonders when a clear difference was perceived between Latin and the emerging Romance languages. Some scholars would argue that the Romance dialects stand in truer historical continuity with the Latin of classical antiquity (through the Vulgar Latin) than the Latin of the medieval church, which was really an artificial language. In fact, the grammar of ecclesiastical Latin was established by non-Romance-language speakers such as the Celts, Anglo-Saxons, and Germans, who learned Latin as a foreign language and then wrote Latin grammars.[6]

Latin liturgy actually reached the apex of its development in the Carolingian Renaissance with the fusion of old Roman and old Gallican elements in the sacramentaries of the seventh and eighth centuries. But it did not stagnate even after this period, since new Latin prayers were added to the Mass liturgy between the ninth and eleventh centuries. Beginning around 1000, Latin sequence hymns were composed to be sung between the Epistle and Gospel on festivals and for other special occasions. Just as Latin secular poetry flourished anew in the twelfth century, so there was a renewal of Latin devotional poetry and hymnody in that period, including "Jesu, dulcis memoria" (Jesus, the sweet thought of you) of Bernard of Clairvaux, stanzas of which are still sung today.

Nevertheless, as Walter Ong has pointed out, Latin became a "learned" language, "a language completely controlled by writing, whereas the new Romance vernaculars had developed out of Latin as languages had always developed, orally."[7] It was a language learned in school, not on a mother's lap. There were no pure oral users of medieval Latin; people who spoke Latin could read and write it. Many could undoubtedly read and write it more fluently than they could speak it in spontaneous conversation. Devoid of "baby talk," it was the language of educated males (very few women learned Latin) that separated the knower from the known. Medieval Latin was an ideal language for abstract thought, which is why it was the language of scholastic theology and later of science. As a liturgical language it also expressed an objectivity in the divine-human relationship that lacked the intimacy of the vernacular. But this may be why the faithful had to look eventually to other sources than the liturgy to nurture their faith relationship with God.

By the beginning of the ninth century, because of the incorporation of newly evangelized peoples into the Catholic Church and the development of new vernaculars, the need to use vernacular languages was recognized, especially in preaching to the unschooled population. But because of the insistence on retaining Latin as the language of liturgy and theology, even as vernacular languages were developing in western Europe, other means of incorporating vernacular elements into the Latin liturgy had to be found.

Preaching in the Vernacular

One of the first signs that Latin could no longer be used exclusively in the Frankish realm is found in a decree from a council of Tours in 813 that bishops should translate their sermons into the *rustica romana lingua* (i.e., Old French) or into German so that they would be understood by the people. The same kinds of instructions were being given in Spain and Italy in the tenth century.[8] Thus, preaching in cathedral churches in these countries was in the vernacular by the tenth century, even though the vernacular was used for preaching earlier in the mission fields, at least through interpreters. We should not underestimate the difficulty of translating sermons into vernaculars that were only in the early stages of development or of finding vernacular words and concepts that could express the words and concepts of the Christian Scriptures and doctrines.

Note that these decrees concerned the sermons of the bishops. The bishops had been the principal preachers in the ancient church, because they were the teachers of the faith. This worked well enough in places where bishops were numerous and dioceses were small. In the larger dioceses north of Italy, it became necessary to extend preaching privileges to presbyters or priests who pastored churches in towns and villages without bishops, and eventually even to deacons. Preaching licenses were given to university-educated clergy.

Throughout the Middle Ages, collections of homilies were also made available for less-educated parish priests to read at mass to their congregations. The same practice was employed in the Lutheran Reformation in the sixteenth century, when it was discerned that ordinary parish priests were unable to explain the new doctrines to their parishioners or practice a strictly exegetical approach to the Scriptures. Hence the reformers continued the practice of providing church postils—collections of sermons on the readings of the church year—for parish pastors to read to their congregations until more educated, university-trained clergy could be provided.

With the rise of the mendicant orders such as the Franciscans, Dominicans, Carmelites, and Augustinians in the thirteenth century, preaching missions were undertaken by members of these orders, who often became celebrities.[9] Their sermons had the character of the revival preaching known in American evangelicalism. They were often preached outdoors in the plaza in front of the city church amid much festivity. A celebrated preacher like the Dominican Vincent Ferrar would be met at the city gates by the townspeople, including magistrates, clergy, and even bishops, who escorted him to a pulpit that had been set in the town square, in front of the great church or cathedral. Such preachers often traveled with an entourage of ordered priests and notaries who could hear confessions and record legal reconciliations that resulted from the fiery sermons that summoned repentance with images of the last judgment, the pains of hell, or the sufferings of Christ.[10] Because the friars supported themselves by begging, they were often accused of trying to encourage larger contributions by making their sermons more entertaining.

Vernacular Translations of the Bible

The primary text of the liturgy is the Bible. The Western church entered the Middle Ages with a vernacular version of the Bible in the form of the Vulgate Latin translated by Jerome. While the Bible in the Eastern church was translated into other vernaculars, the Vulgate Latin remained the standard liturgical text in the West. Yet parts of the Vulgate Latin Bible were translated because preachers who based their sermons on the readings of the mass had to make reference to those texts. Both Old and Middle English provide large chunks of texts that rendered the Latin Bible into the vernacular.[11] Studying these translations provides a lively picture of how literate clergy used preaching, pictures, songs, stories, and theater to bring the Scriptures into the understanding of "lewd" people.

The practice of preachers glossing or paraphrasing biblical texts is attested by Geoffrey Chaucer in "The Summoner's Tale," which also provides a satirical glimpse into popular attitudes toward friars. The friar drops into a sick man's house to solicit a donation, greets the sick man's wife with a not-so-holy kiss, and asks what's for lunch while comparing his evangelical poverty with the layman's comfortable lifestyle. The friar assures the layman that he has been in the parish today on a preaching mission:

> I have today been at youre chirche at messe,
> And seyd a sermon after my symple wit,
> Nat al after the text of holy write,
> For it is hard to yow as I suppose,
> And therefore wol I teche yow all the glose.
> Glosyng is a glorious thyng certeyn,
> For lettre sleeth so as we clerkes seyn.
> [For "the letter slayeth" as we clergy say (1 Corinthians 3:6).][12]

The sick man finally agrees to give the friar a donation, which turns out to be a fart.

There is also evidence of glossing (or farsing) the texts of the Epistles read in the masses of the Christmas Octave. These poetic stanzas are in early Romance dialects in France. They obviously represent an effort on the part of the clergy to help the unschooled laity understand what the Epistles are saying.[13] This use of the vulgar tongue to interpolate the Epistles, restricted to the Christmas Octave, may also represent an effort on the part of the clergy to reinforce the Christian celebration at a time when pre-Christian elements were bound to reemerge and impose themselves on the Christian celebrations.

The widespread practice of glossing the biblical texts with other texts was found objectionable by late medieval reform groups such as the Lollards. Like the later Protestants, they castigated the popular practice of glossing, farsing, or paraphrasing texts and produced their own literal translations of the Bible. Unlike the later Protestant reformers, who were inspired by the Renaissance humanists to return to the original languages and translate the Bible from Hebrew and Greek rather than from the Vulgate Latin, the Lollards did not produce compelling vernacular versions.[14] Ironically, the literal translations of the Latin Vulgate Bible produced in the Catholic Church after the Council of Trent compare more favorably with the literal Lollard translations than with the splendid translations of the great reformers, whose work had a profound impact on the development of modern languages (e.g., German, Swedish, English, French).

The Office of Prone

There was plenty of preaching in the vernacular during the Middle Ages. The great churches often had endowed pulpits by the end of the Middle Ages. Some of the great reformers began their reforming careers as called preachers in these churches. Martin Luther was divided in his opinion as to "whether the sermon in the vernacular comes after the Creed or before the Introit of the Mass; although it might be argued that since the Gospel is the voice crying in the wilderness and calling unbelievers to faith, it seems particularly fitting to preach before Mass."[15] His seeming preference for preaching before the Mass reflects the preaching missions that were conducted by religious orders such as his own Augustinians in the late Middle Ages. His words indicate that he was also aware that preaching before the Mass was evangelistic preaching calling for repentance.

Luther also mentions preaching after the creed within the order of the Mass. While the purpose of the homily within the mass liturgy was to explicate the readings and therefore in ancient times followed the Gospel, the creed was interpolated between the Gospel and the sermon in the medieval mass and sometimes served as the subject for exposition.[16] In this sense, the importation of the creed into the Roman mass served catechetical purposes. Toward the late Middle Ages, the sermon was framed in a pulpit office that included other catechetical elements, such as the Pater Noster and the Ave Maria, as well as parish announcements and intercessions. This pulpit office was known as Prone, from the French word for "intercessions" (*prône*).

The Office of Prone included vernacular elements such as the announcements and intercessions as well as the sermon. The parish announcements included reading the banns of marriage and stating the particular intentions being prayed for at the mass that day. Then, as now, the announcements probably elicited considerable attention from the congregants. They led into vernacular intercessory prayers, which the French called *prône* and the English called *bedes* (bids).[17] This was a solemn form of prayer in which the priest called on the people to pray for the pope, the bishops, and clergy, including himself; for the king, lords, and commons; for the mayor and other authorities in the town or village; for "all our good parisshens"; for those with special needs such as travelers, pilgrims, and prisoners; for "all women that be with chylde in this parysshe or any other"; and finally for the household that was going to provide the holy loaf (not for Communion but for parish fellowship). The second half of the bedes included the faithful departed, both recently deceased parishioners and special benefactors of the church. The names of benefactors of the parish were recorded on a bede-roll that was read once a year at the annual requiem for all the benefactors of the church. As Eamon Duffy notes, there was far more to this than a simple desire for perpetual intercession; the catalog of the endowments and particular gifts to the parish gave the parishioners a sense of continuity and security in their place.[18] The intercessory prayers could conclude with a prayer of general confession of sins and an absolution, as continued to be the case in various Reformation liturgies in Germany and Scandinavia.[19] At the end of the bids, the priest would give notice of any feast or fast days in the coming week.

The Office of Prone was thus a piece of vernacular liturgy that passed into Reformation usage. It served as the basis of Ulrich Zwingli's liturgy of the word at Zurich in 1523.[20] It also served as the framework of the pulpit office in German and Scandinavian Lutheran mass orders. It is possible that Prone was also a place where vernacular carols were sung, since in Lutheran practice, the principal hymn of the service was sung surrounding the sermon. Some stanzas were sung as the preacher went from the altar and mounted the pulpit; other stanzas were sung at the conclusion of the pulpit office. As we shall see, however, vernacular hymn singing was no invention of the Reformation; it found a place several centuries before the Reformation.

Vernacular Songs in the Mass

As the last chapter described, strophic Latin hymns were used primarily in the Divine Office and for processions. Strophic Latin hymns did not find a place in the mass liturgy until the development of sequence hymns between the Epistle and Gospel in about 1000. The original sequences were textless musical elaborations of the final -*ah* of *hallelujah*. But texts began to be added as tropes, or additions to the authorized texts. Tropes were becoming popular in the ninth century.[21] Hundreds of sequences were composed all over western Europe from the eleventh to the thirteenth century, and even beyond. Some of the melodies of sequences even found their way into secular vocal and instrumental music in the Middle Ages.[22]

New musicological research has shown that almost as soon as these Latin sequence hymns were interpolated into the Mass after the Alleluia or gradual tract, vernacular hymns based on them appeared, especially in German. Thus, the Easter sequence "Victimae paschali laudes" (Christians to the paschal victim) by Wipo of Burgundy (c. 1000–1050), chaplain to Emperor Henry III, inspired the German carol "Christ ist erstanden" (Christ is arisen, c. 1100), which in turn provided the basis of Martin Luther's "Christ lag in Todesbanden" (Christ Jesus lay in death's strong bands) (tune as well as text). The "Veni Sancte Spiritus" (Come, Holy Spirit) sequence for Pentecost, attributed to Pope Innocent III (1164–1216), was the source of "Nun bitten wir den Heiligen Geist" (Now we implore the Holy Ghost), attributed to Brother Berthold of Regensburg (d. 1272), to which Luther added three stanzas. Thomas Aquinas's sequence hymn for the feast of Corpus Christi, "Lauda Sion Salvatorem" (Zion praise the Savior), served as the basis for "Gott sei gelobet" (O God be praised), to which Luther added two stanzas. In the case of these and numerous other vernacular songs, which served as the sources for later Reformation chorales, the people actually sang these songs either interspersed with stanzas of the Latin sequence sung by the choir or following the Latin sequence sung by the choir.

Besides these well-known examples, there is other evidence of vernacular singing at various points in the Mass, cited by William Anthony Ruff.[23] Berthold of Regensburg in the thirteenth century mentions a vernacular trinitarian strophe being sung after the creed. Medieval decrees from several locales prohibiting the singing of vernacular songs in conjunction with the principal parts of the Mass show that such singing was actually being done.[24] These German songs were devotional commentaries on the meaning of the Mass as a memorial of the passion of Christ. It became customary to sing a German song at the time of the creed and the sermon. The well-known German credo-hymn that Luther knew and used in his German Mass (1526), "Wir glauben all' an einen Gott" (We all believe in one true God), appears with its melody in a fifteenth-century manuscript. The very idea of Luther's German Mass might have been to extract these German songs that had been sung alongside the Latin texts of the Mass and make them integral to the order of the Mass. Nor was this idea original with Luther, since the Bohemian Brethren had already developed a vernacular liturgy based on songs sixty years before Luther's German Mass. In actual Lutheran practice, vernacular hymns could be sung in addition to or in place of Latin chants. Phillip Melanchthon testifies concerning the evangelical mass in the Augsburg Confession, Article 24 (1530), "In certain places German hymns are sung in addition to the Latin responses for the instruction and edification of the people." This might mean that the medieval practice was being continued, not that the Lutherans had invented something new. It certainly would not have served the purposes of the Augsburg Confession to highlight new practices when it was claiming, "We have introduced nothing, either in doctrine or in ceremonies, that is contrary to Holy Scripture or the universal Christian church."[25] In fact, the singing of German hymns and songs simultaneously with the celebration of the Latin mass continued in German Catholic practice during and after the Reformation.[26]

The background of the Lutheran chorale is primarily the sequence hymn. But French carols were based on the processions sung as the clergy and choirs left the chancel at the end of Vespers and other liturgical services. The origin of these carols, in turn, was the line dance known as the *carole*. Indeed, French clergy danced the *caroles* upon the great labyrinths at Chartres and other Gothic cathedrals.[27] In England carols were also sung in civil processions, a function that persisted in the carols of "The Boar's Head." Some carols, like "The Holly and the Ivy," give evidence of the survival of pre-Christian fertility rites. The Franciscans promoted carols with more Christian themes as part of their preaching missions.[28]

Praying the Mass in the Vernacular

In addition to the vernacular sermon, announcements, and prayers of the pulpit office, vernacular carols interjected into the sequences or other moments in the mass liturgy, and portions of the Latin Bible rendered in the vernacular in sermons, the late Middle Ages saw a proliferation of vernacular lay people's mass books, which provided prayers and other texts for personal use to help the laity participate more fully in the Mass. Lay participation in the Mass had become limited by the late Middle Ages to responding to certain key gestures or phrases, by changing posture such as kneeling or standing, and by singing carols, at least on feast days. Church authorities felt that this was inadequate. As literature developed in the vernacular languages and literacy increased, church authorities approved the private production and use of devotional books, which provided paraphrases of the mass texts and moralizing meditations on the parts of the Mass. Books of Hours (*Horae*) or primers, which usually contained collections of psalms and a daily prayer office, sometimes also contained sections of guidance on the Mass, with appropriate prayers. Since the elevation of the host was the high point of the lay experience of the Mass, many of the devotions in these primers were preoccupied with the elevation and the benefits to be derived from gazing at the host.[29]

These devotional books originated in France. Edmund Bishop traced them back as far as Benedict of Aniane in Carolingian times and the development of supplementary devotions to the divine office that originated in the monasteries.[30] English works for the laity were often translations from the French. The famous rhyming *Lay Folk's Mass Book*, for example, probably originated in Norman French and was translated in the fourteenth century. The prayers were to be said while kneeling with raised hands, although the need for personal diversity was recognized:

Knel and halde up thy hands,
And with inclinacyon
Behalde the Eleuacyon.
Swylke prayere than thou take,
As the likes best forto make.
Many men praayes sere,
like men prayes on his manere.
Schorte prayer soulde be with-owten drede
And there-with a pater-noster and crede.[31]

The use of these private devotional books (at least by the literate) has suggested to historians of late medieval religion that the lay experience of the Mass was becoming privatized. Indeed, the clergy who wrote these books were not aiming to give their readers an understanding of what the clergy and choir were saying, but to tell them when to stand, when to kneel, and to elicit devotional feelings appropriate to each moment of the Mass. Thus, the lay people's mass book or office book was designed to help them do what was appropriate to their role in the liturgy rather than to connect with what the clergy were doing. Moreover, Colin Richmond suggested that the gentry who could read were being drawn away from the rest of the parishioners in the assembly who were illiterate or could not afford to buy a mass book or primer. (Primers especially were customized for the buyer, who made a selection of materials to be included, and therefore were quite expensive and were often preserved as family heirlooms.) Such folk, said Richmond, by reading a devotional book instead of following the movements and gestures of the priest, and "in becoming isolated from their neighbors, were also insulating themselves against communal religion."[32] Pamela Graves carried the thought even further, arguing that the primers and mass books encouraged lay people "to muster their own thoughts, rather than construct a communal memory of the passion through the action of the mass."[33]

Eamon Duffy, in contrast, noted that it was the gentry who paid for the vestments, vessels, processional crosses, candlesticks, and other accoutrements that enriched the parish's eucharistic worship, and even some of the altars and chapels along the side aisles of the nave.[34] This would suggest that rather than withdrawing from communal worship the rural gentry and urban elite tended to dominate it. Moreover, the lay devotional books tended to draw on the same images, metaphors, and phrases derived from the mass liturgy that were also reflected in the paintings, carvings, and windows of the church building. So the illiterate gazing at the rood screen and the literate reading a learned vernacular or Latin prayer reflecting on the wounds of Jesus would have responded in much the same way when summoned from their gazing or reading by the ringing of the sacring bell to adore the host at its elevation. Both would have embraced a shared symbolic world.

This was a world that focused on the passion of Christ for the forgiveness of sins and reconciliation between God and humanity, which are the fruits of the Mass. In the words of *The Lay Folk's Mass Book*,

Welcome, lorde, in fourme of brede
For me thou sufferde herd deede;
Als thou bore the crowne of thorne
Thou suffer me noghte be forlorne.[35]

Whether worshipers were reading a devotional book, looking at pictures, reciting prayers, whispering to a neighbor, or waiting on the church porch, they were summoned by the ringing of the sacring bell to the moment of the elevation, the exchange of peace or kissing of the pax board, and, at high points of the year such as Christmas and Easter, to the reception of Holy Communion. The Mass was still a work that all the people did together. And whether they got it from the devotional books or the homilies of the priest, the laity still understood at a basic level what was happening: Jesus Christ, true God and true man, had come among them in sacramental bread and wine, bringing the grace of his passion to his sinful and suffering people.

Thus, the view that the lay people were shut out from the medieval mass rests on a narrow understanding of "participation" that sees liturgy only as text and limits participation to speaking roles. In any event, the accusation has been greatly exaggerated. The laity have always found ways to participate in the liturgy, whether it was in their language or not, and they have always derived meaning from the liturgy, whether it was the intended meaning or not. Furthermore, the laity in worship were surrounded by other "vernaculars" than language, not least of which were the church buildings themselves and the liturgical art that decorated them.

Latin and Vernacular in Contention

Nevertheless, by the beginning of the sixteenth century, there was widespread agitation to put the Bible and the liturgy also into vernacular languages. A booklet (*libellus*) written by two Venetian Camaldese (Paolo Giustiniani and Pietro Quirini) and addressed to Pope Leo X in 1513 proposed a sweeping reform of clerical life and education that would include "translation of the Bible into modern languages and a vernacular liturgy."[36] The Protestant Reformation represented a determination to put liturgy into the language of the people. Yet even among Protestants, there was a certain reserve. Lutherans, for example, did not totally abandon the use of liturgical Latin. Latin services continued to be held in city churches, schools, and universities, even up until the eighteenth century, while vernacular services were held in villages and rural places (although often with great resistance from the villagers and peasants).[37] In 1560, Queen Elizabeth I of England authorized the publication of a Latin version of the *Book of Common Prayer* for use in the universities. Even in Protestant countries, Latin continued to be taught in the schools and practiced in the law courts, and for this reason, Martin Luther would not abandon Latin services entirely, "because the young are my chief concern."[38]

Nevertheless, Protestant services were increasingly in the vernacular, either in whole or in part. The Catholic Church, in reaction, retreated from vernacularization, but not entirely. The Council of Trent eventually refused to sanction the use of vernacular in the Roman liturgy, but this rejection represented more a determination on the part of the bishops to shore up the authority of the Roman Catholic Church than a view that Latin possessed some sort of sacred power. Moreover, it is apparent that the council fathers recognized the validity of the reform-ers' concern for more thorough catechesis in order to ensure better participation in worship. As the recommendations of the council's twenty-second session show, a new principle was being proposed: *cel-ebrate* the liturgy in Latin, but *explain* it in the vernacular. "The holy council commands pastors and all who have the *cura animarum* (the cure of souls) that they, either themselves or through others, explain frequently during the celebration of the mass some of the things read during the mass."[39] However, efforts to produce translations of the Roman liturgy so that the people could follow the Mass in their own language were met with resistance by the Holy See.

CHAPTER 9

The Medieval Liturgical Calendar

This chapter covers a long span of time and a great deal of material. The Western Middle Ages are conventionally regarded as spanning nearly a thousand years between the pontificate of Gregory the Great (590–604) and the sixteenth-century Reformation. Scholars argue for more or less time at both ends, but this time span will serve the purpose of this chapter. We will look at the calendar from the lay perspective, since the days and seasons of the church year and the customs observed in connection with those days and seasons shaped the lives and world-view of medieval Christians as profoundly as anything.

In the culture of Christendom that emerged in the medieval West, the liturgical calendar played an important role in the everyday lives of ordinary people, since there was little difference between the civil calendar and the church calendar. The acceptance of the church calendar in its broad outline of festivals and seasons throughout the Christian world also contributed tremendously to the unity of Europe. Yet within a universally accepted calendar, there was plenty of room for local variations and special days of local significance.

The Day, the Week, the Seasons, and the Year

The annual calendar is governed by subunits of time that have acquired social significance. The day is the basic unit of the calendar, and even the "hours" of the day received special significance as a result of the influence of Benedictine monasticism on western European social life. Benedict devised a *Rule* (c. 530–540) that divided the daily life of the monk into equal segments of prayer, work, and rest. Monks lived according to a fixed routine, and the tolling of the monastery bell for the "hours of prayer" had an impact also on the daily lives of people who lived in the countryside surrounding the monasteries. It is thought that the first mechanical clocks were alarm clocks whose purpose was to awaken sacristans to ring the monastery bells. The purpose of synchronizing the schedules of the monks in terms of praying, eating, working, and sleeping was to develop an intensely communal life. But the discipline of this routine also spread to the general population, so that times of praying, eating, working, and sleeping became fairly uniform throughout European society.

While the same routines were followed on most days, not all days were equal, and this accounted for variations in the routine. We have seen that Sunday, the Lord's Day, acquired special significance in Christianity as a day of worship and rest. Other days also acquired special significance as commemorations of events in the life of Christ and the death days of the saints (which marked their birth into eternal life). Some dates were established by universal usage throughout the church; other dates were established by local authority. The establishment of saints' days could be politically highly charged and was done as much by royal decree or civic legislation as by papal proclamation. Local authorities strove to provide fitting sanctity for "holy days" by decreeing time off from work, the closing of usurers' shops (banks), the suspension of the collection of debts, and the removal of prostitutes from public view. Crimes committed on a holy day often received a harsher punishment than crimes committed on ordinary days.[1]

The church strove to replace the names of the days of the week inherited from Roman antiquity with its own system. The Romans preserved the Babylonian astrological week in which the seven days were named after the seven known planets. Church leaders tried to get Christian societies to accept the liturgical nomenclature. In the liturgical system, Sunday was the "Lord's Day" (*Dominica*) and Saturday remained the "Sabbath" (*Sabbato*). The other days of the week used the simple ordinal numbers found in Genesis 1 and in the liturgical books, with Monday as the "second day" (*feria secunda*), Tuesday as the "third day" (*feria tertia*), etc. Only Portugal fully adopted the biblical/liturgical enumeration; Iceland and a few other places did so partially. Spain, France, and Italy accepted Sabbath and Lord's Day but retained the planetary names for weekdays. England and Germany not only retained the planetary designations, but even replaced most of the Roman names with comparable Norse deities except for Saturday, for which there was no Nordic equivalent.[2]

Language differences also affected the vernacular designations of major festivals and liturgical seasons. The Gothic language was much more accepting of Christian loanwords from Greek and Latin than were Old English or Anglo-Saxon, which tended to "baptize" pagan words rather than borrow from Latin. Thus, despite massive exposure to Latin and Romance languages, English speakers still use the Germanic words *Lent* (*Lengten* = "lengthening" of days, or spring) and *Easter* (*Eostre*), rather than *Quadragesima* and *Pascha*. The origin of the English word *Easter* is uncertain. In the eighth century, the Venerable Bede (c. 673–735) guessed that it was derived from Eostre, the Anglo-Saxon goddess of spring, although more modern theories suggest that it comes from a Germanic word meaning "east." In spite of the borrowed Latin for "Christmas" (*Christi missa*), "Yuletide" is still known and used. The German *Weihnachten* (consecrated nights) may be a holdover from the pre-Christian solstice celebration. The German name for Lent, however, reflects the character of the season: *Fastenzeit* ("fasting time"). Thus, in the very names of the days and seasons, we see the mixture of Christian and pagan perspectives that shaped the medieval mind-set.

The liturgical calendar, based on historical commemorations, was superimposed on the natural calendar. In western Europe, the solar cycle establishing four seasons of the year was more important than the lunar calendar dividing the year into months. The fact that Christian feasts coincided with natural phenomena such as the winter and summer solstices (the Nativity of our Lord and the Nativity of John the Baptist) and the spring equinox (Easter) reinforced the blending of systems.

Most societies find it desirable to have a date on which the new year begins. In medieval Europe there were different new year's days. The Roman designation of January 1 as the day of the new year was not widespread in trans-Alpine Europe, although it remained in use in Rome. The liturgical calendar began with Advent, but this was a Gallican development. We have seen that the original Gallican Advent was a season of six or seven weeks, beginning near Saint Martin's Day (November 11) and often called "Saint Martin's Lent" (*Quadragesima*

Sancti Martini). If this were the civil new year, it would have made the year begin at harvest time in many localities, but spring is much preferred as a time of new beginnings. In Coventry, it seems that the new year began at Candlemas (February 2, the Feast of the Presentation of Jesus forty days after his nativity), when the city's pastures were opened for private use. In Venice the new year coincided with the beginning of the sailing season.

The day much more preferred for the new year in England and some other countries was the Annunciation (March 25). This was also the date of the spring equinox. The annunciation was regarded theologically as the date of the beginning of the new creation in terms of the incarnation and the redemptive sacrifice of Christ (the Annunciation often coincided with Holy Week and even with Good Friday). This mystically tied together the old creation and the new. Geoffrey Chaucer, in "The Nun's Priest's Tale" of his *Canterbury Tales*, speaks of "the month in which the world bigan, / That highte March, when God first maked man" (II.367–68). The Annunciation remained the date of the new year in England and in British North America until 1752, when the Gregorian calendar was adopted.

Advent, Christmas, and Epiphany

The liturgical year began with the season of Advent, even though the civil year began on January 1 or March 25. We have seen that Advent developed in Gaul as a forty-day season beginning on Saint Martin's Day (November 11), possibly as an initiatory season replicating Lent. When Roman liturgical books were imported into the Frankish Kingdom, they lacked propers for the Advent season, which then had to be supplied from local sacramentaries and lectionaries. A telltale sign of the Gallican provenance of Advent is that some of the classic Advent collects are addressed to Christ, whereas Roman collects would always be addressed to God the Father "through Jesus Christ, your Son, our Lord."

As the influence of Franco-German emperors waxed and the influence of Roman popes waned, the Germanic rulers were able to reverse the flow of influence and impose trans-Alpine practices on Rome. One of the consequences of this development was that around 1000 C.E., a universal four-week Advent season took shape. It began four Sundays before Christmas, usually the Sunday closest to Saint Andrew's Day

(November 30). Remnants of the older six-week Advent lingered in the lectionaries in the eschatological readings that marked the end of one church year and began the new church year. Advent was a penitential season, but not quite as penitential as Lent. For example, in the mass, the Gloria in Excelsis was suppressed during Advent, but not the Alleluia. The Third Sunday of Advent (*Gaudete*) acquired an especially joyous character.

We have seen that Christmas may not have originated simply as a Constantinian adaptation of Christianity to the growing sun cult in the late Roman Empire. It may have originated from calendrical calculations related to the time of Christ's conception (the Feast of the Annunciation, March 25). Nevertheless, in the old Julian calendar, December 25 was the winter solstice. It was not possible to keep solstice observances completely out of the Christmas celebration, especially in the northern European countries. The burning of the Yule log (Yule was the month of December) was originally a pagan custom designed to chase away the demons of ice and snow, but burning of the log continued in Christian homes.[3] Homes were decorated with greens, and lighted candles were placed in the windows. The Yule tree was an undecorated fir tree placed in the house at the onset of winter. It is to be distinguished from the Christmas tree, which originated as a prop for the Paradise Play performed on the Feast of Adam and Eve (December 24).[4] Decorated with fruits and nuts, and later with candles, the Christmas tree was not known outside of Germany until the nineteenth century. The Yule log may be the distant origin of the Advent wreath, which seems to have been first used by Lutherans in eastern Germany in the sixteenth century.

The liturgical books provided three masses for Christmas: at midnight (the Mass of the Angels), at dawn (the Mass of the Shepherds), and at midday (the Mass of the Incarnation). In the fifteenth century, mystery plays, performed on December 25, acted out the story of the nativity in the Gospel of Luke. This tradition of drama and pageant has continued up until the present time and is often the primary focus of parochial Christmas celebrations.

The Christmas season lasted for twelve days, culminating in the Feast of the Epiphany on January 6. In the Eastern church, the Epiphany celebration included themes of Christ's baptism and his first miracle of turning water into wine at the wedding feast at Cana. In the Western church, Epiphany commemorated the visit of the Magi to the

Christ-child. Between the thirteenth and the fifteenth centuries, the adoration of the Christ-child and the holy family had received an emphasis that would have been foreign to the ancient church or even to the early Middle Ages. According to tradition, Francis of Assisi promoted the use of the crèche or nativity scene as a way of inspiring devotion. The cult of the Christ-child was promoted by Franciscan preachers during the fourteenth and fifteenth centuries. Eventually every town had its own crèche. Carol singing accompanied the use of the crèche and grew in popularity during this same time period. This practice also seems to have been promoted by the Franciscans.

The whole twelve days between December 25 and January 6 were a time of feasting, reflecting the late fall harvests and culling of the herds. Several days within this season received special emphasis and were accompanied by special customs.

Saint Stephen the Martyr and Deacon was commemorated on December 26. It was a general custom among European farmers to decorate their horses and bring them to the church for a special blessing. Later in the day, the whole family went for a festive wagon or sleigh ride.

Saint John the Apostle and Evangelist was commemorated on December 27. Reflecting the Gospel of John's first sign of Jesus, turning water into wine at the wedding feast at Cana, wine was blessed on this day, and toasts were made "in the love of Saint John."

The slaughter of the Holy Innocents was observed on December 28. Liturgy on this day had a penitential character. But the Christmas revelries prompted the playfulness of electing a boy bishop, since the day became a special devotion for students and choirboys.

The Feast of Fools (*Festum Fatuorum*) was introduced in the eleventh century to keep the clergy away from Christmas revels. One of their number was elected a "Bishop of Fools." Dressed in pontifical regalia, he presided over the choir offices during Christmas week. Many pranks were played on him and by him on the others.

The Feast of the Ass (*Festum Asinarium*) was an outgrowth of the Feast of Fools. It provided pageants that celebrated all the donkeys connected with events in the Bible. These two feasts were suppressed by the fifteenth century. But the song "Oriente partibus" (From orient country came / A lordly ass of highest fame) originated from this pageant.

The Feast of the Circumcision on January 1 was of Gallican origin. The Roman church did not at first accept such a major festival on

January 1 because that was the Roman New Year's Day, and the church would not have done anything to encourage additional merrymaking on this day. In fact, in the Roman liturgical calendar, the Octave of Christmas was a Feast of Mary because of the papal practice of celebrating a station mass on January 1 at the Church of Saint Mary Major. But the Feast of the Circumcision and Name of Jesus overshadowed the Roman Feast of Mary. Because the Christ-child received his name on this day, the feast became associated in medieval devotion with the honor of the Holy Name. Bernard of Clairvaux wrote his famous hymn "Jesu Dulcis Memoria" (How Sweet the Thought of Jesus) as an act of devotion to the Holy Name. A common medieval custom was the blessing of the family by the father in token of God's blessing for the new year. As each family member knelt before him, the father made the sign of the cross over his wife and children.

The old Roman custom of giving presents at the beginning of the new year survived in all the Latin countries. But under Christian liturgical influence, the preferred date for gift giving was transferred from January 1 to January 6, the Feast of the Epiphany, especially in Italy and Spain. Only in France was January 1 retained as the day of gift giving.

From Epiphany to Ash Wednesday

The Feast of the Epiphany originated in the East as early as the third century. January 6 was the date of the winter solstice in the Egyptian calendar, which was twelve days behind the Julian calendar. The feast day was established in Gaul and Spain during the fourth century at about the same time as the Roman Christmas was being established. While in the East the feast focused on the Baptism of Christ and the blessing of water, as well as on the first miracle of Christ at Cana, in the West the theme of the Adoration of the Magi soon became dominant. Not surprisingly, in the early medieval West the people's attention was focused on the persons of the magi. The Gospel of Matthew does not tell us how many wise men there were. The East had a tradition of twelve magi, but the West settled on three—one for each gift. On the basis of Psalm 72 and Isaiah 60, the wise men were turned into kings. In the book *Collectanea et Flores*, ascribed to the Venerable Bede, an earlier legend of their names and physical characteristics is recorded. And so the names of Melchior (an old man with white hair, who offered the gift of gold), Gaspar (a young man with a ruddy complexion, who offered the gift of incense), and Balthasar (a black man with a heavy beard, who offered the gift of myrrh) entered into the Western lexicon. Their story was acted out in the popular mystery play called "The Office of the Star," which, like the Nativity Play, originated as part of the liturgical office. But because of the tendency to ham up the character of King Herod, the play eventually was put outside the church building. The blessing of water was not practiced in the West, but the Roman Rite popularized a blessing of the home.

An important liturgical custom on the Feast of the Epiphany was the Proclamation of the Feasts, which announced the date of Easter for that year and all of the days in the calendar dependent on the date of Easter. This oral calendar was proclaimed on Epiphany not just because it was at the beginning of the year—not every country celebrated the new year on January 1—but because the dates of the rest of the days in the church year after the Epiphany (except festivals and commemorations that had assigned dates) depended on the date of Easter.

A day of special devotion for medieval Christians was Candlemas (February 2), officially known as the Presentation of Jesus in the Temple and the Purification of Mary. The popular name Candlemas comes from the blessing of the parish's supply of candles for the year. This day was particularly celebrated as a feast of light, deriving from the day's Gospel, in which old Simeon greets the Christ-child in the Temple and utters his canticle, which has entered the liturgical tradition as the Nunc Dimittis ("Lord, now let your servant depart in peace"). Simeon hails the Christ-child as "the light for enlightening the nations and the glory of your people Israel." Even in the Middle Ages, popular lore regarded Candlemas as a weather forecast, although without the help of groundhogs:

> If Candlemas be fair and bright,
> Come, Winter, have another flight;
> If Candlemas brings clouds and rain,
> Go, Winter, and come not again.

The Candlemas procession was one of the three or four great liturgical processions of the year in which the whole community participated (the others being Palm Sunday, Rogationtide, and Corpus Christi). All of the parishioners brought candles to the church, where some of the candles were contributed for the church's use during the year, and a penny for the parish priest. The prayers of blessing suggest that apo-tropaic powers were recognized in the wax. Parishioners lit the candles in their homes during thunderstorms and in time of illness, and they placed candles in the hands of the dying to ward off the devil. All of the candles (including the paschal candle) were blessed on this day and were then carried in a great procession around the church as the Nunc Dimittis was sung. The Candlemass commenced after the procession.[5]

Other saints' days in early February held special attraction for medi-eval people. On Saint Blasius' Day (February 3), horses and cattle drank blessed water to protect them from future maladies. Bread was distributed on Saint Agatha's Day (February 5). The hagiography of Saint Dorothea (February 6) told how she protected young plants from frost. Saint Valentine's Day (February 14) was, and still is, the festival celebrating sexual love. This festival season ended with the Chair of Saint Peter (February 22), which became the occasion for the parish priest to bless oats for cattle and the last day to gather dead winter wood to be used for spring and summer fires.

The time just before Ash Wednesday was Carnival time through-out Europe (meaning "farewell to meat" before the great Lenten fast began). Much of the church year depended on the date of Easter, which could vary from March 22 to April 25, since it was based on the lunar calendar. Easter Day was always the first Sunday after the first full moon of spring (theoretically after Passover). This meant that the forty days of Lent, beginning with Ash Wednesday, could occur as early as February 4. When Lent arrived early, Carnival time was pushed back into January, and there was almost nonstop feasting between December 25 and the beginning of Lent.

Carnival was a very popular and important part of medieval and early modern European social life. As Edward Muir has written, among all the popular lay festivals, Carnival "produced the richest symbolic imagery; had the greatest influence on European culture, especially on comic drama; and celebrated the materiality of everyday life, the realm of the body."[6] If the purely liturgical festivals were rituals of the upper body, Carnival was a ritual of the lower body. Carnival involved feasting and drinking, entertainment in the forms of circuses and plays, races and other games, masquerades and dances, and generally was a time given to revelry and ribaldry. Even before the Reformation, Carnival was celebrated more in southern Europe than in northern Europe, since February is not a pleasant time to frolic outside in places like

Scotland and Norway. Carnival-like celebrations occurred in the northern countries at Midsummer. Since *Carnival* literally means "farewell to meat" (from the Latin *carnem levare*) before the arrival of Lent and the time of fasting, meat was a prime ingredient of Carnival, and butchers' guilds took a primary role in the organization of the events. Given the sexual images and practices of Carnival, it is not surprising that Carnival was a prime time for weddings. Apparently in early medieval Venice, all marriages were solemnized during Carnival time. Given the masquerades and opportunities for playacting both on stage and off, Carnival was also a time of reversal of roles, when the poor acted rich and the rich acted poor. It was a "safety valve" for built-up tensions in society and provided an opportunity for subjects to express resentment to authorities without fear of reprisal. Since this opportunity for rebelliousness was an annual ritual, it helped reinforce the social order. Yet it also served as what Victor Turner called a "liminal" experience on the margins of respectability that served to renew the established order.[7]

Lent and Holy Week

On Ash Wednesday all of the excesses of Carnival came to an abrupt halt. Probably with many sins to confess, the faithful went to church to be shriven (make confession) and to receive the mark of penitence with the imposition of ashes. The ashes were made from the burning of the previous year's Palm Sunday branches. The use of ashes as a mark of penitence goes back to the public penance of the ancient church, which made reference to Old Testament examples of sitting in ashes (Jonah 3:5–9; Jeremiah 6:26–25, 34). Enrollment into the *Ordo poenitentium* (order of penitents) forty fast days before Easter was an official rite in the Roman Church as early as the fourth century, and the custom soon spread to other churches. Being a public penitent meant being excommunicated (cut off from communion) during the period of penitence. The penitents were led out of the church on Ash Wednesday and were not readmitted until Maundy Thursday. (The word "quarantine" comes from the "forty" of *quadrigesima*.) However, the practice of public penance was dying out by the sixth century, even though it remained officially on the books. The practice of private confession that emerged from the monasteries, especially in the Irish tradition, was slow in gaining acceptance as an alternative. Not until the Fourth Lateran Council in 1215 was making confession to a priest laid on all the faithful who had attained an "age of discretion" (usually age seven) in preparation for receiving communion on Easter. By this time, however, all of the faithful were receiving ashes on Ash Wednesday as a way of entering into the time of penitence. The penitential practices of Lent laid on all the faithful included the three "notable duties" of Matthew 6: almsgiving, prayer, and fasting.

By late antiquity the forty-day fast before Easter in imitation of Jesus' forty days of fasting in the wilderness after his baptism was well established in both Eastern and Western churches. Sunday was never a fast day in the Christian tradition because it was the Lord's Day and therefore the day of the Eucharist. One does not normally feast and fast at the same time. This is why the Eastern churches do not celebrate the Eucharist on a fast day, such as the days of Lent, until the time of fasting is ended.[8] In the Eastern church, Saturday was not a fast day either. This was a remembrance that the seventh day of the week had been the Old Testament Sabbath, and therefore a day of joy and celebration. Hence, the forty days began earlier in the Eastern calendar than in the Western calendar, since Saturdays as well as Sundays were not reckoned in the counting of fast days. However, in the Eastern church, a less strict fast was maintained even on Saturdays and Sundays during Lent or *Quadragesima*.

The standard Christian fast, as Pope Gregory the Great wrote to Augustine of Canterbury, was abstinence from flesh meat and from all products that come from flesh, such as milk, cheese, eggs, and butter.[9] This remained the standard fast for a thousand years and was laid on all except those whose health was a concern. In strict practice, no food was taken until the end of the day. After the eighth century, this one evening meal was advanced to the time of the Office of None (about 3 P.M.). A noon meal did not become a general practice until the fourteenth century. When eating the main meal of the day at noon became a general practice, the evening meal became lighter fare (as it continues to be in Europe) and was pushed later into the evening. Toward the end of the Middle Ages in the West, this new social reality was taken into account in laws governing fasting so that lay people as well as monks were eating three times a day but abstaining as far as possible from the proscribed foods on fast days. In spite of a universal Christian tradition of fasting, common sense governed the application of fast laws in local situations. For example, abstinence from *lacticinia* (milk foods), which included butter, cheese, and eggs, was never strictly enforced in Britain, Ireland, and the Scandinavian countries because of the lack of oil and other products that could serve as substitutes. But people who needed to eat milk foods often gave extra alms for the building of churches. One of the steeples of the Rouen Cathedral in France is called "the butter tower."

Lent had originally been a time of preparation for solemn public baptism at Easter. By the early Middle Ages, with infant baptism becoming a norm and the concern to baptize infants as soon after birth as possible, Easter baptism became less common. However, almost as if in compensation for the loss of the initiatory character of Lent, it became a time for matchmaking and announcing the engagements of young people. Easter Day became an occasion for weddings, especially in Ireland.[10] Certainly this custom, combined with dances and games with eggs and balls on Easter Day, is a throwback to the fertility rites associated with the spring equinox in pre-Christian Europe.

Palm Sunday

The sixth Sunday of Lent was called Palm Sunday. It was a day of great ceremony on which the triumphal entry of Jesus into Jerusalem to the acclamation of his disciples was ritually reenacted. This entailed a great procession around the church, in which everyone participated. Liturgical Uses of different local churches resulted in different ceremonies. Few were as elaborate as those of Salisbury (Sarum).[11] In the Sarum Use, the officiating priest wore a red silk cope, and his assistants were vested in albs. They were followed by the choir and the people, everyone carrying blessed branches. The branches were called "palms" but were usually whatever branches were available in the locale. The procession was headed by a veiled cross and made its way through the west choir door of the cathedral, went around the cloister, and continued out through the canons' door to the first station—the extreme eastern point of the northern churchyard before the cross. The choir sang antiphons as the crowd processed. At the station the deacon read the Gospel from Matthew 21:1–9. Then there appeared a second procession, which had left the church during the distribution of palms and had taken a different route. This procession was headed by two banners and an unveiled cross onto which were tied green branches; it also included relics of the saints and a hanging pyx with a consecrated host. In the medieval mind, the consecrated host stood in for Christ himself, whose body was really present in the bread. Singing additional antiphons, the merged procession went around the church to the second station, although the veiled cross disappeared. At this station the choirboys sang the hymn "All Glory, Laud, and Honor." At the end of each stanza, the choirboys threw down cakes and flowers while repeating the refrain. Then the procession went through the cloister to the third station. At this station three clerks of higher rank turned to the people and sang *Unus autem ex ipsis* ("But one of them named Caiaphas…"). Then a ceremony took place that is not mentioned in the *Sarum Processional* but is mentioned in other Sarum books: the officiant opened the main church doors with the cross.[12] The procession moved through the nave to the fourth station, unveiling the rood (the large wooden cross suspended above the threshold between the nave and the chancel) as it went. At this station the celebrant began the antiphon ("Hail, our King, Son of David"), genuflected, and kissed the ground. The choir passed into its stalls, and as the procession ended, the cross on the high altar was uncovered and remained so for the rest of the day. High Mass followed.

In the Mass there was a striking departure from the usual Sunday ritual. The entire Passion according to Saint Matthew was chanted (by three clerks in churches that had the resources), with the words of Jesus sung by a bass, the words of the evangelist or narrator by a tenor, and the words of the crowds by an alto. This dramatic rendering of the Passion Narrative set the scene for the rest of Holy Week, which reenacted the passion, death, and resurrection of Christ, using dramatic rituals.

Maundy Thursday

Lent officially ended on the afternoon of Maundy Thursday. A second and more ancient fast was then observed over the next three days. The Jerusalem church bequeathed two eucharistic celebrations on Maundy Thursday: one in the afternoon to break the Lenten fast; the other in the early evening to commemorate the anniversary of the Lord's Supper. These two celebrations were also observed in Rome in the titular churches, but in papal practice, three masses were celebrated on Maundy Thursday: the morning mass of the reconciliation of penitents, the afternoon mass of the blessing of oils, and the evening mass of the Lord's Supper. The reconciliation of penitents and the blessing of oils were episcopal rites and were not celebrated in parish churches. The term *Maundy Thursday* is English and comes from the practice of the *Mandatum,* or foot washing, that was practiced in the Sarum Rite. The foot washing was practiced in Milan but not in Rome. After the seventh century, it was added to the Roman Rite but did not always take place during the celebration of the Mass. In Roman practice, the pope washed the feet of twelve lesser clergy and thirteen poor men during the Vespers of Holy Thursday. In the rest of Europe, bishops, abbots, and pastors engaged in this ritual, sometimes washing the feet of lower clergy, sometimes washing the feet of paupers. Paupers were undoubtedly pleased to participate, since they usually received alms for their effort.[13]

This foot-washing ritual was not always a part of the evening mass of the Lord's Supper, but the evening mass was considered the proper beginning of the Triduum (the liturgy of the Three Days). This was the last mass celebrated before Easter, since it was not the custom of the church, East or West, to celebrate the Eucharist on Good Friday. Instead, Holy Communion was distributed from the sacrament reserved after the evening mass. The practice of setting aside the hosts for distribution on Good Friday led to a complicated ceremony involving the following elements:

1. *A procession with the sacrament to a place of reservation*—In medieval devotion to the Eucharist outside of the Mass, this became an altar of repose, banked with candles and flowers.

2. *The practice of prayer before the reserved sacrament*—In medieval devotion, this came to be called the Forty Hours' Devotion, referring to the length of time Jesus' body lay in the tomb.

3. *A ritualized "burial" of a consecrated host (and/or a wooden cross)*—This was buried in a symbolic tomb or "holy sepulcher." Every church was required to provide a sepulcher, and the expenses for making, maintaining, lighting, and keeping watch survive in the financial accounts kept by many churchwardens.[14]

4. *The stripping of the altars of their linens and candles while the main altar was washed with water and wine (a symbol of Christ's blood washing the world clean)*—Every detail of this action was allegorized in popular teaching.

In the seventh century, after the evening mass there was a prayer service, which really anticipated Matins/Lauds. Its name derived from the words of the responsory, *Tenebrae factae sunt* ("It became dark" or "Shadows fell"). The practice of extinguishing candles during the singing of psalms and the reading from Lamentations characterized this service. Also there was a dramatic noise at the end—sometimes a striking of the benches to represent the scourging of Christ, in other places a loud noise representing the earthquake that rent the tomb of Christ. The exact reason for the extinguishing of lights is unknown. Some have suggested that it was because of the approach of dawn. More likely it was done for dramatic effect. In any event, the Tenebrae services of the Wednesday, Thursday, and Friday of Holy Week belong to the changes required in the prayer offices to accommodate the special liturgies of the Triduum. They do not belong to the Triduum itself.

Good Friday

The medieval Good Friday liturgy comprises three parts: the chanting of the Passion Narrative, the veneration of the cross, and communion from the reserved sacrament (the mass of the presanctified). Liturgical books in Rome suggest that there was a difference between the papal liturgy and the presbyteral liturgies at the *tituli* and *parochiae*. The presbyteral liturgy included the reading of the Passion according to John, a brief veneration of the cross, and communion from the reserved sacrament (Word and Sacrament). The papal liturgy included the solemn bidding prayers after the liturgy of the word and a procession with the cross, ending with its veneration. This liturgy did not include general communion from the reserved sacrament.

In western and northern Europe from the ninth century on, the veneration of the cross became more elaborate. The cross was veiled and was slowly uncovered during the procession. Once it was placed, Reproaches (known as *Improperia*), found in the *Pontificale Romano-Germanicum* (c. 950), were sung. These coupled scriptural descriptions of God's gracious acts toward his people (here identified with Christ) with descriptions of the various sufferings endured by Christ, concluding with the words, "O my people, what have I done to you? In what have I afflicted you? Answer me." These reproaches contained a strongly anti-Semitic tone, which, combined with the Passion according to John and the bidding prayer for the Jews, gave the whole Good Friday liturgy an anti-Jewish character that sometimes sparked violence against the Jews during the Middle Ages. The hymns of Venantius Fortunatus, "Pange, lingua, glorioso proelium certaminis" (Sing, My Tongue, the Glorious Battle Telling) and "Vexilla regis prodeunt" (The

Royal Banners Forward Go) were sung continuously while the people came forward to kiss the cross. "Creeping to the cross" became one of the frequent targets of the Protestant reformers, so there can be no doubt about the high place it held in lay devotion.

As the dramatic service of Tenebrae followed the evening mass of the Lord's Supper on Holy Thursday, so on Good Friday the late medieval popular devotion known as the Stations or Way of the Cross followed the Good Friday liturgy. This devotion was promoted by the Franciscans, who advocated representational devotions, such as the manger scene. Another paraliturgical devotion that became popular in the late Middle Ages was the Burial of Christ, in which a consecrated host was buried in a "sepulcher," which might be a walled recess, tomb, or vaulted enclosure.[15] In Venice this became a vast funeral procession through the streets with a coffin containing a consecrated host that would be buried in a tabernacle in the great Cathedral of Saint Mark. This representational piety has been called the "culmination of the pictorial mind."[16] The popularity of the Way of the Cross and the Burial of Christ had the effect of moving the Good Friday liturgy from afternoon to morning.

A particularly vivid means of inciting the devotion of the people occurred in Spain in the procession of the flagellants. Men voluntarily processed through the streets, whipping themselves with knotted cords, their clothing flecked with drops of their own blood, in order to identify with the sufferings of Christ in the scourging he received at the hands of the Roman soldiers. In Germany, Wednesday, Thursday, and Friday nights during Holy Week saw children and others noisily driving the spirit of Judas from the churches with rattles, clappers, hammers, and other noisemakers. In contrast, the bells of the churches were silent from Maundy Thursday until Easter morning.

Easter Vigil

The liturgy of the Easter Vigil was expanded during the early Middle Ages in the West but died out as a great public liturgy by the end of the Middle Ages. At first there were no special liturgies during Holy Saturday because of the amount of preparation needed for the Easter Vigil. It took time to prepare the "new fire" for the beginning of the vigil, which was often a bonfire of impressive proportions built in the public square in front of the cathedral or town church. An elaborate ceremony developed for the blessing of the new fire, involving litanies, collects, holy water, and incense.[17] The paschal candle was lit from this new fire and was carried into the church with a triple-sung acclamation of *Lumen Christi* (The light of Christ) with the response *Deo gratias* (Thanks be to God). The massive paschal candle was placed near the ambo, from which was sung the Easter proclamation (*Exsultet*) and Thanksgiving for the Candle. The candle was decorated with a cross and other symbols, and five grains of incense were inserted behind five spikes representing the five wounds of Christ. The Thanksgiving for the Candle became a veritable rehearsal of salvation history. In southern Italy, *Exsultet* scrolls were prepared on which were painted the scenes commemorated in the Thanksgiving. As the *Exsultet* was sung, the scroll was unrolled over the top of the ambo so the congregation could see the images as the deacon sang the text.[18] The early medieval lectionaries reduced the twelve traditional Old Testament readings to four: the creation, the exodus, Isaiah 4, and Deuteronomy 31. To each of these was added a sung response (psalm or canticle) and a collect said by the presiding minister. This service of readings was followed by a procession to the font while the litany of the saints was sung, then a lengthy blessing of water followed by baptisms if there were any.

Then the first mass of Easter began with the singing of the Kyrie and Gloria in Excelsis. The readings for the Mass were usually Colossians 3:1–4 and Matthew 28:1–7. Between the readings, an Alleluia was sung three times by the presider and repeated by the whole congregation, each time on a higher tone. Some elements in the Mass were omitted, such as the creed and the Agnus Dei (two later additions to the Mass). Later still, a brief form of Matins and then Lauds were appended to the mass. The significant dramatic feature at this celebration of Matins/Lauds was the "Visit to the Sepulcher," an early form of liturgical drama known as the *Quem quaeritis*, in which three choir boys acted out the visit of the myrrh-bearing women. They encounter an angel, who tells them that Jesus is not in the tomb; he has risen, and they should tell the rest of the disciples this news.

The two significant developments in the medieval practice of the Vigil were that it was no longer the premier time of the year to celebrate baptism and that a second mass was added on Easter Day. There were fewer adult baptisms, and infants were being baptized as soon after their birth as possible. Also, a second mass on Easter Day was needed to accommodate all the communions that were mandated by the decree of the Fourth Lateran Council (1215) that all Christians should receive communion at least once a year on Easter, after making their confession and receiving absolution. These developments pushed the Vigil up to an earlier hour on Saturday in order to accommodate the number of confessions, so that by the sixteenth century, the Vigil was customarily done on Holy Saturday morning. The Easter Day mass had eclipsed the vigil in importance in the popular mind.

It is not surprising that the Reformation found little reason to continue the liturgies of the Triduum. First, in the ritual processes typical of the Reformation, the candles of Candlemas, ashes of Ash Wednesday, and palms of Palm Sunday were abolished because of superstitions associated with the use of them. Also, the ceremonies of the Triduum, including the Maundy Thursday foot washing and the Good Friday veneration of the cross, were eliminated. Second, the new Reformation emphasis on everyone receiving communion combined with the tradition of Easter as the primary communion time of the year required having communion services on Maundy Thursday, Good Friday, and Easter Day in order to accommodate the number of communicants. Indeed, the reforms of Ulrich Zwingli in Zurich in 1524 specified that the women, children, and men were to receive communion respectively on these three days. In Lutheranism, too, these three days became important occasions on which to receive Holy Communion. In fact, in German Lutheranism, Good Friday became the biggest communion day of the year. This was obviously not communion from the reserved sacrament but a full liturgy of the Word and Lord's Supper (i.e., the Mass) for which propers were provided. Times of preparation for communion, including confession and catechetical examination, were required during Holy Week.

Meanwhile, the Catholic Church did nothing to renew these liturgies in the post-Tridentine liturgical reforms. In fact, Baroque Catholicism, with its adoration piety, placed the Holy Thursday mass of the Lord's Supper in the morning so that the rest of the day could be devoted to the adoration of the reserved sacrament. The Good Friday liturgy was celebrated in the morning so that the afternoon could be devoted to popular devotions such as the burial of "Christ" in the sepulcher, the new Three Hour Devotion on the Seven Last Words of Christ developed by the Jesuits in Latin America, or the communal Way of the Cross. While the *Missale Romanum* of 1570 restored the twelve Old Testament readings of the Easter Vigil, the Vigil continued to be celebrated in the morning so that the rest of the day could be devoted to confessions in preparation for the Easter communions. In plain fact, these liturgies were no longer the great popular celebrations that they had been in late antiquity. They were basically rituals on the books, preserved only because of their antiquity.

From Easter Day through the Day of Pentecost

The scene on Easter morning in the medieval church was a stark contrast to the somberness of Holy Week. The priests appeared in gold vestments. The most precious gold and jeweled vessels of the church were placed on the altar. A little drama took place at Lauds in which choristers knocking on the church door asked the priest to see the body of Jesus of Nazareth, but the choir (representing the angels) sang, "He is not here; for he has risen, just as he said. So go proclaim the news again and again, for he is risen." The bells of the church pealed jubilantly, and the whole community thronged to the Mass to receive their Easter communion.

Just as Easter was preceded by forty days of penance during Lent, so it was followed by forty days of rejoicing during the Easter season, leading up to the Feast of the Ascension. The days before the Ascension constituted Rogationtide, a time of processions to "beat the bounds" of the parish, during which litanies were sung to invoke God's blessing on the seedtime. These Rogation processions were universal in western Europe but varied widely from one locale to another. Thus, they were pliable enough for communities to pour into them what was important to them. They also had achieved great popularity and for that reason were not immediately suppressed by the Protestant Reformation, at least in Germany and England. Rogationtide often occurred close to May 1, with its floral poles and dancing.

The Feast of Pentecost was far more important liturgically and theologically than it became in popular observance. This is probably because it was not associated with an agricultural event such as the Jewish Feast of Weeks (associated with the spring harvest). Nevertheless, it became a time for parish church-ales, parish festivals designed to make money through the sale of alcohol and rich foods.

The Half Year of the Church

The second half of the church year seems quite "empty" in comparison with the ceaseless progression of fasts and feasts that characterized the first half. A trinity of festivals inaugurated this season: the Feast of the Holy Trinity, which is the octave of Pentecost; the Feast of Corpus Christi, which was the delayed octave of Maundy Thursday and one of the most popular days of the year; and the Feast of the Nativity of Saint John the Baptist (June 24), which coincided with the summer solstice and was celebrated with bonfires and dancing in the northern countries in which the sun barely set. As far as Saint John's Day is concerned, the pre-Christian pagan element of Midsummer totally eclipsed the biblical commemoration in popular celebrations. The next chapter will give special attention to the development, practices, and social significance of Corpus Christi.

The routines of the months of July, August, September, and October were broken only by occasional saints' days, the most universal of which were Peter and Paul (June 29) and the Assumption of the Blessed Virgin Mary (August 15).

The end of the church year was ushered in by the dual celebrations of All Saints' Day on November 1 and All Souls' Day on November 2, whose origins I discussed in chapter 4. In the Celtic calendar, November 1 was the beginning of winter. In popular imagination, this was a time when the souls of the departed visited their former homes as ghosts and hobgoblins looking for warmth and hospitality—or revenge. These spirits were greeted with treats and jack-o'-lanterns to placate them or ward them off. This was also a busy time for burial confraternities, who paid for requiem masses for their members and maintained the graves of the faithful departed.

CHAPTER 10

The Eucharistic Body and the Social Body in the Middle Ages

What is the glue that holds a society together? It may be the relationships of kith and kin, ethnic or racial sameness, tribal identity, or commitment to a common set of beliefs. Some kind of governing structure serves to maintain the bonds between people, whether this is a family patriarch, a community council, or a tribal chief. Where diverse families, races, or tribes live together in a single society, we look to a state or imperial government to provide and foster common ties between people. Thus, the Roman Empire provided an overarching governing structure for all the peoples and nations that lived within its borders. It is commonly believed that the church served as a unifying institution that transcended all the disparate, separate, loosely connected, and often feuding political entities of the Western Middle Ages and held them together. After all, church and society were practically coterminus. But this is not specific enough. Emperors and popes, kings and bishops, could be at odds with each other. One thinks of the investiture controversy in the eleventh century between the powerful Pope Gregory VII and the politically astute Emperor Henry IV, which brought the emperor to his knees as a penitent,[1] or of the tug-of-war between King Henry II of England and Archbishop Thomas Becket, which led to the latter's murder.

Something more specific and more unifying than the church as an institution served as the social glue of the Middle Ages: the Eucharist. This should not be surprising, because the Eucharist is the glue that holds the church together. The sacramental body forms the ecclesial body, which is kept in union with the historical body of Christ, the head of the ecclesial body, by receiving his body and blood in the sacrament.

Communion Ecclesiology

This is a reality that the contemporary church struggles to retrieve. Yet it is the earliest and most basic theology of the sacrament—and the earliest and most basic ecclesiology. In 1 Corinthians 10–12, we find both the earliest eucharistic theology and the earliest ecclesiology. All three chapters speak of "the body of Christ" in all three senses: the sacramental body, the historical body of Christ, and the ecclesial body. Paul develops this somatic theology in the context of practical problems in the life of the congregation. He admonishes the Corinthians, who tended to be puffed up with "knowledge" (*gnosis*), that they cannot partake of the sacrifice offered to demons because they are the body of Christ (10:17). But they are the body of Christ because "the bread that we break . . . is a sharing [*koinonia*] in the body of Christ" (10:16), about which the Lord says, "This is my body that is for you" (11:24). Every celebration of the Lord's Supper is a proclamation of the Lord's death until he comes (11:26). The "divisions" (*schismata*) and "factions" (*haireseis*) (11:18, 19) manifested at the Lord's Supper are a scandal. They exist because the Corinthian Christians do not "discern the body" (11:29). As a consequence, they do not eat the Lord's Supper, but their own suppers (11:21). The "body" they fail to discern is the church that is constituted by the sacramental body of Christ in which the Corinthians receive the crucified body of Christ, whose Spirit has apportioned various gifts (*charismata*) for building up the ecclesial body (12:4–11) and joins together baptized Jews and Greeks, slaves and free, who "drink of one Spirit" (12:13–14). The argument here is dense, but the three "bodies" are joined together in an inseparable relationship. The ecclesial body is formed, and its individual members coming from diverse backgrounds are bonded with Christ and with one another by sharing in the sacrament of the body and blood of Christ.

As Jean-Marie-Roger Tillard shows, this communion ecclesiology became a standard teaching in the church of the first five centuries.[2] He shows by thorough documentation that the relationship between the eucharistic body and the ecclesial body was a common assumption of three local churches, represented by Nestorius and Cyril of Alexandria (who disagreed on Christology but not on the relationship between the sacrament and the church), John Chrysostom (Antioch and Constantinople), and Augustine of Hippo (the Latin West). For John Chrysostom, the grace of Communion is that we are united to Christ and to one another. He brings to this communion ecclesiology a sense of the radical leveling of class distinctions in the waters of baptism and at the Lord's Table that is nothing short of revolutionary.[3] At Constantinople, Chrysostom noted the participation of the emperor and beggars at the same table of the Lord. Communion ecclesiology also pervades the writings of Augustine. For example, in *The City of God*, book 10, chapter 6, he discusses the bodily nature of sacrifice and the unity of the body of Jesus Christ, the sacramental body, and the body of the church in one sacrifice offered to God.[4] But Augustine's communion ecclesiology is perhaps most accessible in the sermons he preached to the newly baptized on Easter morning. Hear Augustine the bishop in *Sermon 227*:

> I haven't forgotten my promise. I had promised those of you who have just been baptized a sermon to explain the sacrament of the Lord's Table, which you can see right now, and which you shared in last night. You ought to know what you have received, what you are about to receive, what you ought to receive every day. That bread which you see on the altar, sanctified by the word of God, is the body of Christ. That cup, or rather what the cup contains, sanctified by the word of God, is the blood of Christ. It was by means of these things that the Lord Christ wished to present us with his body and blood, which he shed for our sake for the forgiveness of sins. If you receive them well, you are yourselves what you receive. You see, the Apostle says, "We who are many are one body, for we all partake of the same bread" (1 Cor. 10:17). That's how he explained the sacrament of the Lord's Table; one loaf, one body, is what we all are, many though we be.[5]

The unanimous conviction of the ancient church is that the ecclesial body of Christ is formed, maintained, nourished, and kept in union with Christ by the sacramental body of Christ. Ancient church practice reflected this ecclesiology. Baptism as initiation into the body of Christ was consummated by incorporation into the eucharistic fellowship. The church orders consistently show that the candidates were led from the font into the eucharistic hall, where they were greeted by the bishop and welcomed into the eucharistic fellowship with such gestures as the laying on of hands (an act of designation), anointing (an act of sealing), and the greeting of peace (a gesture of welcome), gestures that serve as the origin of the rite of confirmation performed by the bishop.[6] Canonical public penance served to protect the integrity of the eucharistic fellowship and therefore involved excommunication and reconciliation, which in the Roman Rite occurred respectively on Ash Wednesday and Maundy Thursday.[7] Bishops supervised both initiation and penance because they were the chief eucharistic ministers. This ecclesial and liturgical principle was already promoted by Ignatius of Antioch at the beginning of the second century. The wider church fellowship was established by bishops being in communion with each other. Christians were in communion with one another whose bishops were in communion with each other. Schism between churches was signified by one bishop excommunicating another, the most dramatic one being the mutual excommunications of the bishop of Rome and the patriarch of Constantinople in 1054.

In spite of the increasing temporal and secular authority invested in the bishop, theologians even up through the Middle Ages continued to say that the church hierarchy existed to serve the communion of the church; ordained ministry was never regarded as something in and of itself. The ordained ministry existed to serve the sacraments. Indeed, for Thomas Aquinas (1224–1274), the *res* (reality) of this sacrament "is the unity of the mystical body." He adopts the viewpoint of John of Damascus:

> This sacrament has a . . . significance . . . with regard to the present . . . that is, ecclesiastical unity, into which people are incorporated through this sacrament; that is why it is called *communion* or *synaxis*. For Damascene says, "It is called *communion* because through it we communicate with Christ, both by partaking of his flesh and divinity and by communicating with and being united to one another through it" [*Exposition of the Orthodox Faith* 4:13].[8]

The Eucharist became the central symbol and the source of unity of the medieval *corpus Christianorum* because it is the source and goal of the church's unity. We shall see how the eucharistic controversies of the early Middle Ages shored up the unifying power of the sacrament, how new definitions affected performance of and participation in the sacramental rite, how sacramental community threatened to break down toward the end of the Middle Ages, and how the emergence of the

Corpus Christi festival reasserted the sacramental community in a new social context.

Eucharistic Controversies

Controversies about the real presence of Christ raged between the ninth and the eleventh centuries and resulted in a new dogmatic definition in the early thirteenth century. It began in a dispute between two monks of Corbie, Paschasius Radbertus and Ratramnus (who occupied adjoining cells).[9] The essence of the argument stemmed from an answer to a pastoral question sent to the monastery from a newly founded Saxon church. Whatever the original question, the answer given by Paschasius in *De corpore et sanguine domini* (Concerning the Body and Blood of the Lord, c. 831) was that we receive in the Eucharist the same body of Christ that was conceived in the womb of the Virgin Mary and hung on the cross, and that this body becomes present in the bread through the operation of the priest's words at the Mass. Although this view was probably inspired by the writings of Ambrose of Milan, Paschasius's younger colleague Ratramnus thought that his fellow monk had responded in too literal a fashion. He appealed to the Augustinian-symbolist view that the body of Christ in the sacrament is figurative, an image of a spiritual truth that resided elsewhere.

The realist view of Paschasius gained momentum in the following centuries, no doubt because of the empirical worldview of the western European culture. When Berengar of Tours brought the teachings of Augustine, logic, and grammar forcefully to bear on the issue in the eleventh century in favor of a symbolist view, he was opposed by Lanfranc of Bec, who used Aristotle, logic, and grammar in favor of the realist view.[10] In this new phase of the debate, "sacramental presence" was opposed to "real presence." In the atmosphere of a cultural sea change from the Platonism of late antiquity to the Aristotelianism of the Western Middle Ages, Berengar could not win the debate. In 1059 he was forced to recant and agree to the following statement: "I believe that the bread and wine which are laid on the altar are after the consecration not only a sacrament but also the true body and blood of our Lord Jesus Christ, and they are physically taken up and broken in the hands of the priest and crushed by the teeth of the faithful, not only sacramentally, but in truth."

This formulation was too crass even for Lanfranc. Hugh of Saint Victor in particular felt the tension between "sacrament" and "reality" (*sacramentum et res*). Unable to resolve it, he took a cue from biblical revelation that the incarnation of the Word in Jesus was both a sign and a reality and suggested that the Eucharist is also both sacrament and reality. After another two decades, the 1059 statement was replaced in 1079 with the declaration *Ego Berengarius* ("I, Berengar") which stated:

> Bread and wine . . . through the mystery of the sacred prayer and by the words of the Redeemer are substantially converted (*substantialiter converti*) into the proper and life-giving flesh and blood of our Lord Jesus Christ, and that, after consecration, they are the true body of Christ which was born of the Virgin Mary and hung on the cross for the salvation of the world and which now sits at the right hand of the Father, and the true blood of Christ which was shed from his side, not only as a sign and by virtue of the sacrament, but in their proper nature and true substance.

The idea that the bread and wine are converted into the body and blood of Christ by prayer and the words of Christ provided the first step toward defining the real presence of Christ in the Eucharist by means of the dogma of transubstantiation, promulgated at the Fourth Lateran Council in 1215. The dogmatic constitution, *Caput firmiter*, was really a pronouncement aimed against the Albigensians, Waldensians, and other groups who held antisacramental and anticlerical views, and it simply assumed that the bread and wine are "transubstantiated" into the body and blood of Christ. It is uncertain who first coined the term *transubstantiation*. The dogma speaks of "substance" and "species" but does not use the term *accidents*.[11] It was left to the great theologians of the high scholastic period (Albert the Great, Thomas Aquinas, Bonaventure, Duns Scotus) to bring the categories of Aristotle to bear on this dogma—a matter we can safely avoid discussing in a social history of the liturgy, since these discussions would have eluded the ordinary clergy and people of the church. Indeed, Thomas Aquinas himself felt that it was not necessary to understand the complexities of transubstantiation and said so in the sequence hymn attributed to him for the Feast of Corpus Christi, *Lauda, Sion*:

> That which you do not understand,
> That which you do not see,
> Faith will strengthen beyond the order of things.

But it does serve my purpose to point out that the doctrine of the real presence had an enormous impact on ritual practice. These practices, in turn, had a subtle but profound effect on the theology of the Eucharist.

Eucharistic Matter, Performance, and Participation

The unity that is the *res* of the Eucharist is rooted in ancient practices of table hospitality, the bonding of friends and even of enemies that is formed by eating and drinking together. The Eucharist continued to be discussed as food—how could it be otherwise, since bread and wine are involved?—but now as food that is unlike any other. In the words of James of Vitry (c. 1160/70–1240), "This food is not bodily food but food for the soul; not of the flesh but of the heart."[12]

This special food had to be of the highest-quality wheat and wine and be protected from abuse and ridicule, loss or decay. A whole set of regulations were devised to control the manufacture, use, reservation, and disposal of the eucharistic elements.[13] Baking hosts became a ritualized procedure carried out in religious houses, accompanied by the singing of psalms. The hosts were baked in a vessel coated with wax, rather than in oil and fat, which might fry them. To keep crumbs from falling to the floor during the administration of communion, housling cloths were held under the chins of communicants, who now knelt to receive the host. Consecrated hosts not received by communicants had to be consumed by the priests or servers or stored in a place of reservation to be used later in the communion of the sick. The most usual container for reserving hosts in the Middle Ages were metal boxes called pyxes, which were locked and could be suspended over the altar and operated by a set of pulleys. The hosts in the pyxes had to be changed every eighth day to prevent molding. If less attention was given to the wine in the medieval regulations, it was because by the twelfth century, the cup was not generally administered to lay communicants for fear of spilling the precious blood of Christ in the transmission. The doctrine of concomitance, which held that the whole Christ is received under either species, was developed in the twelfth century to justify communion under one specie. Communicants were given a cup of unconsecrated wine to help wash down the host.

As there were regulations concerning the handling of the eucharistic food, so there were regulations governing the food handlers—the priests. The hard-won *libertas ecclesiae*, which removed clergy from secular supervision and punishment and kept them under the authority of the bishops and the ecclesiastical courts, could be justified only on the basis of the fitting character and the effective work performed by the clergy. Clergy were set aside from the rest of society by a celibate lifestyle, distinctive clothing, and specialized training to do work that society regarded as necessary for its well-being. Priests received special power at their ordination to offer the sacrifice of the Mass for the benefit of the living and the dead. Only the priest could say the words of Christ that made Christ present in the bread and wine. Only the priest could take the life-giving sacrament to the sick. Only the priest could offer the Mass for the repose of the souls of dear ones in purgatory.

Thirteenth-century rubrics directed the priest to say, while holding the host over the chalice at the concluding doxology of the *Canon missae* (Canon of the Mass), "Gratias agimus tibi" (We give thanks to you), giving thanks for the beatified, for those in purgatory, and for the living. There were other places in the canon where the dead could be commemorated, and they would be mentioned by name in votive masses. As Jacques LeGoff has argued, in a system that made sense to everyone except the Lollards, the doctrine of purgatory brought the Mass into the realm of pastoral care.[14] It was believed that masses offered for the dead reduced the time they would spend in purgatory. In acts of charity for the dead, the wealthy endowed perpetual chantries to sing offices in memory of the dead, urban confraternities arranged for votive masses to be offered for their deceased members.[15] Even the poor could afford to have an anniversary mass celebrated for a loved one. John Bossy has stressed, "The devotion, theology, liturgy, architecture, finances, social structure and institutions of late medieval Christianity are inconceivable without the assumption that the friends and relations of the souls in purgatory had an absolute obligation to procure their release, above all by having masses said for them."[16]

The great plagues that struck fourteenth-century Europe left many dead and generated a great demand for requiem and votive masses, which, in turn, produced a great demand for priests. The result was a veritable proletariat of mass-priests, or "altarists," who did no pastoral work other than offering masses. Contributing to the need for mass-priests was the fact that parish priests had more pastoral work to do than to offer all the masses that were increasingly demanded.

Bossy has argued that the two main emphases in the eucharistic theology of the Middle Ages—eucharistic sacrifice and real presence of the body and blood of Christ—served two social purposes. The eucharistic sacrifice, like all sacrifices, represented the social universe as a concatenation of distinct parts that needed to be joined together. The sacrament itself represented and embodied a unity and wholeness that had been achieved.[17] The living and the dead constituted one important social division that needed to be kept in union or for which reconciliation was needed if the living had committed wrongs against the dead when they were alive. Edward Muir writes, "Masses for the dead also provided insurance against molestation by ghosts."[18] Ghosts were personal hauntings; they were understood to be dead relatives who visited their kin to rectify wrongs committed against them while they were alive or to remind the living of their obligations to the dead. The eucharistic sacrifice, given concrete articulation in requiem and votive masses, was a way of making peace between the living and the dead. Sharing in the eucharistic communion was a way of making peace between the living. The fact that the living attended Mass in the presence of Christ himself, really present in the visible host, was a strong encouragement to work out reconciliation between disputing parties even without actually receiving and eating the host.

The doctrine of transubstantiation certainly contributed to a focus on the sacramental elements and on the power of the priest to confect the sacrament. But as I indicated, these ritual developments also affected the theology of the Eucharist in a subtle but profound way. They gave rise to a literalist concern about what the sacrament "is" as a phenomenon and centered popular attention on the "miracle" performed by the priest. Both of these concerns, observed Henri de Lubac, isolated the sacrament from its ecclesial context.[19] In turn, these two foci produced a fused focus in the desire of the people to witness the elevation of the host more than to eat and drink together. The awesomeness of the miracle of transubstantiation produced in the people a sense of unworthiness to receive the host, yet the great benefits of the sacrament made the sacrament an object of desire that could be met by gazing at it in the elevation.[20]

There is no doubt that the elevation of the host was the high point of the Mass for the laity. It occurred at the words in the eucharistic canon, "This is my body which will be given for you," which was pinpointed as the moment at which the bread became the body of Christ. At this point all the senses were brought into play. Bells were rung to signal that the moment of transubstantiation was taking place—both a small sacring bell at the altar and sometimes three peals of a great bell in the tower. At the ringing of the bells, the celebrant and everyone at the altar genuflected before the awesome mystery. At a sung mass, the choir, which had been singing the Sanctus while the priest began reciting the canon, now broke into the *Benedictus qui venit* (Blessed is he who comes in the name of the Lord). Incense was wafted in the direction of the host. Two additional candles were lighted on the altar mensa before the canon, and sometimes additional torches were held aloft, so the people could better see the host. Sometimes a dark curtain was suspended behind the reredos of the altar so that the white host could be seen against it. Even the development of Gothic architecture allowed for light from large stained-glass windows in the apse to illumine the space around the high altar. In churches with rood screens, openings were cut so the laity in the nave could peer into the chancel to see the elevation of the host.

The laity knew no bounds in their enthusiasm for the elevation. Miri Rubin reports the gift in the will of Thomas Goisman, an alderman of Hull, to the Holy Trinity Chapel in 1502, for the construction of a machine that would allow an angel to descend from the roof at the elevation and reascend after the Pater Noster. Churchmen also knew no bounds in describing the benefits of witnessing the elevation. Rubin reports, "In a sermon for a Sunday after Epiphany 1375 Bishop Brinton of Exeter taught that after seeing God's body no need for food would be felt, oaths would be forgiven, eye-sight would not fade, sudden death would not strike one, nor would one age, and one would be protected at every step by angels."[21]

The more the elevation emphasized the miracle of God in Christ present among us in the eucharistic host, the more unworthy the people felt to receive communion. Requests for forgiveness and expressions of unworthiness pervade the texts of the medieval mass. This is seen in the prayers of preparation at the beginning of the mass: *Confiteor* (the confession of sins) at the foot of the altar, followed by *Aufer a nobis* (take away from us our iniquities) as the priest went up to the altar, even after the prayer for forgiveness (*Indulgentium, absolutionem, et remissionem peccatorum*). There were more prayers for forgiveness in the canon (*Nobis quoque peccatoribus*) and before receiving communion (*Domine Jesu Christe . . . libera me . . . ab omnibus iniquitatibus meis, et universis malis*). Expressions of unworthiness are uttered by the priest in the offertory prayers (*Suscipe, sancte Pater* and *In spiritu humilitatis*) and before receiving communion (*Domine, non sum dignus*). While it is true that the people did not recite these prayers, there was still an understanding that the priest was offering the Mass on behalf of the whole Christian assembly. And more than merely reciting affective prayers seeking forgiveness or expressing unworthiness in the presence of the Holy, all the faithful who had attained an age of discretion were required by a canon of the Fourth Lateran Council to make a confession of sins to the priest before receiving communion and to receive communion at least once a year at Easter.[22]

Along with making a confession to the priest was the requirement of setting things right with one's neighbor before receiving one's "rights," as communion came to be called by the laity. The ancient kiss of peace remained in medieval practice or was revived by the invention of the pax board in England in the thirteenth century. This popular practice was welcomed by the clergy and disseminated throughout Christendom by the Franciscans. The pax board was a cross or painted picture of Christ, which the priest kissed after the greeting *Pax domini sit semper vobiscum* (The peace of the Lord be with you always). It was then kissed by another minister or the parish clerk and passed through the congregation, each person kissing it in turn.[23] Kissing the pax signified that all those present had made peace with one another before coming to the mass.

The pax was clearly a substitute for the reception of Holy Communion. While contemporary reformers have justly criticized the reduction in frequency of reception of Holy Communion during the Middle Ages, the Easter communion maintained the sense of the unity of the ecclesial body in the sacramental body as well as any celebration in antiquity—or in our present time. This was prepared for by fasting, by sexual abstinence, by confessing one's sins, by setting right anything that was amiss with one's neighbor, and by giving an extra offering. Easter Day sermons by the parish priest often emphasized the harmony of the community. Indeed, the great prayer of the Easter Vigil known as the *Exsultet*, sung over the great paschal candle, petitioned for "peace during the time of our paschal rejoicing." The difficulty of achieving this peace becomes clear if we think of the deep-seated conflicts between families that the church had to resolve even to get the entire parish to participate in the Easter communion. The intensity of these conflicts was immortalized by Shakespeare in *Romeo and Juliet* in terms of the rivalry between the Capulets and Montagues in Verona. John Bossy indicates that some parish priests, unlike Shakespeare's Friar Lawrence, were sometimes party to such hostilities themselves and had to be pressured to work for the reconciliation that alone could make the Easter communion an expression of the fellowship of the entire parish.[24] After the Easter mass, a great parish feast of paschal lamb or some other meat would be served at tables set up in the nave. This Easter dinner was paid for by a fraternity or guild or, lacking these, would be provided by the parish priest.[25]

The sharing of food after mass, such as unconsecrated bread (known as the pax bread) and wine, was common in parish churches. The bread was baked by parishioners on a rotation system. The man or woman offering the bread brought it to the high altar at Sunday Matins, recited a prayer, and lit a candle. The offerer was mentioned by name in the bidding prayer from the pulpit. The loaf was cut up and shared, along with a cup of wine after the Mass.[26] These activities certainly gave the Sunday mass a communal character that was lacking at weekday masses. Absence from the Sunday mass without good reason was resented by parishioners.

The Breakdown of the Sacramental Community

These ritual dynamics suggest that the medieval mass had not lost its social or corporate dimension just because the people didn't join in reciting texts or singing responses. Even with regard to texts and singing, we have seen that the people were led in reciting basic prayers in the Office of Prone conducted from the pulpit (e.g., Pater Noster, Ave Maria) and that—especially in Germany—they joined in singing carols juxtaposed with festival sequences and perhaps at other points during the mass as well. Nor were there power plays between priest and people. The parish priest was, in fact, one of the people who tended his garden when not ministering to the needs of the parishioners and was, as often as not, supported by the people even in instances of violations of celibacy requirements.[27]

I have referred to the view of John Bossy that the medieval mass served the purpose of working out a complex social algebra designed to maintain the bonds between the living and the dead as well as to make friends out of enemies.[28] Bossy also noted two important reasons why "social integration and unity," perceived as eucharistic goals during the high Middle Ages, came to be "secularized" by the late Middle Ages. First, there was the rise, in the early fifteenth century, of "an asocial mysticism of frequent communion" fostered by the introspective program of the *devotion moderna*,[29] which departed significantly from the medieval laity's norm of an "annual communion" at Easter.[30] In other words, receiving communion became a matter of personal decision that served one's individual spiritual needs rather than a corporate act by which the bonds of community were strengthened. More frequent communions in this context undermined the relationship between the social body and the sacramental body because not everyone was receiving the sacrament simultaneously. So while individuals might confess their sins and make amends with their neighbors, the whole community was not working out reconciliation together. Moreover, people received communion after the Mass or even before the Mass from the reserved sacrament rather than at the point in the Mass itself where the sacrament should be administered. Thus, the quasi-private reception of Holy Communion dissolved the sequential links within the liturgical order (the Lord's Prayer with its embolism and the kiss of peace leading to the administration of Holy Communion), and it obliterated the administration of Holy Communion as the object of the eucharistic celebration.

Second, in reaction to the first development, Bossy pointed to "the tendency to transfer the socially integrative powers of the host away from the Mass as such and into the feast of Corpus Christi, and by way of that feast to the rituals of monarchy and of the secular community."[31] This is because the main event of the Corpus Christi celebration was the procession with the exposed host,[32] but in its retinue came the contingent segments of urban society (for Corpus Christi was a distinctly urban festival), each in their own order: nobility, mayor and magistrates, town council, guilds and fraternities (jockeying for position as close to the host as possible), with prelates, clergy, and religious scattered throughout. These processions became quite complicated and were organized by the leading citizens of a town. Even though the various guilds and fraternities contributed toward the expenses of the event, local nobility often patronized the procession, and town political authorities had to regulate the event in order to maintain law and order. But beyond this, the French kings especially, in their struggle to centralize authority in themselves at the expense of the regional nobility, superimposed the symbols of royal authority on the procession in the coronation city of Reims and took for their own trappings of office the canopy that covered the host, since it was a symbol of majesty. Thus, there was a tendency on the part of political authorities and powers to appropriate for themselves the sanctity of the sacrament.

Corpus Christi: The Reassertion of Sacramental Community

Thus, in contrast to the sociofugal (scattering) impact of the individual's private reception of communion, the Corpus Christi celebration retained a sociopetal (gathering) impact. It drew the community together, and did so around the sacramental body of Christ. It might be claimed, in spite of the secular takeover of the main events, that this festival with its High Mass, procession, fairs, feasting, entertainment, and plays was the final firewall against those forces of personal piety that were displacing, unwittingly, the sacramental body as the glue holding together the social body within the political body that was emerging in the urban centers of fourteenth- and fifteenth-century Europe. It also became a feast that had power to invert, and therefore equalize, social roles.

The inversion of social roles can be traced to the very origin of the feast. The city of Liège was host to many religious houses, including some women's cloisters that had been managed by the Cistercians and Praemonstratensians. As these houses became a financial burden, these religious orders gave up the management of religious houses just at the time when there was an influx of women interested in the religious life. New arrangements had to be made for female religious communities. Some women, called Beguines, who wanted to live lives of poverty and chastity and to follow a penitential discipline, were simply attached to parishes. Into this situation came the new Dominican Order, which set up convents for women who were willing to share the mendicant and scholarly life. The orthodox religiosity of these women was deemed commendable at this time, in the thirteenth century, when the church was being challenged by heretical groups such as the Cathari and Waldensians, who attacked the heart of the medieval system— the clergy and the sacrament. One of these women, Juliana of Liège, received visions of the Eucharist, desired to see established a universal feast of devotion to the sacrament, and shared her dreams with her confessor. Her desire was promoted by the bishop of Liège. These visions inspired Pope Urban IV to authorize the feast of Corpus Christi, which he did in the bull *Transiturus*, issued in 1264. But it seems that this bull was not widely disseminated, and it remained for the Avignon popes to promote the feast in the fourteenth century. The most famous propers for the feast are attributed to Thomas Aquinas, including the sequence "Lauda, Sion" for the Mass and the hymn "Pange lingua corporis" for Vespers. The Dominicans played a role in promoting this set of propers, which eventually eclipsed other propers locally produced.[33]

This new feast fit into the emerging urban culture of the thirteenth and fourteenth centuries. As Mervyn James reminds us, the communities that celebrated Corpus Christi were "deeply divided—riven by an intense competitiveness; by the struggle for honor and worship, status and precedence, power and wealth. Conflict was the dark side of the moon of unity."[34] The tensions within the social body had to be ritually projected and resolved.

As we have seen, the ritual of the Mass provides for expressions of confession of sins and reconciliation among disputing parties to effect peace—both personal and communal—in Holy Communion. But as the corporate character of the Mass lessened toward the late Middle Ages, other rituals had to provide a way of dealing with social conflict and resolution. To a great extent, this role was taken on by the plays that were performed on great festivals throughout the church year, but especially on Corpus Christi. The play cycles (such as the Coventry Plays), in James's opinion, provided a mechanism "by which the tensions implicit in the diachronic rise and fall of occupational communities could be confronted and worked out. In addition, they made available a means by which visual and public recognition could be given to changes in relationships of superiority, dependence or cooperation which existed between occupations."[35] If the Corpus Christi procession legitimated the present political and economic structures that kept society in the hands of the princes, magistrates, and powerful guilds, the play cycles could deal with the reversal of power and fortune under the reign of God. This theme is provided by the content of the Gospels themselves, which along with other biblical stories provided the plots for the plays. The plays went through the whole biblical history of salvation, since Corpus Christi was celebrated at the end of the festival half of the church year—the Thursday after Trinity Sunday (Corpus Christi is the delayed octave of Maundy Thursday)—and was a kind of consummation of everything that had been celebrated from Advent through Pentecost. Not surprisingly, therefore, the last play of the Coventry Cycle was the Doomsday Play, in which God, the judge of all, judges "pope, priest or prince with crown," making the last first and the first last. God's judgment, enacted with delight by the players, made pope and king equal to any priest or peasant, just as the Eucharist itself had leveled all social divisions in the one body of Christ.

CHAPTER 11

The Dissolution of the Social Body in the Reformation Communion

As we have seen, in the Middle Ages the Eucharist, which serves as the expression of ecclesial unity, was the source of social unity in the society of Christendom. This perceived relationship between Eucharist and social unity continued into the first decades of the Reformation. Martin Luther prepared versions of the Mass (Latin, 1523; German, 1525) that eliminated everything that "smacked and savored of sacrifice" in order to promote the sacrament of the altar as the gift of communion, which the people were exhorted to receive more frequently. Ulrich Zwingli designed a communion service in Zurich (1525) in imitation of the Last Supper of Christ, in which the whole congregation assembled four times a year to receive Christ into their hearts and collective lives. Four communions per year would have been an extraordinary display of piety among late-medieval communicants. Various Anabaptist fellowship groups tried to intensify the experience of communion by reviving the foot washing and the kiss of peace.

Second-generation reformers tried to deepen the work of the pioneer reformers. John Calvin tried to articulate a sense in which the Reformed could also affirm the real presence of Christ. He desired to have the Lord's Supper celebrated frequently,[1] but in Geneva he could not persuade the civil authorities to authorize more than four celebrations a year, because they wanted to stay in step with other Reformed cantons. Archbishop Thomas Cranmer, who presided over the imposition of an English rite on the commonwealth during the reign of Edward VI, tried to balance the English concern for continuity first with the more conservative German way (1549) and then with the more radical Swiss approach (1552). It remained for Elizabeth I to guide her divines toward a practice that would be more characteristic of the Anglican *via media* (middle way).

Since the reformers were building on a solid tradition of eucharistic fellowship, their efforts ought to have been more successful than they turned out to be. But Reformation churches were never able to establish social bonds through eucharistic communion as powerfully as had been done by the late medieval practices of the elevation of the host or the Corpus Christi festival. The rejection of the doctrine of transubstantiation could have contributed to the loss of a perceived connection between the sacramental body and the ecclesial body, since the bread and wine were now treated as ordinary bread and wine in Reformed Christianity. Even Lutheranism, which otherwise doggedly held to the doctrine of the real presence of the body and blood of Christ, was ambivalent about the treatment of the sacramental elements. The division of the Protestant movement over the interpretation of the sacrament of unity may have been another cause of the disconnection between sacrament and society. It might also have been the case that the reformers expected more transformation of populations who were now hearing the gospel than the people were able to deliver. Luther, ever the realist among the reformers, admitted as much when he said that a third kind of communion service was needed besides the Latin and German masses—one that "should not be held in a public place for all sorts of people. But those who want to be Christians in earnest and who profess the gospel with hand and mouth should sign their names and meet alone in a house somewhere to pray, to read, to baptize, to receive the sacrament, and to do other Christian works."[2]

Let us recognize that the reformers did not set out to disconnect the eucharistic body from the social body. In his treatise on "The Blessed Sacrament of the Holy and True Body of Christ, and the Brotherhoods" (1519),[3] his first major statement on the Lord's Supper, Luther emphasized the fellowship of the sacrament. He even suggested that a Christian in distress or bearing a heavy burden should "go joyfully to the sacrament of the altar and lay down his woe in the midst of the community [of saints] and seek help from the entire company of the spiritual body—just as a citizen whose property has suffered damage or misfortune at the hands of his enemies makes complaint to his town council and fellow citizens and asks for help." In this same treatise Luther attacked the confraternities or sodalities for looking out after their own fraternal welfare rather than the needs of all people in society.

Also, Carter Lindberg has shown the connection between the work of the community chest and communion practices in many German church orders, specifically the offering for the poor received at Communion.[4] But this practice is "beyond charity" because, contrary to the common stereotype that the reformers separated public and private morality and were indifferent to the ethical import of social structures and institutions, Lindberg contrasts the medieval point of view, formed by a piety of achievement and idealized poverty—either as voluntary renunciation or as almsgiving—with the efforts of the reformers to address the growing problem of begging. In their view the religious endorsement of poverty precluded urban efforts to address this problem. Impelled by their theology, the reformers developed and passed new legislative structures for addressing social welfare needs. The key to their undertakings was the conviction that social ethics is the continuation of community worship. Public worship and public ministry are two aspects of *Gottesdienst*, "the service of God." In other words, "the service of God" was understood by Luther and his colleagues as both God's service to us in Word and Sacrament and our service to God in worship and in love toward our neighbor.

But Yngve Brilioth observed, "At the re-birth of sacramental life at the Reformation, the idea of Communion-fellowship begins by filling the whole service with its inspiration, but ends by being refused a place within it."[5] The connection between Communion and community in popular thinking was undermined by the more individualistic piety inherited from the late Middle Ages combined with practices espoused by the Reformation, including failure to ritualize public reconciliation, fencing the table, an emphasis on hearing the word and its architectural requirements, and the sanctification of civil government. We will look at each of these factors in turn.

A More Individualistic Piety

In spite of the intensely corporate character of medieval life, or perhaps because of it, a strain of individualistic piety began to appear, first in the monastic reforms of the eleventh and twelfth centuries (e.g., Canons Regular, Carthusians, Cistercians, and Praemonstratensians) and then

Plate 1. Christians met to study the word of God and celebrate the sacraments of Christ in private houses during the first several centuries of Christianity. Sometimes the congregation acquired the title to the house and remodeled it to serve the catechetical and liturgical needs of the members. Such a private home was renovated in Dura-Europos on the Roman-Persian border in eastern Syria around 250 C.E. by removing a partition between two rooms to create a larger assembly hall. A third room was converted for use as a baptistery with a canopied pool that was three feet deep. Frescoes on the walls depicted biblical scenes.

Plate 2. Beginning in the fourth century, Christian liturgy was performed in large basilicas (royal halls). Ravenna in northern Italy served as the seat of the Byzantine (Roman) emperor in the West in the sixth century. The basilicas of San Vitale and San Apollinare Nuova in Ravenna are decorated with brilliant mosaic panels illustrating biblical stories and liturgical actions. In this panel the Empress Theodora, wife of Justinian I, and her court are participating in an offertory procession by offering bread for the Eucharist.

Plate 3. The Byzantine Empire was torn apart in the eighth century by a bitter iconoclastic controversy. The Seventh Ecumenical Council held in Nicea in 787 settled the issue by defining that "holy icons . . . should be exhibited in the holy churches of God," including images of Christ, his Mother (the *Theotokos*), saints, and angels, and that "they should be kissed and that they are an object of veneration and honor but not of real worship." Centuries earlier St. Basil of Caesarea had written that "The honor paid to the image passes to the prototype" (*On the Holy Spirit* 18:45). To kiss an icon of Christ or of a saint or of the *Theotokos*, as this Eastern Orthodox woman is doing, is to show love and respect to Jesus Christ himself, or to the saint depicted.

Plate 4. In the late middle ages, affluent lay people commissioned books of the hour to be copied and illustrated for their personal use. Yet these devotional books were related to the liturgical life of the church. This page from such a book prepared for Adelaide of Savoy, Duchess of Burgundy (c. 1460–1465) includes the liturgical calendar for March and depicts a sermon and receiving communion. The type of pulpit and people sitting on the ground suggests that this Dominican friar may be preaching outdoors on a typical late-medieval preaching mission. The lack of a chasuble on the priest suggests that the communicants are receiving the sacrament after mass, which was by the late middle ages when people usually received communion.

Plate 5. A mass at St. Denis Abbey near Paris, a painted wooden panel by the Master of St. Giles. This is the moment of transubstantiation, signaled by the elevation of the host. Note that a monk is pulling back the curtain on the side of the altar so that the king and others in attendance can see the elevation. The black chasuble worn by the priest might indicate that this is a votive requiem mass being celebrated for the repose of the soul of a loved one on the anniversary of the person's death. This was probably the most frequently celebrated type of mass in the Western middle ages, and was vigorously rejected by the Protestant Reformers.

Plate 6. Processions have been a part of Christian liturgical ceremonial at least since the fourth century. In the middle ages processions involving the whole town were common, held to "translate" a saint (move the bones from a grave to a shrine) and to celebrate the feast of Corpus Christi. In this painting of Denis van Alsloot an *Ommeganck* (procession) takes place in Brussels to celebrate the translation of the image of the Virgin of the Sands from Antwerp to Brussels two centuries earlier. The whole city participated—magistrates, guilds, religious orders, and clergy of various ranks.

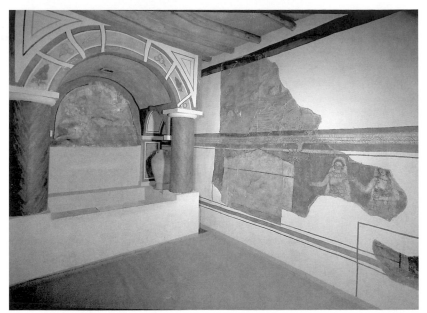

Plate 1. Yale Reconstruction of Dura-Europos, Christian House, Baptistery. Photo: © Yale University Art Gallery. Used by permission. Full caption opposite.

Plate 2. The Court of Empress Theodora. Byzantine Mosaic, 526–551 C.E., S. Vitale, Ravenna, Italy. Photo: © Scala / Art Resource, NY. Full caption opposite.

Plate 3. Woman Kissing Icon in Saint Sophia Cathedral, Veliky Novgorod, Russia. Photo: © Olivier Martel/Corbis. Full caption on page preceding photo gallery.

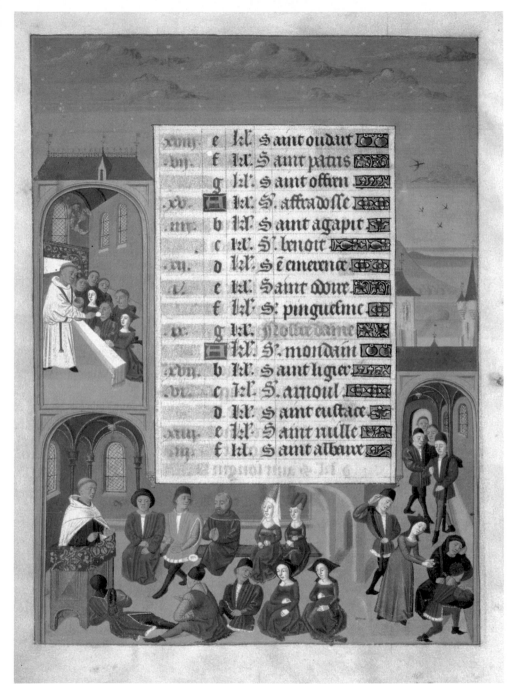

Plate 4. March, Sermon and the Sacrament. The book of hours of Adelaide of Savoy. Musée Condé, Chantilly, France. Photo: R. G. Ojeda © Réunion des Musées Nationaux / Art Resource, NY. Full caption on page preceding photo gallery.

Plate 5. Mass of Saint Giles in the Cathedral of Saint Denis. circa 1500. National Gallery, London. Photo: © Erich Lessing / Art Resource, NY. Full caption on page preceding photo gallery.

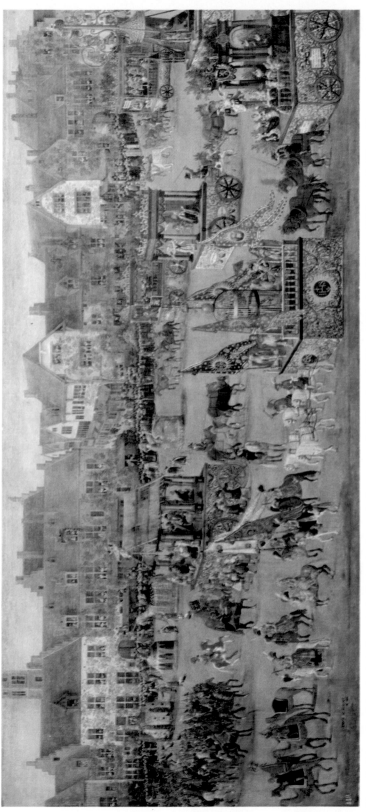

Plate 6. Triumph of the Archduchess Isabella in the Brussels Ommeganck of Sunday, 31 May 1615, detail. Photo: © Victoria & Albert Museum, London / Art Resource, NY. Full caption on page preceding photo gallery.

Plate 7. Charles II of Spain kneeling before the Holy Sacrament. El Escorial, Spain. Photo: © Scala /Art Resource, NY. Full caption on page following photo gallery.

TEMPLE DE LYON, NOMMÉ PARADIS.

Plate 8. The Protestant Church in Lyon, called "The Paradise." Bibliothèque Publique et Universitaire, Geneva, Switzerland. Photo: © Erich Lessing / Art Resource, NY. Full caption on page following photo gallery.

Plate 9. The Lord's Supper in a Scanian Church. Lithograph by Bengt Nordenberg, 1860s. Reprinted from *The Church of Sweden: Past and Present* (Allhem: Malmö, 1960). Full caption on page following photo gallery.

Plate 10. Methodist Camp Meeting. Engraving, 1836. Photo: © Bettman/CORBIS. Full caption on page following photo gallery.

Plate 11. A Village Choir. 1847. Photo: © Victoria & Albert Museum, London / Art Resource, NY. Full caption opposite.

Plate 12. Around the Altar—St. Gregory of Nyssa Episcopal Church, San Francisco. Photo: © David Sanger. Full caption opposite.

Plate 7. The archetypal Roman Catholic devotion of the Baroque Era was adoration of the Blessed Sacrament. In this picture (1685–1688) by Claudio Coello, Charles II of Spain kneels in adoration of the host exposed in a monstrance at Solemn Benediction of the Blessed Sacrament. Solemn Benediction was usually celebrated at the end of Sunday Vespers. The priest is holding the sacrament with a humeral veil. His elaborate cope and the equally elaborate dalmatic of the attending deacon are illustrative of Baroque decorative excesses.

Plate 8. The archetypal Protestant devotion of the post-Reformation Era was listening to sermons. New churches built after the Reformation often elevated the pulpit and placed it in a central place from which it would be easy for everyone to hear the preacher. The pulpit is at the center of this plain auditorium in Calvinist Lyons. Men, women, and children sit apart. Those with Bibles have them open to follow the text. The children will later be catechized on what they have heard. The dog is tolerated as long as it is quiet.

Plate 9. In this scene from southern Sweden, the pastor (priest), after the Preface, Words of Institution, Sanctus, and Lord's Prayer, turned toward the congregation, holding the paten of hosts, and sang the Pax; then the communicants began to come forward to the altar while the congregation sang the Agnus Dei. Note in this lithograph the life size crucifix over the altar; the candles and chalice on the altar; the priest vested in alb and chasuble; the semi-circular altar rail covered with a houseling cloth (also in most Swedish American churches in the nineteenth century); the communicants kneeling at the altar rail; everyone else standing (except for the old woman and the mother with children) and singing with books noticeably wide open, probably the Agnus Dei or communion hymns; the girl leading the blind and lame to the altar.

Plate 10. This 1836 engraving depicts a Methodist camp meeting. Thousands of people gathered in these revival meetings up and down the American frontier to hear preaching, sing hymns, and respond to calls for conversion. The emotional appeals of the preachers often elicited emotional responses from the hearers, as can be seen in several of the women kneeling in prayer. The camp meetings were also occasions for socializing and renewing friendships, as can be seen in the conversations and camaraderie of some of the men on the periphery of the gathering.

Plate 11. *A Village Choir* by Thomas Webster depicts music-making in the west gallery of an Anglican village church about 1820, before the Cambridge Ecclesiological Movement put choir members in cassocks and surplices and placed them in the chancel. There is no organ, but the miscellaneous instruments include a cello, clarinet, and bassoon. The mixed choir includes men and women, boys and girls. There are not enough books, so the singers must share.

Plate 12. A hallmark of mid-twentieth-century liturgical renewal was gathering around the table of the Lord. Churches in the round were built in numbers. Here in Saint Gregory of Nyssa Episcopal Church in San Francisco, the congregation gathers in one space for the liturgy of the word and then processes with dance-like steps to the space in which the eucharistic meal is celebrated. There is no barrier between the people and the altar. Notice the dancing icons on the walls above the gathering.

in the lay movements of the thirteenth and fourteenth centuries (e.g., Beguines and Beghards, Brethren of the Common Life). This inward turn may have been prompted by such social factors as the breakdown of feudalism with all its consequences for civil strife, the emergence of urban life, the contest of states against the church, schism within the church itself, and continuing corruptions of monastic life. The increasing exteriority of worship, such as the multiplication of choral offices that left no time for the *lectio divina*, as well as the sterility of late medieval scholasticism, which did little to feed the hungry soul, contributed to the development of more affective devotions and mystical reflections. This movement received the name *devotio moderna*, and it advocated, in the words of Abbot Gabriel Braso, "perfection as an ideal of life eminently interior, based on self-analysis and individual piety, and independent of exterior means of sanctification."[6]

The most popular promoters of the *devotio moderna* were the Brethren of the Common Life, founded by Gerard Groote (1340–1384), a lay preacher and deacon who declined priestly orders out of humility. The devotionalists encouraged the use of books of the hours, which were books of prayer offices and devotions for lay use. Each book was individualized by its user, selecting from a corpus of offices, psalms, and prayers. The best-known book to come out of this movement was *The Imitation of Christ* by Thomas à Kempis, a work in four parts, three of which dealt with the inner life and one with the Eucharist.

It has been debated to what extent the *devotio moderna* influenced humanism and the Reformation. Martin Luther received his early education in Magdeburg at a boarding school operated by the Brethren of the Common Life. The influence of the *devotio moderna* on the humanists and the reformers was rejected by R. R. Post in a definitive study of the movement.[7] Post pointed out that the Brethren did not do teaching themselves but only provided room and board and devotional guidance for the students, and that they promoted the *contemptus mundi* (contempt of the world) of traditional monasticism, which all the humanists and many reformers rejected. However, their rejection of scholastic theology, their view that Scripture is the center of the devotional life, their concern to have an uncorrupted text of Scripture and the liturgy, their frequent use of private confession as a spiritual discipline growing out of self-examination rather than as an ecclesiastical discipline to preserve the peace of the church, and their emphasis on the frequent reception of Holy Communion are all aspects found in the thought and praxis of Martin Luther.

Especially as regards Holy Communion, Luther encouraged a frequency of reception based on personal need. In his *Large Catechism*, he stated, "Those who claim to be Christians should prepare themselves to receive this blessed sacrament frequently." He did not want people to be coerced or compelled to receive the sacrament. "Nevertheless, let it be understood that people who abstain and absent themselves from the sacrament over a long period of time are not to be considered Christians."[8] *The Apology of the Augsburg Confession* testifies, "In our churches Mass is celebrated every Sunday and on other festivals, when the sacrament is offered *to those who wish for it* after they have been examined and absolved"[9] (italics added). The Lutheran Confession promotes reception of the sacrament as an individual decision based on spiritual need more than as an act of church.

The Reformed, in contrast, did practice the Eucharist as an act of the whole church. Holy Communion was not available on every Sunday and festival, as in Lutheranism, but four times a year on Christmas, Easter, Pentecost, and "Autumn." Indeed, Ulrich Zwingli in Zurich maintained the medieval emphasis on the Easter communion when he introduced his Communion Service during Holy Week in 1525. The practice in Zurich was for the elements to be passed in silence by the ministers to the congregation, who remained seated. This might seem to foster a more communal spirit in the celebration than the Lutheran custom of kneeling at the altar rail, but that communal spirit was mitigated by the practice of reading from John 13 while the congregation communed in silence, listening to the reading. Communicants were supposed to be attuned to the word more than to each other. In the Zwinglian system, the word creates faith; the acts of eating and drinking in a kind of reenactment of the Last Supper support the word. The Lord's Supper is therefore connected with the body of the church only in a secondary way. The supper strengthens faith, and faith defines the church.[10] But no more than Luther did Zwingli provide for the social dimensions of Holy Communion.

Failure to Ritualize Public Reconciliation

Since the first century, participation in the Lord's Supper presupposed that those who shared the supper were reconciled with one another. The kiss of peace was a ritual signifying a state of reconciliation among the communicants. In the late Middle Ages, this was expressed by passing the pax board through the congregation, each person present kissing it. These boards, which were often wooden crosses on which were painted a picture of Christ, were regular liturgical accoutrements by the time of the Reformation in much of Western Europe. Even the pax board was a diminishment of the kiss of peace, because it entailed a sequential kissing of an object, rather than neighbors kissing neighbors, and this failed to force squabbling neighbors and warring families to reconcile with each other before receiving communion, especially at Easter. But the reformers utterly did away with the ritual of the pax.

Luther retained the Pax Domini in his *Formula Missae et Communionis* (1523), interpreting it as the word of absolution in the Mass from Christ to the people. For this reason he preferred to have it sung or said by the celebrant facing the people.[11] But in his *German Mass and Order of Service* (1526), the Pax was eliminated because nothing was to intervene between the words of institution and the administration of Holy Communion. Even the Lord's Prayer was relocated, in the form of a catechesis, to a place before the words of institution. Thomas Cranmer followed Luther's lead, retaining the Pax in the 1549 communion service but eliminating it in the 1552 communion service in order to juxtapose the consecration and the administration. In his *Institutes of the Christian Religion*, Calvin showed an acute sense of the relationship between reconciliation with one's neighbor and unity in Christ, and of the sacrament as the bond of church fellowship. But he failed to provide for any expression of reconciliation in his liturgies. So far as I am aware, only the Anabaptists revived the ancient kiss of peace, but they removed it from its relationship to Holy Communion and placed it at the beginning of the service.[12]

The Pax did not fare much better in Counter-Reformation Catholic practice. After 1600 the Roman Congregation of Rites began treating it as a form of honor rather than as an act of reconciliation. At Solemn High Mass, the celebrant greeted the deacon, the deacon greeted the subdeacon, and so on down through the ecclesiastical ranks. It was confined to the clergy and the choir, except for magistrates or nobility, and it was never given to women. According to Pierre LeBrun, it was largely abandoned because of the complications of precedence it caused.[13] Archbishop Borromeo did the best he could to keep the Pax intact in Milan, as did Bishop Bonner in England during the Marian restoration of Catholicism. But as John Bossy observed, "For the most part the formulators of opinion in early modern Christendom in the

West were markedly concordant in detaching the Eucharist from the rites of social reconciliation."[14]

It should be noted that reformers intended to preserve the communal dimension of Holy Communion. In the post-communion prayer in his German Mass, Luther thanked God for "this thy salutary gift" by which we are strengthened "in faith toward thee, and in fervent love among us all."[15] He advocated placing the communicants in the chancel so that the witness of their presence might encourage others to receive. "God does not care where we stand and it adds nothing to our faith. The communicants, however, ought to be seen and known openly, both by those who do and by those who do not commune, in order that their lives may be better observed, proved, and tested."[16] Embedded in this direction, however, was a practice that would serve to exclude rather than include people in Holy Communion: the fencing of the table.

Fencing the Table

In the earlier citation, *The Apology of the Augsburg Confession* said people receive communion "after they have been examined and absolved." One of the concerns of the Reformation was a stricter "fencing of the table" in terms of who could receive Holy Communion. This generated practices that limited more frequent reception of communion by more people. In Lutheranism it became customary to request permission in person from the pastor to receive communion. Potential communicants were then examined as to their beliefs and their lives. This practice had been recommended by Luther in the section on "The Communion of the People" in his treatise on *The Form of the Mass and Communion for the Church in Wittenberg*.[17] Communicants might be asked questions from the catechism to see if they "understood" the meaning of the sacrament, or they might be "shriven" in confession and absolution. Luther provided a form of individual confession and absolution in his *Small Catechism* and an Exhortation to Confession in his *Large Catechism*.

The Counter-Reformation may have taken more ideas from Luther on the linkage between confession, catechesis, and communion than its promoters would care to admit. In its own way, the Catholic Church took to heart Luther's objection that the scriptural phrase *penitentium agite* means "repent," not "do penance."[18] While the Council of Trent affirmed that the three essential elements in the sacrament of penance are contrition, confession, and satisfaction, it assigned more importance to contrition than to the acts of satisfaction that had been so important to the medieval practice of penance. This is because the emphasis in the use of confession shifted from social sins to personal guilt, from family and community relationships to the individual soul. Archbishop Carlo Borromeo of Milan was instrumental in promoting the practice and attitude toward penance that was to characterize the post-Tridentine Catholic Church. He not only invented the "confessional box," which privatized a ritual that had been conducted in the open in the Middle Ages, but his pastoral instructions to his priests specified that absolution should be refused or delayed where the confessor felt that there was no genuine repentance. Holy Week remained a prime time for making confessions in preparation for one's Easter communion, and priests in Milan were so overburdened with penitents that they could devote no more than a few minutes to each one, and the whole system had to be relaxed.[19] The early Jansenists took up the confessional discipline, but it was perceived by the Jesuits that it worked against more frequent communion. This became an important issue in the Jansenist Controversy in France.[20]

At the same time as the Counter-Reformation Catholic Church was trying to regularize obligatory confession, it tried to establish a mechanism for the catechizing of children where none had existed before. Bishops made it a duty of parish priests to catechize children on Sunday and feast day afternoons and an obligation of parents to send their children to catechism classes. This worked better in towns than in rural parishes. It was once again Borromeo who tried to rectify the problem by requiring Schools of Christian Doctrine to be established in every parish subject to his visitation, under the supervision of the parish pastor. Such schools were established across northern Italy by 1600, but it was not until after 1650 that French dioceses had imposed the requirement of catechization on priests and parents.[21] We note that in Lutheranism, too, the responsibility for catechizing children passed from the head of the household (as specified in Luther's catechism) to the parish pastor.

This linkage of catechesis, confession, and communion was also emphasized in Sweden in the sixteenth century. *The Swedish Church Order* of Archbishop Laurentius Petri (*Den svenska kyrkoordningen 1571*) included chapters "On Penance, Confession and Absolution" ("Om Syndaboot, Scrifftermål och Afflösning"), "On Private Confession"

("Om hemlig Scrifftermål"), "On Public Confession" ("Om uppenbara Scrifft"), and "On Excommunication" ("Om Ban").[22] In its instructions, the *Swedish Church Order* contains some severe directions for fencing the table. Notorious sinners or those living in open sin were to be excluded from communion and could not be restored other than by public penance. Strangers or unknown persons, children under eight or nine, and the insane "as long as they are out of their minds" should not be admitted. As in Luther's instructions, communicants were to give their names to the priest on the previous afternoon or morning of the day of the celebration of Mass so that they could be examined and absolved. "None shall be given the sacrament who cannot give a reason why he comes to communion, or cannot say the Lord's Prayer, Creed, Commandments, etc."[23]

There are two kinds of public confession: a general confession by the whole congregation within the order of the Mass and the *poenitentia publica* for those who have committed gross sins. A list of such sins is provided, along with directions on how the confessor (*poenitentiarius*) is to deal with such sins before giving absolution in the presence of the whole congregation. Laurentius Petri's advice on private confession is both evangelical and pastoral. Priests should be in the church at least a half hour or an hour before mass to receive communicants or hear confessions. They should sit in an open place in the church to avoid scandal. Confessions should not be coerced, but spiritual counsel should be provided. Penances should not be something to recite or a fast, but acts of restitution might be recommended. The ban, or excommunication, "is not an ordinance of man, for Christ himself has instituted and appointed it, as we see in Matthew 18. . . . Therefore it shall neither be despised nor set aside."[24] Nevertheless, Archbishop Petri cautions against a hasty use of excommunication; there should be a delay during which the priest tries to persuade the sinner to repent while also consulting with the bishop or prefect. If this fails and the sinner is excommunicated, the person under the ban shall not attend the church except to hear the sermons; afterward, he shall leave at once.

By the end of the sixteenth century, it became more typical in Swedish practice that the communicants would assemble as a group and the priest would examine them collectively about their knowledge of the catechism and individually about their sins. The penitents had an opportunity to make a private confession, but then a general absolution was declared to the entire group. In time, however, as Christer

Pahlmblad points out, the individual act of confession, or even a prayer of confession other than the general confession in the Mass, fell out of use. It was deemed sufficient to confess to God alone, although the priest continued to examine communicants concerning the church's teaching on repentance and forgiveness.[25] In actuality, this change reflects the process that occurred in the Reformation churches by which *poenitentia*, understood as acts of satisfaction that could be done by the sinner, was replaced by *disciplina*, which was a habit that could be learned.

The Reformed thought that they practically invented *disciplina* and that it was lacking among Lutherans. Discipline had to do with matters of behavior and practice, rather than matters of doctrine or belief. Reformers of all stripes were realizing that traditional practices of penance and ecclesiastical courts had failed to inculcate Christian behavior and that it was better to prevent sin than to punish it. The fact that Lutherans seldom implemented practices of discipline testifies to the Gnesio-Lutheran fear of the third use of the law as a moral guide in that scrupulosity over sanctification might again engender works-righteousness.

Discipline was a concept that developed in Strasbourg under Martin Bucer. In response both to the Anabaptist criticism that the magisterial Reformation had not been a reform of Christian life and to the social disintegration that seemed to be the consequence of the abuse of newfound Christian liberty, Bucer held to the necessity of establishing a scriptural governance of external behavior that would be administered by consistories comprising ecclesiastical and civil representatives. Typical aspects of such governance (requiring civil as well as ecclesiastical legislation) were the sanctification of the Lord's Day and suppression of other feast days that provided too many days off from work, and the establishment of a community chest in order to take care of the needs of the poor and suppress begging and almsgiving. Bucer's untiring insistence on the external government of behavior was less enthusiastically embraced in Germany and England (where he retired in 1549 with the offer of an Oxford professorship from Archbishop Thomas Cranmer, to the relief of Emperor Charles V) than among the Swiss and the Scots. In actuality, however, the inclusion of both spiritual and temporal matters in the work of the consistories failed to be maintained in most places outside of Calvin's Geneva because many gross sins, formerly handled in ecclesiastical courts, came to be covered as crimes, which required reckoning with the civil authorities rather than with God. John Knox's Scottish *Book of Discipline* excluded matters already taken care of by the civil sword.[26]

The *Registers of the Consistory of Geneva in the Time of Calvin* have been published in a critical French edition[27] and in an English translation[28] by teams of scholars working, in both projects, under Robert Kingdon. These records show the pastoral as well as the disciplinary concern of the Genevan Consistory to help lay people understand how to make the transition from Catholic worship to Reformed worship.[29] For example, many people had to be admonished against "muttering" during the sermon, which probably meant saying the prayers that they had previously recited during mass. The records also show that the consistory drew up lists of people who should be denied communion because of bad behavior. They were usually summoned to the consistory a week before communion to see if they had amended their ways. Many were found ready to receive communion. A sentence of excommunication lasted only, in most cases, until the next communion service. Those who tried to receive communion in spite of the ban were called back to the consistory for admonition and punishment. People who had not taken communion during a quarterly communion service were summoned to the consistory to explain their absence. Many of these absentees were found to be ignorant of the new doctrines and practices and were admonished to attend sermons and catechism instruction. Many claimed, however, that they did not understand the sermons, which had become more scholarly and less emotional than the pre-Reformation preaching to which they were accustomed. The reformers were concerned to train a cadre of preachers who would expound the scriptures, word by word, with recourse to the original languages, but they did not take the next step of training congregations to listen to such sermons.

Hearing the Word

We have seen that the medieval church did not lack in preaching. In fact, preaching became a major form of popular entertainment in the late Middle Ages. Celebrated mendicant friars came into towns, greeted with much fanfare. Sometimes pulpits were built out-of-doors, attached to the side of the church building or on a wooden platform erected for the occasion in the town square. These preachers could elicit great emotion with gripping accounts of the terrors of hell or lyrical outpourings of the love of God shown in the passion of Christ, although the transcripts that survive are but a shadow of the oratorical reality. In the Rhineland and other cities of the Holy Roman Empire, there were endowed pulpits in the great churches to which more scholarly preachers were called, such as Johann Geiler of Kaysersberg (1445–1510), who was called to the pulpit of the Strasbourg Cathedral. While these sermons could be earthy, direct, and full of humor, many of the preachers were early advocates of reform. In fact, many of the leading reformers were given pulpits in the chief churches of their cities. In the early 1520s, Luther in the Stadtkirche of Wittenberg, Zwingli in the Grossmünster of Zurich, Andreas Osiander in the cathedral of Nuremberg, Wolfgang Capito, Martin Bucer, and Caspar Helio in the several preaching posts in Strasbourg, Johanes Oecolampadius as Pastor of Basel, and Olavus Petri in the Storkyrka of Stockholm all used their pulpits to advocate reform in doctrine and practice. They also developed a style of preaching that was exegetical rather than topical and served as a powerful example to their colleagues. Some of their sermons were collected into postils that could be used by less capable contemporaries.[30]

New ministers and pastors in Lutheran and Reformed churches were chosen for their knowledge of scripture and skill in public speaking. The custom developed already in the Reformation period of delivering sample sermons that were judged for content and delivery. But these preachers were elected by town councils or consistories rather than by popular vote, and the registers of consistories indicate that it took as much time to develop laity capable of understanding the new type of sermons as preachers capable of delivering them. There were plenty of opportunities to listen to sermons, since preaching services replaced the daily masses. Then, as now, preachers tried to apply the text to current events, which sometimes made the auditors angry.

The centrality of sermons in the life of the church did not necessarily work against the role of the Eucharist in forming the social body. Rather, the spoken word was elevated above ritual actions, which were also impeded by new arrangements of worship spaces.

To encourage more attentive listening to sermons, seating was arranged for the auditors. The seating was somewhat hierarchically arranged, although not exclusively so. Dignitaries such as the town councilmen were seated in chairs close to the pulpit. The rest of the auditors were seated on benches, with women and children closest to the pulpit and the men behind them. However, those who complained that they could not hear the sermons because they were hard of hearing were given seats closer to the pulpit.

Architectural Changes

Seating arrangements sometimes led to the architectural rearrangement of church buildings, since pulpits were often wrapped around a pillar along a side aisle. In Lutheran churches, which retained high altars for Holy Communion from which even the Service of the Word was conducted, benches continued to face toward the chancel. At the time for the sermon, those on benches between the pulpit and the altar got up and turned around to face the pulpit.

In Reformed churches, where Holy Communion was celebrated only four times a year, partitions were removed (such as the rood screen between the nave and the chancel), as well as altars, statues, and other visual aids. The seating was clustered around the pulpit on the long wall.

When new buildings were erected for Protestant worship after the Reformation, form followed function. Especially in Reformed church buildings, the pulpit might be on the long wall with seating arranged around it. In Lutheran church buildings, the pulpit might be erected above the altar-table, although the altar was still arrayed with paraments, crucifix, and candles, and the service (including the reading of the Epistle and Gospel at the Mass) was still conducted at the altar. The preacher would mount the pulpit for the sermon and pulpit office. In England a reading desk for reading the prayer offices was placed under the pulpit. In all of these buildings, galleries were arranged for additional seating, and the pulpits were accordingly elevated.

In England, churches developed a special type of seating known as pews, which could be rented by families of the parish. These were benches enclosed within boxed wainscots, which separated families but within which one also had privacy for devotions. Seating—whether boxed pews or plain benches—had the effect of inhibiting movement or even use of the parish churches for social acts and events such as the passing of the peace and church banquets.[31] Pews limited the interaction of people and privatized the experience of public worship.

Sanctifying Civil Government

Finally, we need to recognize the increased role that the Reformation assigned to the civil government in establishing and preserving social unity. Certainly it is the case that in the struggle between church and state in the late Middle Ages, the state was gaining ground. Kings and other rulers were centralizing power in themselves at the expense of the other nobility, often by aligning themselves with the needs of the common people. The free cities of the Holy Roman Empire had received a substantial measure of self-government, and their city councils made decisions that affected both secular and religious life. But as Luther experienced the intransigence of the papacy and the hierarchy in reforming the church, he turned to the civil authorities, as the chief Christian laymen, to undertake this task in his *Open Letter to the Christian Nobility of the German Nation Concerning the Reform of the Christian Estate* (1520). He called on Emperor Charles V to convene a free general council of the church (free of the leadership of the pope) to consider and enact reforms, appealing to the example of the Roman emperor Constantine, who convened the Council of Nicaea. In 1528 he prevailed on the elector of Saxony to authorize visitations of the parishes in the absence of episcopal visitations, although then visitors were commissioned as electoral officials rather than as ecclesiastical delegates. In his doctrine of the two kingdoms, Luther assigned to civil government those areas of life that concerned legal arrangements, such as marriage, the execution of wills, and the punishment of crimes (including those committed by the clergy), leaving to the church the preaching of the gospel. The state was an agent of God as much as the church was. It administered the law as God's left hand in society, just as the church administered the gospel in Word and Sacrament as God's right hand. The state had a God-given role and a responsibility within the orders of creation.

Rulers like Henry VIII in England and Gustav Vasa in Sweden (neither of whom were fully committed to Reformation doctrines) were not slow to realize how the Reformation served their economic and political interests as they broke relations with the papacy, converted papal annates to taxes payable to the crown, officially assumed temporal governance of the church, disbanded the monasteries and dispersed their lands to friends and allies, dissolved chantries and appropriated their funds into state treasuries, and confiscated parish treasures. Yet this in itself was not enough to transfer the unifying symbol of society from the church's Eucharist to the state. In both England and Sweden, there were popular rebellions against these acts of royal rapacity. Moreover, as Eamon Duffy and Vilhelm Moberg indicate in their social histories, the common people found ways of subverting royal decrees and fooling royal bailiffs by hiding vestments, bells, and church plates, or by rebelling.[32] What mattered was the appropriation of sacred symbols for state use.

On the eve of the Reformation, Sir Thomas More in England had attempted a discussion of Christian politics in the guise of a life of King Richard III. He intuited that the community was held together by common sacred symbols derived from the sacraments, and that a principal duty of a Christian ruler was to respect these symbols and inculcate a sense of reverence toward these objects on the part of their subjects— duties that King Edward IV had performed but Richard III had not. For More, this was an even more critical lapse on the part of Richard than murder and usurpation. Yet even before More penned his book, there were examples of royal appropriation of sacred symbols. Richard III's contemporary, Charles VIII of France, was received by the citizens of Rouen by something like a secular mass. As John Bossy writes,

> Taking advantage of the fact that the arms of their city displayed the *Agnus Dei*, they exploited the source of relevant symbolism available in both the mass and in the text of the Apocalypse. They described their young and otherwise unattractive king as Lamb of God, savior, head of the mystical body of France, guardian of the book with seven seals, fountain of life-giving grace to a dry people, deified bringer of peace; one worthy to receive, without the formality of being slain, blessing and honor, glory and power.[33]

This was one example of a form of entrance processions used by popes and kings known as an *Advent*, some of which were constructed in imitation of the entry of Christ into Jerusalem on Palm Sunday. The imagery of such entrances inevitably compared the pope or the king to Christ and the entered city to Zion.[34]

It was one thing to appropriate sacred symbols to prop up the monarchy; it was another thing for the monarchy to replace sacred symbols with its own symbols. Elizabeth I of England, far from being the moderate she has often been portrayed as being, at the beginning of her reign (1559) issued a set of injuncts that required the removal and destruction not just of "misused images," as were attacked and pulled down in the iconoclastic injunctions of Edward VI's reign, but of "all images . . . all tables." The removal of images and altars also removed unifying symbols of the sacred. The royal coat of arms had already replaced the rood screen group (Christ on the cross, his mother and the beloved disciple at the foot of the cross) during the reign of Edward VI, but these were destroyed by Queen Mary, who ordered that roods be restored (and royal supremacy be ended). When Elizabeth came to the throne, she ordered the bare wooden roods of Mary's time destroyed (there had not been time for many of them to be decorated) and replaced with brightly painted royal coats of arms (she knew her subjects did not like barren churches).

Realizing also that a real presence requires a body, Elizabeth became a master of the development of the royal ceremonial entrance into the form of the royal progress. The progress developed from the medieval custom of kings or queens traveling from castle to castle to receive the hospitality of their subjects and to establish their power throughout the land. Elizabeth devised and starred in a long-running progress throughout her realm in which she transformed herself into the adored object of her subjects. Admittedly, Elizabeth came to the throne in a precarious position. In 1570 she was excommunicated by the pope, who absolved her Catholic subjects from allegiance to her. She was the subject of foreign and domestic plots as well as the Armada dispatched by Philip II of Spain, who had been married to her half-sister Mary. So every summer, she undertook a progress, accompanied by hundreds of courtiers and attendants on horseback and three hundred carts of baggage pulled by teams of six horses each, covering about twelve miles per day and staying in the homes of her subjects along the way. Her travels usually produced an improvement in the infrastructures of towns as well as of the great manor houses in which she stayed. She was greeted in each city with as much pageantry as the town could muster and a festival atmosphere, which included carnivals, picnics, plays, and public ceremonies such as knightings and the bestowing of other awards.[35] Not only did her body replace the eucharistic body as the presence that unified the social body, but her summer progresses eclipsed the Corpus Christi festivals, which still survived at least as civic observances into the 1570s.[36] By the time James I came to the throne, Protestantism was well established in England, Corpus Christi festivals were a thing of the past, and the Stuarts avoided progresses for more private ceremonies and long-winded treatises on the divine right of kings. But by then the state had assumed the function of maintaining social unity that had been formerly provided by the church's Eucharist.

CHAPTER 12

Death Here and Life Hereafter in the Middle Ages and the Reformation

The tendency in recent historical studies has been to view the Reformation of the sixteenth century more in continuity than in discontinuity with the late Middle Ages. The idea of reform itself was rooted in the cycles of renewal that the monasteries went through all during the Middle Ages. Within this context, Heiko Oberman called the Reformation "a medieval event."[1] Steven Ozment dates the age of reform as 1250–1550,[2] while John Bossy sees a coherent history of Christianity in the West from 1400 to 1700.[3] However, the Protestant Reformation also stood in radical discontinuity with the Middle Ages in some important respects, not the least of which was its approach to death.

One of the marks of medieval cultural life in general was its special concern for the welfare of the departed. Certainly a sense of communion with the dead was a part of the Christian cultus from the early centuries in such practices as the commemoration of martyrs and saints on the anniversaries of their deaths and the reading of the diptychs of the living and the dead at the Eucharist. From the time of late antiquity and into the Middle Ages, an immense apparatus developed for the remembrance of the faithful departed and prayers for their eternal welfare. Yet social historian Edward Muir asserts, "The Reformation, particularly in its early phases, can be seen as a forceful rejection of the ritual industry of death with all its expensive commitments to priestly intervention."[4]

A Community of the Living and the Dead

The Reformation approach to the rites of death was in part a reaction to the cultural preoccupation with death in the late Middle Ages. As Johan Huizinga famously wrote, "No other age has so forcefully and continually impressed the idea of death on the whole population as did the fifteenth century, in which the call of the memento mori [reminder of death] echoes throughout the whole of life."[5] This occurred in a time that Huizinga characterized as dominated by "religious excitement and religious fantasy,"[6] in which practices that had a recognized and normal place in traditional Catholic piety were blown into proportions that ceased to make sense, such as when indulgences were counted in millions of years of release from time in purgatory. While the revisionist social historian Eamon Duffy considers Huizinga's account of the morbidity of the period to be "highly colored," he does not challenge Huizinga's fundamental assertion. He observes, "Wherever one turns in the sources for the period one encounters the overwhelming preoccupation of clergy and laity alike, from peasant to prince and from parish clerk to pontiff, with the safe transition of their souls from this world to the next, above all with the shortening and easing of their stay in Purgatory."[7]

The idea of purgatory is that certain sins could be redeemed after death under certain conditions. This concept developed slowly as a source of speculation among North African fathers, based on a few biblical texts such as 2 Maccabees 12:41–46 (the story of the sacrifice ordered by Judas Maccabeus to redeem the sins of soldiers who had fallen in battle), 1 Corinthians 3:11–15 (the purification after death of certain categories of sinners "as if by fire"), and Luke 16:19–31 (the parable of the rich man and Lazarus, which describes places to which the soul goes after death before the resurrection to the final judgment). The doctrine of purgatory may be traced to Origen, who taught that the will of God to save his whole creation extended beyond the limits of earthly life and included opportunities for the purification of the soul in the afterlife toward final salvation, even of the devil and his angels. While rejecting Origen's belief in the universal salvation of all, Augustine of Hippo established the notion of a purgatorial time in which one received punishment for sins and was purified for heaven, and held that it was appropriate to pray for the remission of sins of the dead. Pope Gregory the Great took Augustine's notion about "purgatorial fire," made tentatively and in passing, and made it "something that has to be believed" (*credendus*). It also "has to be believed" (*credendum est*) that the prayers of the faithful avail in obtaining release from purgatorial fire for those who had sinned "not out of malice but out of the error of ignorance."[8]

Gregory contributed immensely to the imagery of purgatory and to the repertoire of apparitions and visions on which later writers drew. The idea of visitations from the dead developed especially on the soil of Celtic Christianity. This element of folk religion certainly fed into the medieval understanding of purgatory and contributed to the concern of the living to provide charity for the dead.

Both All Saints' Day on November 1 and All Souls' Day on November 2 can be closely associated with the medieval preoccupation with the needs of the dead. As we have already noted in chapter 4, All Saints' Day as we know it originated in the seventh century on Celtic soil, where November 1 marked the beginning of winter. Persisting from pagan times into the Christian era were beliefs that, at this time of the year, the dead returned as ghosts to haunt those who had wronged them in life, had not abided by the provisions of their wills, or had not adequately provided for their safe passage in the afterlife. The rituals used by the living for protection included putting food on the graves on All Hallows' Eve to satisfy vengeance-minded souls and hanging jack-o'-lanterns to frighten off demonic spirits. Commemorating all the saints on November 1 can be viewed as a way of countering the negative pagan residue of this folklore with a more positive Christian celebration. Even so, the church countenanced these fears by having the church bells rung throughout the night to ward off evil spirits and having bonfires lit in the churchyards to warm the souls of the dead.[9]

All Souls' Day as we know it originated in the monastery at Cluny in 998, spread quickly throughout Europe, and was joined with All Saints' Day. November 2 became one of the busiest days in the year for burial confraternities, who cleaned and decorated graveyards; for priests, who offered requiem masses for all the faithful departed of the parish and processed through the graveyards to bless the graves; and for monks, who sang prayer offices of the dead for all the benefactors of the monasteries.

In medieval culture, the dead were very much a part of the consciousness of the living. The doctrine of purgatory greatly contributed
to this consciousness. It stemmed from the Christian view that the
dead could receive a second chance before the final judgment, and that
the living could help them receive it. Jacques LeGoff has shown that
purgatory was a remarkable example of human projection, including
the projection of human institutions, into another dimension.[10] This
projection took the form of the "spatialization" of purgatory and the
stretching of the penitential system of the church into the afterlife.
Spatialization refers to the widespread belief that purgatory occupies a
specific space, as imaginatively described in the "Purgatorio" of Dante's
Divine Comedy (although in the popular imagination, the dead were
never very far from the graveyard, which is why there was such a concern to maintain the graveyard as a place of peace and to keep the
burial sites well maintained). In terms of the extension of the church's
penitential system into the afterlife, theologians from the twelfth century on viewed purgatory as a time of extended penance that began
with confession and absolution as one of the "last rites" at the time of
death, so the sinner's attitude at the moment of death assumed dramatic importance.

While one's whole lifetime of good deeds would factor into one's
destination in the afterlife—heaven, hell, or the second chance of purgatory—the dying might try to make up for their sins of commission or
omission by means of deathbed reconciliations and provisions in their
wills for the poor of the parish (who often surrounded the bed of the
dying benefactor, holding candles to ward off the devil from claiming
the soul of the dying). Wills provided not only for the adornment of
parish churches (often making up for forgotten tithes and offerings),
but also, in an effort to hedge one's bets in the afterlife, for the endowment of chantries in which masses and prayer offices would be sung on
the anniversary of one's death. Both the dying in their wills and the living by joining burial confraternities could provide for a certain number
of votive masses to be said for the relief of the soul of the departed in
purgatory. Typically, votive masses for the dead were said on the three
days after the report of a death, on the thirtieth day, and on the anniversary as far in perpetuity as a bequest specified.[11]

Books providing advice on "the art of dying" were popular devotional works in the late Middle Ages. Illustrated with woodcuts and
verses, these books provided commentaries on the rites of visitation
of the sick and burial. Priests were instructed to hold the crucifix over

the eyes of the dying parishioner, interrogate him or her with regard to heresy and trust in Christ's passion, and finally administer "the last rites," which included confession and absolution, anointment of the dying (extreme unction) to complete the effects of penance, and viaticum (last communion).[12]

The doctrine of purgatory eliminated the boundary between earthly life and the afterlife by promoting the view that the soul is judged at death and is escorted to one place or another, to be rejoined with the body when raised in the general resurrection. This was the common view, even though the funeral liturgy held to an older view, expressed in the famous medieval sequence hymn "Dies irae" (Day of Wrath), that judgment occurs at the day of reckoning when the dead are raised and not at the time of death. Social historians may debate the extent to which all these elaborate and expensive provisions reflected individual panic or self-preoccupation at the end of the Middle Ages, as Philippe Ariès claimed,[13] or a continuing expression of social *pietas* toward family and friends, as John Bossy suggested.[14] But certainly the church made a massive accommodation to lay views and concerns that are not reflected in the texts of its liturgy.

Late medieval liturgical books typically provided for a procession from the house of the departed to the church, the prayer office of the dead, the funeral mass followed by the absolution, and a procession to the place of burial, followed by the burial itself. The medieval funeral liturgy was heavily influenced by monastic practices, so details varied from one ritual province to another, but it was pervaded by a somberness that was in contrast with the paschal character of earlier Christian burial rites with their psalms and Alleluias.[15] The following elements were typical.

When the priest and the mourners arrived at the house of the deceased, Psalm 130 (*De profundis*) with its antiphon *Si iniquitates* (If you, Lord, should mark iniquities) was said or sung. Psalm 51 (*Misereri mei*) was sung in procession to the church, ending with *Requiem aeternam* (Rest eternal).

The body was placed before the altar in the church, surrounded by candles. The office of the dead, a form of Matins, was sung in the church, with lessons from Job ending with the Kyrie, the Lord's Prayer, and a series of responses.

The funeral mass was celebrated, at the end of which the ministers went to the bier for the absolutions while the responsory, "Libera me Domine de morte aeterna" (Deliver me, O Lord, from eternal death), and the Kyrie were sung, ending with the Lord's Prayer, the sprinkling of the bier with holy water, and a concluding prayer.

The procession left the church accompanied by the anthem "In paradisum." Upon the procession's arrival at the graveyard, the grave was blessed if this had not been done previously. Then the Benedictus was sung with "Ego sum resurrectio et vita" (I am the resurrection and the life) as the antiphon, followed by the Kyrie, the Lord's Prayer, and the responses as at the office. The priest made the sign of the cross over the grave while the versicle "Requiem aeternam" and its response "Requiescat in pace" were said. On the return from the place of burial to the church, the "De profundis" was again sung with its antiphon.

The Reformation's Critique of the Medieval Way of Death

Martin Luther's act of nailing his Ninety-Five Theses on the door of the Castle Church at Wittenberg on the eve of All Saints' Day was symbolically strategic. The elector Frederick the Wise of Saxony had amassed an extensive collection of relics, which were displayed in the Castle Church on All Saints' Day, to the veneration of which were attached indulgences totaling millions of years. This was also the time of the year when the industry of death was most prominently working. Luther himself was not aware of the financial deal between the House of Hohenzollern and Pope Leo X concerning the plenary indulgence being peddled by the Dominican Friar Johann Tetzel. But he knew that this indulgence was having a negative effect on the practice of penance among his parishioners. Even though Duke Frederick had forbidden his Saxons to cross into Hohenzollern territory to buy them, they were doing so. Oberman reports that drafts of Tetzel's sermons have survived and that what Luther's parishioners were telling him was pretty accurate:[16] "As soon as the coin in the coffer rings, the soul from purgatory springs."[17]

Many of the practices Luther criticized had already been rejected by the theology faculty of the University of Paris. But Luther went beyond complaints about abuses. From the outset he asserted, "When our Lord and Master Jesus Christ said, 'Repent,' he willed the entire life of believers to be one of repentance."[18] He disagreed that the pope has a treasury of merits from the saints to dispense, because the true treasure of the church is the gospel of the glory and grace of God (Thesis 62). Every true Christian participates in this treasure by living a life of repentance and faith. Luther also disagreed that the pope's authority reached into the afterlife, although the pope, like any other Christian, could make intercession for those in purgatory. In his *Explanations of the Ninety-Five Theses* (1518), Luther still professed belief in purgatory along the lines laid down by Augustine.[19] But over time he slowly became skeptical about its reality, due to its lack of scriptural basis and the abuses connected with it. In 1530 he wrote his tract *Rejection of Purgatory* and in the *Smalcald Articles* (1537) that he held purgatory to be "contrary to the fundamental article that Christ alone, and not the work of a man, can help souls. Besides, nothing has been commanded or enjoined upon us with reference to the dead."[20]

The other major Protestant reformers were quick to reject the doctrine of purgatory on the basis of the justification-by-faith/all-sufficient-atonement-of-Christ axis of Reformation theology. Ulrich Zwingli not only found no scriptural warrant for purgatory, but said that it contradicted Mark 16:16, "Whoever believes and is baptized shall be saved." John Calvin later added that purgatory is a "terrible blasphemy of Christ" because it denies that "the blood of Christ is the sole satisfaction for the sins of believers, the sole expiation, the sole purgation."[21] The unique situation in England, according to Diarmaid MacCulloch, is that King Henry VIII rejected the doctrine of purgatory, and therefore dissolved the chantries, without replacing it with the doctrine of justification. Not until the publication of the *Book of Homilies* in 1547, early in the reign of the boy king Edward VI, was justification by faith made a central tenet of the English Reformation.[22]

The Protestant reformers were convinced that the idea of purgatory developed because of uncertainty about God's justification of sinners. They saw no basis for that uncertainty in the promises made in Christ—for example, "Very truly, I tell you, anyone who hears my word and believes him who sent me has eternal life, and does not come under judgment, but has passed from death to life" (John 5:26) and, "So if anyone is in Christ, there is a new creation: everything old has passed away; see, everything has become new" (2 Corinthians 5:17). Jesus' parable of the rich man and Lazarus shows that between life here and life hereafter lies an abyss that does not allow communication between the living and the dead (Luke 16:19–31). Moreover, there is a qualitative difference between life on earth and life hereafter, where "in the resurrection they neither marry nor are given in marriage" (Matthew 22:30). These New Testament statements do not allow a projection of earthly life into eternal life, nor an alteration of judgment after death.

Unlike the medieval scholastic theologians, the New Testament writers were reluctant to make any statements concerning the whereabouts of the dead. Therefore, the reformers were not willing to engage in speculation either. Drawing on Pauline language, they were content to speak of "falling asleep in Christ." Luther's views on this have not been interpreted uniformly but it seems that he did not regard death as a conscious state. Perhaps one of his best statements on the evangelical view of death is made in a preface to *Christian Songs Latin and German, for Use at Funerals* (1542):

> But we Christians, who have been redeemed from all this through the precious blood of God's Son, should train and accustom ourselves in faith to despise death and regard it as a deep, strong, sweet sleep; to consider the coffin as nothing other than our Lord Jesus' bosom or Paradise, the grave as nothing other than a soft couch of ease or rest. As verily, before God, it truly is just this; for he testifies, John 11:11: Lazarus, our friend, sleeps; Matthew 9:24: The maiden is not dead, she sleeps. Thus, too, St. Paul in 1 Corinthians 15, removes from sight all hateful aspects of death as related to our mortal body and brings forward nothing but charming and joyful aspects of the promised life. He says there [vv. 42ff.]: It is sown in corruption and will rise in incorruption; it is sown in dishonor (that is, a hateful, shameful form) and will rise in glory; it is sown in weakness and will rise in strength; it is sown in the natural body and will rise a spiritual body.[23]

Martin Schalling expressed this same view in his masterful hymn of comfort with which Johann Sebastian Bach concluded his *Saint John Passion*:

> Lord, let at last thine angels come,
> To Abr'hams bosom bear me home,
> That I might die unfearing;
> And in its narrow chamber keep
> My body safe in peaceful sleep
> Until thy reappearing.
> And then from death awaken me,
> That these mine eyes with joy may see,
> O Son of God, thy glorious face,
> My Savior and my fount of grace.

Lord Jesus Christ,
My prayer attend, my prayer attend,
And I will praise thee without end.[24]

Implementing Reform

The comfort of God's promise of eternal life in Christ looms large in the works of J. S. Bach.[25] But two hundred years before the time Bach's choirboys stood at the open grave of a Leipzig citizen, singing the unaccompanied motet "Jesu, meine Freude" (Jesu, my joy), a "revolution" had occurred in the pastoral and liturgical practices surrounding death. As early as 1519, Luther said in a sermon on preparing for death that the dying should meditate on God's grace and the promise of salvation in Christ; one should brood on one's sins during one's lifetime, not on one's deathbed. Writing against the fear of death, Calvin held, "No one has made much progress in the school of Christ who does not look forward with joy to the day of death and final resurrection" (*Institutes* III, 9:5). The sermons preached by the reformers at the funerals of notable public figures became models on how to extol examples of holy living and holy dying.

A change in teaching required a change in practice. This could come about only as the Reformation was implemented by civil authorities. The typical process by which the Reformation was implemented in the imperial cities of the Holy Roman Empire was that a celebrated preacher was called to an endowed pulpit and preached the ideas of reform from the city's Great Church. This led to deliberations concerning changes in practice in the city council, in which a full public debate was held between the reformers and the papal party, after which a vote was taken by the council on measures to implement reform.[26] This process was at work in the 1520s in Nuremberg, one of the first cities to officially embrace the Reformation by civil decree.

As late as October 1, 1517, Pope Leo X granted full absolution to any Nuremberg citizen who donated a sum equal to a day's cost of living. Yet less than a year earlier, in 1516, the vicar general of the Augustinians, Johannes von Staupitz, had attacked indulgences and drew attention to God's mercy in Advent sermons preached in Nuremberg, and his views were well received. The city's churches called Reformation-minded preachers, including Andreas Osiander in 1521. Wolfgang Volprecht was made prior of the Augustinian monastery. Lazarus

Spengler, the clerk of the city council, became a leading lay leader of the Reformation. The celebrated artisans Albrecht Dürer and Hans Sachs were sympathetic to Reformation ideas. Since the imperial court was located in Nuremberg and three imperial diets were held in the city between 1522 and 1524, Reformation ideas were preached in full hearing of the imperial establishment. The papal nuncio to the imperial court demanded the arrest of the preachers, but they were protected by the city council.[27]

Yet not every citizen was of the same mind as to the course of the Reformation in Nuremberg. Hans Sachs probably summed up various attitudes in a pamphlet published in 1524 in the form of a dialogue in which a zealous Lutheran (Peter) was criticized by a moderate evangelical (Hans) and a traditional Catholic (Ulrich, Peter's father-in-law), who charged that the new faith was nothing more than an abusive ridicule of tradition, a bigoted mockery of practices that pious Christians had previously held dear, including fasting, confession, pilgrimages, indulgences, good works, and vigils and masses for the dead. Hans warns that self-righteous dismissals of tradition, regardless of the truth of the criticism, only cause people to dig in their heels. It would be better, he said to Peter, "to give unknowing people some consoling words about Christ" and not forbid "those things which Christ leaves us free to do."[28] It may be that the clergy of the city heeded the words of Hans Sachs's pamphlet and, anticipating resistance and complaints, circulated for the benefit of the laity a detailed justification of the changes they were proposing. Among the practices to be rejected were the Latin mass ("pure blasphemy"), anniversary masses for the dead (the product of "clerical greed" and "shameful lay ignorance"), funeral masses ("if the common person properly understood these, he would not give a 'good morning' for one"), singing vigils for the dead ("if the common person only understood these, he would not pay a dollar for a year's worth"), purgatory ("it is nothing"), the *Salve Regina* (Hail, Queen of Heaven), consecrated salt, holy water ("a mockery of Christ"), and the singing of Matins and Compline.[29] As the city council debated the proposed changes, however, it became clear that the moderate position of Hans Sachs would prevail through the advocacy of the influential Lazarus Spengler. Thus, while votive masses, funeral masses, anniversary masses, vigils for the dead, and purgatory were set aside, many traditional elements remained in Lutheran practice.

While there were undoubtedly "Ulriches" and other Catholics in the cities and the small principalities of Germany who did not agree with the Reformation, the decisions made by city councils and local princes could claim a degree of civic consensus. This was much harder to achieve in large, diverse countries like England, where the Reformation was ruthlessly implemented under the regime of Lord Protector Somerset early in the reign of the boy king, Edward VI. Commissioners implementing the royal injunctions forbade the wearing of black copes over their surplices in the rites of death, the ringing of death knells, the "immeasurable ringing for ded persones at their burialls, and at the feast of All Sowles," and confiscated the endowed livings and accoutrements of chantries, which were suppressed by the Chantry Act of 1547.[30] The abolition of images and the confiscation of vestments and church plates also struck at the late medieval connection between the living and the dead, since many of these objects in parish churches had been bequeathed in the wills of deceased parishioners. The suppression of the chantries not only drastically reduced the number of employed priests (those not needed were pensioned off), but sometimes threatened the infrastructures of towns, since income from endowed chantries may have also covered the costs of maintaining local hospitals, bridges, and water supplies. The combination of the assault on piety and the local economy by heavy-handed royal commissioners led to local outbreaks of rebellion, the most serious of which took place in the West Country of England with the promulgation of the English *Book of Common Prayer* in 1549.[31] The thousands of men of Cornwall and Devon who took up arms against the royal commissioners considered themselves to be devout defenders of the old faith and its practices, who found the religious changes coming at too fast a pace. But they were bloodily put down by foreign troops fighting under the flag of the King of England.

Reformation Rites of Death

In reforming the rites of death, the Lutheran Reformation churches generally abandoned services in the church at the time of death but provided for rites of committal at the cemetery, at which psalms in the vernacular were sung and sermons were preached. The preachers and church orders pleaded not only for a simplification of the rites but also for less extravagant burial practices so that the poor would not be embarrassed.

The Brandenburg-Nuremberg Church Order of 1533 was influential on subsequent church orders. During the procession to the grave site, the canticle Benedictus or Psalm 40 was sung. This was followed by the medieval hymn "In media vita" (In the Midst of Life We Are in Death), or the antiphon "Ego sum resurrectio et vita" (I am the resurrection and the life), or a German hymn such as Luther's translation of "In media vita": *Mitten wir im Leben sind mit dem Tod umfangen* (In the midst of earthly life snares of death surround us). The burial then took place in silence and was followed by a sermon either at the grave or back at the house of the deceased.

The more conservative Mark Brandenburg Church Order of 1540 had the German "Media vita" (*Mitten wir im Leben sind*) and "De profundis" ("Aus tiefer Not," or Out of the depths I cry to you, O Lord) sung in procession to the grave following the processional cross, and concluded with the "Libera me" and the burial. After this there was a brief service in the church, beginning with the Nunc Dimittis and followed by lessons from Job 19 and 1 Corinthians 15, with Latin responses or German hymns between the readings. The Benedictus with the antiphon "Ego sum resurrectio" was then sung, followed by a collect in German, a response "Si bono suscepimus" ("Shall we receive good at the hands of the Lord, and shall we not receive evil?"), the anthem "Si enim credimus" (If we believe), leading to the Epistle (1 Thessalonians 4:12–17) and Gospel (John 11:21–27). The order concluded with a repetition of "Si bono suscepimus."[32]

In 1543 Philipp Melanchthon and Martin Bucer prepared a church order for the archbishop-elector of Cologne, Hermann von Wied. Archbishop Hermann specified that Brandenburg-Nuremberg was to be followed, but the reformers also used other church orders, including Mark Brandenburg.[33] While the Reformation of Cologne (*Einfaltigs Bedencken* or *Pia Deliberatio*) was never implemented because Archbishop Hermann was deposed by his chapter in 1546, it had an enormous influence as a literary source of the *Book of Common Prayer* of the Church of England. Thomas Cranmer followed developments in Germany with great interest. He had been an ambassador of King Henry VIII to the imperial court at Nuremberg in 1532 and was very attentive to the liturgical changes being implemented there. He continued correspondence with the continental reformers after being appointed archbishop of Canterbury in 1533. He had the Cologne Church Order translated into English under the title *A Simple and Religious Consultation of Archbishop Hermann* in 1547 (revised 1548) on the eve of the implementation of liturgical changes in England.

Its influence was not so evident in the burial rites of the 1549 prayer book, which retained in English much of the traditional scheme: procession to the church or grave, the burial proper, a brief office of the dead, and a funeral communion service. The service at the grave included some of the material in the German rites, such as scripture sentences from Archbishop Hermann's Consultation, an English version of "In media vita" ("In the myddest of our lyvynge / Death compaseth us rounde about," by Miles Coverdale), and the choice of readings. The Sarum *Dirige* was also retained. In the 1552 prayer book, the funeral communion service was abolished. The Order for the Burial of the Dead was conducted at the grave. It included the scripture sentences of 1549, "In the midest of lyfe we bee in death," the committal, the lesson from 1 Corinthians 15, a Kyrie (suffrages omitted), the Lord's Prayer, and two collects.[34]

Two important aspects of death and burial found in the 1549 prayer book are suppressed in the 1552 prayer book: prayers for the dead and attention to the body of the deceased. While the prayers for the dead in the first prayer book were cautiously worded, they did express a sense of community between the living and the dead, "they with us and we with them." But in his influential 1550 *Censura* (Examination) of the *Book of Common Prayer*, Martin Bucer, who had been given a professorship at Oxford, criticized prayers to the dead. Admitting that "this custom of praying for the faithful departed is a very ancient one," he nevertheless asserted, "Our place is to prefer divine authority to all human authority. . . . Now there is no part of scripture which teaches us to pray for the dead, either by word or example. And it is forbidden to add or take away anything from scripture."[35] Also, in the committal of the body to the earth, Cranmer translated the text from the Sarum Rite as follows: "I commend thy soule to God the father almighty, and thy body to the grounde, earth to earth, asshes to asshes, dust to dust."[36] The dead could still be spoken to directly in 1549. But in the more Reformed prayer book of 1552, the dead were no longer a part of the living. They could not be prayed for or spoken to. In the committal text, the priest turned away from the corpse and faced the living when he said, "Forasmuche as it hathe pleased almightie God of his great mercy to take unto himselfe the soule of our dere brother here departed: we therefore commit his body to the ground, earth to earth, asshes to asshes, dust to dust."[37] Here the dead person is spoken about, not to. Likewise, in the final prayer of the 1552 Burial Service, reworked from a prayer in the 1549 "celebracion of the holy communion when there is a burial of the dead," the phrase "both thys our brother, and we, may be found acceptable in thy sight" has become "we maye be founde acceptable in thy syghte." The boundaries of human community have been redrawn to exclude the dead.

The 1552 prayer book had a very brief career at this point in history, because King Edward VI died in 1553 and was succeeded by Mary Tudor, who restored the state of religion as it had existed at the end of the reign of her father, Henry VIII, except for reestablishing a relationship with the papacy in Rome. Marian religion was not totally reactionary; her archbishop of Canterbury, Reginald Cardinal Pole, was a leading advocate of Catholic reform. But many traditional customs related to death and burial were restored. When Elizabeth I succeeded her half-sister in 1558, an Act of Uniformity restoring the *Book of Common Prayer* passed Parliament in 1559 by only three votes. Elizabeth wisely proceeded cautiously to eliminate the Catholic practices that had been restored during Mary's reign.[38] But requiem masses and even funeral communions were suppressed. The bell could toll to announce a death, but the tolling of the bell to invite prayers for the deceased was forbidden.

The elimination of prayer offices and masses for the dead changed the provisions of last wills and testaments. After the Reformation, wills often provided for community charities rather than for religious foundations. As Eamon Duffy notes, it cannot be said that the change in wills represents a change in doctrinal conviction, since the state religion made no provision for those things for which Catholics had provided in their wills.[39] As if by compensation, since fewer accoutrements were needed or desired for the liturgical enrichment of parish churches, people made provision for the building of elaborate monuments in memory of themselves and their families, which eventually cluttered the aisles and bays of parish churches and cathedrals, perhaps in the belief that these memorials of the dead would not be confiscated by rapacious rulers. This was the case not only in England but in other countries as well.

One of the religious tensions of Elizabeth's reign was the presence within the Church of England of a "puritan" party that desired a more thorough reform of practice and life. Puritan clergy objected to the "skudding" of the minister to the churchyard stile to meet the funeral cortege and preferred a service in the church with no ceremonies or prayers connected with the burial. Puritans objected that the prayer book required the minister to bury every person "in sure and certayne hope of resurreccion to eternal lyfe, through our Lord Jesus Christ." Were all the dead elect? Puritan ministers were increasingly reluctant to read the Burial Office over the bodies of drunkards, adulterers, or other notorious sinners.

These objections persisted for a hundred years. As the English Presbyterian Richard Baxter (1615–1691) put it, "It is a confusion perilous to the living, that we are to assume that all we bury be of one sort, viz., elect and saved: when contrarily, we see multitudes die without any such signs of repentance as rational charity can judge sincere."[40] However, James Pilkington, bishop of Durham during Elizabeth's reign, declared (probably for most English parishioners) that "the comely using of these [rites of the dead] in God's church is a great comfort to all Christians, and the want of them a token of God's wrath and plague."[41] This was one of the major controversies of the Savoy Conference (1661), which met at the time of the Restoration of king, bishops, and prayer book after the period of the Puritan Commonwealth to decide on the content of the new prayer book. The Anglican victory over the Presbyterians on this point is reflected in the alteration of the prayer "Almighty God, with whom do live the spirits of them that depart . . . ," from "in whome the soules of them that be elected" (1552, 1559) to "with whom the souls of the faithful," (1662) implying that if one dare not presume to say that any man is damned, then it is better to be charitable and hope in the mercy of God.

CHAPTER 13

The Ecclesiastical Captivity of Marriage

The church did not enter the world with a rite of marriage. Not surprisingly, marriage was the most difficult of the rites of passage for the church to control. As with the rites of death, the cultural practices of the societies out of which Christians were drawn exercised an enormous influence on Christian practice. It was easier to control the rites of death. At the moment of death, the dying and the deceased's kin were anxiously concerned about the deceased's eternal welfare. This gave the church considerable leverage in guiding the dying toward a "good death" and assuring the bereaved about the deceased's status in the afterlife. In the case of marriage, however, the church's interests were often at cross-purposes with the interests of the families involved. This is because marriages, as often as not, were family or political arrangements worked out by the fathers of the bride and groom, and the church's interests did not always coincide with the interests of families. For example, during the Middle Ages, the church was interested in effecting reconciliation between disputing families or warring nations in order to promote social harmony or peace between neighbors. By developing categories of persons related by blood or marriage with whom one might not marry and encoding these categories in canon and civil law, the church forced families to move beyond their own circles to find spouses for their children. The parish priest's involvement in marriage was often less a matter of officiating at a rite of marriage than of inquiring whether there were any impediments to the marriage—and forwarding to the bishop or to Rome requests for dispensations from these impediments—and publishing the banns of marriage at mass on three successive Sundays to see whether there were any personal or legal objections to the marriage.[1]

Medieval Rites of Marriage

We have little information about Christian rites of marriage in the first three centuries, and not much more information in the next three centuries.[2] We may assume that Christians continued to observe the customs of the cultures from which they came, whether Jewish, Greek, or Roman. Some marriage customs associated with the ancient Romans—such as the use of betrothal rings, betrothal dinners, the wearing of a bridal veil and a floral crown, the solemn declaration before witnesses of the groom's and bride's intention to become husband and wife, the exchange of gifts, the wedding banquet, and the bride being carried over the threshold of her new home—remain a part of Western wedding practices, transmitted by the church from ancient to modern society. With some help from the writings of the church fathers about marriage, we can make educated guesses as to how the received rites were christianized and what Christian rites of marriage were like as they developed. We can see that in Christian weddings, the bishop or some other clergy replaced the Roman *auspex nuptiarum* as the officiant and the *pronuba* as the priest who blessed the marriage bed. Certainly the Eucharist was substituted for the offering of the sacrifice of the hearth, and this required the presence of the bishop or a presbyter.

The wife who married a pagan was placed in a religiously compromised situation, since by custom she was supposed to sacrifice to the gods of the hearth in her husband's home. The religious compromises that were required when Christians married pagans undoubtedly contributed to the church's desire to prohibit Christians from marrying non-Christians once the church was in a position to exert social control. Also, since there were more eligible women than men in the church, highborn Christian women were put at a disadvantage, since women who married beneath their status lost their own status and assumed their husband's.[3] It is no wonder that church fathers recommended virginity.

By the time of the sacramentaries in the early medieval West, we have prayers for nuptial masses and for blessing the couple before they received communion and before they entered their marriage bed. In fact, there is a proliferation of marriage prayers and blessings in the sacramentaries and missals of western Europe.[4] But here is a classic case where having rites in the books does not mean that everyone actually used them. The important aspects of the marriage rites were the legal aspects. These aspects included the exchange of vows; the exchange of rings and other gifts of espousal, often between families and not just between the bride and groom; and the kiss of peace, which might be delayed until the Pax in the nuptial mass. These were threshold rituals performed on the church porch, not before the altar. Or they might be performed at the threshold of a private house and be witnessed by a magistrate and not by a priest. Some families were happy to keep the clergy away from their marriage arrangements.

Many of the lower-class weddings were not solemnized at the church at all. The rites could be quite informal. Edward Muir reports that in Wales, the bride and groom simply jumped across a broom placed aslant in the threshold of the bridal cottage, but they could not touch the broom or the doorjamb, and the act had to be witnessed. Interestingly, divorce could be obtained just as easily by jumping back over a broom, still making sure that neither the broom nor the doorjamb was touched, and in the presence of witnesses.[5] Christopher Brooke gives the story of a saddler in York named John Beke, who simply sat down next to Marjory, asked, "Do you wish to be my wife?" and upon her affirmative answer, took her hand and said, "Marjory, here I take you as my wife, for better or worse, to have and to hold until the end of my life; and of this I give you my faith," and she said the same to him. They kissed and were then regarded as husband and wife.[6] An analysis of notary registers shows that in the fifteenth century, the vast majority of weddings took place outside of a church: 73 percent in Ely, 92 percent in Canterbury, 98 percent in Toulouse.[7]

In the early Middle Ages, the number of sacraments recognized by the church floated around from between two or three to eleven or twelve. In 1215, The Fourth Lateran Council set the number of sacraments at seven. Marriage was included among the seven. The scholastic theology of the period, drawing on the categories of Aristotle, defined the form and matter of each sacrament. The theologians defined the form of marriage as the giving of mutual consent and its matter as conjugal consummation. Canon law since this time held that the exchange of vows and conjugal consummation constituted the form and matter of marriage. This was the case with or without the benefit of clergy. It is not surprising that the majority of marriages were celebrated outside the church, although noble and royal families with some sense of public responsibility for the maintenance of Christendom required the services of bishops and archbishops.

According to John Bossy, two developments toward the end of the Middle Ages enlarged the role of the priest in the rite of marriage. First, there was growing fear of diabolical intervention for which apotropaic acts were desired. As in baptism the exorcisms of infants increased in importance in popular perception, so in marriage the blessing of the marriage bed was desired.[8] This was because the sexual organs were considered especially vulnerable to diabolical intervention; failure to perform sexually could lead to recrimination, hostility, and adultery. The church was desirous to have the priest bless the marriage bed, since otherwise many magical remedies were applied from the folk culture to ensure the fertility of the wife or to prevent the impotence of the husband.[9] If the priest was not available to bless the bridal chamber, priestly intervention in the marriage rite at the church became more desirable. This led to the blessing of the ring before it was placed on the bride's fourth finger. It now became a talisman of fidelity, and perhaps also of fertility, and not only a symbol of social alliance.

Second, since canon law held that the exchange of consent and conjugal consummation between two physically qualified individuals in any circumstance constituted the sacrament of marriage, many young people took advantage of this to get married without parental consent. But in view of the clandestine character of such weddings, it was deemed beneficial even by young people to have the priest witness the exchange of vows and provide a blessing. The secret marriage of Romeo and Juliet before Friar Lawrence in Shakespeare's play testifies to this practice. This growing practice, of course, exacerbated the tug-of-war between the fathers and priests, since it made the priest a surrogate father.[10]

The Reformation Critique of Marriage

Much of the social critique of the Reformation was bound up with the institution of marriage. Luther and his followers objected to the cloister, with its glorification of virginity and celibacy, as the ideal state of Christian life. Nor did they regard the cloister as the best solution to the problem of unmarried daughters. They taught that marriage and parenthood were equally honorable Christian vocations. Laws were enacted prohibiting the placement of boys and girls in cloisters, and as cloisters were dissolved, monks and nuns were married, returned to their families, or pensioned off.[11]

Most of the reformers testified to the sanctity of marriage by providing the personal example of marrying and producing children. In cities and territories that adopted the Reformation, most of the clergy became married with children in short order. By 1525 Luther and all his associates at Wittenberg had married and established households. This may have been the area that produced the greatest social revolution in the Protestant Reformation.

We cannot assume that everyone immediately accepted the new reality of married clergy. Although more and more of the laity were willing to tolerate illicit relationships between priests and concubines in the late Middle Ages, and were even willing to help pay the fee to legitimize a poor parish priest's children, the actual marriage of priests undoubtedly created confusion, and perhaps even anxiety, among many of the laity. Whatever the sexual irregularities celibacy might produce, it indicated a unique sacred status. A married priest was just like another neighbor, and the parishioners lost confidence that he was in more of a position to intercede on their behalf with God than anyone else. The reformers, of course, might say that the priest isn't supposed to be in a position to intercede more than anyone else; everyone must stand before God on the basis of his or her own faith. Yet it is noteworthy that King Henry VIII of England, even after his break with the papacy, his introduction of reforms in the church, and his own multiple marriages, still required clerical celibacy. The fact that Protestant preachers railed against celibacy for several generations, even when they were all married, suggests that the idea of a married clergy was not sitting well with all the laity.[12]

Luther not only encouraged monks and nuns and priests to marry, but he criticized church law for preventing many potential marriages by defining so many impediments to marriage within a broad spectrum of biological, legal, and spiritual relationships. As he noted in *The Babylonian Captivity of the Church* (1520), the church normally required a dispensation for a marriage to occur between couples who were related by blood or marriage, as distant as third cousins. "Spiritual affinity" prevented the marriage of a godparent to a godchild and to all the siblings of the godchild. Adoption also produced an impediment to marriage. Nor could a Christian marry a non-Christian. Sometimes physical infirmities were deemed impediments and required dispensations by the church.[13] Luther points out that the list of prohibited marriages in Leviticus 18:6–18 includes only twelve categories. Any marriages contracted outside of those prohibitions should not be prevented by church law, for "marriage is superior to any laws."

Luther also criticized church law for encouraging immature marriages by its recognition of "secret" marriages among youth (the minimum age was twelve for girls, fourteen for boys) without the knowledge and consent of their parents and without public witnesses. In Lutheran and Reformed cities and territories, new marriage laws required both parental consent and a public witnessing of the vows before a magistrate, but preferably in the church as a public place, before the marriage could be considered legal. On the other hand, Luther strongly defended the right of young people to marry whomever they pleased. Persons arranging a marriage should consider the wishes of all family members, especially those of the putative bride or groom. A 1524 tract stated Luther's pastoral position even in its title: "Parents Should Neither Compel nor Hinder the Marriage of Their Children and Children Should Not Marry without the Consent of Their Parents." He urged youth confronted with the "outrageous injustice" of a forced marriage to turn to the magistrates for help or, if that recourse failed, to flee to another country and marry their chosen mate there.[14] Parents who find a prospective marriage objectionable should go along with it if their arguments against it fail and let their obstinate children learn by experience the wisdom of their parents.[15]

Luther regarded marriage as a "worldly estate," although instituted by God, rather than a sacrament of Christ. As such, it could and should be regulated by the state. Marriages contracted before a civil magistrate were as valid as those contracted before a priest in the church. However, the idea of making marriage as noble an estate for Christians as the monastic profession, along with the desire to exercise pastoral care in marriage, led Luther to recommend that it be celebrated in a church.

Luther revised the rite of marriage accordingly. As he looked at the variety of marriage rites in use in Christendom, he was led to say in the preface to his 1529 *Order of Marriage for Common Pastors*, "Many lands, many customs."[16] He understood that marriage rites varied greatly from one district to another. He was disposed to leave unchanged the customs of various places, as long as common prayer and God's blessing were prominent, "but not tomfoolery or pagan spectacle." Luther left intact the customs of publishing the banns in the Sunday service before the wedding. He also retained the statement of intention and exchange of rings at the church door, with the pronouncement "What God has joined together, let not man put asunder" (Matthew 19:6) and the announcement of the marriage. Then the couple moved to the altar, not for the nuptial mass, but for Scripture reading (Genesis 2:18, 21–24, and a catena of other passages woven into an address to the bride and groom) and prayer.[17] The nuptial mass fell into the category of a votive mass, and votive masses (masses offered for special intentions) had been abolished. Martin Bucer of Strassburg, however, found a way to retain the communion of the bride and groom by having the marriage rite take place at the Sunday morning service of Holy Communion.

Reformed orders of marriage generally followed Luther's, although we note several differences. Calvin's marriage rite for Geneva presupposes reforms that had already been undertaken by Farel. Weddings took place on Sunday, unless it was one of the four Sundays during the year when the Lord's Supper was celebrated. Calvin would not even open up the possibility of the old concept of the votive mass being retained. Calvin's order used far more words of instruction and admonition than Luther's; it used Matthew 19 rather than Genesis 2 as a primary reading; and the distinction between the church door and the chancel was not retained. One other critical item that was missing was the exchange of wedding rings.[18] Luther's order did not include a blessing of the rings, but it did provide for the exchange of rings. This omission of any reference to rings in Calvin's order may have been a means of curbing the superstitions that had come to be associated with the ring in the late Middle Ages, especially regarding fertility. Edward Muir reports that among several remedies for impotence was the man urinating through his wife's wedding ring. If that also failed, however, he should "piss through the keyhole of the church in which he was married."[19] Reformed rites would not allow for the blessing of inanimate objects, nor for the blessing of the marriage bed.

We should note that Calvin was the lawyer among the major reformers and was more interested in revising the marriage laws than some of the other reformers had been. In the Geneva Marriage Ordinance of

1545, previous ecclesiastical and civil laws were merged into one system. Marriage was regulated jointly by the civil magistracy, which granted the betrothal license, and the church consistory, which approved the wedding ceremony. Sexual intercourse before marriage was forbidden in Geneva; therefore, the time between betrothal and the wedding ceremony should be as short as possible (three to six weeks). Cohabitation before the wedding was also banned in Geneva, and pregnant brides had to wear a veil as a sign of shame. The adorning of the bride's hair was discouraged. Rowdy celebrations were discouraged. Dancing and lewd songs were punishable, although they undoubtedly went on behind closed doors.[20]

Catholic Regulation of Marriage

The problem of the clandestine marriages of youth contributed to the Protestant solution of not only requiring parental consent but also celebrating the marriage publicly in the church. This same problem contributed to a similar Catholic solution. The bishops who assembled at the Council of Trent in 1563 faced a dilemma when they considered marriage doctrine and practice. They had to respond to Luther theologically, since he had denied the sacramental character of marriage and had drastically reduced the number of impediments to marriage. But Catholic parents, especially in France, were running to the Protestants in droves because they agreed that youth should not be contracting marriage without parental consent. Some bishops, especially from France and Spain, argued that the church should declare clandestine marriages invalid; a smaller number, mostly Italian, supported by the papacy, defended the traditional theology of marriage. The compromise seemed to be to increase the age at which marriage without parental consent was legal. The Italians argued for age eighteen for women, age twenty for men. The French wanted a higher age, such as age twenty-five for women and age thirty for men. But this still left unanswered the question of what to do about the secret marriages of those who were older but for whom parental consent and social rites were lacking. The council was hopelessly deadlocked.

Finally, the papal legate, Cardinal Morone, came up with a proposal that deserves a place of special recognition in the history of chairing meetings. He proposed that clandestine marriages be declared invalid, but that the definition of clandestinity be changed. "Clandestine marriages" were to be those contracted outside the church. In the future, all marriages were to be contracted in the church, before the parish priest and witnesses, after the publication of three banns. All other marriages, even if contracted before a priest, were to be considered null and void. Moreover, couples were encouraged, though not required, to wait to fulfill conjugal relations until after the marriage had been blessed at a nuptial mass. This proposal was decreed by the Council of Trent as the only way to break through the impasse created by the pastoral issue of how to deal with clandestine marriages. This decree had the effect of sweeping away a theology of marriage that the church had held for a thousand years—namely, that marriage is contracted by mutual consent and fulfilled by the conjugal act. As John Bossy commented, "It transformed marriage from a social process which the Church guaranteed to an ecclesiastical process which it administered."[21]

It is difficult to understate the radical assault on the contractual traditions of kinship morality undertaken by the Council of Trent in its insistence that marriages be performed before the parish priest in the parish church, that there could be individual liberty in the choice of partners since free consent was required of both marriage partners, and in declaring clandestine marriages undertaken by minors to be valid, although illegal.[22] The council also removed many of the impediments to marriage growing out of blood relationships but reinforced the impediment of spiritual relationships (e.g., sponsors of baptism or confirmation could not marry their candidate). The parish pastor was required to determine whether the couple freely consented to the marriage and whether any impediments were present. In addition, the parish was now required to keep registers of marriages and baptisms performed in the parish; the two lists were necessary in order to check on spiritual relationships. In a separate action, the council also imposed requirements of training, behavior, and age on godparents, and reduced the number of baptismal sponsors to one or one of each sex. It took more than a century for the Tridentine decrees concerning marriage and baptismal sponsorship to be implemented in many parts of the Catholic world, since families resisted this ecclesiastical assault on their centuries-old privileges of arranging the marriages of their children and choosing their children's godparents.

Marriage Celebrated in the Church Building

The ritual implications of the decrees on marriage became evident in the revised *Rituale Romanus* of 1614, which swept aside centuries of tradition throughout Europe by moving the marriage rite from the church door to before the altar, where there would be no question that marriage was a sacramental act that needed to be solemnized by the parish priest. This ritual change was resisted by secular governments, civil officials, and clergy loyal to local rites (such as the Gallican Rite) throughout the seventeenth century. Ironically, the new Roman Ritual bore a resemblance to the Anglican *Book of Common Prayer*, which had also enhanced the role of the parish priest and abolished the location of the marriage rite at the church door. Instead, a rubric in the 1549 prayer book says, "The persones to be maried shal come into the bodie of ye churche, with their frendes and neighbours."[23] This rubric is unchanged in the 1552 prayer book.

The ritual importance of this change is that marriage lost its liminal or threshold character betwixt and between the sacred and the profane.[24] It became totally a sacred rite. By contrast, the Reformed churches were guided by the idea that marriage is a civil contract, not a sacrament, and could be celebrated anywhere. But since the church building also served as the community meetinghouse and was not regarded as a sacred place, most Reformed marriages were also celebrated in the church building. Only Lutheranism, for a time, continued to recognize the liminal betwixt-and-between character of marriage as symbolized by its solemnization at the church door but its blessing at the altar and its dual character as a social arrangement instituted by God, a civil contract placed under the word of God.

CHAPTER 14

Liturgy and Confessional Identity

The liturgical reforms of the Reformation were part and parcel of the reforms in doctrine and life. Before the modern age, with its divisions of life between public and private and its promotion of individual self-actualization through a series of social choices (including choice of creed and worship), life was conceived as a unified whole. Liturgy was not only the public arena of encounter between God and God's people in proclamation and prayer, it also established in the hearts and minds of the faithful the beliefs of the church. Reforms of the liturgy among Lutherans, Anabaptists, the Reformed, Anglicans, and Roman Catholics (somewhat in that chronological order) served the interests of doctrine. For example, one could not believe in the sole mediating role of Christ with God the Father and also invoke the aid of the saints. One could not emphasize the Eucharist as Christ's gift of communion and also emphasize the Eucharist as a sacrifice offered by the church, especially for special intentions in votive masses. But not only did liturgy correlate with doctrine, it formed one in the faith. It made a difference whether altars on which the sacrifice of the Mass had been offered remained intact or were replaced with communion tables.[1] It made a difference whether the pastor elevated the bread or broke it. The elevation reinforced a belief in the real presence; the breaking of bread reinforced the idea of Holy Communion as the expression of the church's fellowship.

These liturgical practices became concrete ways in which ordinary lay people could distinguish between confessions, especially between Lutherans and Reformed. If the subtleties of eucharistic debate eluded ordinary worshipers, they knew whether the officiating pastor was Lutheran or Reformed depending on whether he elevated the host and chalice or broke the bread.

Worshipers were not above reacting immediately and violently if the wrong ceremony was used, perhaps by grabbing the cleric and escorting him unceremoniously out of the church. Iconoclastic efforts on the part of Reformed princes and pastors in Lutheran lands also stirred the people to civil unrest. The worst outbreak of mob action occurred in Berlin in 1614, when the Calvinist margrave Johann Sigismund ordered the removal of all crucifixes, pictures, altars, and the baptismal font from the cathedral two weeks before Easter. On Palm Sunday at the early service, the Reformed preacher celebrated the cleansing of the house of God of all leftover papal idolatry. At the noon service, the Lutheran preacher mounted the pulpit and castigated what had been done, stirring up the congregation into a frenzy that spilled into the streets and required all the margrave's efforts throughout Holy Week to restore order.[2]

If we, in the ecumenical conversations of the late twentieth century, have come to see that some of these positions need not be mutually exclusive, that was not so apparent in the battle over confessions in the sixteenth century. The Reformation period understood completely the patristic statement that "the law of prayer should constitute the law of belief" (*Lex orandi, lex credendi*).

Lex Orandi, Lex Credendi

The axiom *Lex orandi, lex credendi* was formulated in the fifth century by the lay monk Prosper of Aquitaine, a disciple of Augustine of Hippo, in his now-famous clause *ut legem credendi lex statuat supplicandi* ("so that the law of prayer may establish a law for belief").[3] By use of this principle, Prosper sought to "prove" the need for the "grace of Christ" against the Semipelagians by appealing to the intercessory prayers of the church (actually the bidding prayer in the Roman Good Friday liturgy). He argued that such a prayer shows we are utterly dependent on the grace of God to accomplish that for which we pray, since we are impotent to accomplish by our power the things we petition in prayer. In using this kind of argument, Prosper was following his mentor, Augustine, who argued the case for the doctrine of original sin against the Donatists on the basis of the fact that infants are exorcized before baptism, which implies that they are in the power of the devil, and that infants are baptized, which implies that they are born in sin that must be forgiven.[4] This appeal to liturgy to "prove" doctrine, usually in controversy with heresies, is but the polemical use of a methodology used by the ancient fathers that also served irenic purposes. In their mystagogical homilies, ancient bishops explained the meanings of the sacraments to the newly baptized during the week after Easter. These homilies explicated the sacramental rites of Christian initiation that the neophytes had just experienced. These homilies are the primary sources of the sacramental theology of the church fathers.

It has also been pointed out that there are examples of doctrinal influence on liturgical development in the ancient church, so that what was done in the Reformation was not a total reversal of procedure. In some cases there was a give-and-take between liturgy and belief that resulted in subtle influences of one on the other. For example, Irenaeus turned to the earthly elements of the Eucharist in his polemics against the Gnostics for "proof" concerning the doctrines of the goodness of creation, of the incarnation, and of the resurrection of the body.[5] This was a typical appeal to the *lex orandi*. But as Josef Jungmann pointed out,[6] Irenaeus's discussion of the Eucharist as "our oblation to God," the offering of the "first fruits" of God's own creatures to God, probably contributed to the development of the offertory procession (i.e., bringing the offerings of bread and wine to the altar). Or again, the "recapitulatory" use of creeds in the liturgy may also be taken as an example of doctrinal influence on the liturgy. Yet we know that baptismal confessions of faith used in local churches served as the basis of the text of the creed that was approved by the Council of Nicaea in 325.[7] The Nicene-Constantinopolitan Creed was first introduced into the Eucharist in Constantinople during the patriarchate of Timothy (511–517) as a way of disavowing accusations of Monophysite tendencies.[8] It was thus first used regularly in the liturgy by those who needed to show their loyalty to the doctrinal decisions of the early ecumenical councils. The original anti-Arian thrust of the creed was employed in the West when it was added to the Eucharist in Visigothic Spain to mark the conversion of King Reccared from Arianism to Catholicism in 589. The Council of Toledo in that year decreed that the Nicene Creed should be recited by the people at every mass, a decision perhaps influenced by the Byzantine model. Jungmann also demonstrated how anti-Arian concerns led to the expansion of the conclusions of prayers in both the East and the West to show the coequality of the persons of the Godhead in response to Arian appeals to the termination of prayers "through Jesus Christ our Lord" as proof of the Son's subordination to the Father.[9] To this ancient appeal to the mediatorship of Jesus Christ was added "who lives and reigns with you and the Holy Spirit, one God, world without end." Thus, theological concerns influenced the actual texts of prayers.

Since liturgy involves actions as well as words, ceremonies were sometimes added to the liturgy to reinforce doctrine. The dogma of transubstantiation was promulgated at the Fourth Lateran Council in 1215 to resolve three centuries of eucharistic controversy in the Western church. This dogmatic decision had the effect of promoting practices of adoration such as kneeling at the sound of the Sanctus bells and elevating the host after the recitation of the *Verba consecrationis* (the words of institution).[10] Yet behind both the dogma of transubstantiation and the practices of eucharistic adoration lies the Western liturgical tradition of placing Christ's words of institution in the center of the eucharistic canon, and the corresponding lack of any comparable consecratory formula such as an epiclesis of the Holy Spirit. Thus, we again see a give-and-take in the mutual influences of liturgy and doctrine, practice and profession.

But the axiom *Lex orandi, lex credendi* is not just about the influence of liturgy on doctrine or of doctrine on liturgy.[11] As Aidan Kavanagh points out, if the issue of the relationship between the *lex orandi* and the *lex credendi* turns on the matter of "influence," then the debate becomes a tug-of-war over whether liturgy should exercise control over doctrine or doctrine should exercise control over liturgy. This is not what the relationship between the *lex orandi* and the *lex credendi* is all about. When Prosper said, "Let the law of prayer *establish* the law of belief," he wasn't dealing with the question of influence but of primacy. Prayer is a primary theological activity because it enacts one's faith relationship with God, whereas doctrinal formulations are a secondary theological reflection on the experience of the encounter with God. The idea that prayer should establish belief suggests that doctrine should be a reflection on the faith relationship with God formed in Word and Sacrament and nurtured in prayer and fellowship.

The reciprocal relationship between liturgy and doctrine certainly became a crucial concern in the Reformation of the Western church. While it may seem that the Protestant reformers especially were interested in doctrinal control over the liturgy, it was actually more the case that the reformers were concerned that both liturgy and doctrine should express the relationship with God that was being newly experienced and expressed as a result of fresh interpretations of Holy Scripture. New exegetical insight led both to liturgical revision in the early 1520s and to the proposed doctrine of justification by faith through grace for Christ's sake set forth preeminently in Article IV of the Augsburg Confession (1530). The experience of encounter with a gracious God who makes promises to his elect people had its liturgical corollary in an emphasis on what we receive from God and a de-emphasis on what we offer to God.

This new emphasis did not always require changing liturgical texts or practices. Lutherans especially advocated a conservative reform, relying on preaching and teaching to point out an evangelical use of traditional forms and ceremonies. The Reformed, on the other hand, felt that it was necessary to eliminate many inherited texts and practices; but even they appealed to patristic as well as apostolic example. Only the radical Reformation tried to repristinate the New Testament church and its worship. The Council of Trent retained much of the medieval liturgy. Yet even Roman Catholic liturgical reform produced profound changes in, for example, church architecture, which affected the ordinary Catholic's experience of God in worship.[12]

None of these efforts need be viewed just as an assertion of doctrinal control over the liturgy. Roman Catholicism, in particular, has appealed to the liturgical and devotional basis of doctrine. But Luther, too, could appeal to the core elements in the *Ordo missae* (Order of Mass) and write,

> In these various parts you find nothing about a sacrifice but only praise and thanks. Therefore, we have also kept them in our mass. Particularly the Agnus Dei, above all songs, serves well for the sacrament, for it clearly sings about and praises Christ for having borne our sins and in beautiful, brief words powerfully and sweetly teaches the remembrance of Christ.[13]

A primary aspect of Reformed eucharistic theology was based on the *Sursum corda*—lifting up our hearts on high, seeking heavenly things, where Jesus Christ is seated at the right hand of the Father, rather than fixing our eyes on visible signs that are corrupted through usage.[14] Liturgical reforms can thus be viewed as a way of reestablishing the correlation of liturgy and doctrine as corrected expressions of the faith relationship between God and the believing community.

Liturgy and Confessionalization

The Reformation fractured the body of Christ in the Western church. The result was a multitude of confessions to which princes and their people adhered in the various lands of Europe. The later British and American system of denominationalism was unknown in Reformation Europe. There was one established church or "confession" in each country or territory. But in the schism within the body of Christianity caused by the Reformation, adhering to a particular confession of faith became a self-conscious social act.

Wolfgang Reinhard delineated seven marks of confessional identity: (1) the elaboration of clear theological positions; (2) their promulgation and implementation through synods and visitations; (3) their internalization through schools and seminaries or universities; (4) the use of the printing press to propagate doctrine and censorship to hinder the propagation of the doctrines of other confessions; (5) the development of disciplinary measures through visitations, consistories, and excommunication; (6) the control of the nature of and access to liturgical rites; and (7) the development of confessional languages.[15] Heinz Schilling and R. Po-Chia Hsia have distinguished between confessionalism, or the development of confessions, and confessionalization—the role played by the confessions in society.[16] Reinhard argued that confessionalization contributed to Western individualism, rationalism, social discipline, and bureaucracy. But it was also a move beyond ethnocentricism, since people identified with their confessional brethren in other countries. This is why German historian Ernest Walter Zeeden saw in confessionalization a decisive step in the development of modern Europe.[17] Catholics, Lutherans, and Calvinists felt a bond of unity with brothers and sisters in the faith in other countries and languages beyond their own.

Minority Confessions

This last consideration reminds us that it would be a misconception to think that confessional identities were limited to territories in which those confessions were legally embraced and enforced. Religious minorities could be found in most countries; sometimes they were persecuted, but just as often they were allowed to live in peace. Where they were persecuted, their plight aroused the sympathy, and sometimes the intervention, of confessional brethren in other places, if and when this was feasible. Minority confessions included the Reformed Huguenots scattered throughout the cities and towns of France and Lutherans in Austria. But in some territories, there were also religious majorities living under rulers who did not share their confessions. Greek Orthodoxy existed under Turkish Muslim rule, sometimes even as a majority of the population, as in Greece. Lutherans in Poland were mostly found in Silesia, where they were the majority in some districts. The majority of the Irish remained Catholic even under the supremacy of Protestant English monarchs over the Church of Ireland. The majority of Brandenburgers remained Lutheran when the elector Johann Sigismund officially embraced Calvinism in 1613 and expressed it in his *Confessio Sigismundi*. In all these cases, liturgy as well as confessions of faith became marks of identity for confessional communities.

Suppressed Majorities: Ireland and Brandenburg

In Ireland this was expressed not just in terms of books and texts, but also in the *ways* in which books and texts were used. The majority of the Irish failed to become Protestant even though they were ruled by English Protestant monarchs. The Irish Act of Uniformity in 1560 had to bow to the reality of the lack of a Gaelic prayer book and a Gaelic translation of the Bible and provided that ministers ignorant of English could use the more conservative Latin version of the *Book of Common Prayer* that had been prepared for the universities in England.[18] The Latin prayer book provided for reservation of the sacrament for the sick and a requiem Eucharist, as in the 1549 prayer book. With lax enforcement of uniformity, many Irish priests "counterfeited the Mass" to conceal from their congregations the full extent of the reforms officially required. Thus, the Protestant prayer book was used to preserve Catholic identity until newly trained Catholic priests could return from studies in Louvain to hold clandestine Catholic masses in Ireland.[19]

In Brandenburg, the conservative liturgical reforms sought by Elector Joachim II in the Mark Brandenburg Church Order (1540) were embraced by the people as marks of authentic Lutheranism against the Calvinism of later electors. Johann Sigismund and his successors, Reformed ministers at the Potsdam court of Margrave, sought to eradicate from the hearts and minds of the people "the childish superstition" that Christ's true body and blood were in the bread and wine by eliminating communion wafers, altars, candles, mass vestments, and copes, as well as the practices of singing the words of institution while facing the altar and genuflecting at the altar. The Lutherans therefore clung to these uses all the more assiduously.[20] The elevation of the eucharistic bread became even more dramatically an act of ostension, sometimes with the addition of words such as "See, dear Christians, this is the true body of Christ given for us, and this the true blood of Christ shed for us."[21] The Reformed, on the other hand, insisted on the ceremonial breaking of the bread (*fractio panis*) to signify the absence of a newly created Christ in the bread. Any minister who broke the bread at the altar could easily be identified as Reformed by the congregation. So the very act of breaking the bread at the communion could provoke a riot. In some places, the people publicly ridiculed the Reformed by spreading their coats on the street and reenacting the breaking of bread on them.[22] Ritual thus served as a sign of confessional identity.

Confessional Enforcement of Liturgy in England and Scandinavia

Liturgy was used by the reformers to promote the reform of doctrine, worship, and Christian life. But what could be accomplished quickly in German imperial cities or Swiss cantons or small German principalities took much longer in far-flung kingdoms. In England the Act of Uniformity in 1549 imposed a single vernacular prayer book on a realm where heretofore five different Latin rites had been in use. The prayer book and its attendant ceremonies were widely accepted in London and southeast England, but rebellion broke out in Devon and Cornwall, where the people did not speak "the king's English." These rebels also wanted a restoration of the old ceremonies and customs that had been abolished in the Injunctions of 1547.[23] Besides this rocky beginning came the vicissitudes of changing religious policy in the succession of the reigns of Edward VI (the 1549 *Book of Common Prayer* was authorized, and then a more Reformed prayer book was authorized in 1552), Mary I (the prayer book was abolished, and the Roman Rite restored), and Elizabeth I (the 1552 prayer book was restored with a few amendments and authorized by an Act of Uniformity in 1559). Despite this, the *Book of Common Prayer* gained a broad acceptance among the English people. Ironically, this was because many of the exiles who returned to England after the death of Mary I found the restored prayer book of 1559 still too unreformed after their experiences in Geneva, Frankfurt, and other centers of the Reformed confession. Their opposition to its provisions helped the *Book of Common Prayer* to gain more widespread acceptance in the 1570s and 1580s. As Eamon Duffy commented, "The prayer-book itself, from a weapon to break down the structures of traditional religion, became in many places their last redoubt. As the godly [i.e., the Puritans] came to see in the prayer-book, with its saints' days, its kneeling, its litany, its prescribed fasts, its signing with the Cross, little else but the rags of popery, and sought their abandonment, so adherence to the prayer-book became one way of preserving such observances."[24]

In the countries that embraced Lutheranism, implementing evangelical liturgical orders was a slow process for two reasons: first, the books and materials needed for such an order were not all produced at once, and second, Reformation ideas spread by German merchants in the 1520s primarily in the port cities of Riga, Stockholm, Malmö, Copenhagen, and Bergen did not affect people in the hinterland or in fishing villages along the coasts. The very slowness in spreading evangelical liturgical orders elsewhere may have influenced the English reformers to include all basic liturgical orders and propers in one vernacular prayer book. But as in western and northern England, resistance to liturgical revision was especially strong in the more remote regions of Norway and Sweden.

In Denmark, the Catholic ecclesiastical order was abolished by King Christian III in one fell swoop in 1536. A new church order was prepared and was sent to Wittenberg for Martin Luther's advice and consent. In 1537, the elector of Saxony sent Johannes Bugenhagen to Copenhagen, at King Christian's request, to assist in the final version of the *Danish Church Order*. Bugenhagen had already assisted in the preparation of several church orders for north German cities and territories. The Danish Church Order was implemented in 1537 with the celebration of a Danish mass and the consecration of seven new bishops or superintendents for Denmark and Norway. The church order was approved by the Diet in 1539 and translated into Danish in 1542. This church order allowed considerable flexibility to local pastors, since the order of the Mass was not complete in all its details. In typical Lutheran fashion, priests had to consult other books—in some cases pre-Reformation missals, in other cases new evangelical handbooks and hymnals as these appeared—to supply texts of prayers and music to fill out the order prescribed in the church order. Printed editions of the *Danish Altar Book*, such as Peder Palladius's edition of 1555, also gave further rubrics and texts. Thus, in the first few decades of the Reformation, parish priests in Denmark could introduce change at a pace the people could tolerate.

In Norway King Christian III urged church leaders to go slow in implementing the church order, since the country was largely unprepared for change, most parishes continued to be served by pre-Reformation Catholic priests, and in any event, the Bible, liturgical material, and a catechism had yet to appear in the Norwegian language. Even so, as a fully provisioned Norwegian liturgy became possible and as the merchant class, especially in the trading ports, embraced "the new religion," peasants often remained largely Catholic in their piety as well as in their spiritual practices for decades and even centuries, even though they had to suffer serious persecution as a result.[25]

In Iceland, which was also under Danish administration, the *Danish Church Order* met with outright resistance from the two most powerful men in the country, Ögmundur Palsson, the bishop of Skálholt, and Jon Arason, the bishop of Hólar. In 1539, a young new bishop, Gizur Einarsson, was appointed by King Christian III to succeed the old and blind Bishop Palsson in the diocese of Skálholt. Einarsson was among a group of young men in Skálholt who had secretly studied Lutheran teachings. Another of these young men, Oddur Gottskálksson, had also secretly translated the New Testament into Icelandic. But when young Bishop Einarsson failed to get the church order adopted, as he had promised, the king sent an army to Iceland in 1541 to force the situation. Shortly thereafter, the Diocese of Skálholt adopted the church order, and Bishop Einarsson was then consecrated in Copenhagen. But he still encountered opposition and died at the age of forty in 1548. The majority in the cathedral chapter supported a Catholic candidate for bishop, but the king appointed the Lutheran candidate, Marteinn Einarsson. When the new Bishop Einarsson returned to Iceland, he was captured by Bishop Arason, who also tried to seize Skálholt by force but failed. In November 1550, Arason was defeated, captured, and beheaded along with two of his sons. This ended official resistance to the Reformation in Iceland. But the degree of the immediate acceptance of or continuing resistance to the Reformation among the people has yet to be told. The Reformation could not be implemented until all the books needed in an evangelical church could be printed. A complete Icelandic translation of the Bible was published in 1584, an Icelandic hymnal was printed in 1589, and an Icelandic ritual book, or *Graduale*, was promulgated in 1594, all under the direction of Bishop Gudbrandur Thorláksson in Hólar.

Only when all of these resources were available could a truly evangelical liturgy be celebrated and the evangelical faith take root among the people.[26] Yet even though the *Graduale*, entitled *Ein Almeneleg Messusöngsbók*, provided the musical traditions of both the German mass and the traditional plainsong setting, including the provision of Latin introits and parts of the ordinary,[27] still people stayed away from church because they objected to the changes. Icelandic pastors tell of families who thought it was politically wise to send representatives of the family to Sunday services. When these delegates returned home, the rest of the family inquired, "What did the priest say today?" This inquiry was made more out of suspicion of change than out of pious interest.

A Gradual Approach: Sweden and the Baltic Countries

In Sweden, the reformer Olavus Petri, who had been a student at Wittenberg in 1516–1518, prepared a translation of the New Testament, a catechism, and a *Swedish Manual* and *Swedish Mass* between 1526 and 1531. But the *Swedish Mass* was authorized only for use in Stockholm. This was a 1530 decision of the city council, on which Olavus Petri served as secretary. But King Gustav I Vasa, who understood the conservative attitude of his subjects, refused to authorize it for use throughout the kingdom. Even when a synod in Uppsala approved the use of the Swedish Mass throughout the realm in 1536, each municipality and parish was free to embrace the Swedish Mass or continue the use of the Latin Mass.

Christer Pahlmblad has searched parish records to find evidence of the introduction of the Swedish Mass. Two such instances are telling: the Mass was celebrated in Swedish for the first time in Skellefteå, a town on the coast some three hundred kilometers north of Stockholm, on Christmas Day in 1536, "but it was not welcomed," and in the parish church of Umeå in the same vicinity for the first time on Candlemas in 1537, where the reaction was the same. In both parishes, the Latin Mass continued along with the Swedish Mass into the 1540s.[28] Over a period of years between 1535 and 1571, Archbishop Laurentius Petri merged the Swedish Low Mass with the Latin High Mass, so that by the time his church order was promulgated in 1571 under the authority of King Johan III, this evangelical form of the Mass had gained widespread acceptance. In typical Lutheran fashion, however, Latin elements in the Mass were not entirely abandoned but could be permissively used.[29]

Lutheranism entered Latvia and Estonia (Livonia) already in the early 1520s and made much more headway in Livonia than in Poland or Lithuania. At first Lutheran teaching, presented in a radical form by Melchior Hoffman, was accompanied by the iconoclastic destruction of liturgical art and the plundering of churches and monasteries. It was in the interest of the Order of Teutonic Knights, who constituted the ruling class, and the town councils to maintain order so as to keep the Russians or Poles from overrunning the country. City councils took over the supervision of the progress of the Reformation in Riga and Tallinn.[30] A church order was prepared in 1529 by Johann Briessmann (1488–1549), a disciple of Luther and the reformer of Königsberg, who was called as preacher at the cathedral in Riga in 1527. Briessmann's order embodied elements of the church order of Königsberg, which Briessmann had helped to prepare. It was more widely implemented in other towns in 1533. In spite of the radical beginnings of the Reformation in Livonia, the Riga church order had a conservative character. Many pre-Reformation practices were left untouched.[31] It was written in German; the record of the Reformation in Latvian and Estonian is practically nonexistent. But churches were turned over to the indigenous people for evangelical services held in Latvian and Estonian. The fact that Dominicans preached against the Reformation in both Estonian and German indicates that Reformation ideas were being spread among the indigenous people, and in the countryside as well as in the towns. Even so, the social improvements experienced in other countries that adopted the Reformation were not felt among the indigenous peoples of Livonia; the ruling class kept their hold on power.[32] Even residual elements of Catholic church life, including functioning monasteries, remained intact until the country was occupied by Sweden in 1565.

The Counter-Reformation: The Case of Poland

The Council of Trent had to react to the proliferation of Protestant church orders and also respond to the need for liturgical reform. The council fathers entrusted the revision of the missal and breviary to the pope, and the Roman Curia imposed the use of the Diocese of Rome on the whole Catholic Church in communion with the bishop of Rome by making the Breviary and Missal of Pope Pius V the standard for every church. But the use of the *Roman Breviary* of 1568 and the *Roman Missal* of 1570 was not required in dioceses whose liturgical rites were more than two hundred years old. In Italy, Spain, Germany, Belgium, and France, a number of major dioceses took advantage of this exception; they included Milan, Toledo, Braga, Trier, Cologne, Liège, Lyons, and many French dioceses that claimed the use of the Gallican Rite.[33] The dioceses of central Italy in the Papal States were used to the Roman Rite, but we may conclude that much of the rest of Catholic Europe was unaffected by post-Tridentine liturgical changes.[34]

Poland, in contrast, represents an interesting case of the gradual implementation of the Counter-Reformation to regain Catholic control over the combined Kingdom of Poland–Grand Duchy of Lithuania. In the sixteenth century, this vast region included a substantial non-Christian minority of Jews and Tartar Muslims. Also, Lutheranism took hold in Silesia, in the port cities, and in the Duchy of East Prussia (ruled by the House of Hohenzollern as vassals, in this instance, to the King of Poland), where German was spoken. Many of the Polish nobility embraced Calvinism because of Calvin's emphasis on the governing role of the lay elder and because the French reformer represented an alternative for those who held the Germans in antipathy. A sizable group of the Bohemian Brethren also sought refuge in Poland, where religious toleration was a matter of law (the *Pacta conventa*). These three Protestant groups banded together in the *Consensus Sendomiriensis* of 1570 to protect themselves against possible Catholic repression (up to one-sixth of the parishes were held by Protestants), to strengthen the Protestant position in the Diet (Protestants held a majority of the seats), and to promote mutual understanding.[35]

The spirit of Renaissance humanism was a powerful influence on Poland, including the Catholic majority. Desiderius Erasmus was able to say, "Poland is devoted to me." This influence can be seen in the development of Polish literature and in new church architecture, which reflected the neoclassical buildings being erected in Renaissance Rome, such as the Jesuit Church of the Gesù. But a different spirit was introduced with the election of Sigismund III Vasa as king in 1587. Sigismund was the son of King Johan III of Sweden and Queen Katherina Jagellonica and the nephew of King Sigismund II Augustus.

He had been raised as a Catholic in the humanistic Lutheran court of his father and was heir to the throne of Poland. It was his great desire to return Sweden to the Catholic fold, and to this end he amassed an army of Jesuits in Poland to implement not just a Catholic Reformation but the Counter-Reformation. Sigismund succeeded his father as king of Sweden in 1593, but in anticipation of his arrival, the Swedish Church and Estates adopted the Augsburg Confession and restricted non-Lutheran worship in the country to Sigismund's court. A headstrong Vasa, Sigismund would not abide by the conditions of the Accession Charter, left for Poland after his coronation, and returned to Sweden in 1596 with troops to secure his position. After being defeated in a brief civil war led by his uncle, Duke Karl (later King Karl IX), Sigismund lost the Swedish crown in 1599, but he always harbored the hope of recovering this kingdom for the Catholic Church. He also lost Polish territory to Czar Ivan IV ("the Terrible") and to his cousin, King Gustav II Adolf of Sweden, who turned the Baltic Sea into a Swedish lake.[36]

In the meantime, there were more than four hundred and fifty Jesuits in Poland in about 1600, and the most powerful Catholic preacher of the age, the Jesuit Piotr Skarga (1536–1612), was the chaplain to Sigismund's court. Not only had King Sigismund III, in effect, repudiated the oath of toleration he took at his coronation, but also the Protestants continued to be plagued with conflicts and divisions, and the Polish bishop Stanislaw Cardinal Hosius (1505–1579), who had presided as one of five presidents over the last session of the Council of Trent, implemented a series of aggressive reforms in his diocese of Warmia (Ermeland), which modeled a renewed Catholicism. Therefore, the *Confessio fidei catholicae christiana* (Confession of faith of Catholic Christianity) became well established in Poland by the beginning of the seventeenth century.[37]

Thus Poland, a center of Catholic renewal in the early sixteenth century, became a bastion of the Counter-Reformation by the end of the sixteenth century. The liturgical books of the *Roman Breviary* (1568), *Roman Missal* (1570), and *Roman Ritual* (1614) were established as the liturgical counterpart of this confession of faith, making due allowances for local popular customs. These books were well established in Poland as the liturgical expression of the Counter-Reformation. The same situation pertained in Lithuania, since there were no liturgical uses more than two hundred years old. Lithuania's conversion from paganism had been as recent as 1385.[38]

Liturgy, Meaning, and Belief

Liturgy has been used to promote confessional identity because liturgy encodes meaning. For this meaning to be communicated, liturgy must be performed.[39] This seems like a simple and obvious thing to say, but it should not be taken for granted, especially in our own secular age, when the temptation is to lose confidence in the liturgy because it no longer seems to be meaningful to people. But we should consider the alternative. We have records or descriptions of the rites performed in ancient Ur or Thebes. They possess only an antiquarian or anthropological interest, because they are no longer performed. They are liturgies of the dead. Liturgies are living when people inject their own living bodies into performing them. Liturgies must be done in order to be real.

In performing liturgies, the performers both transmit and receive the meaning that the liturgy encodes. That is to say, if I proclaim the gospel in the liturgy or celebrate the sacraments, I am both transmitting the message of the gospel and the sacraments and receiving the message that I proclaim and celebrate. I not only receive the message; I accept it. I cannot reject it without ceasing to perform the liturgy. This obvious truth about liturgical rites applies both to ministers and people, since both have liturgical roles in proclaiming the gospel and celebrating the sacraments. People must be present and participate in the liturgy if it is to be a living rite and communicate a meaning. But the very fact that people are present and participate in the liturgy implies an acceptance of its meaning. And the act of participating in the performance of a liturgy opens one to the possibility of being exposed to the meanings encoded in that liturgy.

Let us recognize that people do not have to accept what the liturgy means. They are usually free *not* to participate in rituals if they choose not to do so. In the modern age, with the claims that secular culture exerts on people, many people choose not to participate in the liturgy, so they avoid accepting its meaning. If enough people stay away from the church's liturgy, it will no longer be a living rite. It will be as dead as the liturgies of Zeus or Thor. Those gods are also dead because they have no worshipers. The gods need worshipers. The true God wants worshipers. That is why the God of Israel delivered his people from bondage of Egypt, so that they would be free to worship him in the desert or in the promised land (see Exodus 3:18). The servant-son of this God commissioned his disciples to round up worshipers for the true God from among all the nations.

Precisely because refusal to participate in worship is always a possibility, participation in the liturgy does imply a public acceptance of the meaning encoded by the liturgy. But public acceptance does not imply belief, since belief is an inward state that is knowable only subjectively, if at all. One usually participates in a liturgy because one believes, but participation does not imply belief; it only implies public acceptance. Inward belief cannot be outwardly observed. It is undoubtedly true that many people have participated in liturgy who have not inwardly believed what was being said or done, or have simply gone through the motions of participation without that participation affecting their everyday lives. Some people have refused to participate in liturgy because of belief—because they did not believe the meanings that a particular liturgy communicated. This has often been done at great personal cost if one was avoiding a liturgy in which public participation was legally required. People have been jailed, fined, and even executed for avoiding participation in liturgies with whose doctrinal content they disagreed.

Liturgy can survive for a long time just on public acceptance. But a liturgical order that is not supported by the inner convictions of at least a core of its devotees is in danger of falling into desuetude, of sooner or later becoming a dead letter. Gaining public acceptance of its confessions was sufficient as the first task of the Reformation. This was accomplished by means of liturgical promulgation of official church orders. But a second step was needed to bring people to the point of inner conviction. This was accomplished through preaching, massive catechization, and rooting liturgy in the culture of the people, especially through use of the vernacular language. A case can be made that this was pretty much accomplished by the end of the sixteenth century. At this point, the confessional communities settled into an established orthodoxy. Orthodox Reformation liturgies, especially in the Catholic and Lutheran traditions, could be splendidly celebrated, and generally were during the Baroque period. But at the point at which even Reformation liturgy was becoming moribund, popular religion or Pietism emerged to "convert the outward orthodox confession into an inner living theology of the heart."[40]

CHAPTER 15

Popular Devotions, Pious Communities, and Holy Communion

Sometime in the seventeenth century, the modern world as we know it dawned. The *ancien régime* held out for the divine right of kings and promoted established religion, but secularization occurred in politics, education, the arts, and other aspects of social life and thought. To some degree, this can be attributed to the fragmentation of the Western church into competing churches, which inevitably undermined theological authority. The competition of confessions contributed to the fierce religious wars of the century (especially the Thirty Years' War on the continent of Europe and the English Civil War) and unprecedented persecution of religious minorities (especially the persecution of the French Huguenots when King Louis XIV revoked the Edict of Nantes). This violent competition of confessions contrasted with some degree of religious toleration toward the end of the century in places like the Netherlands, the Kingdom of Prussia, and the proprietary British colonies of Maryland and Pennsylvania in North America.

The post-Reformation period has been termed religiously the Age of Confessionalism and politically the Age of Absolutism. I termed it the Age of Certainty, after René Descartes' philosophic means of arriving at certainty by doubting everything.[1] The seventeenth century was a time when, as John Donne wrote, "New Philosophy calls all in doubt." Certainty was achieved in all areas of life by responding to the doubts that were raised concerning, for example, theological orthodoxy (note the emergence of dissenters in every tradition) and political absolutism (note the republican experiments). Expressions of theological orthodoxy and political absolutism may have been a way of protesting the doubts raised by new scientific discoveries, new political ideas, and new religious insights.

Donne's line "New Philosophy calls all in doubt" appeared in the first of two poems written to eulogize Elizabeth Drury, the daughter of Donne's patron Sir Robert Drury, on the occasion of her death at the age of fifteen. In the first anniversary poem, "An Anatomie of the World" (1611), Donne analyzed the state of the world from the standpoint of the untimely death of a young woman of noted virtue. The poem is a prime example of the *contemptus mundi* (contempt of the world) that was a feature of late medieval piety lingering into the seventeenth century. Each section of the poem ends, "Shee, shee is dead; shee's dead; when thou knowest this," followed by a statement of the world's corruption: "Thou knowest how poor a trifling thing man is . . . Thou knowest how lame a cripple this world is . . . Thou knowest how ugly a monster this world is . . . Thou knowest how wan a Ghost this our world is . . . Thou knowest how drie a Cinder this world is."[2]

John Donne the Protestant, drawing on Archbishop John Whitgift's Lambeth Article (1583) assuring eternal salvation to those who had received justifying faith, could be certain that Elizabeth Drury's soul was in heaven. But ordinary Christians did not feel such an assurance because Protestant preachers continued to threaten eternal punishments to the disbelieving and unrepentant. Threats came also from Lutheran preachers who used the law/gospel dialectic to instill fear of punishment/trust in the Savior.[3] Both Protestant and Catholic preachers read Augustine and emphasized his doctrines of original sin and human depravity. John Donne was, in fact, an avid reader of Augustine and Bernard. The English public would have been familiar with the Bernard of the *memento mori* (remembrance of death) because of the 1616 translation of "The Complaint or Dialogue, Betwixt the soul and The Bodies of a damned man" by the Puritan pastor William Crashaw, father of the poet Richard Crashaw.

Ironically, while the religious confessions claimed the absolute certainty of faith, the Reformation's assault on routine conformity to religious tradition and the Counter-Reformation's banishment of superstitious folk observances produced in many people disturbing questions related to the certainty of faith.[4] Even the Reformation's hard-won answers to the question of salvation—Lutheranism's doctrine of justification by faith alone, Calvinism's doctrine of predestination, Catholicism's affirmation of salvation by grace-inspired good works—failed to satisfy seventeenth-century spiritual yearning. Johann Arndt (1555–1621) drew sanctification into Luther's doctrine of justification; Blaise Pascal (1623–1662) championed Jansenism's neo-Augustinian predestination against Jesuitical Semipelagianism; John Bunyan's (1628–1688) pilgrim trod a perilous course through the wilderness of this world to the city of God and saw a side path to hell at the very gates of heaven. The vast Catholic literature on preparing for death also held out the possibility of failure at the end, even for believers.

In response to this uncertainty, the devout gravitated toward popular devotions and joined pious groups as ways of asserting their faith and receiving the support of fellow believers for their religious pilgrimages on earth. Popular devotions have also been called "paraliturgical devotions" to indicate that they flourish alongside of official liturgy. "Popular devotions" means that they are practiced by the people, with or without official ecclesiastical approval. "Popular" does not necessarily mean that the devotions so designated are practiced by a great majority of the people, although there certainly was widespread participation in the devotions that emerged among Catholics and Protestants. Popular devotions in the form of ritual acts were practiced by Roman Catholics. Forms of devotion practiced by Protestants included the use of hymns and metrical psalms in household devotions.

Popular Devotions

It is not possible to define popular or paraliturgical devotions as such until there is a definition of official liturgy, since "popular" or "paraliturgical" suggests that these devotions were practiced alongside or in addition to official liturgy. Paraliturgical devotions were defined as such in the Roman Catholic Church after the promulgation of official liturgical books by the Roman See following the Council of Trent.[5]

The Council of Trent had defined those issues in liturgical and sacramental practice that called for reform and renewal, but left it to the pope to supervise the revision of liturgical books. It had decreed that all local churches (dioceses) whose own liturgical usage was less than two hundred years old had to conform to the reformed Roman Rite. These exempted dioceses included Milan (Ambrosian Rite), Toledo

(Visigothic Rite), and the usages of many dioceses in France (elements of the Gallican Rite, some of which were revived so that French dioceses would not have to conform to the Roman Rite).[6] In fact, the decrees of the Council of Trent were slow to be implemented almost anywhere outside of the Papal States. The emperors in Germany and the kings of France and of Spain found the Tridentine reforms either too much of an infringement on their prerogatives or too inadequate a response to Protestant objections to Catholic practices.

Nevertheless, the Roman Curia embarked on the production of reformed liturgical books. The official books promulgated were the *Roman Breviary of Pope Pius V* (1568), the *Roman Missal of Pope Pius V* (1750), the *Roman Pontifical* (1596—a book of services led by bishops), the *Episcopal Ceremonial* (1600—a book of rubrics describing the ceremonies performed by and honors due to bishops), and the *Roman Ritual* (1614—a pastor's handbook of occasional services). As Carl Dehne has explained, "Whatever did not find a place in the books of the new worldwide Roman Rite—no matter how widely practiced in other parts of the Latin West and no matter what its propriety and utility—was considered in a legal sense non-liturgical."[7] Yet nonliturgical or, more properly, paraliturgical devotions of a popular nature flourished alongside the official liturgies of the church. These rites were paraliturgical simply because they weren't included in the official books. But many of them were sanctioned by the highest authorities in the Roman Catholic Church.

Popular devotions that were almost universally practiced by Roman Catholics throughout the centuries after the Council of Trent included penitential processions, the Rosary of the Blessed Virgin Mary, the Way of the Cross, Solemn Benediction of the Blessed Sacrament, Forty Hours Devotion and Perpetual Adoration of the Blessed Sacrament, eucharistic communion in honor of the Sacred Heart of Jesus on the first Fridays of nine consecutive months, and novenas (nine consecutive days of prayer) for various occasions or in honor of various heavenly patrons. This list is not exhaustive, but in the paragraphs that follow I will try to describe each of these and then provide an assessment of the value of paraliturgical devotions and popular religion.

Penitential Processions

Liturgical processions have been used to produce communal cohesion. The Corpus Christi procession did this in a spectacular way. Processions were also used during the sixteenth century to compensate for sacrilegious acts such as the destruction of statues of Christ or of the Virgin Mary. As early as 1528, King Francis I of France personally participated in such a procession designed to make reparation for the desecration of a statue of the Virgin Mary. Another procession in which the king participated as a penitent occurred in 1535 to make reparation for a Protestant poster that blasphemed the blessed sacrament of the altar, in which the blessed sacrament and every relic available was carried through the streets by priests and acolytes while people stood with lighted torches along the route of the procession.[8]

Toward the end of the sixteenth century, lay brothers in eucharistic confraternities mounted elaborate processions in which the eucharistic host was carried in a pyx under a canopy. But more disturbing were the confraternities of penitents who processed through the streets wearing hoods to conceal their identities while flagellating themselves. This practice, which had emerged in the fourteenth century, had died out by the sixteenth century except in a few pockets of northern Italy and southern France. By the end of the sixteenth century, it was revived throughout France and Spain. The Jesuits used this piety of suffering during their revival missions in the late sixteenth and early seventeenth centuries. At the conclusion of a mission, the men would remain inside the church building, beating themselves with iron chains while the women and children stayed outside screaming for mercy from God.[9] Holy Thursday in Spain was marked with ritual dramatizations of suffering from sunset to midnight as men and women, young and old, anticipated the passion of Christ by sharing a simple meal and then walking through the streets barefooted while flagellating themselves.

Marian Pilgrimages

Pilgrimages had long been undertaken to give thanks, express penance, or seek the intercession of a saint. They came under the scathing denunciation of the Protestant reformers and declined sharply during the early sixteenth century. But they flourished anew by the end of the sixteenth and into the seventeenth centuries. Most of the pilgrimage sites in Europe brought pilgrimages to the shrine of a saint. After the Council of Trent, the most popular pilgrimage sites were those devoted to the Virgin Mary.

In Italy, the Marian shrine at Loreto, which contained the house from Nazareth in which the Angel Gabriel had announced to the Virgin Mary that she would bear the Son of God, was revitalized in the second half of the sixteenth century. The famous composer at the court of Munich, Orlando di Lasso, wrote a setting of the Litany of Loreto in 1575, a series of invocations to Our Lady of Loreto prayed every Saturday at the Holy House. Famous pilgrims to Loreto included Francis Xavier, Carlo Borromeo, Francis de Sales, Montaigne (who left a votive offering in 1580), Duke Maximilian of Bavaria (1593), and Emperor Ferdinand II (1598). Chapels modeled after the chapel at Loreto were replicated throughout southern Germany. The Hapsburgs constructed an imitation of the Holy House for the use of the Augustinians in Vienna.

Marian shrines were very popular with German Catholics. Duke William of Bavaria in 1579 revitalized the shrine of Our Lady of Altötting when he founded an archconfraternity whose members promised to make a pilgrimage to the site every four years. This helped to draw thousands of pilgrims to the shrine each year, and Jesuit and Franciscan houses were established at the site to minister to them.[10]

The Rosary of the Blessed Virgin Mary

Part and parcel of Marian devotion was praying the Rosary. The Rosary was a medieval devotion that gained great popularity among post-Tridentine Catholics. It combines the petition of familiar prayers almost in a mantra fashion with meditation on selected mysteries of salvation. The prayers used are fifteen "decades" (tens) of *Ave Maria* (Hail Mary), each preceded by a *Pater noster* (Our Father) and concluded by a *Gloria Patri* (Glory be to the Father). The fifteen mysteries or topics of meditation are grounded in three series of five (usually prayed separately), as follows:

- The Joyful Mysteries—annunciation, visitation, nativity, presentation, meeting in the temple

- The Sorrowful Mysteries—Jesus' agony, scourging, crowning with thorns, carrying the cross, death on the cross

- The Glorious Mysteries—Jesus' resurrection, Jesus' ascension, the descent of the Spirit, assumption of the Virgin Mary, crowning of the Virgin Mary, and glorification of all the saints

The origin of the Rosary is popularly ascribed to Dominic (d. 1221), the founder of the Dominicans. Certainly the Dominicans did the most to propagate the praying of the Rosary, but the attribution to Dominic cannot be sustained. The most that can be said is that this devotion grew out of the Marian devotions that flourished from the twelfth century on and was used both as a form of prayer and as a form of instruction by the Order of Preachers.[11] The fifteen mysteries of the Rosary seem to have been popularized in a series of woodcuts from German Dominican circles in the late fifteenth century. The mysteries constitute a comprehensive digest of the main events in salvation history and a summary of the liturgical year. A bull of Pope Pius V in 1569 confirmed the devotion, and the introduction of a Feast Day for Our Lady of the Rosary into the Roman calendar in 1573 helped to standardize its use throughout the Catholic Church.

The Way of the Cross

The Way of the Cross consists of a series of stations at which pictures or tableaux depicting scenes in the passion of Christ provide a focus for meditation. The roots of this devotion can probably be traced back to late antiquity, when Christian pilgrims to the Holy Land followed the way of the cross from the location of the site of Pilate's judgment to Calvary, and probably wanted to replicate it when they returned home. It was a devotion championed by the Franciscans, who were given custody of the holy places in Palestine in 1342. They saw it as part of their mission to promote this devotion and had tableaux erected in their own church buildings. The devotion spread rapidly to other churches. The number of stations varied widely from place to place and was finally stabilized at fourteen when the devotion was regulated by Pope Clement XII in 1731. Nine of the stations depict biblical scenes; five are legendary.[12]

The Way of the Cross has also been described as "a poor man's pilgrimage" that enabled the devout to follow the stations within or around their parish church without having to travel all the way to Jerusalem. Some stations were arrayed along the internal side walls of church buildings; others were erected outside the church building along a pathway and required traveling a little distance from one station to the next. The stations can be followed by an individual or a group, silently or with singing between stations, with or without texts.

Particular texts for use with the Way of the Cross have never been prescribed. However, an antiphon from the veneration of the cross in the Good Friday liturgy came to be used at each station, along with whatever other readings one might use: "V/ We adore your cross, O Lord, and praise your resurrection; R/ For through the cross joy has come to the whole world." This piece of solid liturgical text was joined with stanzas of the medieval hymn *Stabat mater* that have been sung in procession from one station to the next. This hymn, like the devotion itself, is of Franciscan provenance. It has sometimes been assigned to the authorship of Bonaventure. This hymn was used exclusively in popular devotions until 1727, when Pope Benedict XIII extended the Feast of Our Lady of Sorrows to the whole Roman Catholic Church and admitted the *Stabat mater* into the Roman Missal. In the opinion of Joseph Jungmann, the *Stabat mater* "actually exhibits a character that is not properly liturgical, an accent that is emotionally lyrical rather than hymnic, and in its immersion in the sufferings of Christ—reminiscent of St. Francis' mysticism—it shows traces of individual piety, of Franciscan devotion to the Passion and our Lady hardly consonant with the objective spirit of common prayer."[13] In other words, it is a hymn more suitable to paraliturgical devotion than to official liturgy. The Way of the Cross (*Via Crucis*) has been greatly elaborated in Hispanic practice as a street procession with stations on Good Friday.

Solemn Benediction of the Blessed Sacrament

Some have regarded the Solemn Benediction of the Blessed Sacrament as the hallmark of Baroque devotion, although it was never included in the *Roman Ritual* of 1614 or sanctioned by the Sacred Congregation of Rites, which even insisted in a decree of May 31, 1642, that exposition of the reserved sacrament be severely limited, especially as regards private exposition.[14] But Solemn Benediction reflected culturally the age of royal absolutism, which reached a high point in the long reign of King Louis XIV of France (1643–1715). Comparable to the throne of the sun king was the throne of the King of kings in the tabernacle, often several feet high, on the high Baroque altar no longer partially concealed by a rood screen. The natural instinct would be to genuflect before the sacramental presence of Christ the King.

In spite of its lack of official recognition, the roots of Solemn Benediction of the Blessed Sacrament are located in the liturgy of the hours and in the Corpus Christi procession. "Benediction" refers to a blessing with the exposed sacrament. In the fourteenth century, it became very popular to perform devotions (*laude*) in the presence of the reserved sacrament exposed to view at the end of Vespers or Compline. At some point the custom developed of taking the pyx or monstrance in which the reserved sacrament was kept and blessing the worshipers with it. This probably followed in the wake of the practice of blessing the people with the sacrament exposed in the monstrance at a station in the Corpus Christi procession. Soon the occasions at which this kind of blessing was given began to multiply, including processions on Christmas, Palm Sunday, Easter, Pentecost, All Saints, at the dedication of a church, as well as at the coronation of a monarch, at the occasion of victory in battle or war, and deliverance from calamity or disease.[15] Some pastors and bishops in southern Germany and northern Italy complained as late as the end of the sixteenth century that people blessed their crops with the reserved sacrament. It was precisely this kind of abuse with which the Congregation of Rites was dealing.

In spite of the lack of an official ritual of solemn benediction, a standard ritual did develop and flourish during the seventeenth century. It was modeled on the rite of exposition and benediction in the Corpus Christi procession provided in the 1614 *Rituale*. It consisted of an incensation, the *Tantum ergo* (We before him bending), stanzas from the hymn "Pange lingua corporis" of Thomas Aquinas, the Corpus Christi collect, and the blessing of the people with the monstrance in the form of a cross. This rite was typically performed at the end of Sunday Solemn Vespers. In spite of official reluctance to countenance devotions involving the exposition of the sacrament, such devotions spread through eucharistic confraternities and religious orders dedicated to the Adoration of the Blessed Sacrament.

Forty Hours Devotion and Perpetual Adoration of the Blessed Sacrament

Like the devotions we have already considered, it is difficult to be precise about the origins of the Forty Hours Devotion. But it probably emerged early in the sixteenth century, perhaps in Milan. There, in 1527, Gian Antonio Belotti preached a series of Lenten sermons in which he urged Christians to spend forty hours before the reserved sacrament in order to seek God's help during a time of war. Belotti seems to have recommended doing this devotion four times a year, at Easter, Pentecost, the Feast of the Assumption, and Christmas. The idea was taken up by the Capuchin Joseph von Ferno, who added a new element of transferring the reserved sacrament from church to church, with forty hours of devotion in each place, so that by rotation there would be perpetual adoration of the Blessed Sacrament throughout the year.[16] The devotion was championed and spread by Antony Maria Zaccaria, a member of the Clerks Regular of Saint Paul. In 1550, the Oratorian Philip Neri introduced the Forty Hours Devotion in Rome, and from there, it spread rapidly. The reforming archbishop Charles Borromeo (d. 1584) could speak of the Forty Hours as if it were ancient custom and continued to promote it in the archdiocese of Milan. It came to be associated with Carnival time, at the beginning of Lent.

While this devotion was developed and championed by clerics, it quickly became a popular custom among the laity. Its communal character is seen in the practice whereby lay people signed up to take their turn as part of the Forty Hours and relieved one another. By the end of the sixteenth century, popes were granting generous indulgences to those who participated in this devotional relay. In the eighteenth century, too, papal approbation of this devotion was renewed in the *Instructio Clementina*, which outlined all the rites and ceremonies that were to be observed during the Forty Hours.[17]

The instruction specified that during the Forty Hours, the sacrament is to be exposed on the principal altar of the church, and all other images and statues near the high altar are to be covered. Relics are also to be removed from the high altar during the time of exposition. Candles are to be kept burning continuously, and no other masses are to be celebrated at the altar of exposition other than the masses that begin and end the period of the Forty Hours. These opening and closing masses are to be the votive Mass of the Blessed Sacrament, and may be accompanied with processions with the sacrament, litanies, and prayers. No requiem masses are to be celebrated in the church at which the Forty Hours Devotion is being done, and if there are other private masses being celebrated, bells may not be rung during their celebration. While these instructions really applied to the diocese of Rome, they were commended to others and were widely implemented.[18]

Devotion to the Sacred Heart of Jesus

As with other devotions, the roots of the Devotion to the Sacred Heart of Jesus lie in the Middle Ages, in this case, devotion to the wounds of Christ. But two seventeenth-century French religious gave abiding form to the devotions to and liturgy of the Sacred Heart. John Eudes (1601–1680) was a priest of the Oratory of Jesus until he founded the Oratory of Jesus and Mary in 1643 because he saw that devotion to Jesus and his mother were indistinguishable. His writings dramatically depict the sufferings of Christ on our behalf. In 1668 he composed propers for an office and mass of the Sacred Heart. The collect for the mass prays "that our hearts being consumed in unity among themselves and with the Heart of Jesus, we may perform all our works in His humility and charity."[19]

The other champion of the devotion to the Sacred Heart was the Visitation Sister Margaret Mary Alacoque (1647–1690), who had several revelations of the Sacred Heart in visions between 1673 and 1675. She came to understand that in reparation for the ingratitude of the Christian people for the love of Christ, she was to receive communion on the first Friday of each month and to spend each Thursday night from 11 P.M. until midnight prostrate in prayer to share the sadness that our Lord experienced in the Garden of Gethsemane. A holy death was promised to those who received communion on nine consecutive first Fridays. A final vision led her to petition that on the Friday after the octave of Corpus Christi, a special feast in honor of the Sacred Heart be celebrated in reparation for the indignities Christ experienced in the expositions of the Blessed Sacrament on the altars of the world. It is from Sister Margaret Mary's visions that the devotion of receiving communion on nine consecutive first Fridays and having a Thursday evening holy hour in memory of Jesus' agony in Gethsemane became a popular devotion.

This devotion, like the others, spread rapidly. Upon the petition of Polish bishops, Pope Clement XIII approved a mass and office for the feast of the Sacred Heart on the Friday after the octave of Corpus Christi in 1765. In 1778 Pope Pius VI approved other propers for Austria, Venice, and Spain. Pope Pius IX made it a universal feast in 1856.[20]

Novenas

According to the dates in the previous paragraph, the official approval of the devotion to the Sacred Heart came in the eighteenth century, during the Age of Enlightenment. There is no doubt that the Roman See used this devotion as a counter to the spirit of the Enlightenment. As we will see in the next chapter, Enlightenment reformers found it necessary to counter these devotions in order to promote their agendas for liturgical reform. In addition, the eighteenth century witnessed another paraliturgical popular devotion: the practice of novenas.

Novenas can be traced to Father Alphonsus Liguori (1696–1787). The scion of a noble Neapolitan family, he abandoned law to become a priest in 1726, founded the Order of Redemptorists in 1732, and became Bishop of Sant' Agatha dei Goti. In many ways his concerns and writings paralleled those of the Protestant Pietists of the period. He opposed both Jansenist rigorism, which discouraged frequent communion, and Jesuit rationalism, which encouraged it. He became famous for his writings in moral theology, but his greatest impact was the book *Visits to the Blessed Sacrament and the Blessed Virgin*, first published in 1745. This book went through two thousand editions in the next two centuries and had a tremendous impact on Roman Catholic piety, leading it in an individualistic and emotional direction that could only be regarded as antithetical to the spirit of the liturgy.[21] Much of it centered on private spiritual communion and a loving embrace of Jesus through contemplation. While Liguori encouraged frequent reception of Holy Communion, the amount of preparation he recommended in order to receive the sacrament worthily actually discouraged it. For most devout souls of the time, communion was limited to "spiritual communion," expressed in terms of "desire."

The book contains thirty-one forms that are to be used at visits to the reserved sacrament or during mass, one for each day of the month. Each form includes three devotions to be used at the beginning, during, and at the end of the visit to the reserved sacrament or during mass, plus one for a visit to the image of the Virgin Mary. The prayer forms are very simple and direct and were easy to memorize; an example is the short ejaculation, "My Jesus: Thou hast given Thyself entirely to me: I give my whole being to Thee."[22] The fact that the faithful did memorize these prayers made it easy for worshipers to attend to their own devotion during mass instead of attending to the liturgy of the church. Because of the popularity of these devotions, it was also difficult for liturgical reformers in the eighteenth century, as well as in the twentieth century after the Second Vatican Council, to wean the people away from their private devotions in order to participate more consciously in the actions of the Mass.

Liguori also made use of a form that began to appear in the seventeenth century: the novena. The novena was a private or public devotion spread over nine days. Liguori provided devotional material for novenas for Christmas, on the Sacred Heart of Jesus, and for All Souls' Day. These devotions focus on the content of these days but draw a moralistic application for the individual.

Some novenas, such as those held in conjunction with the Feast of the Virgin of Guadalupe on December 12 in Mexico and among Mexican-Americans, have actually had an impact on whole seasons of the church year. The Novena to the Virgin of Guadalupe consists of nine days of special prayers, devotions, and preparations for the December 12 celebration between December 3 and 11. Within this period are the Solemnity of the Immaculate Conception (December 8) and the optional memorial of the now-sainted Juan Diego Cuauhlatoatzin (December 9), the Native American peasant who received the vision of Our Lady of Guadalupe. The December 12 celebration is followed by the Novena of Las Posadas, nine days of special prayer, devotion, and preparation for the Nativity of Christ on December 25, during which the search of Mary and Joseph for shelter is reenacted in towns, neighborhoods, and parishes. As Maxwell Johnson has pointed out, this gives much of the Advent season among Latinos a Marian emphasis, even though the official Roman Catholic liturgical emphasis during Advent is on the Second Coming of Christ, the ministry and preaching of John the Baptist, and the Annunciation.[23]

The Value of Paraliturgical Devotions

It remains to say something about the value of these devotions. They all provided an emotional expression of religiosity that may have been lacking in the official liturgies of the church, at least in the manner in which these liturgies were performed. The official liturgies, both Protestant and Catholic, appealed more to the head than to the heart. Dramatic elements in the official liturgies that could have appealed to the emotions, such as the foot washing on Maundy Thursday, the Reproaches and Veneration of the Cross in the ancient Good Friday liturgy, and the great light service at the beginning of the Easter Vigil, were either observed in ways that didn't engage the people or, in the case of Protestantism, suppressed them. As Carl Dehne observed,

> While the [Catholic] clergy were picking their way through the rubrical thicket of the prescribed Easter Vigil, anticipated early in the morning of Holy Saturday in the chancels of nearly empty churches, the popular paschal worship of the northern churches focused on the absolutely obvious public vigil before the hidden reserved Eucharist in remembrance of the Lord's burial, and on the evidently triumphal eucharistic procession at dawn on Easter Sunday in commemoration of his rising from the dead.[24]

It should also be noted that many of the popular devotions might have become pieces of official liturgy but failed to be included in post-

Tridentine Roman liturgical books because they were not practices of the diocese of Rome.

Songs at Home and in Church

Catholics sought God through intense physical sensations. For Protestants, concerned to understand the word of God through attention to texts, devotion was expressed less through the physical body than through the mind. Yet the sensual was not totally neglected. The way to the mind was through hearing; faith comes from what is heard; what was heard was often sung.

Luther prized music next to the word of God because music heightens the word. Hymns (actually chorales and spiritual songs) became an important form of Protestant popular religion. In his *German Mass and Order of Communion* (1526), Luther gave impetus to congregational song by replacing texts of the ordinary of the Mass with versifications set to chorales. Already in his Latin *Form of the Mass and Communion for the Church at Wittenberg* (1523), he called for composers to produce songs for evangelical worship. Luther himself contributed thirty-six songs to the emerging body of Protestant hymnody. The publication of the so-called *Babst Gesangbuch* in Leipzig (1545) was a significant expansion of the early Reformation practice, which had drawn primarily on pre-Reformation hymnic traditions. Luther wrote a preface to this hymnal on the basis of what it included from the 1543 Klug hymnal, but he never actually saw the completed edition of the Babst hymnal (he died in 1546). The "Psalms and Spiritual Songs Composed by Pious Christians" added to the initial Babst collection included songs drawn from the Bohemian Brethren and the adoption or imitation of the Geneva Psalter. This opened the floodgates to new hymn writing because of the general assumption that Luther had approved the Babst hymnal *in toto*.

The more diversified collection of the Babst hymnal proved providential in the long run, because the original core of Lutheran liturgical hymnody became frozen and eventually proved emotionally insufficient in the wake of bitter theological disputes, war, plague, inflation, and the successes of the Catholic Reformation. Many pastors complained that hymn singing by the congregation was becoming lackluster. Perhaps for this reason, as well as because choral settings of the standard chorales were being composed, choirs assumed a greater role in singing the liturgy and chorales in many churches, and congregational participation began to decrease. Even the standard liturgical hymns of the German Lied (Song) Mass were sung by the choir or parish clerk, albeit with the intention that the people would catch on and join in singing them.[25]

We should understand that not every parish church was endowed with choirs. Choirs flourished primarily in cathedrals and large city churches where there were Latin schools, since the choirs were composed primarily of boys and men. In these places, pieces of Latin liturgy survived in Lutheran worship because there were choirs to sing the traditional introits, graduals, and canticles of the Mass and the prayer offices. In Sweden, where congregational hymn singing developed slower than in Germany and the Prose Mass was preferred to the Song Mass, the church order of Archbishop Laurentius Petri specified that choirs would sing parts of the liturgy in Latin. This provision was encouraged during the reign of Johan III (1568–1592). As late as 1620, new Latin choir books were published in Sweden. But in Denmark and Norway there were fewer cities than in Germany and Sweden, and fewer cathedrals, city churches, and Latin schools. There were only five cathedrals in all of Norway, and two of these (Nidaros or Trondhjem and Hamar) acquired organs only in the sixteenth century. Most village churches throughout Scandinavia remained without organs during the sixteenth century and well into the seventeenth century. Moreover, the chapter office of Precentor or Ludimagister (liturgical director) was changed in the Reformation church to posts as lecturers in theology. Thus, the rich liturgical life of the pre-Reformation church, including its musical life, was not maintained.

One of the strangest developments in the overseas provinces of the Danish Empire was in Iceland, where there seemed to be paid quartets to sing even the hymns while the people kept their mouths shut. Not even this arrangement was provided in Norway, in part because the rural people seemed suspicious of four-part singing. For the most part, the liturgy was sung by the priest and an assistant, sometimes called *djäkn* (deacon) or *klockare*, who sang the dialogical responses. We cannot assume that the German tradition of congregational singing, which preceded the Reformation, flourished everywhere. Nor can we assume that even this tradition was comparable to the congregational singing with which we are familiar today, because of complaints from Luther and others that the congregation was not learning the new hymns and songs. Hymnals were provided to choirs and parish clerks but not to the congregations (unless individuals bought their own books for use at home).

Hymnody flourished anew, especially in Germany, during the seventeenth century, but more for use in home devotions than in church services. This includes the mystical hymns of Philipp Nicolai (1556–1608), "Wake, Awake, for Night Is Flying" and "How Brightly Shines the Morning Star," which were included in Nicolai's devotional book *Mirror of Joy* (1606), written during a time of fear of plague in Unna, Westphalia. They mark the transition to the seventeenth century's warmer lyrics and fresh melodies, which were used in domestic settings before they found a place in public worship. The sufferings of the Thirty Years' War produced a wealth of hymnody, including Johann Heermann's (1585–1647) passion chorale "Ah, Holy Jesu, How Hast Thou Offended?" and Martin Rinkart's (1586–1649) "Now Thank We All Our God" (which may originally have been sung as a family table grace). Heermann and Rinkart were pastors, but lay people also were writing hymns. Johann Franck (1618–1677), a lawyer who became mayor of Guben in Brandenburg in 1661, wrote the great communion hymn "Soul, Adorn Yourself with Gladness" and "Jesu, Priceless Treasure." Probably the greatest Lutheran hymn writer of the seventeenth century was Paul Gerhardt (1607–1676), who expressed a quiet confidence in God's love that is often lacking in earlier Lutheran hymns, as in "Jesus, Your Boundless Love to Me" and "O Lord, How Shall I Meet You." It is not surprising that he felt a kinship with the medieval mystic Bernard of Clairvaux and added stanzas to the verses attributed to Saint Bernard, "O Sacred Head, Now Wounded." Gerhardt's lyrics were memorably set to music by the cantor of Saint Nicholas Church in Berlin, Johann Crüger (1598–1662). A Reformed hymn writer who made a great contribution to Lutheran hymnody was Joachim Neander (1650–1680), author of "Praise to the Lord, the Almighty" and composer of numerous hymn tunes.

All of these hymn writers are regarded as precursors of Pietism. Except for the Reformed poets Neander and Tersteegen, these hymn writers were orthodox Lutherans. Nicolai and Gerhardt especially were known for their intense anti-Calvinism. But the hymns of the seventeenth century, sung primarily in households, paved the way for the reception of the Pietist program of group meetings. The market for hymns is indicated by the gargantuan size of hymnals toward the end of the seventeenth century. For example, the Dresden Hymnal of 1622 had 276 hymns but grew to a collection of 1,505 in the 1673 edition. The Lüneberg Hymnal of 1635 contained 355 hymns; the 1694 edition had 2,055 hymns. The most famous Pietist hymnals were Johann Anatasii Freylinghausen's *Geistliches Gesangbuch* (1704) and his *Neues Geistreiches Gesangbuch* (1714), which were combined in 1741 in the Halle hymnal (named after the Halle Orphanage, which published and distributed it throughout Germany). Known also as the *Freylinghausen Gesangbuch*, this collection of 1,581 lyrics set to 597 different melodies and figured basses was also brought to the British North American colonies in the mid-eighteenth century by German Lutheran and Reformed immigrants. The great Dutch Reformed mystic and poet Gerhard Tersteegen (1697–1769) took over Neander's *Bundes-Lieder* (Songs of the Covenant) and tripled its size, contributing about one hundred hymns of his own, including "God Himself Is Present."[26] These hymnals were entrepreneurial products, not official church books. They were published without the permission of ecclesiastical authorities and flourished beyond theological censorship and control. Nevertheless, many of the hymns in these collections were sung in the Lutheran liturgies under pastors with Pietist leanings and in orthodox Saxony.

In Denmark the greatest hymn writer of this period was Bishop Thomas Kingo (1634–1703), who advanced hymnody beyond the Reformation chorales by drawing on secular airs. The last remnants of Gregorian chant disappeared with the *Danmark og Norgis Kirke-Ritual* (1685), which offered a service consisting musically only of hymns. An official new hymnal, published by Kingo in 1699, had the same spirit as the Freylinghausen collection and was used throughout Denmark, Norway, and the Faroe Islands. It engendered for the first time since the Reformation a popular liturgical tradition in these countries.[27]

Pious Communities

Some popular devotions were embraced by pious groups whose very existence on the margins of church life gave them a sense of what anthropologist Victor Turner called liminality, the sense of being "betwixt and between" defined states of culture.[28] Like monks and friars of earlier times, Catholic confraternities and Protestant *collegia pietatis* (colleges of piety) provided what Turner called *communitas*, over against the social structure of the institutional church. In his *Pia*

Desideria (Pious Desires, 1675), written as an extended preface to an edition of the works of Johann Arndt, Lutheran pastor Philipp Jacob Spener proposed the formation of dedicated groups of lay persons who would study the Scriptures and encourage one another by exhortation and prayer in the life of sanctification.[29] Protestant Pietists gathered in *collegia pietatis* to encourage one another in the godly life through Bible study and prayer, just as Catholics had gathered in eucharistic confraternities to encourage one another to more frequent reception of communion, to adoration of the reserved sacrament, or to participate in vigils such as the Forty Hours Devotion. Protestant Pietists also turned toward works of charity in the care of the poor, the sick, orphans, and widows in the eighteenth century, most notably demonstrated in the charitable institutions founded at Halle under August Hermann Francke,[30] just as Catholic confraternities had provided welfare and funeral benefits to their members and sponsored hospitals, nursing care, and prison ministries. Protestant ecclesiastical authorities sought to control the activities of the *collegia pietatis*, just as Roman Catholic authorities had sought to regulate the number and activities of the confraternities.[31]

Louis Châtellier showed that "the Europe of the devout" encompassed hundreds of sacramental and Marian sodalities.[32] In the large urban areas of Italy by 1600, it is estimated that up to one half of all males belonged to a confraternity. There were also confraternities of women and adolescents. Some confraternities, especially those developed by the Jesuits, were based in colleges rather than in parishes, but included townspeople as well as students and embraced people of different social ranks, both married and unmarried. The Marian Congregations sponsored by the Jesuits were noted for their disciplines of daily mass, monthly communions, weekly meetings, ascetical practices, and charitable works.[33] The Company of the Holy Sacrament, organized in Paris in 1629, enrolled more than four thousand members throughout France at the height of its prestige and included such notable churchmen as Vincent de Paul, Bishop Bousset, and François Fénelon.

It is interesting that each confessional group created paraliturgical devotions around the core liturgical feature that was most important to them: Protestants held devotional meetings to focus on the word of God; Catholics conducted group devotions focused on the sacrament of the altar. The very fact that ardent lay people sought out this supplementary support indicates that they did not deem the official liturgies as sufficient for their spiritual needs. Still, their pious devotions were an extreme extension of their confessional identities. The Catholic use of processions, veneration of the Blessed Sacrament, devotion to Mary and the saints, and masses for the dead reaffirmed these rituals in the face of Protestants' condemnations of such practices. Protestant Pietists gathered to study the Bible and discuss sermons, that is, to focus on the word shorn of all external ornamentation. Meeting in pastors' studies or private homes, these conventicles were not even surrounded by such liturgical art as continued to flourish in Lutheran church buildings. Reformation iconoclasm was not only an attack on works of art and sacred objects; it was also an attack on rituals that made use of images and objects.[34]

Reception of Holy Communion

One ritual that could not be dispensed with, although it could be altered considerably in religious perception, was the celebration and reception of Holy Communion.[35] Martin Luther and John Calvin both desired a more frequent celebration of Holy Communion, as did the Council of Trent. In the case of Luther, Holy Communion would be offered as long as there were communicants who desired to receive the sacrament. Calvin experienced in Strasbourg a schema of celebration of the Lord's Supper that was at least monthly in parish churches and every Sunday in the cathedral, but he inherited in Geneva a practice in Reformed Switzerland of celebrating the Lord's Supper four times a year and never was able to persuade the authorities to increase the frequency of celebration. In the Roman Catholic Church, mass was celebrated daily. The issue was to persuade the faithful to receive communion more frequently. Yet a new penitential emphasis was also evident in the teachings of the Council of Trent, and this was the strand emphasized in Antoine Arnauld's *De la Fréquente Communion* (Concerning Frequent Communion, 1643).

This six-hundred-page work, typical of the Jansenist method of collecting, translating, and analyzing copious primary sources on any given topic, was less about the frequency of receiving communion than about why frequent communion should be avoided. It was directed primarily to confessors and spiritual directors for whom the relationship between confession of sins and reception of communion was a primary concern.

In this work, which went through many printings and editions, Arnauld advocated a return to strict penitential demands, which he believed lax confessors were not observing. Strict penitence severely curtailed the frequent reception of communion for most Christians, even those not guilty of "mortal sins" but simply "attached" to "venial sins."[36]

In Arnauld's theology, baptism effects union with Christ. This union is maintained by the gift of the Holy Spirit received in baptism. The Spirit "impels" the baptized to the Eucharist, which is given as the "perfect-ing food" to those who are spiritually "healthy." Arnauld did not believe that communicants must be in such a state of spiritual health that they would be perfect, as one would be in heaven. But post-baptismal sin repels the sanctifying Spirit, who "impels" the sinner to penance instead of to the table as a way of restoring the spiritual integrity necessary for participation in the Eucharist. The practices of penance place the peni-tent in a situation like the Israelites wandering in the wilderness, the centurion and the woman with an issue of blood seeking Jesus' aid, or the prodigal son who stood "afar" from his father. In penance, "hunger" for the Eucharist is awakened and purified. The baptized, who should be drawn to the Eucharist, instead withdraw from it in order to desire communion all the more. In acts of penance, they develop the spiritual disciplines that will make them more worthy communicants.[37]

Arnauld applied this not just to individuals but to the whole church. He argued that the early church had a forceful spiritual renewal, begin-ning at Pentecost, and could therefore partake of the Eucharist even daily, as we see in the book of Acts. But as time went on, the people, especially the clergy, experienced a spiritual decline, and the need for penance increased. While frequent communion remained and remains a goal for the Christian, it became more difficult to attain this goal because the church embroiled its members in careless and sinful liv-ing from which only penitential withdrawal from the sacrament could free them.[38] The schisms of the church produced by the Protestant Reformation also worked to press the church toward acts of penitence including withdrawal from eucharistic communion, since the eucharis-tic communion of the whole church has been broken.

Not surprisingly, a bitter argument swirled around Arnauld's book and some of the aspects of the Tridentine reform it attempted to rep-resent. Arnauld's thesis flew in the face of the desire of the Tridentine reform to encourage more frequent reception of the sacrament. Those who countered Arnauld's argument were forced to dissociate the "unworthiness" of individuals from the "worthiness" of the church as a whole. Fénelon, for one, in his "Letter on Frequent Communion,"[39] argued that the church of the present age is no more or less worthy than the church of earlier ages; the Spirit works in all ages to bring the baptized to the Eucharist. If there is any difference between the church of the present age and the church of the early centuries, it is that the church of today is at peace rather than under persecution. This naturally produces a spiritual complacence, which can be combated through more ardent acts of devotion, including more frequent reception of communion.

It is noteworthy that Fénelon wrote after the expulsion of Protestants from France by the revocation of the Edict of Nantes. Therefore, individual need became the sole determination for deciding about reception of communion; broken fellowship was no longer present. For example, Calvin had argued that the Reformed Church could celebrate and receive communion more frequently because it was purged of the corruptions of the past.[40] Celebration of Holy Communion among the Reformed was for the purpose of social cohesion as well as for meeting the spiritual needs of the members. The Reformed retained the system of quarterly communions precisely in order to prepare the whole church, not just individuals, for the celebration of the Lord's Supper. Among both Catholics and Protestants, however, by the end of the seventeenth century, the needs of the individual came to dominate preparation for Holy Communion, whether by means of visits to the Blessed Sacrament among Catholics or preparatory sermons, exhortations, and acts of corporate confession among Protestants.

Protestants had their own version of retreat from frequent communion through rigorous acts of enumerating sins and confessing them. The Huguenot Jean Claude wrote a popular work, translated into English as *A Treatise of Self-Examination in Order to the Worthy Receiving of the Holy Communion Together with Suitable Prayers* (London, 1683), that took hold of 1 Corinthians 11:28 and aimed the exhortation to "examine oneself" toward an elaborately interior scrutiny also practiced by the Puritans.

Nevertheless, the appeal to individual need paid off in terms of increased eucharistic devotion and reception of Holy Communion among both Catholics and Protestants in the early eighteenth century. Confession and communion were joined together for both Catholics and Protestants. For Roman Catholics, the privacy of confession ensured by the development of the confessional box increased the number of people availing themselves of the sacrament of penance and therefore the number of communicants. Boxes were introduced in Cologne in 1662. As of 1663, 27.8 percent of Cologne parishes had confessional boxes; by 1743 they were found in 88.4 percent of parishes.[41] In the early eighteenth century, there was growth in the number of confraternities devoted to the Eucharist. Rural missions throughout Europe undertaken by Jesuits and Capuchins extended confraternities to rural parishes, where they had been previously lacking. Confraternity members received communion more frequently than other Catholics, some month, or bimonthly.[42]

Also in the early eighteenth century, the number of communions increased in Lutheranism. It is difficult to know how frequently individuals received communion, since registration was connected with going to confession, but the number of communicants could have been higher than the number of confessions. In orthodox Leipzig, communion registrations indicate that there were often more than two hundred communicants every Sunday and holy day at each of the city's churches. In the Saint Thomas and Saint Nicholas churches, fifteen thousand to twenty thousand registered communicants per year were typical in the first half of the eighteenth century.[43] This number decreased precipitously toward the end of the eighteenth century under rationalism, when the sacraments were de-emphasized and Communion was tacked on to the service of the word for those who wished to remain to receive communion. Roman Catholics usually did not receive communion at mass either, but after mass.

The Reformed tradition aimed at preparing all church members to receive communion when it was offered. Among Anglicans and Presbyterians, this was two to four times per year. The *Book of Common Prayer* provided an exhortation to be read by the priest, announcing the next communion and inviting parishioners to avail themselves of the sacrament. Among Congregationalists, communion was offered monthly. But there were proposals to stagger the Sundays on which communion was offered in various meetinghouses in places, like Boston, where there were several meetinghouses. In this way, some ardent members could receive communion almost weekly by attending different meetinghouses.[44]

Receiving communion thus became a matter of personal decision more than of church discipline. It was viewed more as a way of meeting spiritual needs than a matter of constituting the church and renewing its life and mission. This was an approach to receiving communion that can be traced back to the late medieval *devotio moderna*. But as reformers appealed to the Christian's need for the sacrament and emphasized its spiritual benefits (e.g., forgiveness of sins), the reason for receiving communion became more personal and less communal. The emphasis on meeting individual spiritual need signaled the dawning of the modern age also for the churches.

CHAPTER 16

Worship Awakening

The Age of Enlightenment has been regarded as a time when, because of the ascendancy of science and reason, religion and faith did not fare well. Some historians have seen in the Age of Enlightenment "the rise of modern paganism."[1] Certainly deism (David Hume) and even atheism (Voltaire) among the elite did not bode well for orthodox religion. Yet the upsurge in popular religion late in the seventeenth century that was expressed in Roman Catholic popular devotions and in the hymns and prayer meetings of Protestant Pietism continued throughout the eighteenth century. The Age of Enlightenment also experienced powerful religious movements that can be regarded as reactions to the emphasis on rationalism yet also reflected the Enlightenment's equal emphasis on experience, its challenge to authority, and its demotion of ritual in favor of moral behavior. These movements included the Wesleyan revivals in England and the Great Awakening in the British North American colonies.

Pietism continued to develop in Germany throughout the Age of Enlightenment. The elector of Brandenburg, King Friedrich Wilhelm I of Prussia (1688–1740), sanctioned the establishment of the Pietist University and Mission Center at Halle, under the leadership of August Hermann Francke (1663–1727). The king appointed known Pietists to the head of other educational institutions that had formerly been controlled by orthodox Lutherans. Pietism's emphasis on a life of service served the interests of the Great Elector, who wanted to convert the independent-minded Prussian Lutheran nobility into a court-oriented civil service and thereby enhance royal absolutism. The

Wesleyan revivals in Great Britain spawned the Methodist movement, which gained adherents among the poorer classes of society and provided a pattern of addressing the social ills caused by the Industrial Revolution and urbanization. The "Great Awakening" in the British North American colonies launched a pattern of religious revivals that practically defined the history of Christianity in America. We may also note in this same time period the rise of the mystical sect known as Hassidism within Polish Judaism and the birth of Reform Judaism in Prussia.

Each of these movements emphasized a personal and emotional faith.[2] Each can be seen as a reaction to the inability of the official cultus to meet the personal religious needs of the worshipers. The very idea that personal religious needs should be met is a modern idea that slowly emerged over the course of several centuries in the practice of self-examination in the late medieval *devotio moderna*, the cultivation of self-development encouraged by Renaissance humanism, the Reformation's doctrine of justification on the basis of one's faith alone, and the option of religious "choice" in the post-Reformation fracturing of Christendom into confessional churches.

Religious choice was not uniformly available in all European countries. It was difficult to be anything other than Roman Catholic in Spain and Italy or anything other than Lutheran in the Nordic countries. But in spite of terrible outbursts of persecution, it was possible to be Protestant in predominantly Catholic France. In the small German states, one could move to the territory of a neighboring prince whose confession was one's own. In many of the free cities of the Holy Roman Empire, worship facilities existed for both Protestants and Catholics. The Toleration Act in Great Britain in 1689 reduced (although it did not entirely remove) legal penalties for those who did not subscribe to the Articles of Religion of the Church of England, particularly Catholics and dissenters. This act at the beginning of the Age of Enlightenment may be viewed as the birth of modern denominationalism. Toleration of Protestants was not legally enacted in France until 1787, on the eve of the revolution. Many groups that experienced persecution in other places during the seventeenth century found refuge in the Netherlands, which was the most religiously tolerant country. But toleration was also the policy of King Frederick II the Great of Prussia, and it was emulated by Emperor Joseph II of Austria.

Many groups emigrated to the British colonies in North America to seek freedom of religious practice. They included, first, Puritan separatists and dissenters, who settled in New England; Baptists, who founded Rhode Island; Catholics, who settled in Maryland; and English Quakers, German Lutherans and Reformed, Mennonites, and other Anabaptist groups, who settled primarily in Pennsylvania. Swedish Lutherans were already settled along the Delaware River and Dutch Reformed along the Hudson River from previous Swedish and Dutch colonies. Among others coming from Great Britain, we need to remember that while the Church of England was episcopalian, the equally established Church of Scotland was presbyterian. The southern colonies were heavily Anglican along the coast, the Presbyterians headed to back country along the Appalachians, and Lutherans expelled from Salzburg were settled in Georgia as a buffer between coastal settlements and Native Americans.[3]

Many of the groups that settled in the New World strongly represented an ethos that emphasized personal religious experience and response. Even the Lutherans were organized by a mission pastor from the Pietist center at Halle in Brandenburg, Henry Melchior Muhlenberg (1711–1787), who was dispatched to keep the Lutheran settlers from being ministered to by Count Nicholas von Zinzendorf, the even more Pietistic bishop of the Moravians, who had settled the Moravians on his estate and developed the community called Herrnhut. The very conditions of life on the American frontier produced an individualistic spirit, since the pioneers who ventured beyond the settlements on the seaboard were cut off from communally exerted authority.

The First Great Awakening

The Great Awakening can be regarded, from a social historical perspective, as an effort to tame the rougher edges of the American frontier spirit. The term *Great Awakening*, describing the revivals that occurred in the 1740s, was first used in the 1840s by evangelicals eager to establish a legitimizing line of descent for their own religious revivals, which began in the frontier camp meetings of the early nineteenth century and which they termed "the Second Great Awakening." The religious revivals known as the First Great Awakening occurred primarily in New England and New Jersey in the late 1730s and 1740s but spread to other colonies as well.

To be sure, the awakenings can be regarded, theologically, as a reaction to the rationalism that was assaulting orthodox Congregationalism (threatened by Unitarianism) and Presbyterianism (threatened by deism). But we also need to take seriously the religious conditions of life in colonial America—or, rather, irreligious life. Most settlers on the frontier arrived ahead of government and without a church. The journals of clergymen like the Lutheran Henry Melchior Muhlenberg and the Anglican Charles Woodmason tell of a back-country under-world (not that far from the coastal settlements) that took advantage of the absence of government and church. This included squatters, runaway debtors, idlers, gamblers, and outright criminals whom they encountered on their horseback journeys to far-flung settlements to try to minister to scattered congregations.[4] They reported the comments of vagrants and travelers who sat in taverns and uttered atheistic and anticlerical sentiments. Christianity had enormous resources for cop-ing with the hardships of everyday life, but these had to be applied to a population lucky to have an elementary school education and barely rising above literacy. The politeness of settled society wore thin on the frontier, and the frontier was never far from settled society.

Ministering in the hills of western Massachusetts, the Puritan minis-ter and intellectual Jonathan Edwards (1703–1758) rebuked the youth of his Northampton congregation for holding a dance on the Sabbath. In sermons, Bible studies, and home visitations, Edwards stressed the dangers of damnation and the promise of salvation. He was amazed at the results, as more than three hundred young men and women claimed conversion experiences and applied for church membership. Edwards was a young pastor when the revival broke out in 1738. He had been building on the half-century ministry of his predecessor, Edward Taylor (1642?–1729). Puritanism itself could be considered a revival move-ment, since the congregations admitted only the converted to their membership. But Edwards considered the revivals to be nothing less than "the surprising works of God," and he carefully analyzed the per-manence of the "religious affections" in a book that became a textbook for future awakenings.[5]

As the revivals spread from Northampton, emotion became a more pronounced aspect of public worship. It brought a new dominance of preaching in Puritan worship and ended the former practice of the congregation questioning the sermon.[6] The sermon was no longer to be reflected upon theologically, but acted upon in a response of faith commitment.

Earlier, in New Jersey, the preaching of the Dutch Reformed min-ister Theodore Freylinghuysen (1692–1748) prompted revival and controversy. William Tennent Sr. (1673–1746), a Presbyterian minister from Ireland living in Pennsylvania, agreed with Freylinghuysen's emphasis on experiential regeneration and created an academy in his home, called by his opponents the "Log College," where he trained his sons, Gilbert, John, and William, and other men for the ministry. The graduates of this Log College, with their emphasis on being born again, distressed more conservative Presbyterians.[7]

The stage was set for the arrival of George Whitefield (1714–1770), the fiery Anglican priest with theatrical training and a magnificent voice. Whitefield had been associated with the Wesleyan revival and open-air preaching in England. He arrived in Delaware in 1739 for the second of his four preaching tours in America. Since he was already famous before he arrived, his itinerary and revival services were reported in colonial newspapers. They created, in effect, the first media event in American history. As in England, Whitefield often preached outdoors because no church building was large enough to hold the crowds that he attracted. Benjamin Franklin estimated that Whitefield preached to twenty thousand people in Philadelphia and could be heard by all. His revival services brought together more people than had ever been brought together in one place before in colonial America. Whitefield's willingness to preach in any church reinforced the Pietist notion that religious experience transcends doctrinal differences. Not a profound theologian, Whitefield originally began preaching as an Arminian but was persuaded by Jonathan Edwards and Gilbert Tennent to embrace Calvinist predestinarianism so that he would be welcomed in Congregationalist, Presbyterian, and Baptist churches. But his basic message remained unchanged: the necessity of an experience of new birth.[8]

The awakening produced such novelties as itinerant preachers, lay preachers, preaching for the conversion experience, and controversies over admitting the unconverted to Holy Communion.[9] Probably the greatest fruit of the awakening was a missionary spirit, which was embraced by most of the churches in America. This spirit played a role in the taming of the frontier as it moved steadily west and in the conversion of Native Americans. But it also reinforced the Enlightenment idea that worship is primarily for the edification of the people. This taught people to look for what they get out of worship more than for what they put into it.

Presbyterian Communion Seasons in Scotland

Revivalism did not originate in America. Puritanism itself was a kind of revival movement, since only the converted could be included in the covenant community. The agenda of Pietism was to "convert the outward orthodox profession into a living theology of the heart." But an important precursor to American revivalism was the "sacramental seasons" held by the Presbyterians in the Scottish highlands. As early as the 1620s, people gathered from all over a district for several days of preparation for the quarterly reception of Holy Communion. The days were spent in services of confession in which preaching aimed at repentance. The purpose of the gathering was preparation for partaking of the Lord's Supper together, after which profound thanksgiving was expressed. These gatherings were held in barns or, in the summer, outdoors in the fields. Ministers from the surrounding communities participated in these gatherings, and often an itinerant guest preacher was brought in from outside the area to deliver a series of sermons. The Presbyterians who came to the middle colonies brought this tradition with them. It is the background of the camp meetings on the frontier from western New York State, through western Pennsylvania, Maryland, Virginia, North Carolina, and to eastern Ohio, Kentucky, and Tennessee that formed the Second Great Awakening.

Frontier Camp Meetings and the Second Great Awakening

The first great camp meeting was organized by the Reverend James McGready (1758?–1817), a Presbyterian who had ministered in western North Carolina, at his Gaspar River Church in Logan County, Kentucky, in July 1800. This outdoor service lasted several days and ended with the "altar call" to the Lord's Supper. Another Presbyterian who attended, Barton Warren Stone (1772–1844), was impressed by what he saw at Gaspar River and announced a great meeting to be held at Cane Ridge, Kentucky, on August 6, 1801. When the day arrived, so did a crowd estimated at anywhere from ten thousand to twenty-five thousand, along with ministers from several non-Presbyterian traditions, including Baptists and Methodists. The event lasted six or seven days and finally had to be terminated because sufficient supplies could not be provided for such an unexpected crowd. The phenomena that occurred there, and which Barton Stone wrote up, were described as the greatest outpouring of the Holy Spirit since the Day of Pentecost. Stone wrote of "bodily agitation or exercises," "the falling exercise," "the jerks," "the dancing exercise," "the barking exercise," "the laughing exercise," "the running exercise," and "the singing exercise."[10] Sydney Ahlstrom has said, "The Cane Ridge meeting has challenged descriptive powers of many historians, yet none has risen fully to the occasion." He suggests:

> One must first try to re-create the scene: the milling crowds of hardened frontier farmers, tobacco-chewing, tough-spoken, notoriously profane, famous for their alcoholic thirst; their scarcely demure wives and large broods of children; the rough clearing, the rows of wagons and crude improvised tents with horses staked out behind; the gesticulating speaker on a rude platform, or perhaps simply a preacher holding forth from a fallen tree. At night, when the forest's edge was limned by the flickering light of many campfires, the effects of apparent miracles would be heightened. For men and women accustomed to retiring and rising with the birds, these turbulent nights must have been especially awe-inspiring. And underlying every other conditioning circumstance was the immense loneliness of the frontier farmer's life and the exhilaration of participating in so large a social occasion.[11]

The Packaging of Revivalism

While the Presbyterians had been in the forefront of the first camp meetings, the Old Light Presbyterians associated with the College of New Jersey (Princeton) distanced themselves from preaching for conversion, while the Congregationalists, Methodists, and Baptists encouraged it. It was a Presbyterian, Charles Grandison Finney (1792–1875), who became "the father of modern revivalism." Born in Warren, Ohio, he grew up in central New York, returned to Warren for his secondary education, kept school for a while, and then practiced law in Adams, New York. In disputes with a Presbyterian minister friend, George W. Gale (later to be the founder of Knox College in Galesburg, Illinois), Finney began to read the Scriptures and experienced a conversion in 1821. He immediately began preaching without a formal theological education. He was a Christian lawyer with "a retainer from the Lord Jesus Christ to plead his cause." His persuasive powers and success led the local Saint Lawrence Presbytery to license him as a preacher.

He was soon holding spectacular evangelistic meetings in Rome, Utica, Troy, and other cities along the newly opened Erie Canal. His growing fame led him to other states and finally to New York City in 1832. Finney held forth in a theater that Lewis Tappan and others had rented for him, which they called the Second Presbyterian Church. But even its "freeness" was not free enough for Finney. Experiencing the resistance to his theology by the Princeton faculty and the criticism of prominent ministers like Lyman Beecher, Finney withdrew to the Broadway Tabernacle, which had been built for him. But his tenure there was short, because his health was poor and he was increasingly taken up with the movement to abolish slavery. In 1835 he was called as professor of theology at the newly founded Oberlin College in Ohio. He served as president of the college from 1851 to 1866 and made it a center of revival theology and Christian social activism.

Finney practiced the "new measures" he would write about in his *Lectures on the Revival of Religion* (1835). His speech was tough, direct, forceful, and inescapably popular; he argued his case like a lawyer. He believed that human sin was voluntary and therefore avoidable; hence "entire sanctification" was a human possibility. The point of the revival was to lead sinners to this conviction and possibility. Moreover, he declared in his *Lectures*, "Revival is not a miracle, or dependent on a miracle in any sense. It is a purely philosophical [i.e., scientific] result of the right use of the constituted means." Finney did not believe that Jesus had instituted or the apostles had laid down in the New Testament any measures or order of worship that must be followed. Rather, we are free to do what it takes to save souls. The essential test of any measure, according to Finney, was "Does it work?" In Finney's pragmatic ethos, if something works, keep it; if it doesn't, discard it and try something new.[12]

Finney's contribution was to package the practices that had proved successful in the frontier camp meetings and move them indoors. This affected everything about Reformed and Free Church worship. The worship space was arranged in a semicircle around a platform on which was placed a small reading stand, rather than a large pulpit. Three chairs were placed behind the lectern: one for the worship leader, one for the song leader, and one for the visiting preacher. A quartet of singers could be placed to the side, or a whole choir could be arranged in a kind of gallery behind the ministers. Finney used music to make an impact on the worshipers. His introduction of choirs was itself controversial within the Reformed tradition. Within this purpose, even the pipe organ had a use. Holy Communion was demoted to a table placed beneath the lectern. The "altar call" no longer led to the table but to "the anxious bench" at the front of the church, where those seeking a conversion experience could be prayed over.[13]

As James White pointed out, this order of worship was easily divided into three sections: "preliminaries," including songs, testimonials, and prayer; the sermons; and a harvest of souls. This order of service found acceptance in almost all Protestant traditions except the Episcopal and Lutheran, and in African American as well as white churches. Some traditions, among them the Methodists and Presbyterians, might include more in the "preliminaries," such as the Apostles' Creed and Lord's Prayer and readings from scripture. If an offering needed to be received, that could be done before the sermon. But the sermon always came at the climax of the service and was followed by some kind of call to conversion or discipleship. This has remained the pattern of Sunday-morning and evening revival services in nonliturgical Protestant churches. The same pattern was followed in the Billy Graham Evangelistic Crusades and now in the Willow Creek Community Church in Barrington, Illinois, which in turn has become a model for other churches that want to offer "seeker services."

This point needs to be understood clearly. The style of music and the character of preaching may differ from one tradition to another. For example, African American worship has a uniqueness that deserves its own chapter in a social history of liturgy because of the important role worship has played in the African American community. The biblical story of the exodus of Israel from Egypt has been especially important in African American worship.[14] There are characteristics of African American worship that transcend denominations and worship traditions, whether those traditions are revival, liturgical, or Pentecostal. These characteristics include its participatory character notwithstanding the dominant role of the pastor, the emotional range of the music, and the affective and interactive character of the preaching.[15] But the order of service is roughly the same in African American churches as in other nonliturgical Protestant churches: praise and prayer, Scripture and preaching, response and blessing.

Successive Waves of Revival in America

Revivalism has been a continuing feature of Protestant worship in the United States, but it was necessary to stoke the fires of revivalism from time to time. By the 1840s the fires of the Second Great Awakening warmed into political action in the abolition and temperance movements. This was aligned with and supported by the millennialism of the same period. The Civil War (1861–1865) was waged with all the fervor of religious crusades, sparked by the activist movements associated with the revivals (especially abolition in the Northern states).

In the aftermath of the Civil War, preachers stayed away from social issues. Many rejoiced in the "gospel of wealth" evidenced in the new factories, the growth of the cities, the expansion of the middle class, and millionaires who bestowed their benefactions on museums, seminaries, and churches. But industrialization and urbanization produced new social problems, which were addressed by the home mission movement and the Salvation Army. Dwight L. Moody (1837–1899) became the leading revivalist of the post–Civil War era. A lay businessman, Moody became involved in the YMCA and efforts to save people "from" the city. While on business for the YMCA in England in 1872, he was asked to substitute in a London pulpit. Some four hundred people responded to his invitation to discipleship at the end of his sermon. Seeing possibilities in this, Moody teamed up with the musician Ira David Sankey (1840–1908) and embarked on a crusade in Great Britain in 1873–1875. It is estimated that Moody and Sankey reached three million to four million people on that crusade. Upon his return to the United States, Moody preached to thousands of people in Brooklyn and Philadelphia and then set out on a cross-continental railroad campaign funded by leading entrepreneurs.[16] The "gospel songs" of Sankey and others became staple Protestant favorites for the next seventy-five years.

In the early twentieth century, the fires of revival were stoked again, this time by Billy Sunday (William Ashley Sunday, 1863–1935). Born in Iowa, he came to Chicago to play baseball with the Chicago White-Stockings, was converted, and began work as the assistant secretary of the Chicago YMCA in 1891. Two years later, he signed on with a revival team touring the smaller cities of America. Soon he began his own preaching campaign, and by 1900 he was preaching in the larger cities. By 1904 he could demand that expense money be raised and arrangements be made before he would arrive in a city with his campaign. In his peak year, 1917, he preached in New York City to 1,443,000 people in a ten-week campaign and listed 98,264 converts. Using physical activities such as furniture smashing and an unbroken torrent of harsh words aimed at the familiar sins of the world (high society, worldly amusements, filthy habits, pliable politicians, liberal preachers, trashy immigrants, and especially the "booze traffic"), his call for fighting men of God was met with many responses to the "altar call." By this time, the professionalization of evangelistic campaigns had made it possible for "decent Americans" to respond painlessly. Billy called them forward as his musician, Homer Rodheaver (1880–1955), led his choir in singing softly,[17] a pattern that would later be used in the Billy Graham crusades.

Catholic Revivalism

Embedded in the preaching of celebrated revival preachers (and mainline preachers like Lyman Beecher as well) was an anti-Catholicism that reflected Protestant reaction to the waves of Irish and German and later southern and eastern European immigrants, who swelled the ranks of the Roman Catholic Church in America. In the 1850s the American, or "Know Nothing," Party attained political power in several states on a platform of temperance, property rights for married women, ignoring slavery, and anti-Catholicism ("down with rum, Romanism, and rebellion").

Protestants fought the new waves of immigrants with a combination of intimidation (even burning church buildings) and efforts to convert Catholics (especially through the public school system). Catholic prelates fought back by building a competing system of parochial schools so that Catholic children would not have to be exposed to Protestant prayers and the reading of the King James Version of the Bible in the classroom. At the same time, they promoted a practice of popular devotions that steered clear of superstitious views the immigrants may have brought with them while also helping uneducated immigrants to identify themselves as Catholics, and they conducted revival missions of their own.[18] These Catholic revivals were conducted by priests in preaching orders, who came into a parish for a few days to conduct a preaching mission. Large crosses and signs were posted outside church buildings during the revivals, and special liturgies were conducted. Catholic revival preachers sounded the themes of judgment and hellfire and called for personal conversion, just as Protestant revivalists did. But the emotional response was not an unmediated personal relationship with Jesus; it was anchored in sacramental observance. As J. William Frost has noted, "Catholic revivalism was an urban ritual and did not have the rural and nostalgic flavor of Protestant revivals."[19]

Post–World War II Revivalism

America's involvement in World War I, the conflicts between liberal Christianity and fundamentalism, Prohibition, the Great Depression, and World War II absorbed the religious energies of America while evangelical revivalism made a slow retreat. After World War II, significant changes occurred in the United States and the world, including the phenomenal growth of the suburbs, the development of television and other electronic media, the stress of the Cold War, and anxiety over the atomic bomb. Conditions were right for a revival of revivalism.

The revival that came was associated with Billy Graham (William Franklin Graham, born 1918), a native North Carolinian and conservative Reformed Presbyterian, who attended Wheaton College in Illinois and, after graduation, began a radio ministry in Chicago associated with Moody Bible Institute. A Los Angeles tent meeting in 1949 catapulted him into national prominence as a preacher and evangelist. In 1950 he organized the Billy Graham Evangelistic Association and by 1956 was using all available forms of mass media to advertise his crusades and get his message out. His televised crusades in arenas in major cities enabled him to preach to millions at a time. Preparation for the crusades enabled Graham to enter into partnership with local churches in a way that had not been done by previous evangelists. The Graham organization made an effort to refer converts to local churches. Like the great evangelists before him, Graham teamed up with the musicians, in this case Cliff Barrow and the singer George Beverly Shea. They popularized the Swedish folk song "How Great Thou Art," which was taken into the repertoire of every Protestant congregation. As in the Billy Sunday revivals, people came forward at Graham's invitation at the end of his sermons to make a "decision for Christ" while the choir sang softly "Just as I Am." While previous evangelists had the support of leading businessmen, Billy Graham was sought after as a religious adviser to every president of the United States from Eisenhower to Clinton. He was especially close to Lyndon Johnson and Richard Nixon. Revivalism and the civil religion were seldom more closely allied.

The general revival of religion in the 1950s eventuated in the planting of congregations and the building of thousands of new church buildings in the burgeoning suburbs to which Americans moved by the millions with the help of G.I. loans and good jobs in flourishing industries. American church membership was at an all-time high.

The Church Growth Movement and Seeker Services

Just as the Billy Graham crusades were gaining momentum in the United States and throughout the world, at the high point of religious affiliation in the United States, the growth of new suburban congregations, and the expansion of facilities in older urban congregations, the baby boomers for whom these facilities were built began to leave the churches in droves. In the United States, sociological studies have shown that 60 percent of the baby boom generation born between 1946 and 1964 left their church of origin during and after the 1960s. While a pattern of young adults drifting away from church existed throughout U.S. social history, fewer have returned to church later in life than previously, and many who have returned have migrated to other churches or religions.[20]

It should be noted that this tremendous loss of millions of members occurred even though many churches in the 1960s and 1970s engaged in efforts to "make worship relevant." The Roman Catholic Church led the way, in the aftermath of the Second Vatican Council, with reformed vernacular liturgies and by inculturating Christian worship into popular American culture with its folk masses in the 1960s and 1970s. Other churches that embraced the liturgical renewal movement of the twentieth century (which will be dealt with in chapter 18) also discarded archaic language and employed more contemporary forms of architecture and music. These efforts were not considered evangelistic in the sense of reaching out to the unchurched. The folk masses and renewed liturgies of the 1960s and 1970s were really designed to meet the needs and desires of church members who were becoming as "bored" with the tradition as those who left the church altogether. Ignazio Silone spoke for his generation worldwide when he wrote:

One fine Sunday some of us stopped going to Mass, not because Catholic dogma seemed to us, all of a sudden, false, but because the people who went began to bore us and we were drawn to the company of those who stayed away . . . what characterized our revolt was the choice of comrades. . . . Without the slightest attempt at resistance, indeed with the well-known fervor of neophytes, one accepts the language, symbols, organization, discipline, tactics, programs and doctrine of the party to which one's new comrades belong. It is hardly surprising that rarely should anything learned in the catechism and schoolbooks hinder one's docile acceptance of the new orthodoxy. Indeed, one does not even feel the need of refuting them, because all of that has become part of the world one has left behind. They are neither true nor false; they are "bourgeois," dead leaves.[21]

The argument here is peer influence, an influence that can trump all others. Granted that some of these new comrades left the church because of real disagreements with its doctrines, one cannot help but feel that the main reason people left was simply that they had grown distrustful of any institutions. Worship experiences alone had little to do with their search for something else.

But worship experiences had something to do with their return to church. During the 1980s, new-paradigm churches designed "seeker services" to attract and hold the unchurched, based on the order of worship with which they were familiar in the evangelical tradition (frontier revival). The pioneers were the Garden Grove Community Church in Anaheim, California (known as the "Crystal Cathedral"), pastored by Robert Schuller (Reformed Church in America), and the Willow Creek Community Church in Barrington, Illinois, pastored by Bill Hybels (Wheaton College). In each case, Schuller and Hybels discovered what had turned people away from churches and determined not to offer those things. In each case, they began holding services in neutral settings—Schuller in a drive-in movie lot and Hybels in a movie theater. They were soon drawing thousands of people to Sunday and weekend services. These models were copied by mainline Protestant congregations during the 1990s. Two of the most successful were the Community Church of Joy in suburban Phoenix, Arizona, pastored by Walt Kallestad (Evangelical Lutheran Church in America), and Saddleback Community Church in Orange County, California, pastored by Rick Warren (Southern Baptist).

These services intentionally employed popular cultural expressions, especially forms of popular music but also architectural settings, that were familiar to the unchurched to whom these churches were appealing. These seeker services were developed as a form of evangelistic outreach to the large portion of the population in the baby boom generation that had become unchurched. The Crystal Cathedral model still had some traces of traditional worship: Schuller had installed a magnificent pipe organ and continued to wear an academic gown in his Reformed tradition. Willow Creek's format was simpler: a half hour of praise band music (sometimes with a drama) followed by a forty-five-minute message, strictly timed. Pastor Rick Warren of the Saddleback Community Church advocates doing away with everything that smacks of the traditional images of "church," especially pipe organs and hymns.[22] In their place have appeared rock combos that perform Christian contemporary music designed to reach the generation nurtured by rock music and who attended rock concerts. Pastors Walt Kallestad and Timothy Wright of the Community Church of Joy speak unapologetically about using the entertainment culture in evangelism and worship.[23] These weekend services are advertised for "seekers"; the faithful gather midweek for a more hardcore Christian message, baptism, and Holy Communion.

With a nod to the tradition of the camp meeting, Willow Creek's campus is located in a bucolic exurban area with a chapel-auditorium on a hillside above a lake. The thousands of people who attend weekend services arrive by car, and the parking lots are as large as those of the largest suburban shopping malls. Parking lot attendants direct traffic to expedite finding parking and getting into the building on time for the service and the simultaneously held "Promiseland" children's education. The ample concourses are staffed with information booths advertising Willow Creek's myriad small groups and ministry activities. A food court provides a full breakfast or brunch to the Sunday crowds. The praise band, drama group, and speaker are amplified by sight as well as sound on large projection screens, on which may also be shown the lyrics of the song the congregation is invited to join in singing. Willow Creek has its imitators in thousands of evangelical and mainline churches that also try to be seeker-friendly.[24] Some older congregations that cannot start from scratch with the unchurched offer "contemporary" as well as "traditional" services. Others that don't have the staff to offer two or more different kinds of services practice a "blended" service that combines both traditional and contemporary elements (by which is usually meant different musical styles).

The model of these "megachurches" coincided with the principles of the church growth movement that originated in the studies of Donald McGavran, a Disciples of Christ missionary in India in the 1950s. McGavran wanted to know why some missions grew and others didn't. His research resulted in a number of books that outline principles for creating the conditions necessary for missionary success. In the early 1960s, McGavran returned to the United States and became a member of the faculty of Fuller Theological Seminary. The principles of "church growth" that he developed were originally taught as missiological theory but were applied to the North American cultural context beginning in the 1970s. Encouraged by successful models in reaching the unchurched provided by the megachurches, "church growth" in theory and practice exploded beyond its association with Fuller Seminary. While McGavran himself did not think these principles would affect worship, worship was massively affected by being turned into an evangelistic tool that made use of the expressions of contemporary popular culture to target particular audiences.

The church growth movement, combined with the examples of the successful megachurches, has provided know-how for target marketing to the baby boom generation and has produced generation-specific worship. The baby boomers were born into highly affluent Western societies with seemingly limitless possibilities. Wade Clark Roof found that even though many boomers did not achieve all of their goals, 86 percent of these self-believing Americans believed that there was no limit to what human beings could do if they really put their minds to it. Further, 71 percent held that a person who was strong and determined could pretty much control what happens in life. And 66 percent agreed that if someone does not succeed in life, it's usually the person's own fault.[25] But their own children have experienced limitations and failures in economies that could not boom forever, family dysfunction and widespread depression caused in large part by their parents' failed marriages, and mass death around the world caused by ethnic cleansing, genocide, politically sponsored starvation, the AIDS epidemic, and global terrorism. Generation X and their millennial younger siblings have come to regard modernity with its positivistic philosophy as a dead end, opting instead for postmodern relativism and nihilism.

This significant change in philosophic outlook reminds us that generations are not defined just by being born within a certain historical time frame. They are formed by people who share a common experience during the formative phase of their lives. Strauss and Howe note that what happens to a generation, particularly in its youth and young adulthood, shapes a peer personality. Thus, "a generation has collective attitudes about family life, sex roles, institutions, politics, religion, lifestyle, and the future."[26] The baby boomers came of age in a time of unparalleled affluence. They participated in gender, educational, political, and religious revolutions, and then turned within themselves to find meaning and purpose. But we must remember that they experienced in their formative years in the 1950s the tensions of the Cold War, the threat of nuclear holocaust, anticommunist paranoia in the United States, and largely unrecognized discrimination against minorities, women, the poor, homosexuals, and anybody who dared to be different. They grew up with so much tension and suppressed feelings that they were a time bomb set to go off. Not surprisingly, the "soft institutions" of the family and religion were the first to feel the countercultural backlash, and they have pioneered new paradigms of family and religion. But their offspring had very different formative social experiences.

Differences between generations are real; that's why there can be clashes between them. Churches need to consider more carefully the impact of embracing the mission strategy of designing worship and congregational life for particular generations. Generational dynamics are not static. Strauss and Howe say that each generation negotiates its own passage through four main stages of its life cycle: youth, young adulthood, midlife, and old age. Many aspects of generational dynamics are temporary and change as the generation goes through the next stage in life. Church leaders who have targeted specific generations need to constantly adapt to the life changes of the generation they have recruited into church membership. They also need to recognize that what appeals to one generation will not necessarily appeal to the next generation. Many seeker services based on strategies developed in the 1980s risk becoming outdated. Many Generation Xers born since 1965 have gravitated to the "praise and worship" services that grew out of the Pentecostal tradition and the charismatic movement of the 1970s. There has also been evidence of an interest in traditional worship and a retrieval of old rituals among those who were reaching adulthood toward the end of the twentieth century.

Pentecostalism

We need to back up here to consider the contribution of Pentecostalism to the revival spirit in America and around the world. Pentecostal worship depends on an immediate experience of the Holy Spirit and therefore has a theological heritage in groups such as the Quakers, the Shakers, and the holiness movement that came out of Methodism with its emphasis on "Christian perfection" or the "second blessing," premillennialism, and the "faith healing" movement.[27]

But the first sign of Pentecostalism as we know it occurred on January 1, 1901, when Bethel Bible College student Agnes S. Ozman began to speak in tongues. Her experience was soon shared with other members of her class in Topeka, Kansas, and the director of the school, Charles Fox Parham (1873–1929). Parham began to incorporate ecstatic phenomena into revival services he conducted in Kansas and Texas. He taught that the experience of speaking in tongues was the sign that a person had received the Holy Spirit. It was the assurance of salvation for which the holiness movement had been looking. This idea was taken up by the black Holiness preacher William J. Seymour (1870–1922), who was associate pastor of a Nazarene Church in Los Angeles. Disagreement with the senior pastor (a woman) forced him to open his own church, the Apostolic Faith Gospel Mission on Azusa Street in 1906. It was from this mission that the Pentecostal explosion moved in all directions and into all segments of society.[28]

The Azusa Street revival was as formative of Pentecostalism as the Cane Ridge Camp Meeting had been of evangelical revivalism a century earlier. Every day for nearly three years, the Azusa Street revival persisted, attracting seekers, hecklers, spiritualists, and people of all races from every walk of life. The *Los Angeles Times* covered the revival as a major media event but could conceal neither its scorn nor its own sensationalist rhetoric: "Weird Babel of Tongues—New Sect of Fanatics Is Breaking Loose—Wild Scene Last Night on Azusa Street—Gurgle of Wordless Talk by a Sister," screamed the headlines. Nor in a day of strict segregation did the *Times* overlook the racial mix of those who gathered in the mission. The *Times* reported the "shouts of an old colored 'mammy'; in a frenzy of religious zeal," who, in "the strangest harangue ever uttered," cried out, "'You-oo-oo gou-loo-loo come under the bloo-oo-oo boo-loo' . . . Colored people and a sprinkling of whites compose the congregation, and night is hideous in the neighborhood by the howling of worshippers, who spend hours swaying forth and back in a nerve-wracking attitude of prayer and supplication. They claim to have the 'gift of tongues' and to be able to comprehend the babble."[29]

The Pentecostal movement was characterized from the beginning by its appeal to people of different races—blacks, whites, and Latinos. Some sociologists have analyzed the movement as a lower-class religious protest against the social exclusiveness and cold rationalism of middle-class mainline Protestant denominations.[30] The class-based explanation, however, is belied by the fact that Pentecostalism has embraced middle-class and even affluent members as well as those who are on the margins of society. As James F. White has suggested, Pentecostalism is "the first postenlightenment tradition."[31] It is a massive rejection of rational religion that, by the beginning of the twenty-first century, has become a worldwide movement embracing a half billion adherents.

For its first fifty years, the Pentecostal movement had little influence on the mainline Protestant churches. But in the early 1960s, a charismatic movement, which included speaking in tongues and healing, made an impact in both Roman Catholic and Protestant churches. Charismatic renewal surfaced among Roman Catholics on the campuses of Duquesne and Notre Dame Universities in the late 1960s. It caused serious internal conflict in thousands of Baptist, Episcopal, Lutheran, Methodist, and Presbyterian congregations over both the charismatic activities and the belief that "the full gospel" included the "baptism in the Holy Spirit," the outward sign of which is speaking in tongues.[32]

Pentecostal and charismatic worship theoretically follows no order or structure, since ministers and people must follow the promptings of the Holy Spirit. Prayer and praise are constant components of this worship, and they can break out at any time. The act of worship is actually more prominent in Pentecostal and charismatic services than the act of preaching.

The Praise and Worship Movement

The church that connected with post-Enlightenment or postmodern youth was the Vineyard Fellowship. The late John Wimber had previously been a member of the Yorba Linda Friends Church, an evangelical Quaker congregation, and then a pastor in the Calvary Chapel movement. His charismatic practice and theology led him to found a new church, the Anaheim Vineyard Fellowship, and later to spearhead a new denomination, the Vineyard Association of Churches.[33]

Under the influence of the Vineyard, the Pentecostal-inspired "praise and worship" service actually follows a pattern that is not so different from the revival service. There is an opening section of congregational singing, prayer, and announcements (usually twenty to forty-five minutes), followed by the sermon, followed by "ministry time" that may include prayer and charismatic activity. Singing is a very important ingredient in the service, and the song leader actually functions as the worship leader. The song leader decides how many songs should be sung, how long the singing should go on, when people should stand, and when they should sit. The idea is to have a flow of songs that leads in a particular direction and prepares the congregation for the "message."

The Vineyard uses five distinct themes in a medley of free-flowing praise: (1) invitation, (2) engagement, (3) exaltation, (4) adoration, and (5) intimacy.[34] The music may begin with upbeat gathering songs praising God, then shift to quieter reflection on being in the presence of God, and finally move to very subdued songs whose words address God directly and personally. If Holy Communion is celebrated, it may be administered during this worship and praise medley at the point at which songs of intimacy with Jesus are sung. In the typical Vineyard order of service, announcements, the message, and ministry to personal needs follow. This is the same order followed in evangelical seeker services, but Vineyard worship is more participatory. People more readily join in the singing and freely make use of bodily gestures such as raising hands, clapping, kneeling, hugging, or crying during praise and worship.

A distinction is made between "praise" and "worship" in that praise is about God, worship is directed to God. The songs sung in these services tend to mimic the trends in popular music, providing a Christian alternative to secular music, which has taken the name "Christian music." The contemporary Christian worship music industry has become a big business in itself. For a while it was dominated by four big labels (Maranatha! Music, Mercy Publishing, Integrity Music, and EMI Christian Music Group and its Christian Worship Music label, Worship Together), but the creation of Christian Copyright Licensing Inc. has made it possible for smaller independent companies to enter the market.[35]

The praise choruses and more exuberant styles of praise and worship have had an impact on Protestant worship in the late twentieth century, just as the revival services did in the nineteenth century, and denominations have begun to publish their own collections of "Christian music." It seems fitting that worship in this tradition, which has been so tied to American culture, should finally become a business in itself, since commercialism and consumerism have been hallmarks of American culture. The fact that popular Christian music is tied in with the recording industry and is really music for performers rather than for participants, and therefore for entertainment rather than worship, does not dissuade leaders of the praise and worship movement from using it, since entertainment is also an important feature of contemporary American culture, and their goal is to reach the culture. In the next chapter we will trace through this same historical time period a more countercultural form of Christian worship.

CHAPTER 17

Liturgical Restoration

The movements of worship awakening, described in the previous chapter, trace their origin to the Age of Enlightenment, yet they may be said to have been "in, but not of" the Enlightenment. Revivals countered the spirit of rationalism, but not in the name of orthodoxy; rather, they aimed at producing a conversion experience. This chapter looks at liturgical movements that were quite different from those stemming from the Great Awakenings. They have their genesis in an explicit reaction to the Enlightenment. Therefore, we must look at Enlightenment religion to see what the restorationists were reacting against.

The Enlightenment's Assault on Traditional Religion

Persons in positions of leadership in church and state reflected the Enlightenment's emphasis on reason and tried to create a "reasonable Christianity," including "reasonable" proposals for worship renewal. For example, as mentioned in the previous chapter, King Friedrich Wilhelm I of Prussia used Pietism to advance reforms in church and society. The King of Prussia had reason to champion the Pietists. The House of Hohenzollern had been Calvinist since the early seventeenth century, ruling a territory that was overwhelmingly Lutheran (including Brandenburg, East Prussia, and Silesia). But the expansion of the Kingdom of Prussia also enlarged the Reformed population. It was useful to the Hohenzollerns to pursue a policy of religious toleration, and the Pietists were known for their disinclination to engage in confessional diatribes. Toleration was expanded under his son Friedrich II (Frederick the Great, King of Prussia 1740–1786), who encouraged religious refugees—even Jesuits after the suppression of the Society by Pope Clement XIV in 1773—to settle in his dominions.

Frederick the Great was an adherent of Christian Wolff, a patron of Voltaire, a correspondent with Diderot and the Encyclopedists. His father had suppressed the more "Catholic" features of Lutheranism in his realm, such as vestments and altars that offended his Reformed ministers. Frederick II was content to leave ecclesiastical matters to the bishops and consistories, but his religious organization of the army shows his liturgical preferences: daily hymn singing, morning and evening devotions, and communion twice a month. His greatest contribution to changes in the religious life of his realm was seeing that the clergy received a rationalist education. His professor of philosophy at the University of Königsberg, Immanuel Kant, after the king's death and in the face of reaction, defended *Religion within the Limits of Reason Alone* (1793). While Kant saw no value in the sacraments as supernatural ordinances, he saw their social usefulness as rites of initiation and communal bonding.[1]

Johann Sebastian Bach (1685–1750), as cantor of Saint Thomas Church and School in Leipzig, was on a collision course with the rector of the Thomasschule as soon as the rationalist Johann August Ernesti was appointed, over the role of worship and the kind of resources needed to support each view. Cantor Bach believed that worship is rendered "to the glory of God alone" (*soli Deo gloria*) and that a "well-ordered church music" was needed to support such worship. This might require the removal of untalented choristers. Rector Ernesti believed that worship exists to edify the congregation and that the important thing is that any who wished could sing in the choir.[2] This is a conflict that has played out in many congregations ever since that time.

Günther Stiller, in his study of liturgical life in Leipzig during and after the cantorship of Bach, shows the vitality of worship and sacramental practice in that orthodox Lutheran city during Bach's tenure and its rapid deterioration during the superintendency of Johann Georg Rosenmüller, who served as chief pastor in Leipzig's churches after 1785. As noted in chapter fifteen, annual communion attendance held at fifteen thousand to twenty thousand in each of the two principal churches of the city (Saint Thomas and Saint Nicholas) in the period from 1723 to 1743. From 1786 the number of communicants did not rise above ten thousand.[3] Communion ceased to be an integral part of the chief Sunday service; it was tacked on to the service of the word for those who desired to receive the sacrament after the rest of the congregation was dismissed. Also, the number of extra services on church festivals and prayer offices during the week were cut back drastically after 1786 because of the decline in worship attendance. It is apparent that the changes were either chasing the people away in droves or were not drawing them back.

Throughout Germany there was an assault on the Lutheran liturgy toward the end of the eighteenth century. A revolution in education, especially in Prussia, eliminated the old Latin schools, but with the closing of the Latin schools, the institutional foundations of church music were undermined. "Foolish frills" such as liturgical vestments, candles, ornamentation in churches, and chanting of texts were put aside. The only texts that remained chanted in the Lutheran liturgy by the beginning of the nineteenth century in most places were the Lord's Prayer and the Words of Institution and sometimes the Preface. The pericope system of lectionary readings was steadily abandoned by pastors, who were given more direct control over the liturgy. This also led to the breakdown of the church year. In 1816 a new church festival was made official by King Friedrich Wilhelm III: *Totenfest* or Memorial Day.[4] Liturgical prayers in Lutheran agendas throughout Germany were changed to reflect the spirit of the age.[5]

The Holy Roman Emperor, Joseph II (1765–90), made similar efforts to bring Catholicism under the Enlightenment. Under the Hapsburgs, there was also an attempt to make worship more relevant to the people. Joseph II could enact changes only in the hereditary Hapsburg lands of Austria, Hungary, and Belgium, but these lands were ruled jointly with his mother, Empress Maria Teresa, until her death in 1780.

Joseph recognized the need for toleration in order to attract and hold needed talent such as Frederick II was attracting to Prussia (and to keep Frederick II from luring persecuted Protestants to his territory), but Maria Teresa, embodying the *Pietas Austriaca*, resisted it. After her death, he was able to enact a Patent of Toleration in 1781. But Joseph became alarmed at the number of Protestants who registered their adherence to one of the tolerated confessions. So "his enduring monument was a Hapsburg monarchy which combined toleration with a good deal of intolerance"[6]

Upon the death of Maria Teresa, Joseph set up an Ecclesiastical Affairs Commission to create new dioceses that would be under his jurisdiction rather than that of the prince-archbishops of Salzburg and Passau. A total of 255 new parishes were created in Lower Austria, 121 in Upper Austria, 180 in Styria, and 83 in Carinthia. The new parishes were to have schools that children would be required to attend. The parish priests were to have adequate stipends to match new expectations. To pay for all this, Joseph dipped into monastic endowments and closed about one-third of the religious houses in Austria. Some of the monks were absorbed into the renewed parish priesthood; others were pensioned off; women religious were sent home. With the sale of monastery and diocesan seminary properties, Joseph erected new general seminaries with enlightened curricula in which the teaching was in the vernacular. The people went along with all this. But they resisted vigorously when their emperor cut processions, curtailed unauthorized pilgrimages, and required the dead to be buried in sacks in common graves outside of towns and cities rather than in coffins in private burial plots, in the interests of public health and reducing the financial strains on the poor caused by expensive burials.[7] His law required churches to provide coffins to transport corpses to the cemetery, but then the bodies would be buried in sacks and the coffins returned to the church for reuse.

Joseph regarded unnecessary grandeur and ostentation as a sign of false piety. In this regard he embraced the church music reforms championed by the "enlightened" Pope Benedict XIV, who in 1749 issued an encyclical promoting plainsong as the ideal church music and tolerating polyphony with organ or other instrumental accompaniment as long as it avoided theatrical effects and didn't obscure the comprehensibility of the text. A Viennese court decree of 1754 forbade the use of trumpets and drums in the service. This was honored more in the breach than in observance until 1782, when Prince-Archbishop of Salzburg Colloredo ordered instrumental music to be replaced by German songs. The next year he vetoed the epistle sonatas and instructed his court composer Michael Haydn to prepare simple settings of the graduals and offertories to be sung by the choir. During this period neither Michael nor his brother Franz Joseph Haydn wrote any mass settings. Wolfgang Amadeus Mozart (1756–1791) abandoned a C-minor Mass he was working on in 1783. But toward the end of his life he sought the position of kapellmeister at Saint Stephen's Cathedral in Vienna and began composing the kind of unadorned church music preferred in Josephine

Catholicism, such as the motet *Ave Verum*. At his untimely death in 1791, Mozart received a Josephine-style burial, not the pauper's burial that many of his romantic biographers assumed because he was buried in an unmarked common grave.[8]

In the meantime, Joseph II's brother Leopold, Duke of Tuscany and destined to succeed Joseph at his untimely death, initiated liturgical reforms with the assistance of Scipone de' Ricci, a Jansenist who had been vicar-general of the diocese of Florence and became bishop of Pistoia and Prato in 1780. Ricci wanted to make the parishes the center of liturgical life, which meant getting rid of the competition from private shrines and chapels in the houses of religious orders. He wanted to abolish private masses, which meant reforming the whole system of mass stipends. He wanted to reinstitute the communion of the people during the Mass and not from the reserved sacrament after the Mass was ended. He knew that vernacular liturgy was not a possibility, but he wanted missals printed with vernacular translations in parallel columns with the Latin texts so that the people could follow and participate as they were able. Since most of the clergy of these dioceses supported their bishop, a synod was held in Pistoia in 1786 to enact these and other resolutions. The synod adopted the Gallican Articles of 1682, which affirmed the independence of diocesan bishops from the papacy and held that bishops rule with the assent of their clergy. Religious orders were to be amalgamated into one order that followed the Benedictine Rule according to the use at Port-Royal. Marriages in the mountain villages were to be more strictly regulated to prevent people from marrying relatives. As in the case of Joseph's reforms, however, the people rebelled when changes affected customary practices and popular devotions. When Leopold moved to Vienna to succeed his brother, he advised his successor in Tuscany that Bishop Ricci was a liability and to reward him with a good pension. In any event, the pope withheld his approval of the resolutions from the Synod of Pistoia.[9]

The situation in France in the eighteenth century called for reforms such as Joseph II had implemented in Austria. The population was expanding rapidly, and new parishes were needed, especially in urban areas, but entrenched interests in the parishes prevented the subdivision of established parish boundaries. Police reports indicate increasing incidents of irreligious behavior as processions were mocked and pilgrimage shrines were allowed to fall into disrepair, but there was little support from the government to shore up traditional religious practices. The number and quality of parish priests declined after 1745, and many priests blamed the bishops for not recruiting more and better candidates, which might have been helped by improving the economic situation of the parish clergy. The parish clergy embraced the Jansenist idea that the bishops should govern subject to the consent of their clergy. Their social position was further undermined when, in 1787, Protestants gained the right to marry according to their own customs.

The Church and the French Revolution

In the financial crisis that precipitated the calling of the Estates-General into session, the bishops declined to bail out the monarchy by selling off church property, and this set the stage for the more radical actions of the National Assembly when it convened in 1789.[10] It is unlikely that most members of the Estates-General wanted to assault the church, but it inherited the full force of the financial crisis from which the church had declined to save the monarchy. In the early phase of the resulting revolution, the bourgeoisie of the Third Estate, who had the greatest number of individual votes in the Assembly, with the support of the parish priests, abolished the feudal dues, which deprived the pope of his annates. This also deprived the clergy of their tithes, but other legislation nationalized the church lands and from the revenues provided salaries for the parish clergy. The next step was to suspend monastic vows taken after October 28, 1789. Religious houses were closed, and monks were given liberal pensions; nuns were not affected by these laws. In the Civil Constitution of the Clergy, passed on July 12, 1790, the historic dioceses were reconfigured to match the division of France into *départements*, and the clergy were officially made civil servants whose salaries were paid by the state. This produced a major schism between jurors, who signed the constitution, and nonjurors, who refused to sign.[11]

A second phase of the revolution began in 1792, when radicals gained control of the National Assembly, deposed the king, and organized a republican convention. A reign of terror was commenced against political opponents, including the nonjurors, who were given fifteen days to leave France. Estimates of the nonjurors who went into exile range from twenty thousand to forty thousand, but many were apprehended and executed before they could leave the country. King Louis XVI and Queen Marie Antoinette and thousands of nobles also were executed. The state took over from the churches schools which, at the elementary level, were free and compulsory. Christianity was replaced with a religion of nationalism and reason. The Church of Saint Genevieve was converted into a civil Pantheon, to hold the ashes of Voltaire. The Cathedral of Notre Dame was converted into a "Temple of Reason." The church year festivals were abolished and replaced with deistic festivals, such as the Festival to the Supreme Being instituted by Robespierre. Many churches were closed.

But, just as in the case of Joseph II's reforms in Austria and Leopold's reforms in Tuscany, there was a popular reaction to this assault on traditional religion. A startling revival of religion occurred in the winter of 1794–1795. Bishop Grégoire ignited this revival by making a long speech in the republican convention, calling for freedom of worship, including for Protestants. He then resumed episcopal functions and reopened the churches of his diocese as of January 1, 1795. He issued a proclamation of reconciliation between Christianity and the revolution. The clergy convened a national council in 1797 and reorganized on the basis of the Civil Constitution and the Gallican Articles, basically creating a national church without state support. The bourgeoisie supported the Constitutional clergy, but many of the peasants preferred the papalists, and exiled priests began to return in droves to minister to them. Papalist Roman Catholics, however, were split between those who supported King Louis XVIII and those who accepted the revolution.

Reactions to the Enlightenment

Some historians see the Age of Enlightenment ending with the French Revolution. This was particularly the case among those who regarded the Enlightenment as a French movement. But if the Enlightenment is seen as a pan-European (even a trans-Atlantic) movement, then the picture is different. Revolution was a part of the Enlightenment.[12] At the very beginning of this historical age was the Glorious Revolution in Great Britain in 1688, in which regime change was accomplished with very little bloodshed. The revolutions in public policy, including religious toleration and liturgical "reforms," enacted by the Enlightenment despots, Frederick II in Prussia and Joseph II in Austria, were a significant part of the age. The American Revolution was led by men who were conversant in the theories of government and the nature of humanity propounded by David Hume, John Locke, Jean-Jacques Rousseau, and Voltaire. The French Revolution was a product of Enlightenment thinking, even though it resulted in a very bloody regime change. The administration of Napoléon Bonaparte (1770–1821) as first consul and emperor of the French can be seen as consistent with and even extending the political and religious reforms undertaken by Frederick II and Joseph II. In a nod to the papalists, however, Napoléon restored relations with the papacy on his terms and brought the pope to Paris to preside at his coronation in 1804.

The reaction of the great Viennese composer Ludwig van Beethoven (1770–1827) to Napoléon's self-crowning as emperor of the French is well known. He tore up the title page of his revolutionary Third Symphony (1803), which had been subtitled "Bonaparte." When the symphony was published in 1806, it was given the subtitle "Eroica" and was described as having been "composed to celebrate the memory of a great man." Beethoven, like many of his contemporaries (the English poet William Wordsworth, for example), became disillusioned with revolution. What is less well known is Beethoven's approach to the problem of church music, since he was not a churchgoer and wrote very little church music or even sacred music in general. It is not so well understood why he wrote so little church music. The reason is that he simply found the standard church music of the time, even the best examples in the great masses of Franz Josef Haydn and Wolfgang Amadeus Mozart, too operatic and too sentimental for their purpose and the texts they set. His one effort to produce a mass setting, his Mass in C, commissioned in 1807 by Prince Anton Esterhazy (of the same family who had employed Haydn for several decades), became the occasion of his greatest public humiliation when the prince asked him, after its first performance, "Well, Beethoven, what's this?" "This" was a setting of the Roman Catholic Mass that avoided the operatic tendencies and sentimental character of the conventional church music of that era. It really was an attempt to express the Enlightenment principles of church music. Beethoven had a devil of a time getting it published and finally just gave it to Breitkopf & Härtel in 1809 as a present. Even at this, it wasn't published until 1811.

In the meantime, during 1809 he noted in his diary, "In the old church modes the devotion is divine . . . and may God permit me to express it some day." That "some day" came when Beethoven decided to compose a mass to celebrate the ecclesiastical elevation of his pupil and patron, Archduke Rudolf, to the rank of archbishop and the dignity of cardinal. Thus began the four-year musical odyssey (1818–1822) of composing the *Missa Solemnis*, which Beethoven regarded as "the greatest work which I have composed." But it began with Beethoven noting in his diary, "In order to write true church music . . . look through all the monastic church chorales and also the strophes in the most correct translations and perfect prosody in all Christian-Catholic psalms and hymns generally." He immersed himself in the music of Palestrina, Handel, J. S. Bach, and C. P. E. Bach, and this is reflected in the finished result. Of course, what Beethoven finally produced was an immense symphonic work with chorus and soloists of such profound musical complexity, scope, and duration, and calling for such huge musical forces, that it could not be easily presented even in a cathedral as an actual mass setting. But even as church music that could not easily be performed in a church service, it marked the departure from the church music of the Age of Enlightenment that would characterize the romantic restoration. It was an effort to bring the models of the past to the rescue of the present, and it really had as much to do with glorifying God as edifying man, even to the point of concluding the exuberant Gloria in Excelsis Deo with shouts of *Gloria! Gloria!* to balance the twice-repeated *Credo! Credo!* that followed.

The Restoration of Benedictine Monasteries and Roman Catholic Liturgy

Even after the fall of Napoléon, the Catholic Church in France remained a state institution. There was a movement led by Félicité de Lamennais (1782–1854) to separate church and state in order to gain more freedom for the church, but this movement was resisted by the French bishops, and Lamennais appealed to Rome. Forced to take sides, Pope Gregory XVI mildly rebuked Lamennais, who eventually left the church. Nevertheless, in this period of the restoration of the Bourbon monarchy under King Louis Phillippe (1815–1830), several religious orders were restored. Along with these restorations came the formation of new religious orders that ministered to the urban poor; these included the Oblates of Mary Immaculate, founded by Eugene de Mazenod, and the Society of Saint Vincent de Paul, founded by Frédéric Ozanam.

The liturgical restoration movement is regarded as beginning with the formation of a new Benedictine monastery at Solesmes in 1833 by Dom Prosper Guéranger (1805–1875).[13] Under his leadership, Solesmes became a center of historical liturgical study and the revival of Gregorian chant. Guéranger was part of the movement to form a closer relationship between the French church and the papacy. His *Institutiones liturgiques* (1840), volume 2, was a thinly veiled polemic against the Gallican rites in favor of the Roman Rite. Pope Pius IX supported the work of Solesmes, made Guéranger its abbot, and strove against the resistance of the French bishops to establish the Roman Rite in France. It cannot be said that the liturgical movement associated with Guéranger had a great impact on parochial liturgical life, other than lending the considerable prestige of Solesmes to the introduction of the Roman Rite. But Solesmes became a model of how the Roman Rite should be celebrated, and its (romanticized) singing of Gregorian chant was adopted by everyone. Other Benedictine monasteries were founded, and they, too, embraced Solesmes' liturgical life as the ideal. These monasteries became the centers of liturgical renewal in the early twentieth century.

Roman Liturgy in America

The experience of the Roman Catholic Church in France during the revolution and Napoleonic Era had an impact on Catholicism in the United States. In the early American republic, Catholics were few, there was no bishop, and their pastoral needs were served mostly by Jesuits. In a sense, they were in the same position as the Protestant Episcopal Church, which formed after the American Revolution. Catholics built houses of worship that were as plain as the Protestant meetinghouses and elected trustees to look after them. Charles Carroll (1737–1832) of Maryland held the first vicar apostolate assigned by Rome to the United States of America, and he became bishop of Baltimore in 1788.

The lay trustees sought to share authority and responsibility in the maintenance of the church buildings and in the calling of priests to serve parishes, much as the landed gentry did in Europe. Bishop Carroll was opposed to sharing authority with the lay trustees, but he compromised with them. After Bishop Carroll, all subsequent bishops were foreign born. In the aftermath of the French Revolution, they were not disposed to sharing the governance of the church with elected lay leaders. Between 1790 and 1860, ten million immigrants came to the United States. Forty percent of these were Irish and German. Most of the Irish and about a third of the Germans were Roman Catholics. After the Civil War, they would be joined by millions of other Roman Catholic immigrants from southern and eastern Europe. The bishops became the protectors of Catholic immigrants from Protestants, who even formed a political party with anti-Catholicism as a platform (the Know Nothing Party). The parish priests appointed by the bishops served as father figures to their congregations and were addressed as "Father." Immigrants built churches that replicated the churches they had left behind in the cities and towns of Europe. The plain white meetinghouses gave way to ornate neo-Baroque and neo-Gothic structures, often of cathedral proportions, furnished with life-size crucifixes, statues, pictures, candles, incense, and side altars. While a variety of ethnic features marked the church buildings and parish life, the Roman Catholic hierarchy in the United States united the variety of ethnic parishes with a common Roman Catholic liturgy that allowed for no deviation. The priests performed elaborate liturgies not just on Sundays, but throughout the week. Popular devotions such as the Stations of the Cross, the Rosary, the Sacred Heart of Jesus, and various novenas to Our Lady were emphasized, while popular observances that were a part of Irish, Italian, or Polish religious culture were carefully controlled.

A system of parochial schools helped to form a distinctly Catholic culture in a Protestant land.[14]

Lutheran Liturgical Recovery in Germany and America

Lutheranism also was affected by the Napoleonic Wars. One consequence of the wars was the dissolution of the Holy Roman Empire in 1806. No overarching political structure replaced it until Bismarck created the German Empire in 1870 with the Prussian Hohenzollerns as kaisers. The multitude of small German states continued to exist, but the territories of several of them were greatly enlarged. To Prussia, which had already acquired the dignity of kingdom, were now added the kingdoms of Saxony, Württemberg, and Bavaria. The religious consequence of reconfigurations of territory was that strong minority populations were added to the majority population. Thus, Lutheran Franconia with its capital city of Nuremberg was added to Catholic Bavaria and its Catholic Wittelsbach rulers. Reformed Westphalia was added to Lutheran Prussia with its Reformed Hohenzollern rulers. Under the German system in which the ruler functioned as *summus episcopus*, Lutheran church administration could be supervised by non-Lutheran rulers. This was not such a problem in Bavaria, since confessional differences between Lutherans and Roman Catholics were quite pronounced (and became even more so). In Prussia the Hohenzollerns moved to create, for administrative purposes, one Protestant church, the Prussian Union of Lutherans and Reformed. Whether to placate his Lutheran subjects, to express his own religious aesthetics, or in response to the enthusiasm for Luther studies occasioned by the three hundredth anniversary of the Reformation in 1817, or all three, King Friedrich Wilhelm III guided the restoration of a mass order in 1822 based on the Lutheran church orders of the sixteenth century.[15] This liturgy was imposed on everyone, both the Reformed and the Lutherans, who since the reign of Frederick the Great had become used to more rationalistic liturgies.

Meanwhile, in Bavaria, a young pastor with high-church inclinations, Wilhelm Löhe (1808–1872), was assigned to the small Franconian village of Neuendettelsau in 1837. There he developed a liturgical life centered in the restored Lutheran liturgy based on sixteenth-century church orders, including the restoration of the prayer offices for the deaconess community, which he founded. Pastors in the mission school, which he also founded in Neuendettelsau, carried his liturgy to the American Midwest (Ohio, Michigan, Iowa).

This is the point at which we jump to the United States. Henry Melchior Muhlenberg, who organized the first Lutheran ministerium and synod in North America in 1748, also prepared a common liturgy for the use of the pastors and congregations. After his death in 1787, this common liturgy was revised in various synods to reflect the rationalist spirit of the age. The result was dislocations in the liturgical order such as occurred in Germany. Beginning in the 1820s, under the emerging leadership of Simon Samuel Schmucker, revivalist influences also entered into Lutheran worship. If revivalism's effects on Lutheran worship were moderate in comparison with its effects on other denominations in America, this can be attributed to the fact that most Lutheran worship in the United States during the nineteenth century continued to be in German. This was not just a matter of cultural conservatism, although Pennsylvania itself was virtually a German-language cocoon. Rather, millions of German immigrants continued to arrive in

North America throughout the nineteenth century. The seminary in Gettysburg, Pennsylvania, could not provide enough German-speaking pastors to meet the demand.

The Germans who settled in the Midwest, however, brought their own liturgies with them, and their own sense of identity. The Saxons who formed the Missouri Synod came to the United States to escape the Prussian Union and eschewed fellowship with Lutherans in Pennsylvania because they shared pastors and buildings with the German Reformed Church. These Saxons also resisted the liturgical recovery spearheaded by King Friedrich Wilhelm III until the end of the nineteenth century. The Franconians who formed the Joint Synod of Ohio brought with them Löhe's *Agende für christliche Gemeinden* (Agenda for Christian Congregations, 1844), which was a better model of historic Lutheran liturgy than the liturgies of the older synods on the East Coast. But there were also English-speaking Lutherans on the East Coast, and beginning in the 1860s, they were interested in recovering a more confessional and liturgical form of Lutheranism. Work proceeded, under the leadership of some fine scholars—Beale Melanchthon Schmucker (the son of Samuel S. Schmucker), George U. Wenner, and Edward T. Horn—to produce an English-language Lutheran Common Service that would be based on the pure Lutheran church orders of the sixteenth century. The language of this liturgy reflected the language of the *Book of Common Prayer*, and the musical setting provided with the text was an eclectic mixture of plainsong, Anglican chant, and historic pieces of Lutheran service music. This Common Service of 1888 was approved by the General Council, the General Synod, and the United Synod of the South and was incorporated into their hymnals. As other synodical bodies produced English-language worship books, the Common Service was included in these hymnals.

The Common Service provides an interesting case study of what happens in restoration. An old liturgy is never restored as it was; groups use a historic liturgy to serve contemporary purposes. The Common Service was a Lutheran liturgy adapted to North America. It was in the English language. It recognized the participatory nature of American Protestant worship. It had the congregation sing liturgical texts that, in the sixteenth century, would have been sung by choirs. So, for example, the congregation sang the Gloria in Excelsis, most often to an old Scottish chant, not the chorale "All Glory Be to God on High." Amateur choirs were painstakingly trained to sing plainsong settings of introits and graduals.

Popular revivalist hymns were gradually, if not always favorably, removed from hymnals. But even this suppression of revivalism—at least in the church service, if not in the Sunday school—reflected the liturgical culture of the early twentieth century. After World War I there was a move away from revivalism and toward respectability in Protestant worship generally. James F. White wrote that the aesthetic experience replaced the conversion experience as thousands of neo-Gothic churches dotted the landscape while surpliced choirs filled divided chancels before the high altar, which was pushed up against the "east wall."[16] But even by the late nineteenth century, there is evidence of refinement in Lutheran churches in particular and Protestant churches in general in terms of: the return to the earlier practice of preaching from a manuscript; the employment of trained organists and the improvement in church instruments; the embellishment of the chancel with flowers; the introduction of stained glass; scripture scenes painted on the wall behind the altar, which once again assumed the position of the central focal point; and even crosses and lighted candles on the altar.

The Oxford and Cambridge Movements

The "liturgical aesthetics" of the late nineteenth and early twentieth centuries owed a lot to movements within Anglicanism. The Oxford Movement began in 1832 in reaction to the act of British parliament that abolished some dioceses in the Church of Ireland (Anglican). Against an Erastian system in which Parliament, which now seated non-Anglicans, was making decisions affecting the Church of England, the Oxford Tractarians (most famously John Keble, E. B. Pusey, and John Henry Newman) appealed to the apostolic foundation of the church and its governance by bishops in historical succession. They saw the Church *of* England in continuity more than in discontinuity with the Church *in* England since the time of Augustine of Canterbury.[17]

The Oxford Movement was more concerned with theology and ecclesiology than with liturgics. But simultaneously with the Tractarian movement, an ecclesiastical version of romanticism, which was producing a Gothic revival, flourished under the leadership of the Cambridge Camden Society. For three decades after 1839, this society took the lead in enforcing an Anglican orthodoxy concerning church architecture and vestments.[18] Their ideal was the fourteenth-century English village church with its five sections—narthex, baptistery near the church entrance, nave, chancel, and sanctuary. The chancel was filled with lay choirs, who were vested like monks in cassocks and surplices and who at least sang an "anthem" if not settings of the propers and ordinary of the Mass. The high "east wall" altar, now farther removed from the lay worshipers, replaced the communion table. It was appointed with two communion candles on the mensa and six candles on the credence above the mensa. The celebrant was vested for Holy Communion in alb, stole, and chasuble. The chasuble was of "Gothic" cut rather than the Baroque fiddleback version common in the Roman Catholic Church.

It wasn't long until the *Book of Common Prayer* was found to be inadequate (it was, after all, a product of the Reformation). The *English Missal* provided Anglo-Catholics with a way of filling out the prayer book with material from the Sarum (not Tridentine) missal. Holy Communion was celebrated more frequently than had been the case in earlier Anglicanism. At first an 8:00 A.M. Low Mass was added to the parish schedule with morning prayer and sermon at 11:00 A.M. But increasingly morning prayer was replaced as the principal service with the Holy Communion (or Mass or Eucharist, as it was variously called). People began to receive communion more frequently as their highest act of worship. The Anglo-Catholic ethos flourished more pervasively in the United States than in England.

The Liturgy as a Countercultural Force

The historic, sacramental, and communal approach to worship in the liturgical restoration represents a countercultural reaction to the Enlightenment in general and to American religiosity in particular.[19] As we saw in the previous chapter, the dominant religious movement in America since colonial days has been revivalism. Particularly in the nineteenth century, revivalism became associated with the strains of individualism in American life as celebrated by such influential literary figures as Henry David Thoreau, Ralph Waldo Emerson, Emily Dickinson, and Walt Whitman. The great revival preachers of the century all the way through Billy Sunday stressed salvation in the name of Jesus Christ but not in the community of the church.[20] There is little wonder that most Americans have steadfastly held that they don't need the church to have a relationship with God and that they can commune with God as well in nature as in church, especially on the golf course on Sunday morning. As sociologists have noted, in spite of the high percentage of church attendance in America, the experience of the community at worship has not made much of a dent in the individualism and subjectivity that characterizes much American spirituality. To a great extent, this was because the preaching most American Protestants heard in their churches did not counter individualism and subjectivity with an emphasis on the role of the church in Christian life and the sacraments in God's work of salvation. The hymns and songs of revivalism also gained great popularity, and these emphasized the unmediated relationship between "me and Jesus." Indeed, most American Protestants have had difficulty perceiving the sacraments as "means of grace." The theology of baptismal regeneration has especially fared poorly in American Protestantism because the very ordo of revival worship led to the response of the individual to the word. Baptism was simply an outward sign of one's decision for Christ.

The liturgical restoration movement was at odds with this whole approach to faith and worship. It emphasized the role of the church as the community of salvation and the sacraments as God's acts of saving grace. Baptism was understood to be God's act of regeneration, not just an outward sign of one's decision for Christ. Holy Communion was not just an option for the spiritually stalwart; everyone was encouraged to receive communion more frequently. Worshipers were not just acted upon; they were invited to be the actors of worship. As we shall see in the next chapter, the liturgical renewal movement actually took steps to make the liturgy once again the public work of the people, and some of the practices of renewal were jarring to worshipers in Protestant congregations as well as in Roman Catholic parishes. But while active participation in the liturgy was required in the agenda of liturgical renewal, it was consistently encouraged in the agenda of liturgical restoration. We saw that this was the case in the Common Service of American Lutheranism. But the *moto proprio* (an order setting something in motion) on church music, *Tra le sollecitudini* (Among the cares of the pastoral office...), written by Pope Pius X in 1903 (with the collaboration of the Jesuit Angelo De Santi), which emphasized the need to recover Gregorian chant as restored at Solesmes in parish worship, also encouraged worshipers to join in singing the responses.[21] In these ways liturgical restoration was also a restoration of the people's participation in the liturgy.

However, except for beloved hymns, the music in which the people were to participate was not necessarily popular. Nor was the kind of music recommended for choirs the most popular kind of "serious music": Bach instead of Handel for Lutherans, Palestrina instead of Gounod for Roman Catholics. Bach's Easter cantata, "Christ lag in Todesbanden" (Christ Jesus Lay in Death's Strong Bands), was not as much of a crowd-pleaser than Handel's "Hallelujah" chorus from *Messiah*. For that matter, even within the spectrum of contemporary late-nineteenth-century sacred music, Anton Bruckner's unaccompanied motets were not as popular with parish choirs as the more sentimental operatic-style arias of Charles Gounod, César Franck, and Camille Saint-Saëns.

The liturgical restoration churches resisted the use of music that came out of secular culture, even the secular high culture. This often set up conflict between pastors and their people over what items were appropriate for use in church for occasional services, such as weddings and funerals. The worst battles were fought over what music was appropriate in a church wedding. Many pastors and church musicians waged a battle to discourage the use of the "Bridal Chorus" from Richard Wagner's *Lohengrin* as processional music for Christian marriage services, pointing to the disastrous marriage in that opera. To be sure, few brides and grooms planning a marriage service were familiar with the opera. Ironically, by the middle of the twentieth century, this wedding music acquired other (i.e., romantic, emotional) associations from its use in films, which pastors and musicians felt clouded the institution of marriage with unwanted sentimentality. The same strictures applied to the "Wedding March" from Felix Mendelssohn's incidental music to *A Midsummer Night's Dream*. For funerals, families often requested hymns and songs that emphasized the personal relationship between the believer and Jesus, such as "Rock of Ages, Cleft for Me" or "I Go to the Garden Alone," rather than hymns that sounded the themes of Christ's triumph over death and the believer's inclusion in the communion of saints.

Music has become the touchstone of the worship wars of the late twentieth century. Liturgical restorationists have preferred chant and classical church music. Church musicians have regarded saccharine songs as inappropriate because they blunt the hard edges of the gospel's challenges. They have argued that rock music trades on an eroticism that is completely out of place in Christian worship. But because rock music is bound up with the identity of post-1960s generations, worship leaders in the revival tradition have been willing to use it in their effort to attract the unchurched. The restorationists, however, continue to insist on the use of a high musical culture. They have resisted the use of electronic instruments in liturgical worship, primarily because electronic amplification of instruments and singers discourages congregational participation. Vibrating wind columns generated by the pipe organ and other acoustic instruments attracts the vibrating wind column of the human voice. It is ironic that worship that seems to reek of "establishment" should be so countercultural in North American society, pitting its preference for "high culture" against the widespread appeal of popular culture.

We should also note, however, that the countercultural stance of early Christianity was really a stance against civil religion. Christians were not persecuted because they didn't participate in classical pagan cults but because they didn't participate in the civil cult. Doing so would have compromised their confession that "Jesus is Lord" (*Kyrios, Dominus*), a term that was applied to the deified emperor. Even in a christianized society, there has been an uneasy relationship between the liturgical celebration of the gospel of the kingdom of God and the civil religion, which always has naturalistic or humanistic tendencies.

American civil religion has posed no less a threat to Christian liturgical integrity.[22] One of the most vexing sources of conflict in local congregations is whether to display the national flag in the worship space. This practice gained popularity during the nineteenth century in the revivalists' embrace of patriotic and social causes. The churches and the civil religion have often coalesced in America in an effort to make common cause between Christianity and patriotism. This worked as long as it was perceived that America's cause was just; when that was in doubt, pastors, especially in the liturgical churches, also doubted the wisdom of displaying an emblem with as many emotional ties to the civil religion as the national flag. Some tried to mitigate the influence of the American flag in the chancel by balancing it with the Christian flag or a denominational flag. Others posted the flags of many countries in order to show the transnational character of the church and its worship. A few were successful in removing the flag entirely, at least from the worship space, if not from the church property.

A similar countercultural issue was whether or not to observe the kind of church year calendar that had developed under revivalism in its partnership with the civil religion. This calendar included New Year's Day, Decoration or Memorial Day, Mother's Day, Children's Day, Father's

Day, Independence Day, Labor Day, Rally Day (for Sunday school advancement), and more recently, Veterans' Day. In the Reformed and Free Church traditions that had abolished the entire church year, with the possible exceptions of Christmas and Easter, the calendar was wide open to be filled in with these civil, national, and self-congratulatory festivals. The liturgical churches had a historic church year calendar and accompanying lectionary that would not be reconciled with these events. Since these days were observed in civil society (even those that had emerged in Protestant practice, like Mother's Day), Christians in liturgical churches also expected some recognition of these days, even if they collided with major Christian festivals (e.g. Mother's Day or Memorial Day coinciding with Pentecost).

Evidence of a Continuing Restoration Approach

As described in the next chapter, liturgical renewal continued some of the countercultural emphases of the liturgical restoration movement, including the use of a church year calendar and lectionary that made no explicit allowance for civil and humanitarian holidays. But there is also a sense in which liturgical renewal made peace with some features of contemporary culture. Especially in the liturgical inculturation that occurred after the Second Vatican Council, the Roman Catholic Church opened the door of worship to folk music. In fact, a lyrical worship music with a popular quality has emerged in Roman Catholic worship. The use of a folk music style seemed appropriate in a liturgical setting that emphasized the role of the folk in worship. In the wake of the new emphasis on the assembly, a common complaint of those who objected to liturgical renewal was that transcendence was being diminished in favor of a radical immanence.

Precisely for these reasons, some liturgical parishes refused to embrace the agenda of liturgical renewal. In Episcopal, Lutheran, and Roman Catholic traditions, there were parishes and congregations that resisted the agenda of liturgical renewal. In the Episcopal Church in the U.S.A. and the Anglican Church of Canada, this may be expressed in the retention of east wall high altars rather than freestanding altars, the preference for the traditional language of the prayer book, and resistance to the liturgical role of women.[23] Of course, in a number of Anglo-Catholic parishes in the United States and Canada, one will find solemn celebrations of the liturgy with the requisite number of and properly attired liturgical ministers, "smells and bells,"[24] and fully sung settings of the ordinary and propers that embrace features of liturgical renewal. But in "restoration" churches, there would be little inclination to use inclusive God-language and a preference for the traditional language.

Among Lutherans, liturgical renewal has been a slower process. Many congregations that use *Lutheran Book of Worship* or *Lutheran Worship* have not fully implemented the vision of renewal that these books project. The liturgical role of women in Missouri Synod congregations is limited or nonexistent, although it is fully embraced in the Evangelical Lutheran Church in America and the Evangelical Lutheran Church in Canada. Liturgical renewal has been limited in European Lutheran churches in terms of an action-oriented liturgy with a diversification of liturgical roles, except in some parishes in Sweden and Finland.

Recent Roman Catholic critics have charged that some practices associated with liturgical renewal have gone further than was intended in the Constitution on the Sacred Liturgy in such things as the choice of church music, the demeaning of popular devotions, and the rejection of the eastward orientation of the altar.[25] In recent years there has been a growing preference for Latin masses in the Roman Catholic Church, not only among older Catholics who remember the Mass before Vatican II, but also among younger worshipers who never experienced pre-Vatican II Catholic worship but who find much contemporary Catholic worship banal and lacking in a sense of transcendence. In some dioceses certain parishes have been granted permission by their local bishop to have Latin masses.[26] These parishes may offer both the Novum Ordo mass in Latin and a post-Tridentine Latin mass celebrated in the old style. They are noted for the high quality of the choral music sung at the Sunday and festival masses, which are well attended by a surprising number of young adults and young families who have grown up knowing only the post–Vatican II liturgical renewal. These worshipers, mostly well educated and with highly cultivated but very particular aesthetic sensibilities, have obviously determined that something is lacking in the worship they have experienced in ordinary Roman Catholic parishes.

It is important to note, however, that they are restoring something that never really existed in actual practice. Conversations with liturgists and musicians who remember the period before the Second Vatican Council indicate that the average large local Roman Catholic parish was fortunate to have a solemn choral mass with one priest at the altar on Sundays, though on high feast days, there might be a vested deacon and subdeacon. The more adventurous might have sung the psalm-tone reductions of the propers. Choirs were often big and sang a lot of four-part music and occasionally some of the plainchant ordinaries. There were liturgies during which the choir and congregation just sang hymns and motets straight through the whole mass, seemingly unrelated to what the priest was doing silently at the altar. However, use of the great polyphonic mass ordinaries and of the florid propers out of the *Graduale Romanum* and the occasional orchestral mass ordinaries was reserved for the diocesan cathedral and only for such events as consecration of bishops. The kind of solemn high masses sung at restored "Tridentine masses" every Sunday and feast day, with complete propers from the *Graduale Romanum* and polyphonic ordinaries, were simply unknown in local parishes and many cathedrals, whose parishioners in any event preferred attending spoken low masses to sung high masses.

Thus, it can be said that many young Catholic worshipers at the beginning of the twenty-first century are looking for an experience of God in worship and authority in community that is not so different from other young seekers who are drawn to Pentecostal praise and worship or who seek to retrieve aspects of the Great Tradition in the worship of emerging churches. Against the background of these developments, we need to review the agenda of the liturgical renewal movement of the twentieth century.

CHAPTER 18

Liturgical Renewal

The liturgical renewal movement may be distinguished from the liturgical restoration movement in this way: liturgical restoration sought to recover the order, texts, and rubrics of historical liturgical rites and put them in place; liturgical renewal sought to recover the liturgy's essential character as the public work of the people. The primary agenda, therefore, was to give the assembly an essential liturgical role. The congregants could not be bystanders; they had to be participants in the "full, conscious, and active" sense called for by the Constitution on the Sacred Liturgy, promulgated by the Second Vatican Council on November 22, 1963.

Certainly there has never been a time in the history of the liturgy when the participation of the people was not desired in some way, shape, or form. The Protestant Reformation returned to the people more overt verbal participation than they had experienced previously by means of singing the chorales or the psalms of the metrical psalter. After the Council of Trent, Catholic liturgical reformers encouraged the people to learn and join in the dialogical responses. As we have seen, the Common Service, drafted for Lutheran Churches in America in 1888, provided an even fuller measure of congregational participation than the sixteenth-century models on which it was based. The *motu proprio* of Pope Pius X, *Tra le sollectitudini* (Among the cares of the pastoral office...), issued on November 22, 1903, was written to address abuses in church music. It once again held up Gregorian chant as the ideal musical setting of the Roman mass, but it also encouraged the people to join in singing the chants and responses. In both cases,

Lutheran and Roman Catholic liturgical restorationists operated with a romantic ideal that perhaps went beyond the historical evidence. The people had not historically joined in singing the major chants; that was the role of the choir.

So liturgical renewal was not just a matter of holding up the ideal of "the full, conscious and active participation of the people" in the sense of giving the people a role in the liturgy. They had never been without a liturgical role. But liturgical renewal sought to make the people's work a pastoral reality and discovered that it sometimes required building a bridge between the historic liturgical rites and the cultures in which the people lived and moved and had their being. This awareness came by way of conferences, institutes, and publications through which a massive effort was made to help the people understand the liturgy and participate in it more meaningfully. Enabling the participation of the people required, it was concluded, a number of significant reforms, especially in the Roman Catholic Church, not the least of which was putting the liturgy into the vernacular language of the people. Only such a step would enable the people to move from silence to verbal participation.[1]

The First Calls for Renewal

In 1909, Dom Lambert Beauduin of Mont César Monastery in Louvain, Belgium, gave an address on "The True Prayer of the Church." He sought to address the issue of the excessive individualism and privatism that was a product of Western cultural development since the Enlightenment and that he found pervasive in Roman Catholic piety. The answer was the renewal of the liturgy as the corporate life of the people of God. At a liturgical week in Louvain in 1911, scholarly papers were shared concerning the nature of participation in the liturgy. In spite of these two events, Ernest B. Koenker held that the liturgical movement as we know it today can be traced to the first Liturgical Week held for laity at the Maria Laach Monastery in Germany during Holy Week 1914.[2] This conference was the setting for the introduction of the dialogue mass, in which the people were taught to respond to the celebrant. The response to this venture was immediate and favorable among the culturally elite classes, and the dialogue mass soon won popularity among the working classes as well.

From the beginning, the liturgical renewal movement was led by scholars who had a passionate pastoral concern to renew the liturgy in the corporate life of the people. The scholarly work of the early pioneers of the liturgical renewal movement was different from the scholarly work of liturgical restoration. If the restoration scholarship served to establish the rites, renewal scholarship sought to recover the practice of the rites. This sometimes required peeling away the accretions of the received liturgical formularies in order to get back to older models in which the people did participate more fully in the sacred mysteries. After a century of the scholarship that supported liturgical renewal, we are now more aware that romantic biases colored the interpretation of the data, and we must now proceed more cautiously with historical claims.[3] Nevertheless, the intention from the outset was to provide a solid historical and theological foundation for liturgical renewal.

Certainly the Maria Laach Monastery under Abbot Idlefons Herwegen (1874–1946) made a profound contribution to liturgical scholarship and to liturgical theology in terms of Don Odo Casel's mystery theology. This initial work was interrupted by the First World War. After the war, however, Dr. Pius Parsch at Klosterneuburg in Austria produced a great popularizing work, including biblical publications, devotional literature, periodicals, and sermons.

The liturgical renewal movement spread to the United States already in the 1920s through the contacts of Saint John's Abbey in Collegeville, Minnesota. Dom Virgil Michel (1890–1938) went to Europe in the early 1920s to study philosophy at San Anselmo in Rome and at Louvain. He met Beauduin and Herwegen and was captivated by their work in pastoral liturgics. When he returned to Saint John's Abbey in 1925, he founded the periodical *Orates Fratres* (which became *Worship* magazine in 1951). He also saw to the establishment of the Liturgical Press at Collegeville and launched the Popular Liturgical Library, which produced books dealing with liturgy, social action, sociology, economics, politics, education, art, architecture, and philosophy and thereby helped promote the idea that liturgical renewal and social renewal are related. Significantly, while all of this pastoral liturgical effort emanating from Louvain, Maria Laach, Collegeville, and other centers was largely Benedictine, it promoted liturgical renewal for the whole Catholic Church, especially in the parish. Because the effort was generated from Benedictine abbeys, there was a certain unintended elitist aura about it. Liturgical renewal made slower headway in the Roman

Catholic Church in America because it lacked the support of the hierarchy, which the movement enjoyed in Belgium, Germany, and Austria. We cannot discount the possibility that the American Catholic hierarchy, drawn mostly from working-class families, found the Benedictine leadership too elitist.

Conferences, Institutes, Journals

The Benedictines in Collegeville regarded the liturgical weeks held in Louvain and Maria Laach as models to be followed. A Liturgical Day was held at Saint John's Abbey in 1929, drawing more than four hundred people. Virgil Michel's idea was to expand this into a full liturgical week, but the effort was undoubtedly curtailed by the economic downturn of the Great Depression. Unfortunately, Dom Michel never lived to see the first American Liturgical Week, held in Chicago in 1940. That this week occurred at all after the death of Dom Michel was due to the efforts of Father Michael Ducey, O.S.B. The first three annual Benedictine Liturgical Weeks were held under his administration. An organization called the Benedictine Liturgical Conference was organized, composed of abbots of all the Benedictine houses in the United States, to promote an annual Liturgical Week. In 1943, the Benedictines decided to give up their "ownership" of the National Liturgical Weeks in favor of an independent board of directors. They thus brought to birth the Liturgical Conference in the United States, which would be a major agent of liturgical renewal in America. An independent board brought into the leadership of the liturgical renewal movement priests from other religious orders, including Gerard Ellard, S.J.; diocesan priests, such as Monsignor Martin Hellriegel and Father H. A. Reinhold; academic priests, such as Father Frederick McManus of Catholic University and Father Gerard Sloyan of Temple University; and lay persons, including Mary Perkins and Virginia Sloyan. Some prominent Catholic bishops also lent their support by participating in the Liturgical Weeks; they included Samuel Cardinal Stritch, archbishop of Chicago, who hosted the first National Liturgical Week in 1940.

The National Liturgical Weeks held between 1940 and 1968 brought together participants from all over the United States, including priests, religious, and lay people. By the 1960s there was a growing ecumenical participation. After the first few years, each of the weeks attracted several thousand participants, but the 1963 Liturgical Week attracted more than thirteen thousand participants, and the 1964 Liturgical Week attracted more than twenty thousand. That was, of course, the year after the promulgation of the Constitution on the Sacred Liturgy. Attendance remained at high levels through the last National Liturgical Week, due both to the liturgical renewal stemming from the council and the civil rights movement in the United States. The places and topics of the Liturgical Weeks were as follows:

1940	Chicago	The Living Parish: Active and Intelligent Participation of the Laity in the Liturgy
1941	Saint Paul, MN	The Living Parish: One in Worship, Charity, and Action
1942	Saint Meinrad Archabbey, IN	The Praise of God
1943	Hartford, CT	Sacrifice
1944	New York	Liturgy and Catholic Life
1945	New Orleans	Catholic Liturgy in Peace and Reconstruction
1946	Denver	The Family in Christ
1947	Portland, OR	Christ's Sacrifice and Ours
1948	Boston	The New Man in Christ
1949	Saint Louis, MO	Sanctification of Sunday
1950	Conception Abbey, MO	For Pastors and People: The Divine Office and the Mass
1951	Dubuque, IA	The Priesthood of Christ
1952	Cleveland, OH	The New Easter Vigil
1953	Grand Rapids, MI	Saint Pius X and Social Worship
1954	Milwaukee, WI	Mary in the Liturgy
1955	Worchester, MA	The New Ritual/Liturgy and Social Order
1956	London, ON	People's Participation/Holy Week
1957	Saint John's Abbey	Education and the Liturgy
1958	Cincinnati, OH	The Church Year
1959	Notre Dame University	Participation in the Mass

1960	Pittsburgh	The Liturgy and Unity in Christ
1961	Oklahoma City	Bible, Life, and Worship
1962	Seattle	Thy Kingdom Come: Christian Hope in the Modern World
1963	Philadelphia	The Renewal of Christian Education
1964	Saint Louis, MO	The Challenge of the Council: Person, Parish, World
1965	Baltimore, Portland, Chicago	Jesus Christ Reforms His Church (Three conferences held because of the size of the 1964 conference.)
1966	Houston	Worship in the City of Man
1967	Kansas City, MO	Experiments in Community
1968	Washington, D.C.	Revolution: Christian Responses

Many of the Liturgical Weeks, including those of 1940, 1941, 1946, 1960, and 1967, focused on the idea of Christian community. Social and political conditions in America and the world obviously dictated the agendas in 1945, 1946, and 1968. In fact, before his assassination, Martin Luther King Jr. had been scheduled to speak at the 1968 Liturgical Week. Liturgical legislation from Rome determined the topics in 1948 (the encyclical of Pope Pius XII, *Mediator Dei*, issued in 1947), 1952 (the restored Easter Vigil, 1951), 1955, 1956 (the restored liturgies of Holy Week), 1959, 1964 (The Constitution on the Sacred Liturgy), and 1965 (The Constitution on the Church). The 1953 Liturgical Week was a celebration of the fiftieth anniversary of Pius X's *motu proprio*. In 1954 the conference took explicit note of the pervasive Marian piety in American Catholicism and tried to integrate it into the liturgy. The 1961 week in Oklahoma City took cognizance of the role of the Bible in Christian life and worship; the week was also held in a region of Protestant fundamentalism.

After 1968 there were no more Liturgical Weeks. The major reforms that the National Liturgical Conference had called for had been expressed in the Constitution on the Sacred Liturgy and were being implemented in the official liturgical books that began to appear in the late 1960s. The Liturgical Conference became a publishing house, occasionally sponsoring conferences and workshops on practical topics such as the roles of the presiding minister, lector, cantor, and assembly. The conference gave attention to preaching from the lectionary as well as to other liturgical roles. The periodicals *Liturgy* and *Homily Service* continue to be published.

Several societies and institutes in American Lutheranism carried forward the desiderata of liturgical restoration into the agenda of liturgical renewal. The Saint James Society, founded in 1925 in Hoboken, New Jersey, with Pastor Berthold von Schenck as president, was a Missouri Synod society that pressed for the recovery of classical Lutheran liturgy in its church body such as the United Lutheran Church in America had in the Common Service. It published a journal, *Pro Ecclesia Lutherana*, which was replaced by *Una Sancta* in 1943 and continued to be published until 1967. The names of these periodicals indicate the awareness of a correlation between confessional commitments and liturgical life.

In 1947, the then-president of the Saint James Society, Dr. Adolph Wismar, moved to Valparaiso University in Indiana. With the encouragement and support of the university's chancellor, Dr. O. P. Kretzmann, an Institute of Liturgical Studies was founded. Now more than fifty years old and still going strong, the annual institute attracts hundreds of participants to an inter-Lutheran and even ecumenical forum for liturgical renewal.

An inter-Lutheran Society for Worship, Music, and the Arts (LSWMA) was founded after the 1957 assembly of the Lutheran World Federation in Minneapolis. Many pastors and musicians in different church bodies had worked together to provide worship during the assembly and desired to continue working together and fostering the agenda of Lutheran liturgical renewal. Annual conferences were held, mostly on church college campuses, until 1968. The society also published the journal *Response*. Many of those who served on committees of the Inter-Lutheran Commission on Worship in the 1970s were members of LSWMA. It has been argued that one reason the inter-Lutheran venture that produced *Lutheran Book of Worship* in 1978 went so well is that so many of its committee members had a history of working in the LSWMA.[4] In 1979, the Lutheran Society voted to merge with the Liturgical Conference, which made the Liturgical Conference an ecumenical organization dedicated to church unity as well as to liturgical renewal in the local assembly.

The Liturgical Establishment Embraces Renewal

It is evident that the leaders of the liturgical renewal movement were able to move inside the liturgical establishment and exert some influence on the official liturgical books. In 1976, James F. White was able to write, "The most impressive array of resources and talents ever devoted to liturgical reform has been amassed by the Roman Catholic Church since Vatican II. So massive has the work been that it has had to be carried out at three levels: worldwide, international, and national."[5] This massive work of reform of the rites of the Catholic Church also laid the groundwork for liturgical revision in Protestant churches. Protestants had participated in the Second Vatican Council; their views had been taken seriously. After the council, Protestant leaders were willing to consider the pace-setting work of the Roman Catholic Concilium for the Implementation of the Constitution on the Sacred Liturgy, which in 1969 became the Congregation for Divine Worship.

One of the most noteworthy contributions of the Roman Catholic Church to Protestant liturgical renewal was the three-year lectionary for Sundays and festivals, which was adopted with some variants by several Protestant church bodies. It has subsequently been revised by the ecumenical Consultation on Common Texts in an effort to reduce the number of variant readings and make it more "common." The Revised Common Lectionary is now used by a number of Protestant churches around the world.

The process in the Roman Catholic Church was to produce a Latin *editio typica* (typical edition) of the reformed rite. It was then translated into vernacular languages. In some cases, international consultations did the work of translation for national bishops' conferences that used the same language, such as English, French, German, and Spanish. The International Commission on English in the Liturgy (ICEL) produced English translations of Roman liturgies for eleven nations. The ecumenical International Consultation on English Texts (ICET) worked with ICEL to produced *Prayers We Have in Common*. Common texts of the Lord's Prayer, the ecumenical creeds, and a number of liturgical texts have been produced so that Christians worshiping in the English language would be able to say or sing the same words.

The Roman Catholic Church was translating its Latin rites into vernacular languages; there was no need for Roman Catholics to appropriate the archaic Elizabethan language used in many Protestant worship books. It was certainly a shock to many Roman Catholics to attend mass and hear it in their own language for the first time. It was equally a shock for many Protestants to begin hearing a more contemporary speech used in worship. The Episcopal Church, as custodian of Thomas Cranmer's language in the *Book of Common Prayer*, was not prepared to completely abandon that speech. The 1979 prayer book retained the traditional language along with the contemporary English for the collects and prayers, morning prayer, evening prayer, and the Eucharist. *Lutheran Book of Worship* (1978) retained only the traditional text of the Lord's Prayer along with some traditional English versions of hymns. *Lutheran Book of Worship* and *Book of Common Prayer* used gender-inclusive language when referring to the assembly. Coming a decade later, the United Methodist *Book of Worship* (1989) and the Presbyterian *Book of Common Worship* (1989) ventured a little more boldly in the use of inclusive language for God.

It is the nature of committees to compromise, both in terms of various views within the committee and in response to reactions to its work from its constituents. Even granting these dynamics, there is no question that the liturgical establishment in the Roman Catholic, Episcopal, Lutheran, Presbyterian, United Methodist, and other churches was well ahead of its constituents. Sensitive liturgists, looking back on the reforms of the last forty years, are aware that changes were sometimes made too quickly with too little preparation and that mistakes were also made.[6] John Fenwick and Bryan Spinks have noted that the paths to liturgical renewal were somewhat different for Roman Catholics and Protestants. Roman Catholic liturgical renewal meant simplifying and streamlining the Roman Rite. Protestant liturgical renewal required a "radical reshaping" of existing worship practices, especially in churches that had been used to the revival ordo.[7] The fact that liturgical renewal, taken up by the denominational worship staffs, has given the perception of being bureaucratically managed has not gone over well in some denominations more used to congregational freedom in matters of worship. Presbyterian Robb Redman speaks to this issue from within the perspective of the Presbyterian Church.[8] It is certainly the case that the Presbyterian *Book of Common Worship*, which is an outstanding liturgical resource, goes unused in many Presbyterian churches. Others have argued that, in spite of mistakes, the process of renewal is still going on and is an unfinished work.[9] The Renewing Worship project in the Evangelical Lutheran Church in America has been undertaken with the idea of building on the renewal that has already taken place, not departing from it.[10]

Renewed Liturgy: Catholic and Protestant

In what follows, I will try to describe what the renewed liturgy is like in its ideal form.[11]

Setting

There is more of a sense of gathering around the table for the Eucharist than was the case in liturgical restoration. "East wall" altars have been pulled out from the wall. New or renovated churches have placed the altar closer to the people, with the presiding and assisting ministers facing the people across the table. There is also a place for the proclamation of the word. Some ambos have a shelf on the front side that serves as a "throne of the word." The seating for the people may be more circular or at least angled, suggesting a gathered assembly. In Roman Catholic churches, tabernacles for the reserved sacrament have been placed to the side or in a special chapel. Musicians are gathered on the side of the chancel or nave in a position where they can lead the singing without attracting too much attention to themselves but also feel that they are a part of the assembly. The elements for the Eucharist are often placed on a credence table near the entrance to the nave. Banners and pictures are changed for the season in the church year.

Gathering

The prayer of confession in the Roman Mass, formerly said at the foot of the altar, is now integrated with the entrance rite as a troped Kyrie. In *Lutheran Book of Worship* and *Book of Common Prayer*, a Brief Order for Confession and Forgiveness may be used before the service begins. If it is not used, a prayer of confession may be included in the intercessions at the end of the liturgy of the word. A hymn or psalm is sung to accompany the entrance of the ministers. A selection is made from other pieces in the entrance rite to fit the day or season—Kyrie, Glory to God, *Trisagion* (Thrice-holy hymn), or (in *Lutheran Book of Worship*) Worthy Is Christ—or another song of praise may be sung. The gathering rite ends with a prayer of the day offered by the presiding minister. In recent years efforts have been made to provide a proper prayer for every Sunday and festival in the three-year lectionary. The prayer of the day alludes to the readings that will be heard.

The Word

The three-year Lectionary of the Mass and Revised Common Lectionary provide for a first reading from the Old Testament or (during Easter) the book of Acts, psalmody, a second reading from a New Testament epistle, and a Gospel reading. The psalmody is not another reading; it is a response to the first reading and is preferably sung. A typical way in which the psalm is sung is by a cantor or small choir, with the assembly joining on a repeating refrain or antiphon. Headway has been made in getting the whole congregation to chant the psalm in congregations that use *Lutheran Book of Worship*. An Alleluia verse heralds the Gospel.

The Gospel is considered the primary reading. This is reflected in the ritual surrounding the reading. The gospel book may be carried in procession into the midst of the assembly, and the people stand to hear it and surround the reading with acclamations. Over the course of three years, the four Gospels are read almost in their entirety: Matthew in Year A, Mark in Year B, Luke in Year C, and John primarily during the festival seasons of Christmas and Easter. Old Testament readings are chosen primarily for their typological relationship to the Gospel. They are pericopes (cut-out selections) except for an option in the time after Pentecost in the Revised Common Lectionary that provides for a semicontinuous reading of Old Testament books only loosely related to the semicontinuous Gospel readings. Even this more extended relationship between the first reading and the Gospel does not completely abandon the typological method, since the Old Testament books were selected to correlate with particular Gospels. The second reading consists of pericopes during the Advent–Christmas and Lent–Easter cycles but semicontinuous readings of whole epistles during the time after Epiphany and after Pentecost. Practically the entire New Testament and a substantial portion of the Old Testament are read over the course of three years.

The homily or sermon follows immediately and is expected to be an exposition of the readings. There has been a preference for using the typological method also in preaching. In the typological approach, scripture is compared with scripture. Typological exegesis aims at discovering the coherence or basic unity of Scripture with itself, unlike the allegorical approach, which compares Scripture with something outside of Scripture, such as doctrine. This kind of preaching might make use of images found in the readings, relating them in an evocative way to everyday life. But the object of preaching is to put everyday life under the Scriptures, not to find proof texts in the Bible to validate a point, theme, or topic chosen by the preacher. The liturgical preacher aims to help put the contemporary hearers into the situation of the biblical story or bring the biblical story into the context of the contemporary hearers.

Responses to the Word

In the Lutheran tradition, a hymn of the day serves as a commentary on the readings. It is sung after, or even around, the sermon. The Nicene Creed is used on Sundays and festivals. In the Lutheran, Methodist, and Presbyterian traditions, the Apostles' Creed might also be used on Sundays in the time after the Epiphany or after Pentecost. The prayers of the church (thanksgivings and intercessions) also reflect the readings and guide the specifics of the prepared petitions. The petitions are offered by a lay assisting minister with a litany-response to each petition by the assembly. Petitions are included for the church local and universal (its ministers and people), for the nation and the world (the leaders of governments and peoples), for special needs in the community or the world, for the sick and dying, and in thanksgiving for the faithful departed who are remembered that day. Some petitions are written out in advance; others are offered spontaneously by persons in the assembly.

The Meal

In all the renewed liturgies except the Roman Mass, the greeting of peace follows the prayers and introduces the liturgy of the eucharistic meal. The Peace is enacted by the ministers and people, who greet each other verbally and with a handshake or embrace, citing the greeting of the risen Christ to his disciples in John 20:19, 21, and 26 and the greeting of the Apostle to the congregation in Romans 16:16. In its location before the gathering of the gifts, it enacts the reconciliation required by Jesus in Matthew 5:23–24 before the gifts are offered at the altar.

The gifts of the people are collected and presented at the altar while songs are sung by the choir or the assembly. In the medieval mass, a psalm verse served as the offertory antiphon and *Lutheran Book of Worship* Ministers Desk Edition continues that tradition by providing for each Sunday, festival, and day of commemoration texts of offertory verses that may be sung by the choir. Otherwise, general offertory verses are sung by the congregation as gifts are brought forward by representatives of the people. The gifts include not only the money collected for the mission of the church but the bread and the wine for the Eucharist.

Where once in the Western church there was a single "Canon" that served as the eucharistic prayer (the Roman Canon), now several Great Thanksgivings are included in the worship books of each tradition (Roman Catholic, Lutheran, Episcopal, United Methodist, Presbyterian). These eucharistic prayers include an interjection sung by the congregation after the initial act of praise (Preface) called the Sanctus ("Holy, holy, holy"). It is composed of the texts of Isaiah 6:3 and Matthew 21:9 (which is itself a citation of Psalm 118:26).

The West Syrian model of the eucharistic prayer has been preferred in the new compositions because of its trinitarian structure: praise of the Father for his work of creation, remembrance of the Son's work of redemption, invocation of the Holy Spirit for the benefits of communion. Like the West Syrian models, many new eucharistic prayers include citations from the Bible or references to the biblical salvation history. They include an institution narrative based on the four versions of the words of institution in Matthew 26:26–28, Mark 14:22–24, Luke 22:15–20, and 1 Corinthians 11:23–26. Some Lutheran liturgies use only the words of institution after the Preface and Sanctus. Some Reformed liturgies use the words of institution apart from but in addition to a eucharistic prayer. The full eucharistic prayer provides a summary of salvation history in its trinitarian economy comparable to the creed. Omitting the full eucharistic prayer not only reduces the rich meanings of the meal, it is also plainly disobedient, since the dominical institution includes the rubric "He gave thanks." Gregory Dix had argued that the institution narratives are a set of rubrics giving the "shape" of the meal liturgy. That theory is now greeted with skepticism,[12] but there is no doubt that Jesus said some form of Jewish *berakah* (blessing) and *todah* (thanksgiving) at his last supper in the upper room and that the church has continued to give thanks over the bread and cup throughout its history.

The Lord's Prayer follows the eucharistic prayer. The Matthew 6:9–13 version has been preferred for liturgical use. Matthew's version may have already been influenced by liturgical use. The Roman Rite has included the doxology to the prayer, but separates it from the rest of the prayer by an embolism based on "Deliver us from evil."

Sometimes an invitation to communion is given using biblical words. The Roman mass has used "Behold the lamb of God who takes away the sin of the world" (John 1:29) with the response, "Lord, I am not worthy to receive you, but only say the word and I shall be healed" (based on Luke 7:6–7). The *Book of Common Prayer* has "Alleluia. Christ our Passover is sacrificed for us; therefore let us keep the feast. Alleluia" (based on 1 Corinthians 5:7–8).

The greeting of peace in the Roman Mass precedes the administration of Holy Communion. Some Lutherans also prefer to keep the Peace juxtaposed to the meal.

A major reform in the Roman Catholic Church was having people receive communion during the Mass, not after the Mass from the reserved sacrament.

Songs are sung during the administration of the sacrament. The Agnus Dei ("Lamb of God") is the first one, sometimes sung during the breaking of the bread. Additional songs sung during communion may include biblical psalms, canticles, and hymns. The medieval mass included a communion antiphon, which was a psalm verse. A proper communion verse is still provided in the Roman mass. Some Protestant congregations still resist singing during the communion, even though most of the reformers provided for it. This is symptomatic of the fact that many communicants approach the meal in an individualistic rather than a communal spirit.

The people ideally receive both bread and wine in one continuous serving and standing on Sundays in honor of the resurrection. The preference is to use a single loaf of bread for the whole assembly and a common chalice. In reality, other practices are more prevalent, including intinction of the bread into the wine, individual wafers, and individual cups. Even nonwheat bread and nonalcoholic beverages are offered to deal with special needs. It remains an open question which practice best models the emphasis on the community in liturgical renewal. Obviously the one loaf and one cup are good symbols of commonality. On the other hand, being aware of the special needs of some members of the assembly may give one an even better consciousness of community during communion. This will not be true, however, if the distribution occurs with a buffet mentality that each communicant is simply being given his or her personal choice.

Sending

Lutheran Book of Worship provides for a post-communion canticle, either the traditional Lutheran use of the Nunc Dimittis after communion or the new, somewhat didactic "Thank the Lord."

A proper post-communion prayer was provided for each celebration in the old sacramentaries. In the Protestant worship books, a small collection of post-communion prayers is provided, from which one is selected. There are only so many ways to say "thank you" for the gift received and only so many images of the Eucharist, even though it is rich in images. In *Lutheran Book of Worship*, the assisting minister reads the post-communion prayer. In the *Book of Common Prayer*, it is recited by all.

Protestant liturgies have preferred the Aaronic benediction from Numbers 6:24–26, which Luther specified already in his *Form of the Mass and Communion for the Church at Wittenberg* (1523). Otherwise, the standard trinitarian blessing is used. Sometimes the blessing is accompanied by a dismissal that includes a charge to mission in the world. The standard dismissal is, "Go in peace," to which some brief exhortation is added, such as "serve the Lord" or "feed the hungry." The people respond, "Thanks be to God." The old *Ite missa est* of the Roman Mass is practically untranslatable. But it does have a sense of being sent to carry out the mission of the church. The word *missa* gave its name to the Roman Mass. The renewed liturgies envision people departing without further devotions.

Methods of Inculturation

The impact of the Constitution on the Sacred Liturgy (*Sacrosanctam Concilium*) of the Second Vatican Council was heightened by the impact of other documents, such as the Constitution on the Church (*Lumen Gentium*). This document envisioned a church that is open to the world. If liturgy is truly to be "the people's work," it must be done using the cultural expressions of the people who perform it. The vernacularization of the liturgy that *Sacrosanctum Concilium* called for must finally be realized in the inculturation that *Lumen Gentium* called for. But inculturation is a very complex process.

The Philippine liturgical scholar Anscar Chupungco has demonstrated that there is not one approach to contextualization or inculturation, but at least three, which he labels "dynamic equivalence," "creative assimilation," and "organic progression."[13]

Dynamic Equivalence

Chupungco uses the expression *dynamic equivalence* to describe the replacement of one cultural element with another in a way that goes beyond mere translation of texts.[14] The classical Roman Rite itself was undoubtedly an example of this as Latin texts developed in the period spanning the administrations of Popes Gelasius, Vigilius, Leo the Great, and Gregory the Great. These texts replaced the older Greek liturgy that had been used earlier in the church of Rome. They reflected the unique character traits of Roman culture. This was a time of liturgical creativity, since the texts collected into the sacramentaries bearing the names of these popes were, as far as we are aware, original compositions. Examples of dynamic equivalence are not plentiful in liturgical history. Martin Luther's German Mass (1526) is a prime example, since he did not just translate the Latin texts into German but replaced the Latin texts with equivalent German versifications set to chorales that reflected both Gregorian chant and Meistersinger art song traditions. Yet it adhered to the catholic shape of the liturgy. This pattern continues in Lutheran liturgical practice where an equivalent hymn is substituted for the historic liturgical text. The Reformed churches were also noted for their wholesale substitution of the vernacular metrical psalter for the biblical texts of the psalms, expressed par excellence in the Geneva Psalter. This Reformed practice has been picked up in recent Roman Catholic popular uses of the prayer offices in which hymn versifications are substituted for the texts of biblical psalms and canticles, and are undoubtedly used for a similar purpose: to facilitate the participation of the people.

Issues of inculturation have been especially vexing in African and Asian churches, and all three methods of inculturation may be seen to be at work in various rites. An example of dynamic equivalence in the Catholic Mass of Zaïre may be the alternative form of the Western handshake at the greeting of peace (an act of reconciliation), in which persons in the assembly wash their hands in the same bowl of water as a way of saying, "I wash away anything I have against you." An example in the Catholic mass in the Philippines is that the presider and other ministers receive communion after the congregation has received, as a sign of service and solicitude for the needs of the guests such as a host would usually display. This practice goes against the probable form of the institution, in which Jesus, as the host of the Passover meal, would have partaken first before passing the broken loaf and common cup to the other participants. But it captures the servant role of Christ and the idea of the minister serving *in persona Christi*. This practice is becoming more popular in America, where on the one hand, it undoubtedly plugs into anti-elitist and anticlerical biases that have been present in our culture. On the other hand, anyone who has actually worked as a waiter or a server at a banquet knows that the waitstaff should eat first to give them the energy to do their job.

Creative Assimilation

Creative assimilation may be seen in the early patristic period, when church fathers such as Tertullian, Hippolytus, and Ambrose appropriated terminology from civil society for Christian use. Pierre-Marie Gy notes such words as *sacramentum, fidei testatio, initiatio, confessio, absolutio,* and *paenitentia* all entered the Christian liturgical lexicon from civil use.[15] There are also instances of creative assimilation in which the liturgy is simply done using the culture forms and expressions of society at large. This may actually be the most typical form of contextualization. For example, in the seventeenth and early eighteenth centuries, Baroque forms were appropriated for Catholic and Lutheran liturgy without changing the shape of the liturgy or the basic liturgical texts. The liturgy was housed in Baroque architectural settings, and liturgical music took on the character of the new Baroque art form of opera. Ornate altars were moved against the east wall of the church building and looked like thrones for Christ the King patterned after the throne of the Sun King, Louis XIV of France.

Contemporary examples of this form of contextualization or inculturation abound. In North America, the historic liturgy may be set to culturally specific music, as we see in the settings and hymns provided in the African American Catholic worship book *Lead Me, Guide Me* or the African American Lutheran worship book *This Far by Faith*. In Africa itself, African melodies, drums, and dances have been introduced in Catholic and Protestant worship without changing the shape of the liturgy. And, of course, Christian popular music used in some worship services not only relates to forms of popular music but has engendered the so-called "Christian music" that has become one subdivision of the huge contemporary-music industry.

A major issue of inculturation involving creative assimilation may be the use of natural symbolism in connection with major feast days in the calendar in the Southern Hemisphere. We are well aware that Christmas became associated with European symbols of the winter solstice, such as Christmas lights and the Christmas tree. Also, Easter became associated with fertility symbols of the vernal equinox, such as Easter eggs and the Easter bunny. For the most part, of course, these are the trappings of the secular observance of these holidays, although most ordinary Christians don't distinguish between secular and sacred. But shall the churches in the Southern Hemisphere, where Christmas comes at the summer solstice and Easter at the autumnal equinox, continue to employ these culture-specific customs and symbols simply out of nostalgia? Undoubtedly many Northern Hemisphere immigrants to Southern Hemisphere countries like Australia and New Zealand would be happy to manufacture snow for Christmas to celebrate it as they remembered the holiday in their country of origin. But those who are more "naturalized" in these countries might ask if there ways in which the symbolism inherent in the gospel events themselves can be inculturated under different climatic conditions. What difference does it make that the Christmas or Epiphany festival of light occurs when the light is at its zenith rather than at its lowest? How does the reversal of nature affect the festival of the Nativity of Saint John the Baptist on June 24, which is celebrated in northern countries with midsummer fires marking the gradual diminishing of light until Christmas as a reflection of John's statement that Christ must increase and he must decrease? What difference does it make that the resurrection is proclaimed at a time of the year when old life seems to be dying rather than new life emerging? We need to recognize the complexity of climatic differences in different parts of large land masses. But Christians in the Southern Hemisphere have an opportunity to shed some of the cultural baggage of these festivals in order to highlight the theological meanings of these festivals and to find new natural symbols for our Lord's nativity and resurrection.

Organic Progression

Chupungco's "method of organic progression"[16] involves supplementing or completing the liturgical material that is otherwise lacking. This was literally done when the Roman liturgical books were imported into the Frankish Kingdom by the Carolingian rulers. A sacramentary sent by Pope Hadrian to Charlemagne was found to be incomplete because it didn't include propers for masses celebrated in the Frankish church. So a supplement was added to supply what was lacking. The supplement to the *Sacramentarium Hadrianum* was called "Hucusque" ("Up to this point"). "Up to this point" you have the Roman material; after this point, the *lucanae* are filled with Gallican material.[17] Much of this Gallican material gives us the collects for the season of Advent, a season that was not observed in the ancient Roman church.

In recent years, several church bodies have been developing a three-year set of collects or prayers of the day to match the three-year Revised Common Lectionary. The Evangelical Lutheran Church in America's Renewing Worship team working on the church year tried to use historic or traditional collects where these were available and fit the readings; otherwise, we had to write our own or borrow from other new resources.

Local churches know their own pastoral needs and will engage in their own research or exercise creativity in order to provide for those needs. These needs may include sanctifying rites of passage in certain cultures, commemorating saints venerated in certain locales, or providing special liturgical orders for special events such as ecumenical prayer services or interfaith services. Sometimes local additions may be of a controversial character, such as devising rites for recognizing marital divorce or blessing same-sex unions. Many churches are wrestling with the pastoral issue of whether it is theologically permissible to include situations not sanctioned by the Bible within the scope of God's grace.

Multicultural Liturgy

Liturgical renewal, more than revivalism or liturgical restoration, has promoted cross-cultural and multicultural worship experiences. Theologically, Jesus is the Savior of all people and desires that all people find a place in the worship of God the Father through the Holy Spirit. Liturgically, catholic Christianity has desired to embrace all sorts and conditions of people within one assembly rather than fracturing the assembly into different interest groups. Yet we have seen the body of Christ fractured with generation-specific worship, even in the form of "children's church," in which children are segregated from adults for their own worship. We have seen the fracturing of the congregation into different language groups with, say, an English mass at one time and a Spanish mass at another. There is a value in trying to bring the whole congregation into the body of Christ, with all of its diversity, as one assembly for Word and Sacrament. As a matter of pastoral strategy today, it might be necessary to address both children and adults in one liturgy. It might be necessary to use both English and Spanish or some other languages in one liturgy. Doing liturgy in a multigenerational or multicultural assembly requires great sensitivity, especially on the part of the most dominant group.[18]

Local assemblies also use a variety of cultural forms in the selection of music from different times and places or in the use of forms rooted in particular cultures other than their own. I have been impressed by the pervasive use of African American gospel music in parishes in Europe. Predominantly European American congregations have received and enjoyed the gift of African song. Hopefully, it is received as the gift of fellow Christians who live in another culture and is used with gratitude. To the degree that we are able to use the cultural expressions of other Christian communities, local assemblies gain an appreciation of the breadth of the global church.

Responses to the Communications Revolution

Finally, we need to recognize that the Christian church today lives in the midst of a major cultural shift that is affecting all Western or westernized countries: the electronic-communications revolution. The rise of the image is not at the expense of the word as such, but it is at the expense of the written word, and it has already had a profound impact not just on how we deal with information but also on what kind of information we deal with. I don't think we will see an end of books; in fact, more books are being printed today than ever before. But many are a type of book made possible by electronic communication, such as "talked books" (interviews). We are moving from print as the primary means of communication to video as the primary means.

Many critics decry what this is doing to us, just as critics lamented the shift from handwritten manuscripts to printed books in the age of Gutenberg. Whether we recognize it or not, printed matter organizes the way we approach information, just as video does. As Mitchell Stephens points out, writing transforms words into objects: "Words that are written down, not just enunciated, are freed from the individual situations and experiences in which they were embedded."[19] Even the most sensational events can appear in an orderly and calm way in print. Video, by contrast, shows us events in the disjointed and jarring way we often experience them in person. Print drives us within ourselves to reflect on what we think about the information that is being given to us; video images draw us out of ourselves to focus on—to see—the outward reality. Authors of books work hard in their medium of writing to describe outward appearances; photographers, film editors, and webmasters do it with ease. The most important modern novelists (Fyodor Dostoyevsky, James Joyce, Marcel Proust) were explorers of the inner world, the world of our hidden thoughts and feelings. The most successful cinematographers turn on a bright floodlight and show us our psyches in action. The more our approach to reality is informed by video, the more we will focus on outward appearances than on inward thoughts.

But an outward or superficial approach to reality does not have to be less truthful than an in-depth approach. It can also yield insights that don't come as easily through print. For example, Joseph Brodsky described the medium of the book as encouraging a "flight in the direction of . . . autonomy, in the direction of privacy."[20] The more we look within ourselves, the more individualistic and disconnected from others we become. Video has the capability of showing our connectedness with others. In the televising of great events, from the terrorist attacks on the World Trade Center and the Pentagon to the Olympic Games in Sydney or Athens, millions of viewers become instantly connected with one another, forming a global community.

The fact that one focuses on images rather than words does not have to mean that one seeks less truth, but it does open one to a different reality. Eastern Christianity has already shown us the way in this regard. Certainly the Eastern Orthodox liturgy is not lacking in words; it has even more words than Western liturgy. But the words accompany glorious sight. Worshipers are surrounded with images and icons that present to the worshipers—join to them—Christ, his mother, his friends, the apostles, saints, and angels. The icons mediate to the worshiper the historical world of the Bible and the church and the eschatological world of heaven and eternity. The very ambience of the liturgical space draws worshipers outside of themselves into a sense of connectedness with the whole church on earth and in heaven. This certainly has the power to connect with postmodern young people, who, unlike their modern parents and grandparents, see the self in relational terms, not isolated and unaffected by others.[21]

It must have been like this in the Western church, too, before the age of Gutenberg and the practice of placing texts in the hands of worshipers. Liturgy was a much more communal and conserving activity before the importation of the new medium of printed books. What printing did was to make texts cheaply and interchangeably available for the first time. Manuscripts were expensive and few; they were meant to last a long time, and liturgical texts, once put in place, stayed put. Print appeared just in time for the Reformation and its desire to edit worship books. Print made possible a uniformity that never before existed, a uniformity that received political as well as ecclesiastical expression in successive Acts of Uniformity passed by the English Parliament (1549, 1552, 1559) and the establishment of a Congregation of Rites in the Roman Catholic Church to approve all liturgical books. As the new emphasis on preaching in both Protestant and Roman Catholic Churches made benches useful devices for easier listening, so the proliferation of books available even to lay worshipers made pews necessary to hold the liturgical library. Pews filling the worship space inevitably cut down on the amount of communal action and interaction possible in the liturgy. Liturgy became a gathering of people who each focused on their personal relationship with God.

More than this, however, Aidan Kavanagh draws a direct line from printing to "the loosening of the social bond to the extent that liturgical acts become less public acts of unity in faith than skirmishes between ideological special-interest groups."[22] So the history of liturgy since the sixteenth century has been the story of struggles mostly over texts and rubrics between Neogallicans and Romanizers, Puritans and Anglican prayer book users, orthodox and pietists, Enlightenment rationalists and romantic restorationists, traditionalists and renewalists.

The rise of the image now makes possible a print diversification that transcends liturgical special-interest groups. Pastors and worship leaders can download material and photoduplicate their own worship books; many do this week after week. This inevitably results in an editing of texts and music for local use, over which judicatory offices have little control. It is argued that worship folders alleviate worshipers of the need to find their way through cumbersome worship books (which, it is claimed, are not visitor-friendly). They also make possible a pastoral control of the liturgy that was previously unheard of in the liturgical churches. The use of worship books, on the other hand, keeps the liturgy in the hands of the congregation.

Another way in which the electronic communication revolution has affected our liturgical practices is that the style of presidential ministry in the liturgy is influenced by the way we communicate on the telephone, radio, television, audio and video tape: directly and informally. Walter J. Ong argues, "Electronic technology has brought us into the age of 'secondary orality.'"[23] Orality is the mode of thinking shaped by oral communication (communication without written texts), as opposed to the mode of thinking shaped by literacy, or communication through the written word. Secondary orality bears a striking resemblance to primary orality in that the speaker appeals directly to the auditors with as little mediating aid as possible. Preachers leave the pulpit and speak directly to the congregation without manuscript. A group spirit is engendered on the basis of interpersonal rapport between speaker and audience. This is a rhetorical art that has been cultivated since the rise of television. It differs from primary orality in that it is self-consciously chosen by both the speaker and the audience, because there is an alternative: literary communication. The speaker has made a self-conscious decision not to be tied to a written text, and the group has made a self-conscious decision not to turn inward but to be aware of others in the assembly. Thus, the video revolution has contributed in a profound way to the primary agenda of liturgical renewal: to renew the liturgy as the work of the people done together in community.

A New Location of Transcendence

As I noted in the previous chapter, restorationist liturgy is making a comeback today, especially among some of the young who are looking for a sense of transcendence that the practices of liturgical renewal seemingly deprived them of. We might note that many of these young seekers, often now living in urban areas, grew up in the suburbs. The architecture of countless suburban churches tells the story. These are not primarily places of worship but multipurpose buildings that also provide space for education, meetings, and fellowship that sometimes encroaches on the space for worship. The worship space is therefore no longer a "sanctuary," a place of special holiness. The God encountered in this space is no longer "wholly other" than the community that uses the multipurpose room. Either God will be encountered in the

interactions of the community, or God will not be encountered at all in these places.

Young seekers and old reactionaries may look for a more transcendent God in the older Gothic or Baroque churches in the cities. But they also find one another as they come together for liturgy. Those who congregate at Saint John Cantius Church or Old Saint Pat's in the Loop or the Church of the Ascension or Holy Trinity Orthodox Cathedral (all in Chicago) or in "emerging churches" (see Epilogue) form communities of common interest and mutual commitment. They often constitute the kind of community that anthropologist Victor Turner called *communitas*, a social condition in which class structures are removed, social distance is dispelled, and Buberian dialogue leads them to discover the Eternal Thou in relationship with other thous.[24] The vocabulary of *communitas* includes words like *openness, relationships*, and *sharing*. The character of *communitas* is joyful, celebrative, life-affirming. It prizes honesty, openness, and sensitivity on the part of fellow members of a religious community who meet each other in a sacred space, where they gather around holy things and, in that meeting and through those things, meet God.

Renewed liturgy insists that we act together: that we sing along with but also to one another; that we help one another light candles or receive communion; that we discover meaningful others in the room; that we are not just alone with God "up there on the altar" or "deep in our hearts." A fully trinitarian encounter with God suggests that we do indeed find the Father of us all "up there" and the Holy Spirit "deep within" connecting with our spirits, but we also find Christ the Word "dwelling among us full of grace and truth." The God of Christians cannot ever be "wholly other," not since "the Word became flesh" and entered into our human story. The location of transcendence is found in the immanence of the human community formed by the Spirit of the Father and the Son, the community in which and to which the Son of God is present in Word and Sacrament.

Thus has it been throughout the history of the liturgy, especially its social history. God in Christ has been present to, for, and among his people in the symposium of the house church, in the cemetery gatherings around the graves of martyrs, in the great entrance with the gifts into the basilica, in the icons venerated in defiance of an iconoclast emperor, in the host elevated against the splendid backdrop of Gothic stained glass, in the processions through the fields with chanted litanies or the processions through the streets with hymns of adoration, in the word opened up and applied with new force by Reformers, in the devotions of the pious, in the exuberance of the Spirit's awakenings, in the recovery of the great tradition, and in the renewal of the community at prayer and in praise. The people of God have always discovered God in Christ present among themselves when they have assembled to do their public work, where two or three are gathered in his name. That is why the work of the people is discerned to be, at the same time, the work of God.

EPILOGUE

Postmodern Liturgical Retrieval

At the beginning of the twenty-first century, major liturgical movements of the last three centuries are still in place: the revival tradition that began in the Great Awakenings of the eighteenth and early nineteenth centuries; the restoration that began in Roman Catholicism, Lutheranism, and Anglicanism in the nineteenth century; and the liturgical renewal that flourished throughout the twentieth century. But finally we must note a new movement of worship awakening that has characterized the desire of many in the postmodern generations to utilize forms of the past to meet their own spiritual needs. This movement has originated more in the traditional liturgical churches than in the free churches, and it is also characterized more by a desire to retrieve older rituals than just to renew existing ones. But it is also drawing young people who are in tune with contemporary culture. I have termed this the liturgical retrieval movement.[1] It also relates to what Robert Webber has called "ancient/future worship."[2]

Evidence of this movement may be seen in a couple of examples. The universal popularity of Taizé prayer services testifies to the desire of young people to retrieve words and symbols of the tradition, including Latin responses, chants, candles, icons, and incense, by which to express their own encounter with God. A somewhat more formal version of this type of prayer is evident in the Sunday-evening Compline services held in the Anglican/Episcopal cathedrals in Seattle, Washington; Portland, Oregon; and Vancouver, British Columbia, in which hundreds of young people sit quietly in a candle-illuminated atmosphere while the choir sings plainsong settings of psalms and canticles. One Episcopal priest has called these Compline services "Anglican seeker services."

This type of worship resonates with younger generations who also seek out the "alternative worship" in so-called emerging churches. The "emerging church" phenomenon began around 1995 in Great Britain and has spread to Australia and New Zealand.[3] That this movement has yet to make much impact in the United States may be attributed to the fact that this country continues to cling to Enlightenment sensibilities.

Emerging worship tends to be very eclectic, drawing on pieces of art and text and music from a wide variety of sources. The main sources of information about these alternative services may be found on the Internet. By their very nature, emerging churches are likely to be small groups rather than mass gatherings, since part of what makes them unique is consensus building among the participants in terms of deciding on the style and content of their liturgies. Unlike the seeker services, whose format is determined by the pastor, or the praise and worship services, whose flow is determined by the worship leaders, the order of each emerging-worship service is determined by consensus of the assembly. What results is an act of liturgy that truly is "the people's work."

These young worshipers give a lot of attention to the ambience of the worship space, which is all the more necessary if the meeting is held in an all-purpose room. Creativity reigns as they place screens, hang fabrics, and arrange for both picture slides and icons to serve as foci for meditation. The variety of music used ranges from ancient chant to contemporary Christian songs, but less as set pieces than as background for prayer and meditation. This approach does away with the dominance of the organist or the praise band. The shape of the liturgy is not complicated, and leadership is shared. The "experience" is not clergy dominated; vestments are used sparingly, if at all. In contrast to the church-growth seeker services, symbols are not avoided. Candles may be lit, and incense may be burned. The symbols and actions are chosen to connect with people at different levels and to meet different needs. For example, people may have their hands or feet anointed for healing. There has been much experimenting with Holy Communion to reframe it as a fellowship meal among friends. Rubrical directions are rarely given; the spirit of alternative worship is "Just do it."

This alternative worship addresses an undercurrent of unrest in our world that the megachurches did not address with their messages on how to live successfully and that liturgical restoration seemed to keep at a polite distance. Retrieval is the liturgical expression of postmodernism. Postmodern concerns arise less from philosophical disaffection with modernity than from the loss of confidence in holistic symbol systems and organizations.[4] Enlightenment-inspired confidence in rationality is thought to be actually at the root of much of the evil in the modern world, which made humanity and human progress the center of all reality. Rationality and ideologies related to the doctrine of progress have produced genocide, ethnic cleansing, the exploitation of nature, the domination of the world by industrially and technologically advanced countries, and the emergence of a seemingly permanent underclass suppressed by a global economy. Perceptive souls are concluding that humanity is not adequate to be the center of the universe. There have been too many failures, including the failures of the marriages of the parents of Generation X and the millennial generation. But as youth often connect with their grandparents, so the youthful emerging church is rediscovering things that the restorationists recovered. They are finding ways to adapt these ancient rites and symbols as the renewalists did. They are practicing a worship style that is connected to contemporary culture as the revivalists do. Those in the emerging churches may transcend the differences between revival, restoration, and renewal and lead us in a unifying approach to worship in the twenty-first century. My hunch is that retrieval of tradition, combined with instances of inculturation, will also be the way of Christianity in Latin America, Africa, and Asia—"the next Christendom."[5]

Bibliography

The following titles deal with the social history of Christianity or of liturgy and were useful in writing this book. For additional resources, see the notes to the chapters.

Ahlstrom, Sydney E. *A Religious History of the American People.* New Haven: Yale University Press, 1972.

Baldovin, John. *The Urban Character of Christian Worship: The Origins, Development, and Meaning of Stational Liturgy.* Orientalia Christiana Analecta 228. Rome: Pontificium Institutum Studiorum Orientalium, 1987.

———. *Worship: City, Church, and Renewal.* Washington, D.C.: Pastoral Press, 1991.

Bossy, John. *Christianity in the West 1400–1700.* Oxford: Oxford University Press, 1985.

———. "The Counter-Reformation and the People of Catholic Europe," *Past and Present* 47 (1970): 51–70.

———. "The Mass as a Social Institution 1200–1700," *Past and Present* 100 (1983): 29–61.

Bradshaw, Paul F., and Lawrence A. Hoffman, eds. *The Making of Jewish and Christian Worship.* Two Liturgical Traditions 1. Notre Dame, Ind.: University of Notre Dame Press, 1991.

———. *The Search for the Origins of Christian Worship,* 2nd ed. New York: Oxford University Press, 2002.

Brown, Peter. *The Cult of the Saints: Its Rise and Function in Latin Christianity.* Chicago: University of Chicago Press, 1981.

Chupungco, Anscar J. *Liturgical Inculturation: Sacramentals, Religiosity, and Catechesis.* Collegeville, Minn.: Liturgical Press, 1992.

Duffy, Eamon. *The Stripping of the Altars: Traditional Religion in England 1400–1580.* New Haven: Yale University Press, 1992.

———. *The Voices of Morebath: Reformation and Rebellion in an English Village.* New Haven: Yale University Press, 2001.

Fox, Robin Lane. *Pagans and Christians.* New York: Knopf, 1987.

Hen, Yitzhak. *The Royal Patronage of Liturgy in Frankish Gaul to the Death of Charles the Bald (877).* London and Rochester, NY: Boydell Press, 2001.

Hoffman, Lawrence A. *Beyond the Text: A Holistic Approach to Liturgy.* Bloomington: Indiana University Press, 1987.

Hsia, R. Po-Chia. *The World of Catholic Renewal, 1540–1770.* Cambridge: Cambridge University Press, 1998.

Johnson, Maxwell E. *The Virgin of Guadalupe: Theological Reflections of an Anglo-Lutheran Liturgist.* Minneapolis: Fortress Press, 2003.

Kee, Howard Clark et al., *Christianity: A Social and Cultural History*, 2nd ed. Upper Saddle River, N.J.: Prentice Hall, 1998.

Maag, Karen, and John Witvliet, eds. *Worship in Medieval and Early Modern Europe: Change and Continuity in Religious Practice*. Notre Dame, Ind.: University of Notre Dame Press, 2004.

McManners, John, ed. *The Oxford Illustrated History of Christianity*. Oxford: Oxford University Press, 1990.

Meeks, Wayne. *The First Urban Christians: The Social World of the First Christians*. New Haven: Yale University Press, 1983.

———. *The Moral World of the First Christians*. Library of Early Christianity. Philadelphia: Westminster, 1986.

Moeller, Bernd. *Imperial Cities and the Reformation*. Philadelphia: Fortress Press, 1972.

Muir, Edward. *Ritual in Early Modern Europe*. New Approaches to European History. Cambridge: Cambridge University Press, 1997.

Ozment, Steven. *Protestants: The Birth of a Revolution*. New York: Doubleday, 1992.

Quasten, Johannes. *Music and Worship in Pagan and Christian Antiquity*. Translated by Boniface Ramsey. Washington, D.C.: National Association of Pastoral Musicians, 1983.

Redman, Robb. *The Great Worship Awakening: Singing a New Song in the Postmodern Church*. San Francisco: Jossey-Bass, 2002.

Ruben, Miri. *Corpus Christi: The Eucharist in Late Medieval Culture*. Cambridge: Cambridge University Press, 1991.

Salmon, Pierre. *The Breviary through the Centuries*. Translated by Sister David Mary. Collegeville, Minn.: Liturgical Press, 1962.

Senn, Frank C. *Christian Liturgy—Catholic and Evangelical*. Minneapolis: Fortress Press, 1997.

———. "Sacraments and Social History: Postmodern Practice," *Theology Today* 58 (2001): 288–303.

Smith, Dennis. *From Symposium to Eucharist: The Banquet in the Early Christian World*. Minneapolis: Fortress Press, 2003.

Taft, Robert F. "The Frequency of the Eucharist throughout History." In *Beyond East and West: Problems in Liturgical Understanding*, 61–80. Washington, D.C.: Pastoral Press, 1984.

———. "The Order and Place of Lay Communion in the Late Antique and Byzantine East." In *Studia Liturgica Diversa: Essays in Honor of Paul F. Bradshaw*, edited by Maxwell E. Johnson and L. Edward Phillips, 129–52. Portland, Ore.: Pastoral Press, 2004.

Turner, Victor, and Edith Turner. *Image and Pilgrimage in Christian Culture: Anthropological Reflections*. New York: Columbia University Press, 1978.

Wainwright, Geoffrey and Karen B. Westerfield Tucker, eds., *The Oxford History of Christian Worship*. New York: Oxford University Press, 2005.

Ward, W. R. *Christianity under the Ancien Régime, 1648-1789*. Cambridge: Cambridge University Press, 1999.

White, James F. *Protestant Worship: Traditions in Transition*. Louisville: Westminster John Knox, 1989.

———. *Roman Catholic Worship: Trent to Today*. Mahwah, N.J.: Paulist Press, 1995.

Willis, G. G. "Roman Stational Liturgy." In *Further Essays in Early Roman Liturgy*, 1–87. London: SPCK, 1968.

Notes

Introduction: What Is a Social History of the Liturgy?

1. See Wayne Meeks, *The First Urban Christians: The Social World of the Apostle Paul* (New Haven: Yale University Press, 1983).

2. See John F. Baldovin, *The Urban Character of Christian Worship: The Origins, Development, and Meaning of Stational Liturgy*, Orientalia Christiana Analecta 228 (Rome: Pontificum Institutum Studiorum Orientalium, 1987).

3. See Frank C. Senn, *Christian Liturgy—Catholic and Evangelical* (Minneapolis: Fortress Press, 1997).

4. See John F. Baldovin, *Worship: City, Church and Renewal* (Washington, D.C.: Pastoral Press, 1991), 13–27, 29–35.

5. See Eamon Duffy, *The Stripping of the Altars: Traditional Religion in England 1400–1580* (New Haven and London: Yale University Press, 1992), 136–39, 568, 578–79.

6. Vilhelm Moberg, *A History of the Swedish People*, vols. 1 and 2, trans. Paul Britten Austin (New York: Pantheon, 1972, 1973).

7. Howard Zinn, *A People's History of the United States* (New York: HarperCollins, 1980).

8. Arthur Vööbus, *Studies in the History of the Estonian People* (Stockholm: ETSE, 1969ff.).

9. Eamon Duffy, *The Voices of Morebath: Reformation and Rebellion in an English Village* (New Haven: Yale University Press, 2001).

10. Jean-Marie-Roger Tillard, *Flesh of the Church, Flesh of Christ: At the Source of the Ecclesiology of Communion* (Collegeville, Minn.: Liturgical Press, 2001).

1. Sociologically Speaking, What Kind of Group Was the Christian Assembly?

1. See Kurt Schubert, "A Divided Faith: Jewish Religious Parties and Sects," in *The Crucible of Christianity*, ed. Arnold Toynbee, 77–98 (New York: World, 1969).

2. Peter Berger, "The Sociological Study of Sectarianism," *Social Research* 21 (1954): 479.

3. See Wayne A. Meeks, *The Moral World of the First Christians* (Philadelphia: Westminster, 1986), 75ff.

4. See Hans Conzelmann, *Gentiles, Jews, Christians: Polemics and Apologetics in the Greco-Roman Era*, trans. M. Eugene Boring (Minneapolis: Fortress Press, 1992).

5. On the various attitudes within Judaism on the role of the Land of Israel, see W. D. Davies, *The Territorial Dimension of Judaism, with a Symposium and Further Reflection* (Minneapolis: Fortress Press, 1991).

6. See Ferdinand Hahn, *The Worship of the Early Church*, trans. John Reumann (Philadelphia: Fortress Press, 1973), 40–64.

7. See David C. Sim, *The Gospel of Matthew and Christian Judaism: The History and Social Setting of the Matthean Community* (Edinburgh: T & T Clark, 1998).

8. See the text of Benediction No. 12 in C. W. Dugmore, *The Influence of the Synagogue upon the Divine Office* (Westminster: Faith, 1964), 119–20.

9. See Tzvee Zahavy, "The Politics of Piety: Social Conflict and the Emergence of Rabbinic Liturgy," in *Two Liturgical Traditions*. Vol. 1, *The Making of Jewish and Christian Worship*, ed. Paul F. Bradshaw and Lawrence A. Hoffman, 42–68 (Notre Dame, Ind.: University of Notre Dame Press, 1991).

10. While majority opinion among scholars favors Antioch as the place of origin of the *Didache*, strong arguments have also been presented for Egypt and northern Palestine.

11. See Richard Glover, "The *Didache's* Quotations and the Synoptic Gospels," *New Testament Studies* 5 (1958–59): 5ff.

12. See Louis Finkelstein, "The Birkat ha-Mazon," *Jewish Theological Quarterly*, n.s. 19 (1928–29): 211–62.

13. Jean Daniélou, *The Theology of Jewish Christianity*, trans. and ed. John A. Baker (Chicago: Henry Regnery, 1964) is the only treatment of the doctrines and customs of Jewish Christianity in their entirety.

14. See Arthur Vööbus, *History of Asceticism in the Syrian Orient: A Contribution to the History of Culture in the Near East*, vol. 1, *The Origin of Asceticism: Early Monasticism in Persia* (Louvain: Corpus Scriptorum Christianorum Orientalium 184, subsidia 14, 1958).

15. See Karen Armstrong, *Jerusalem: One City, Three Faiths* (New York: Ballantine, 1996), 170.

16. See Robert L. Wilken, *The Land Called Holy: Palestine in Christian History and Thought* (New Haven: Yale University Press, 1992), 65–81.

17. See J. R. Porter, *Jesus Christ: The Jesus of History, the Christ of Faith* (New York: Oxford University Press, 1999), 23.

18. See the fascinating sociological study of the history of Jesus and early Christianity in Rodney Stark, *The Rise of Christianity: A Sociologist Reconsiders History* (Princeton, N.J.: Princeton University Press, 1996).

19. Wayne A. Meeks, *The First Urban Christians: The Social World of the Apostle Paul* (New Haven: Yale University Press, 1983).

20. See Michael Grant, *A Social History of Greece and Rome* (New York: Scribner's, 1992), 5–37.

21. Pedar William Foss, "Kitchens and Dining Rooms at Pompeii: The Spatial and Social Relationship of Cooking to Eating in the Roman Household" (PhD diss., University of Michigan, Ann Arbor, 1994), 99.

22. See Carolyn Osiek and David L. Batch, *Families in the New Testament World: Households and House Churches* (Louisville: Westminster John Knox, 1997), 91–102.

23. See Elaine Pagels, *The Gnostic Gospels* (New York: Vintage, 1979), 48–69.

24. Ramsey MacMullen, *Roman Social Relations* (New Haven: Yale University Press, 1974), 63.

25. See John S. Kloppenborg and Stephen G. Wilson, eds., *Voluntary Associations in the Graeco-Roman World* (New York: Routledge, 1996).

26. Meeks, *The First Urban Christians*, 77ff.

27. See Dennis E. Smith, *From Symposium to Eucharist: The Banquet in the Early Christian World* (Minneapolis: Fortress Press, 2002), 87ff.

28. See Wayne A. Meeks, *The Origins of Christian Morality: The First Two Centuries* (New Haven: Yale University Press, 1993), 18–36.

29. "Letter of Pliny to the Emperor Trajan," in *Documents of the Christian Church*, trans. Henry Bettenson (New York: Oxford University Press, 1947), 6–7.

30. See Smith, *From Symposium to Eucharist*, 97.

31. See the floor plan in Cheslyn Jones, Geoffrey Wainwright, and Edward Yarnold, *The Study of Liturgy* (New York: Oxford University Press, 1978), 481.

32. See Jean Lassus, *Sanctuaires chrétiens de Syria* (Paris: Librairie Orientaliste Paul Geuthner, 1947).

33. See Meeks, *The First Urban Christians*, 81ff.

34. See Robert Wilken, "Collegia, Philosophical Schools, and Theology," in *The Catacombs and the Colosseum*, ed. Stephen Benko and John J. O'Rourke, 268–91 (Valley Forge, Pa.: Judson, 1971).

35. See Robin Lane Fox, *Pagans and Christians* (New York: Knopf, 1987), 51.

36. Clement, *First Letter to the Corinthians* 40, in *Library of Christian Classics*, vol. 1, *Early Christian Fathers*, ed. Cyril C. Richardson (Philadelphia: Westminster, 1953), 62.

37. Ignatius of Antioch, *Letter to the Trallians* 3, in *Early Christian Fathers*, 99.

38. Ignatius of Antioch, *Letter to the Smyrnaeans* 8–9, in *Early Christian Fathers*, 115.

39. See Shayne J. D. Cohen, *From the Maccabees to the Mishnah* (Philadelphia: Westminster, 1987), 221–22.

40. See Fox, *Pagans and Christians*, 493ff.

41. See John F. Baldovin, "The Development of the Monarchical Bishop to 250 A.D.," in *City, Church, and Renewal* (Washington, D.C.: Pastoral Press, 1991), 135–50.

2. Sacraments and Cult

1. Rodney Stark and William Sims Bainbridge, *The Future of Religion: Secularization, Revival, and Cult Formation* (Berkeley: University of California Press, 1985).

2. Peter Berger, "The Sociological Study of Sectarianism," *Social Research* 21 (1954): 479.

3. See Wayne A. Meeks, *The First Urban Christians: The Social World of the Apostle Paul* (New Haven: Yale University Press, 1983), 150ff.

4. Stark and Bainbridge, *The Future of Religion*, 26, 529–30.

5. Victor Turner, *The Ritual Process: Structure and Anti-structure* (Chicago: Aldine, 1969), 94–108.

6. See Peter Brunner, *Worship in the Name of Jesus*, trans. H. M. Bertram (St. Louis: Concordia, 1968), 20–21; and Alexander Schmemann, "Theology and Liturgical Tradition," in *Worship in Scripture and Tradition*, ed. Massey H. Shepherd Jr. (New York: Oxford University Press, 1963), 172.

7. Schmemann, "Theology and Liturgical Tradition," 175.

8. Ibid., 174.

9. See Alexander Schmemann, *For the Life of the World: Sacraments and Orthodoxy* (Crestwood, N.Y.: St. Vladimir's Seminary Press, 1973), 27.

10. See Meeks, *The First Urban Christians*, 74–110; see also Howard Clark Kee, *Christian Origins in Sociological Perspective* (Philadelphia: Westminster, 1980), 74–79.

11. See Aidan Kavanagh, *On Liturgical Theology* (New York: Pueblo, 1984), especially 73ff.

12. See Frank C. Senn, *New Creation: A Liturgical Worldview* (Minneapolis: Fortress Press, 2000), chaps. 1–2.

13. For a survey of this relationship between sacramental cultus and culture, see Frank C. Senn, *Christian Worship and Its Cultural Context* (Philadelphia: Fortress Press, 1983), 38ff.

14. See Senn, *New Creation*, 117–31; also Anscar J. Chapungco, "Liturgy and the Components of Culture," in *Worship and Culture in Dialogue*, ed. S. Anita Stauffer, 153–66 (Geneva: Lutheran World Federation, 1994).

15. See Gordon W. Lathrop, "Baptism in the New Testament and its Cultural Settings," in *Worship and Culture in Dialogue*, 17–38.

16. See John Peter Oleson, "Water Works," *Anchor Bible Dictionary* (New York: Doubleday, 1992), 6:887.

17. See S. Anita Stauffer, *On Baptismal Fonts* (Bramcote, Nottingham: Grove, 1994).

18. For a thorough survey, see Maxwell E. Johnson, *The Rites of Christian Initiation: Their Evolution and Interpretation* (Collegeville, Minn.: Liturgical Press, 1999).

19. Alistair Stewart-Sykes, "Manumission and Baptism in Tertullian's Africa: A Search for the Origin of Confirmation," *Studia Liturgica* 31 (2001): 129–49.

20. Holding to this social interpretation of manumission need not contradict the insight of Aidan Kavanagh, *Confirmation: Origins and Reform* (New York: Pueblo, 1988), that the ritual pattern of "confirmation" derives from the *missa*, or rite of dismissal in the catechumenate and the postbaptismal ceremonies, in *The Apostolic Tradition*.

21. See Joachim Jeremias, *The Eucharistic Words of Jesus*, trans. Norman Perrin (Philadelphia: Fortress Press, 1977).

22. The bibliography on the origins of the eucharistic prayer is long and getting longer. But see as especially seminal Louis Bouyer, *Eucharist*, trans. Charles U. Quinn (Notre Dame, Ind.: University of Notre Dame Press, 1968); Louis Ligier, "The Origins of the Eucharistic Prayer: From the Last Supper to the Eucharist," *Studia Liturgica* 9 (1973): 161–85; and Thomas Talley, "From Berakah to Eucharistia: A Reopening Question," *Worship* 50 (1976): 115–37.

23. See Louis Finkelstein, "The Birkat ha-Mazon," *Jewish Theological Quarterly*, n.s. 19 (1928–29): 211–62.

24. See Dennis R. Lindsay, "Todah and Eucharist: The Celebration of the Lord's Supper as a 'Thank Offering' in the Early Church," *Restoration Quarterly* 39 (1997): 83–100, who refers extensively to Hartmut Gese, "The Origins of the Lord's Supper," in *Essays on Biblical Theology* (Minneapolis: Fortress Press, 1981).

25. This line of development is explored in the work of Cesare Giraudo, whose writings in Italian are summarized in Edward J. Kilmartin, *The Eucharist in the West: History and Theology*, ed. Robert J. Daly (Collegeville, Minn.: Liturgical Press, 1998), 322–23.

26. See *Documents of the Christian Church*, ed. Henry Bettenson (New York: Oxford University Press, 1947), 6–7.

27. See Blake Leyerle, "Meal Customs in the Greco-Roman World," in *Two Liturgical Traditions*, vol. 5, *Passover and Easter: Origin and History to Modern Times*, ed. Paul F. Bradshaw and Lawrence A. Hoffman, 29–61 (Notre Dame, Ind.: University of Notre Dame Press, 1999).

28. See Dennis E. Smith, *From Symposium to Eucharist: The Banquet in the Early Christian World* (Minneapolis: Fortress Press, 2002).

29. See especially Oswyn Murray, "The Greek Symposium in History," in *Tria Corda: Scritti in Onore di Arnaldo Momigliano*, ed. Emilio Gabba, 259–72 (Como: Edizione New Press, 1983).

30. Leyerle, "Meal Customs in the Greco-Roman World," 37.

31. See Frank C. Senn, "Should Christians Celebrate the Passover?" in *Two Liturgical Traditions*, vol. 6, *Passover and Easter: The Symbolic Structuring of Sacred Seasons*, ed. Paul F. Bradshaw and Lawrence A. Hoffman, 183–205 (Notre Dame, Ind.: University of Notre Dame Press, 1999).

32. See Baruch M. Bokser, *The Origin of the Seder* (Berkeley: University of California Press, 1984).

33. See S. Angus, *The Mystery-Religions and Christianity* (London: John Murray, 1925).

34. See Louis Bouyer, *Rite and Man: Natural Sacredness and Christian Liturgy* (Notre Dame, Ind.: University of Notre Dame Press, 1963), 123ff.

35. See D. H. Tripp, "The Mysteries," in *The Study of Liturgy*, ed. Cheslyn Jones, Geoffrey Wainwright, and Edward Yarnold (New York: Oxford University Press, 1978), 54.

36. See Edward Yarnold, "The Fourth and Fifth Centuries," in *The Study of Liturgy*, 109.

37. See Johannes Quasten, *Music and Worship in Pagan and Christian Antiquity*, trans. Boniface Ramsey (Washington, D.C.: National Association of Pastoral Musicians, 1983), 153ff.

38. See Geoffrey Rowell, *The Liturgy of Christian Burial*, Alcuin Club Collections 59 (London: SPCK, 1977), 10–12.

39. See Peter Brown, *The Cult of the Saints: Its Rise and Function in Latin Christianity* (Chicago: University of Chicago Press, 1981), 32ff.

40. See Quasten, *Music and Worship in Pagan and Christian Antiquity*, 168ff.

41. See Brown, *The Cult of the Saints*, 36ff.

42. The definitive history of the Christian altar is Joseph Braun, *Der christliche Altar in seiner geschichtlichen Entwicklung*, 2 vols. (Munich: Koch, 1924). See also Edmund Bishop, *On the History of the Christian Altar* (London: Day, 1905).

3. Apocalypse and Christian Liturgy

1. See Abraham Schalit, "Palestine under the Seleucids and Romans," in *The Crucible of Christianity*, ed. Arnold Toynbee, 65–76 (New York: World, 1969).

2. Norman Golb, *Who Wrote the Dead Sea Scrolls? The Search for the Secret of Qumran* (New York: Scribner, 1995).

3. See D. S. Russell, *The Method & Message of Jewish Apocalyptic, 200 BC–AD 100* (Philadelphia: Westminster, 1964).

4. See Willy Rordorf, *Sunday: The History of the Day of Rest and Worship in the Earliest Centuries of the Christian Church*, trans. A. A. K. Graham

(Philadelphia: Westminster, 1968), 54ff. See also his later study, "Sunday: The Fullness of Christian Liturgical Time," *Studia Liturgica* 14 (1982): 90–96.

5. Rordorf, *Sunday*, 277.

6. See Jean Daniélou, *The Bible and the Liturgy* (Notre Dame, Ind.: University of Notre Dame Press, 1956), 333ff.

7. David E. Aune, in *Revelation* (Word Biblical Commentary 52a [Dallas: WordBooks, 1997]), argues that this scene reflects and deliberately parodies imperial court practice.

8. G. K. Beale, in *The Book of Revelation: A Commentary on the Greek Text*, New International Greek Testament Commentary (Grand Rapids: Eerdmans, 1999), argues that the author of Revelation draws heavily from Old Testament models, especially Ezekiel 1 and Daniel 7.

9. This point is emphasized by Christopher C. Rowland, *Christian Origins: From Messianic Movement to Christian Religion* (London: SPCK, 1985), 293ff.

10. Massey H. Shepherd Jr., *The Paschal Liturgy and the Apocalypse* (Richmond, Va.: John Knox, 1960).

11. Thus, Maxwell E. Johnson, *The Rites of Christian Initiation: Their Evolution and Interpretation* (Collegeville, Minn.: Liturgical Press, 1999), 72. See Paul Bradshaw, "Hippolytus Revisited: The Identity of the So-Called 'Apostolic Tradition,'" *Liturgy* 16 (1) (2000): 8–11.

12. Paul Bradshaw, *The Search for the Origins of Christian Worship*, 2nd ed. (New York: Oxford University Press, 2002), 144–70.

13. Shepherd, *The Paschal Liturgy*, 83.

14. The earliest list of canonical writings is in a fragment of an eighth-century manuscript published by the Italian scholar Muratori in 1740. Judging by the writings that are included, it probably reflects a canon of about 200 C.E. See Hans Conzelmann, *History of Primitive Christianity*, trans. John E. Steely (Nashville: Abingdon, 1973), 176–78.

15. See John G. Gager, *Kingdom and Community: The Social World of Early Christianity* (Englewood Cliffs, N.J.: Prentice Hall, 1975).

16. See Robin Lane Fox, *Pagans and Christians* (New York: Knopf, 1987), 22.

17. Robert Markus, "From Rome to the Barbarian Kingdom (330–700)," in *The Oxford Illustrated History of Christianity*, ed. John McManners (New York: Oxford University Press, 1990), 78ff.

18. See Fox, *Pagans and Christians*, 605ff.

19. See David W. Kling, *The Bible in History: How the Texts Have Shaped the Times* (Oxford: Oxford University Press, 2004), 13–43, for a discussion of Matthew 21:21, Anthony, and the rise of monasticism.

20. See Graham Gould, *The Desert Fathers on Monastic Communities* (Oxford: Clarendon, 1993).

21. See Alexander Schmemann, *Introduction to Liturgical Theology*, trans. Ashleigh E. Moorhouse (London: Faith Press; Portland, Me.: American Orthodox Press, 1966), 103ff.

22. See Robert Taft, *The Liturgy of the Hours in East and West: The Origins of the Divine Office and Its Meaning for Today* (Collegeville, Minn.: Liturgical Press, 1986), 17–19.

23. Bradshaw, in *The Search for the Origins of Christian Worship*, 176–78, stresses that the monastic office represented a development of the older domestic tradition, whereas the cathedral office was a departure from that tradition. Also, not every church father welcomed the unprecedented enthusiasm for psalm singing that emerged during the fourth century.

24. See Schmemann, *Introduction to Liturgical Theology*, 147–48.

25. Ibid., 149–50.

26. Ibid., 150–52.

27. Ibid., 109–110.

4. Times, Occasions, and the Communion of Saints

1. See Gabriele Winkler, "The Appearance of the Light at the Baptism of Jesus and the Origins of the Feast of the Epiphany: An Investigation of Greek, Syriac, Armenian, and Latin Sources," in *Between Memory and Hope: Readings on the Liturgical Year*, ed. Maxwell E. Johnson, 291–347 (Collegeville, Minn.: Liturgical Press, 2000).

2. See Thomas J. Talley, "The Origin of Lent at Alexandria," *Studia Patristica* 18 (1982): 594–612; and Talley, *The Origins of the Liturgical Year* (New York: Pueblo, 1986), 189–214.

3. See J. Gordon Davies, *Holy Week: A History*, Ecumenical Studies in Worship 11 (Richmond, Va.: John Knox, 1963), 9–22.

4. R. H. Connelly, *Didascalia Apostolorum: The Syriac Version Translated and Accompanied by the Vernona Latin Fragments, with an Introduction and Notes* (Oxford: Clarendon, 1920), 124ff.

5. See Ferdinand van der Meer, *Augustine the Bishop*, trans. B. Battershaw and G. R. Lamb (London: Sheed and Ward, 1961), 49–50.

6. See H. Boone Porter, *The Day of Light: The Biblical and Liturgical Meaning of Sunday* (Washington, D.C.: Pastoral Press, 1960).

7. See Joachim Jeremias, *The Eucharistic Words of Jesus*, trans. Norman Perrin (Philadelphia: Fortress Press, 1977), 122–23.

8. Talley, *Origins of the Liturgical Year*, 24–25.

9. The paschal controversy is well documented in Eusebius' *Church History* 23, which contains primary source material, including the letter of the aged Bishop Polycrates of Ephesus defending the Quartodeciman practice. The

Sunday celebration of Easter is not nearly as well defended in the ancient sources.

10. See Paul F. Bradshaw, "The Origins of Easter," in *Two Liturgical Traditions*, vol. 5, *Passover and Easter: Origin and History to Modern Times*, ed. Paul F. Bradshaw and Lawrence A. Hoffman, 92–93 (Notre Dame, Ind.: University of Notre Dame Press, 1999).

11. Ibid., 83–84.

12. There was discrepancy between the East and the West as to whether the Sabbath (Saturday) should be regarded as a fast day. Since the East counted both Saturday and Sunday as feast days, the period of Lent lasts longer in the Eastern churches than in the Western churches.

13. See G. G. Willis, "The Content and Form of the Solemn Prayers," in *Essays in Early Roman Liturgy*, 39–48 (London: SPCK, 1964).

14. See Philip H. Pfatteicher, *Commentary on the Lutheran Book of Worship* (Minneapolis: Augsburg Fortress, 1990), 264ff.

15. For the full description of the Easter Vigil and Christian initiation in Hippo, see van der Meer, *Augustine the Bishop*, 361ff.

16. Ibid., 381.

17. See Robert Cabié, *La Pentecôte: L'évolution de la Cinquantaine pascale au cours des cinq premiers siècles* (Tournai: Desclée, 1964), chap. 3.

18. For an account of this scholarship, see Susan K. Roll, *Toward the Origins of Christmas* (Kampen: Kok Pharos, 1995).

19. Talley, *Origins of the Liturgical Year*, 101.

20. See Louis Duchesne, *Christian Worship: Its Origin and Evolution*, trans. M. L. McClure (London: SPCK, 1923), 257ff.

21. Talley, *Origins of the Liturgical Year*, 121–34.

22. Ibid., 85–103.

23. Ibid., 147–55.

24. See Frank C. Senn, "The Meaning of Advent: Implications for Preaching," *Concordia Theological Monthly* 42 (1971): 653–59.

25. Ibid., 148.

26. See Terrance W. Klein, "Advent and the Evangelical Struggle for Cultural Symbols," *Worship* 69 (1995): 538–56.

27. Leo the Great, *Sermon XVII* (*Nicene and Post-Nicene Fathers* XII.125–26).

28. Ibid., 127.

29. See F. Noguea, "Avent et avènement d'après les anciens sacramentaires," *Questions Liturgiques et Paroissiales* 18 (1937): 233–44.

30. See Michael S. Driscoll, "Cult of the Saints," in *The New Dictionary of Sacramental Worship*, ed. Peter E. Fink, 1137–43 (Collegeville, Minn.: Liturgical Press, 1990).

31. See Peter Brown, *The Cult of the Saints: Its Rise and Function in Latin Christianity* (Chicago: University of Chicago Press, 1981), 86ff.

32. Ibid., 21.

33. Ibid., 101.

34. See James Frazer, *The Golden Bough* (1890; repr., Avenel, N.J.: Gramercy, 1981), 121–49.

5. Sacred Places and Liturgical Art in Late Antique Culture

1. See Eric M. Orlin, *Temples, Religion, and Politics in the Roman Republic* (Leiden: Brill, 1997).

2. See Béatrice Caseau, "Sacred Landscapes," in *Late Antiquity: A Guide to the Postclassical World*, ed. G. W. Bowersock, Peter Brown, and Oleg Grabar (Cambridge, Mass.: Belknap, 1999), 21ff.

3. See Charles Norris Cochrane, *Christianity and Classical Culture* (London: Oxford University Press, 1944), 178.

4. Ibid., 179.

5. See Pierre Chuvin, *A Chronicle of the Last Pagans*, trans. B. A. Archer (Cambridge, Mass.: Harvard University Press, 1990), 57ff.

6. See Richard Krautheimer, "The Constantinian Basilica," *Dumbarton Oaks Papers* 21 (1967): 117–40.

7. Thomas F. Mathews, *The Early Churches of Constantinople: Architecture and Liturgy* (University Park: Pennsylvania State University Press, 1971), 126.

8. Theodore Klauser, *A Short History of the Western Liturgy*, trans. John Haliburton (London: Oxford University Press, 1969), 33ff.

9. See David Holeton, "Vestments," in *The New Westminster Dictionary of Liturgy and Worship*, ed. Paul Bradshaw, 465–71 (Louisville: Westminster John Knox, 2002).

10. See Klauser, *A Short History of the Western Liturgy*, 35.

11. Robert Taft, "The Liturgy of the Great Church," *Dumbarton Oaks Papers* 34/35 (1980/1981): 69.

12. Hans-Joachim Schultz, *The Byzantine Liturgy: Symbolic Structure and Faith Expression*, trans. Matthew J. O'Connell (New York: Pueblo, 1986), 27.

13. Taft, "The Liturgy of the Great Church," 59.

14. See the English translation of the catecheses of Theodore of Mopsuestia in Edward Yarnold, *The Awe-Inspiring Rites of Initiation* (London: St. Paul, 1971).

15. Cited in Peter Brown, *The Cult of the Saints: Its Rise and Function in Latin Christianity* (Chicago: University of Chicago Press, 1981), 7.

16. Cited in Caseau, "Sacred Landscapes," 37.

17. Brown, *The Cult of the Saints*, 9.

18. Cited in ibid., 38.

19. Aidan Kavanagh, *On Liturgical Theology* (New York: Pueblo, 1984), 59.

20. See Paul F. Bradshaw, *The Search for the Origins of Christian Worship*, 2nd ed. (Oxford: Oxford University Press, 2002), 219–20.

21. Kavanagh, *On Liturgical Theology*, 57.

22. John F. Baldovin, "The City as Church, the Church as City," in *Worship: City, Church, and Renewal*, 13–27 (Washington, D.C.: Pastoral Press, 1991).

23. See A. Grabar, *Christian Iconography* (Princeton, N.J.: Princeton University Press, 1968).

24. Schulz, *The Byzantine Liturgy*, 51.

25. See Hans von Campenhausen, "The Theological Problem of Images in the Early Church," in *Tradition and Life in the Church: Essays and Lectures on Church History*, trans. A. V. Littledale (Philadelphia: Fortress Press, 1968), 183.

26. Cited in Schulz, *The Byzantine Liturgy*, 57.

27. See John Julius Norwich, *A Short History of Byzantium* (New York: Knopf, 1997), 111.

28. On the history of the iconoclastic controversy, see Leonid Ouspensky, *Theology of the Icon* (New York: St. Vladimir's Seminary Press, 1978).

29. See the discussion of Germanus's theology of icons in David W. Fagerberg, *What Is Liturgical Theology? A Study in Methodology* (Collegeville, Minn.: Liturgical Press, 1992), 239ff.

30. Cited in John Meyendorff, *Christ in Eastern Christian Thought* (New York: St. Vladimir's Seminary Press, 1971), 49.

31. Von Campenhausen, "The Theological Problem of Images," 192.

32. Ibid., 191.

33. See Jaroslav Pelikan, *The Christian Tradition*, vol. 2, *The Spirit of Eastern Christendom (600–1700)* (Chicago: University of Chicago Press, 1974), 91–145.

34. Ibid., 198.

6. People and Places for Different Liturgies

1. See Geoffrey Grimshaw Willis, *Further Essays in Early Roman Liturgy* (London: SPCK, 1968), 15.

2. Cyril C. Richardson, ed. and trans., *Early Christian Fathers* [*ECF*], The Library of Christian Classics (Philadelphia: Westminster, 1953), 1:178.

3. *ECF*, 115.

4. *To the Trallians* 5:1–2; *ECF*, 99.

5. *To the Magnesians* 7:1–2; *ECF*, 96.

6. See John F. Baldovin, "The Development of the Monarchical Bishop to 250 A.D.," in *City, Church and Renewal*, 151–70 (Washington, D.C.: Pastoral Press, 1991).

7. See Robin Lane Fox, *Pagans and Christians* (New York: Knopf, 1987), 493–517.

8. See John Wilkerson, ed. and trans., *Egeria's Travels* (London: SPCK, 1971), 36ff (newly translated with supporting documents and notes).

9. See Charles Renoux, "Liturgical Ministers at Jerusalem in the Fourth and Fifth Centuries," in *Roles in the Liturgical Assembly*, trans. Matthew J. O'Connell (New York: Pueblo, 1981), 222ff.

10. Eusebius, *The History of the Church*, trans. G. A. Williamson (New York: Barnes and Noble, 1995), 282.

11. The definitive textual edition is in Michel Andrieu, *Les Ordines Romani du haut Moyen-Âge* (Louvain: Spicilegium Sacrum Lovaniense, 1931). For a synopsis, see Willis, *Further Essays*, 16ff.

12. Willis, *Further Essays*, 8–9.

13. On the complicated history of the rite of confirmation, see John D. C. Fisher, *Christian Initiation: Baptism in the Medieval West*, Alcuin Club Collections 47 (London: SPCK, 1965), 71–72, 80–81; John D. C. Fisher, *Confirmation Then and Now*, Alcuin Club Collections 60 (New York: SPCK, 1978), 126ff.; and Maxwell E. Johnson, *The Rites of Christian Initiation: Their Evolution and Interpretation* (Collegeville, Minn.: Liturgical Press, 1999), 203ff.

14. David R. Holeton, "Confirmation in the 1980s," in *Ecumenical Perspectives on Baptism, Eucharist, Ministry*, ed. Max Thurian, Faith and Order Paper 116 (Geneva: World Council of Churches, 1983), 69.

15. I follow here the discussion in Pierre Salmon, *The Breviary through the Centuries*, trans. Sister David Mary (Collegeville, Minn.: Liturgical Press, 1962), 31ff.

16. See Arthur Carl Piepkorn, "A Lutheran View of the Validity of Lutheran Orders," in *Lutherans and Catholics in Dialogue* 4 (New York and Washington: U.S.A. National Committee of the Lutheran World Federation and the U.S. Bishops' Committee for Ecumenical and Interreligious Affairs, 1970), 220ff.

17. In IV *Sent.*, 24.3.3, cited in J. H. Crehan, "Medieval Ordinations," in *The Study of Liturgy*, ed. Cheslyn Jones, Geoffrey Wainwright, and Edward Yarnold (New York: Oxford University Press, 1978), 327.

18. See Frank C. Senn, "The Office of Bishop in the Lutheran Reformation," *dialog* 24 (1985): 119–27.

19. See Louis Bouyer, *A History of Christian Spirituality*, vol. 1, *The Spirituality of the New Testament and the Fathers*, trans. Mary P. Ryan (London: Burns & Oates; Tournai: Desclée, 1963), 303ff.

20. See Arthur Vööbus, *History of Asceticism in the Syrian Orient: A Contribution to the History of Culture in the Near East*, vols. 1–2, Corpus scriptorum christianorum orientalium, Subsidia 14, 17 (Louvain: Secrétariat du CorpusSCO, 1958, 1960).

21. Bouyer, *A History of Christian Spirituality*, 331ff.

22. See James W. McKinnon, "Desert Monasticism and the Later Fourth-Century Psalmodic Movement," *Music and Letters* 75 (1994): 505–21.

23. Alexander Schmemann, *Introduction to Liturgical Theology*, trans. Asheleigh E. Moorhouse (London: Faith Press; Portland, Me.: American Orthodox Press, 1966), 152–61.

24. Salmon, *The Breviary through the Centuries*, 35; see n. 137.

7. Church Music through the Carolingian Renaissance

1. See Ramsey MacMullen, *Christianity and Paganism in the Fourth to Eighth Centuries* (New Haven: Yale University Press, 1997), 103ff.

2. See Johannes Quasten, *Music and Worship in Pagan and Christian Antiquity*, trans. Boniface Ramsey (Washington, D.C.: National Association of Pastoral Musicians, 1983).

3. Odo Casel, "Die *logike thusia* der antiken Mystik in christlich-liturgischer Umdeutung" [The *logike thusia* (reasonable sacrifice) of the Ancient Mystics in Christian-Liturgical Reinterpretation], *Jahrbuch für Liturgiewissenschaft* 4 (1924): 37ff.

4. Edward Foley, *From Age to Age: How Christians Celebrated the Eucharist* (Chicago: Liturgy Training Publications, 1991), 9.

5. Eric Werner, *The Sacred Bridge: Liturgical Parallels in Synagogue and Early Church* (New York: Schocken, 1970), 128–66.

6. See George Wesley Buchanan, *To the Hebrews*, Anchor Bible 36 (Garden City, N.J.: Doubleday, 1972).

7. See William L. Holladay, *The Psalms through Three Thousand Years: Prayerbook of a Cloud of Witnesses* (Minneapolis: Fortress Press, 1993).

8. *Egeria: Diary of a Pilgrimage*, trans. and annotated by George E. Gingras (New York: Newman, 1970), 99–100.

9. John Chrysostom, *Discourses against Judaizing Christians*, trans. Paul W. Harkins (Washington, D.C.: Catholic University Press, 1979), 92.

10. Ibid., 26–27.

11. Michael Peppard, "Musical Instruments and Jewish-Christian Relations in Late Antiquity," *Studia Liturgica* 33 (1) (2003): 20–32.

12. See the citations in Everett Ferguson, "Toward a Patristic Theology of Music," *Studia Patristica* 24 (1993): 266–83.

13. John Chrysostom, *Homilies on the Psalms* 149:2 (Patrologia graeca 23, ed. J.-P. Migne), 1172ff.

14. Quasten, *Music and Worship*, 77ff.

15. Ibid., 87ff.

16. Michel Andrieu, ed., *Les Ordines Romani du haut Moyen Âge*, vol. 5 (Louvain: Spicilegium Sacrum Lovaniense, 1960), 83, 95, 107.

17. Egon Wellesz, *A History of Byzantine Music and Hymnography* (Oxford: Oxford University Press, 1949), 125ff.

18. See Herwig Wolfram, *History of the Goths*, trans. Thomas J. Dunlap (Berkeley: University of California Press, 1988), 19ff.

19. See Edward James, *The Franks* (Oxford: Blackwell, 1988).

20. See Richard Fletcher, *The Barbarian Conversion* (New York: Holt, 1997), 100ff.

21. See Gerald Ellard, *Master Alcuin, Liturgist* (Chicago: Regnery, 1956).

22. See Henry Mayr-Harting, "The West: The Age of Conversion (700–1050)," in *The Oxford Illustrated History of Christianity*, ed. John McManners (Oxford: Oxford University Press, 1990), 101ff.

23. See Yitzhak Hen, *The Royal Patronage of Liturgy in Frankish Gaul*, Henry Bradshaw Society (London: Boydell, 2001).

24. See Cyrille Vogel, *Medieval Liturgy: An Introduction to the Sources*, trans. and ed. William G. Storey and Niels Rasmussen (Washington, D.C.: Pastoral Press, 1986), originally published in French in 1970.

25. Jeffrey Richards, *Consul of God: The Life and Times of Gregory the Great* (London: Routledge, 1980), 121.

26. Ibid.

27. Ibid.

28. S. J. P. van Dijk, "The Urban and Papal Rites in Seventh- and Eighth-Century Rome," *Sacris Erudiri* 12 (1961): 467.

29. Ibid., 568.

30. Richards, *Consul of God*, 121.

31. See Gerald Abraham, *The Concise Oxford History of Music* (Oxford: Oxford University Press, 1985), 59–60.

32. Wellesz, *A History of Byzantine Music and Hymnography*, 61–65.

33. James, *The Franks*, 129ff.

34. See Patrice Cousin, "La psalmodie chorale dans la règle de Sainte Colomban [Choral Psalmody in the Rule of Saint Columban]," in *Mélanges columbaniens actes du Congrés International de Luxeuil* (Paris: Éditions Alsation, 1951), 179–91.

35. Jerome, *De viris illustribus* [Concerning Illustrious Men] (c. 400), ed. E. C. Richardson, in *Texte und Untersuchungen zur Geschichte der altchristlichen Literatur* 14 (1896): 48. Jerome composed this work as a bibliography to show pagans how many excellent writers there were among Christians.

36. See Michael Richter, *Medieval Ireland: The Enduring Tradition* (New York: St. Martin's, 1988), 69ff.

37. Ibid., 85ff.

38. See David N. Power, "Affirmed from Under: Celtic Liturgy and Spirituality," *Studia Liturgica* 27 (1) (1997): 1–32.

39. See John Walton Tyrer, *Historical Survey of Holy Week: Its Services and Ceremonial*, Alcuin Club Collections 29 (London: Oxford University Press, 1932), 56ff.

8. Vernacular Elements in the Medieval Latin Mass

1. This story of protracted missionary enterprise is told in Richard Fletcher, *The Barbarian Conversion: From Paganism to Christianity* (New York: Holt, 1997).

2. See Henry Mayr-Harting, "The West: The Age of Conversion (700–1050)," in *The Oxford Illustrated History of Christianity*, ed. John McManners, 92ff (Oxford: Oxford University Press, 1990).

3. See Irven M. Resnick, "*Lingua Dei, Lingua Hominis:* Sacred Language and Medieval Texts," *Viator* 21 (1990): 51–74.

4. Fletcher, *The Barbarian Conversion*, 355–56.

5. Ibid., 262–68.

6. See the articles in Roger Wright, ed., *Latin and the Romance Languages in the Early Middle Ages* (University Park: Pennsylvania State University Press, 1996), especially 1–5, 103–11.

7. Walter J. Ong, *Orality and Literacy: The Technologizing of the Word* (London: Routledge, 2002), 111.

8. See Blandine-Dominique Berger, *Le drame liturgique de Pâques*, Théologie historique 37 (Paris: Beauchesne, 1976), 90–91.

9. See Johan Huizinga, *The Autumn of the Middle Ages*, trans. Rodney J. Payton and Ulrich Mammitzsch (Chicago: University of Chicago Press, 1996), 221ff.

10. Ibid., 5–6, 221–22.

11. See Minnie Cate Morrell, *A Manual of Old English Biblical Material* (Knoxville: University of Tennessee Press, 1965); and James H. Morey, *Book and Verse: A Guide to Middle English Biblical Literature* (Urbana: University of Illinois Press, 2000). For these and other references, I am indebted to the outstanding series of articles by Peter Jeffrey, "A Chant Historian Reads *Liturgiam Authenticam,*" *Worship* 78, nos. 1–4 (2004): 2–24, 139–64, 236–65, 309–341.

12. Geoffrey Chaucer, "The Summoner's Tale," lines 1788–94, in *A Variorum Edition of the Works of Geoffrey Chaucer*, vol. 2, *The Canterbury Tales, The Summoner's Tale*, ed. John E. Plummer (Norman: University of Oklahoma Press, 1995), 128–30.

13. See Yvonne Cazel, *Les voix du peuple—Verbum Dei: Le bilinguisme latin–langue vulgaire au Moyen Âge*, Publications romanes et françaises 223 (Geneva: Librairie Droz, 1998).

14. See Ann Hudson, "'*Laicus litteratus*': The Paradox of Lollardy," in *Heresy and Literacy, 1000–1530*, ed. Peter Biller and Ann Hudson, 222–36 (Cambridge: Cambridge University Press, 1994).

15. Martin Luther, "An Order of Mass and Communion for the Church at Wittenberg" (1523), in *Luther's Works*, ed. and trans. Ulrich S. Leupold (Philadelphia: Fortress Press, 1965), 53:25.

16. Joseph A. Jungmann, *The Mass of the Roman Rite: Its Origins and Development*, trans. Francis A. Brunner (Westminster, Md.: Christian Classics, 1986), 1:456.

17. John Bossy, *Christianity in the West, 1400–1700* (Oxford: Oxford University Press, 1985), 68.

18. Eamon Duffy, *The Stripping of the Altars: Traditional Religion in England, 1400–1580* (New Haven: Yale University Press, 1992), 334–37.

19. See Christer Pahlmblad, *Mässa på svenska: Den reformatoriska mässan i Sverige mot den senmedeltida bakgrunden*, Bibliotheca Theologiae Practicae 60 (Lund: Arcus Förlag, 1998), 113–65.

20. See Bard Thompson, *Liturgies of the Western Church* (Cleveland: World, 1961), 147–48.

21. See M. Alfred Bichel, "Greek and Latin Hymnody," in *Hymnal Companion to the Lutheran Book of Worship*, ed. Marilyn Kay Stulken (Philadelphia: Fortress Press, 1981), 14.

22. See Donald Jay Grout, *A History of Western Music* (New York: W. W. Norton, 1960), 49.

23. William Anthony Ruff, *Integration and Inconsistencies: The Thesaurus Musicae Sacrae in the Reformed Roman Eucharistic Liturgy* (PhD diss., Karl-Franzois-Universität, Graz, Austria, 1998), 495–96.

24. See Jungmann, *The Mass of the Roman Rite*, 1:146.

25. *The Book of Concord*, ed. and trans. Theodore G. Tappert (Philadelphia: Fortress Press, 1959), 56, 95.

26. See Jungmann, *The Mass of the Roman Rite*, 1:147.

27. See Hugo Rahner, *Man at Play*, trans. Brian Battershaw and Edward Quinn (New York: Herder and Herder, 1967), 83–86.

28. See David L. Jeffrey, *The Early English Lyric and Franciscan Spirituality* (Lincoln: University of Nebraska Press, 1975).

29. See Duffy, *The Stripping of the Altars*, 117ff.

30. Edmund Bishop, "On the Origin of the Prymer," in *Liturgica Historica*, 211–37 (Oxford: Oxford University Press, 1918).

31. T. F. Simmons, ed., *The Lay Folk's Mass Book* (London: Early English Tract Society, 1879), 38–40, lines 224–32.

32. Colin Richmond, "Religion and the Fifteenth Century Gentleman," in *The Church, Politics, and Patronage in the Fifteenth Century*, ed. Barrie Dobson, 193–208 (Gloucester: A. Sutton, 1984).

33. Pamela Graves, "Social Space in the English Medieval Parish Church," *Economy and Society* 18 (1989): 297–322.

34. Duffy, *The Stripping of the Altars*, 122.

35. 24. *The Lay Folk's Mass Book*, 40; lines 237–40.

36. See Francoise Waquet, *Latin or the Empire of a Sign*, trans. John Howe (New York: Verso, 2001), 44.

37. Christer Pahlmblad, in *Mässa på svenska,* concludes that the celebration of mass in Swedish in the 1530s and 1540s is scant. The 1549 Prayer Book Rebellion of the Devon and Cornish men is well documented in Eamon Duffy, *The Voices of Morebath: Reformation and Rebellion in an English Village* (New Haven: Yale University Press, 2001), 127–41.

38. Martin Luther, "The German Mass and Order of Services," *Luther's Works,* ed. and trans. Ulrich S. Leupold (Philadelphia: Fortress Press, 1965), 53:63.

39. "On the Sacrifice of the Mass," session 22, *The Canons and Decrees of the Council of Trent,* trans. H. J. Schroeder (Rockford, Ill.: Tan, 1978), chap. 8.

9. The Medieval Liturgical Calendar

1. See Edward Muir, *Ritual in Early Modern Europe* (Cambridge: Cambridge University Press, 1997), 74ff.

2. See Eviatar Zerubavel, *The Seven Day Circle: The History and Meaning of the Week* (New York: Free Press, 1985), 5–26.

3. See James George Frazer, *The Golden Bough: A Study in Magic and Religion* (New York: Macmillan, 1922), 638.

4. See Francis X. Weiser, *Handbook of Christian Feasts and Customs* (New York: Harcourt, Brace, and World, 1952), 98ff.

5. See Eamon Duffy, *The Stripping of the Altars: Traditional Religion in England 1400–1580* (New Haven: Yale University Press, 1992), 15ff.

6. Muir, *Ritual in Early Modern Europe,* 86ff.

7. See Victor Turner, *The Ritual Structure: Structure and Anti-Structure* (Chicago: Aldine, 1969), 94ff.

8. See Robert Taft, *Beyond East and West: Problems in Liturgical Understanding* (Washington, D.C.: Pastoral Press, 1984), 66–68.

9. Gregory the Great, *Epist. ad Augustinum Angl. Episc.* (Patrologia latina 77:1351).

10. See Weiser, *Handbook of Christian Feasts and Customs,* 185.

11. See *Processionale ad usum Insignis ac Praeclarae Ecclesiae Sarum* (Leeds: McCorquodate, 1882; repr. 1969), 43ff.

12. See John W. Tyrer, *Historical Survey of Holy Week,* Alcuin Club Collections 29 (London: Oxford University Press, 1932), 60.

13. See Peter Jeffrey, "*Mandatum ovum Do Vovis*: Toward a Renewal of the Holy Thursday Footwashing Rite," *Worship* 64 (1990): 107–41.

14. Duffy, *The Stripping of the Altars,* 31ff.

15. See J. Gordon Davies, *Holy Week: A Short History* (Richmond, Va.: John Knox, 1963), 52.

16. See Kenneth Stevenson, *Jerusalem Revisited: The Liturgical Meaning of Holy Week* (Washington, D.C.: Pastoral Press, 1988), 65.

17. A. J. MacGregor, *Fire and Light in the Western Triduum* (Collegeville, Minn.: Liturgical Press, 1992), 135–72.

18. See Myrtilla Avery, *The Exsultet Rolls of South Italy* (Princeton, N.J.: Princeton University Press, 1936).

10. The Eucharistic Body and the Social Body in the Middle Ages

1. See Isnard Wilhelm Frank, *A Concise History of the Medieval Church*, trans. John Bowden (New York: Continuum, 1995), 65ff.

2. See Jean-Marie-Roger Tillard, *The Flesh of the Church, Flesh of Christ: At the Source of the Ecclesiology of Communion* (Collegeville, Minn.: Liturgical Press, 2001).

3. Ibid., 68ff.

4. Augustine of Hippo, *The City of God*, trans. Henry Bettenson (Harmondsworth, England: Penguin, 1972), 379–80.

5. Augustine, *The Works of Saint Augustine*, ed. John E. Rotelle, pt. 2, *Sermons*, trans. Edmund Hill (Brooklyn: New City, 1990), 6:254.

6. See Aidan Kavanagh, *Confirmation: Origins and Reform* (New York: Pueblo, 1988), 39–78.

7. See Ephrem Carr and Duane Etiene, "The Rite of Public Reconciliation of Penitents in the Roman Pontifical," *Resonance* 1/2, 2/1 (1965/1966): 8–34.

8. *Summa Theologica*, q. 73, a. 4. Cited in Tillard, *Flesh of the Church*, 53–54.

9. On the eucharistic debates of the early Middle Ages, see Gary Macy, *The Theologies of the Eucharist in the Early Scholastic Period* (Oxford: Oxford University Press, 1984).

10. See Richard W. Southern, "Lanfranc of Bec and Berengar of Tours," in *Studies in Medieval History Presented to Frederick Maurice Powicke*, ed. Richard W. Hunt, William A. Pantin, and Richard W. Southern, 27–48 (Oxford: Oxford University Press, 1948).

11. See Hermann Sasse, *This Is My Body: Luther's Contention for the Real Presence in the Sacrament of the Altar* (Minneapolis: Augsburg, 1959), 41.

12. James of Vitry, *De sacramentis*, cited in Macy, *The Theologies of the Eucharist*, 214.

13. See Miri Rubin, *Corpus Christi: The Eucharist in Late Medieval Culture* (Cambridge: Cambridge University Press, 1991), 35ff.

14. See Jacques LeGoff, *The Birth of Purgatory*, trans. Arthur Goldhammar (Chicago: University of Chicago Press, 1948), 213–20, 289–95.

15. See K. L. Wood-Legh, *Perpetual Chantries in Britain* (Cambridge: Cambridge University Press, 1965).

16. John Bossy, "The Mass as a Social Institution 1200–1700," *Past and Present* 100 (1983): 42.

17. Ibid., 34ff.

18. Edward Muir, *Ritual in Early Modern Europe*, New Approaches to European History (Cambridge: Cambridge University Press, 1997), 51.

19. Henri de Lubac, *Corpus mysticum: L'eucharistie et l'église au Moyen Âge* (Paris: Aubier-Montaigne, 1949).

20. See Rubin, *Corpus Christi*, 150ff.

21. Ibid., 62–63.

22. See Oscar D. Watkins, *A History of Penance* (New York: Longmans, Green, 1920; repr. 1960), 2:748.

23. See John Bossy, *Christianity in the West 1400–1700* (Oxford: Oxford University Press, 1985), 70.

24. See John Bossy, "The Counter-Reformation and the People of Catholic Europe," *Past and Present* 47 (1970): 55–56.

25. Ibid., 71.

26. See Eamon Duffy, *The Stripping of the Altars: Traditional Religion in England 1400–1580* (New Haven: Yale University Press, 1992), 125.

27. See Bossy, *Christianity in the West*, 65.

28. See John Bossy, "The Mass as a Social Institution 1200–1700," op. cit., 29–61.

29. On the practices of the *devotio moderna*, see Steven Ozment, *The Age of Reform 1250–1550: An Intellectual and Religious History of Late Medieval and Reformation Europe* (New Haven: Yale University Press, 1980), 96–98. The devotional classic that best epitomizes this movement is Thomas à Kempis's *Imitation of Christ*, a work in four parts, three of which deal with the inner life, and the fourth with the Eucharist.

30. Bossy, "The Mass as a Social Institution," 59.

31. Ibid.

32. On the development of the feast of Corpus Christi, see Rubin, *Corpus Christi*, 164ff; and Nathan Mitchell, *Cult and Controversy: The Worship of the Eucharist outside Mass* (Collegeville, Minn.: Liturgical Press, 1982), 172–76.

33. Rubin, *Corpus Christi*, 185ff.

34. Mervyn James, "Ritual, Drama and Social Body in the Late Medieval English Town," *Past and Present* 98 (February 1983): 3–29; here 8.

35. Ibid., 9.

11. The Dissolution of the Social Body in the Reformation Communion

1. John Calvin, *Institutes of the Christian Religion*, trans. Henry Beveridge II (Grand Rapids: Eerdmans, 1957), 600–601.

2. Martin Luther, "The German Mass and Order of Service," in *Luther's Works*, ed. Ulrich S. Leupold (Philadelphia: Fortress Press, 1965), 53:64.

3. Martin Luther, "The Blessed Sacrament of the Holy and True Body of Christ, and the Brotherhoods," *Luther's Works*, ed. E. Theodore Bachman, trans. Jeremiah F. Schindel (Philadelphia: Fortress Press, 1960), 35:53–54.

4. Carter Lindberg, *Beyond Charity: Reformation Initiatives for the Poor* (Minneapolis: Fortress Press, 1993).

5. Yngve Brilioth, *Eucharistic Faith and Practice, Evangelical and Catholic*, trans. A. G. Hebert (London: SPCK, 1965), 134.

6. Gabriel M. Braso, *Liturgy and Spirituality*, 2nd ed., trans. Leonard J. Doyle (Collegeville, Minn.: Liturgical Press, 1971), 42.

7. R. R. Post, *The Modern Devotion: Confrontation with Reformation and Humanism* (Leiden: Brill, 1968), 675–80.

8. Martin Luther, *The Large Catechism*, in *The Book of Concord*, ed. and trans. Theodore G. Tappert (Philadelphia: Fortress Press, 1959), 451.

9. Phillip Melanchthon, *The Apology of the Augsburg Confession*, XXIV.1, in *The Book of Concord*, 249.

10. See Ulrich Zwingli, *Exposition of the Faith*, in *Zwingli and Bullinger*, trans. G. Bromiley, The Library of Christian Classics, 24:259–65 (Philadelphia: Westminster, 1953), which deals with the purpose of the Lord's Supper and the sacraments in general.

11. *Luther's Works* 53:28–29.

12. See C. P. Clasen, *The Anabaptists: A Social History* (Ithaca, N.Y.: Cornell University Press, 1972), 147–48, 280.

13. Pierre Le Brun, *Explication de la messe* (Paris, 1726), 1:595, n. 597.

14. John Bossy, "The Mass as a Social Institution 1200–1700," *Past and Present* 100 (1983): 58.

15. *Luther's Works*, 53:84.

16. Ibid., 33–34.

17. Ibid., 32ff.

18. See Roland Bainton, *Here I Stand* (New York: Abingdon; Nashville: Cokesbury, 1955), 67.

19. See R. Po-Chia Hsia, *The World of Catholic Renewal 1540–1770* (Cambridge and New York: Cambridge University Press, 1998), 198–200.

20. See Jean Laporte, *La doctrine de Port-Royal: La morale* II (Paris: Vrin, 1952), 232–33.

21. See John Bossy, "The Counter-Reformation and the People of Catholic Europe," *Past and Present* 47 (1970): 63ff.

22. Sven Kjöllerström, ed., *Den svenska kyrkoordningen 1571* (Lund: Håkan Ohlsson, 1971), 65ff., 67ff., 74–75, 81ff.

23. See Brilioth, *Eucharistic Faith and Practice*, 252–53.

24. Kjöllerström, *Den svenska kyrkoordningen*, 81.

25. Christer Pahlmblad, *Mässa på svenska: Den reformatoriska mässan i*

Sverige mot den senmedeltida bakgrunden, Bibliotheca theologiae practicae 60 (Lund: Arcus Förlag, 1998), 166ff.

26. See John Bossy, *Christianity in the West 1400–1700* (Oxford: Oxford University Press, 1985), 126ff.

27. Geneva: Librairie Droz, 1996.

28. Grand Rapids: Eerdmans, 2000.

29. See Robert Kingdon, "Worship in Geneva before and after the Reformation," in *Worship in Medieval and Early Modern Europe: Change and Continuity in Religious Practice*, ed. Karin Maag and John D. Witvliet, 41–62 (Notre Dame, Ind.: University of Notre Dame Press, 2004).

30. See Hilary S. D. Smith, "Preaching and Sermons," in *The Oxford Encyclopedia of the Reformation*, ed. Hans J. Hillerbrand, 3:323–32 (Oxford: Oxford University Press, 1996).

31. See Bossy, *Christianity in the West*, 142.

32. See Eamon Duffy, *The Stripping of the Altars: Traditional Religion in England 1400–1580* (New Haven: Yale University Press, 1992), 478ff.; and Vilhelm Moberg, *A History of the Swedish People: From Renaissance to Revolution*, trans. Paul Britten Austin (New York: Pantheon, 1973), 168ff., 174ff.

33. Bossy, *Christianity in the West*, 154–55.

34. See Edward Muir, *Ritual in Early Modern Europe* (Cambridge: Cambridge University Press, 1997), 242–43.

35. Read a description of a progress to Norwich in 1578 in *What Life Was Like in the Realm of Elizabeth* (Alexandria, Va.: Time-Life Books, n.d.), 54–57.

36. See Duffy, *The Stripping of the Altars*, 579–80.

12. Death Here and Life Hereafter in the Middle Ages and the Reformation

1. Heiko A. Oberman, *Luther: Man between God and the Devil*, trans. Eileen Walliser-Schwarzbart (New York: Doubleday, 1992), 50ff.

2. Steven Ozment, *The Age of Reform 1250–1550: An Intellectual and Religious History of Late Medieval and Reformation Europe* (New Haven: Yale University Press, 1980).

3. John Bossy, *Christianity in the West 1400–1700* (Oxford: Oxford University Press, 1985).

4. Edward Muir, *Ritual in Early Modern Europe* (Cambridge: Cambridge University Press, 1997), 52.

5. Johan Huizinga, *The Autumn of the Middle Ages*, trans. Rodney J. Payton and Ulrich Mammitzsch (Chicago: University of Chicago Press, 1996), 156.

6. Ibid., 220ff.

7. Eamon Duffy, *The Stripping of the Altars: Traditional Religion in England 1400–1580* (New Haven: Yale University Press, 1992), 301.

8. Jaroslav Pelikan, *The Christian Tradition: The Emergence of the Catholic Tradition (100–600)* (Chicago: University of Chicago Press, 1971), 1:355.

9. See Muir, *Ritual in Early Modern Europe*, 70–72.

10. Jacques Le Goff, *The Medieval Imagination*, trans. Arthur Goldhammer (Chicago: University of Chicago Press, 1988), 67–77.

11. See Joseph A. Jungmann, *The Mass of the Roman Rite: Its Origins and Development*, trans. Francis A. Brunner (Westminster, Md.: Christian Classics, 1986), 1:217–19.

12. Bernhard Poschmann, *Penance and the Anointing of the Sick*, trans. and rev. by Francis Courtney (New York: Herder and Herder, 1964), 245.

13. Philippe Ariès, *The Hour of Our Death*, trans. Helen Weaver (New York: Knopf, 1981).

14. Bossy, *Christianity in the West*, 28.

15. See Geoffrey Rowell, *The Liturgy of Christian Burial*, Alcuin Club Collections 59 (London: SPCK, 1977), 70ff.

16. Oberman, *Luther*, 187ff.

17. Roland Bainton, *Here I Stand* (New York: Abingdon, 1950), 78.

18. Martin Luther, "Ninety-Five Theses," in *Luther's Works* (Philadelphia: Fortress Press, 1957), 31:25.

19. Ibid., 126.

20. "Smalcald Articles," in *The Book of Concord*, ed. and trans. Theodore G. Tappert (Philadelphia: Fortress Press, 1959), 295.

21. John Calvin, *Institutes of the Christian Religion*, III:5.6, trans. Henry Beveridge (Grand Rapids: Eerdmans, 1957), 1:576.

22. Diarmaid MacCulloch, *The Boy King Edward VI and the Protestant Reformation* (New York: Palgrave, 2001), 4–5.

23. *Works of Martin Luther* 6 (Philadelphia: Muhlenberg Press, 1932), 287.

24. *Lutheran Book of Worship* (Minneapolis: Augsburg, 1978), hymn 325.

25. See Calvin R. Stapert, *My Only Comfort: Death, Deliverance, and Discipleship in the Music of Bach* (Grand Rapids: Eerdmans, 2000).

26. See Bernd Moeller, *Imperial Cities and the Reformation: Three Essays*, ed. and trans. H. C. Erik Midelfort and Mark U. Edwards Jr. (Philadelphia: Fortress Press, 1972), 63ff.

27. See Günter Vogler, "Nuremberg," in *The Oxford Encyclopedia of the Reformation*, ed. Hans J. Hillerbrand, 3:160–63 (Oxford: Oxford University Press, 1996).

28. See Steven Ozment, *Protestants: The Birth of a Revolution* (New York: Doubleday, 1992), 62.

29. Ibid., 63.

30. See Eamon Duffy, *The Voices of Morebath: Reformation and Rebellion in an English Village* (New Haven: Yale University Press, 2001), 120–21.

31. Ibid., 123, 127ff.

32. Rowell, *The Liturgy of Christian Burial*, 74ff.

33. F. E. Brightman, *The English Rite* (London: Rivingtons, 1915), 1: cxxvii.

34. Rowell, *The Liturgy of Christian Burial*, 84ff.

35. E. C. Whitaker, *Martin Bucer and the Book of Common Prayer*, Alcuin Club Collections 55 (Great Wakering, UK: Mayhew-McCrimmon, 1974), 50, 52.

36. *The First and Second Prayer Books of King Edward VI*, Everyman Library 448 (London: Dent; New York: Dutton, 1910; repr. 1968), 269–70.

37. Ibid., 424–25.

38. See Rowell, *The Liturgy of Christian Burial*, 89–90.

39. Duffy, *The Voices of Morebath*, 504ff.

40. Richard Baxter, *Reliquiae Baxterianae* (London, 1696), 2:315.

41. *The Works of James Pilkington*, ed. J. Scholefield (London: Parker Society, 1842), 317–18.

13. The Ecclesiastical Captivity of Marriage

1. See John Bossy, *Christianity in the West 1400–1700* (Oxford: Oxford University Press, 1985), 19ff.

2. See Kenneth Stevenson, *Nuptial Blessing: A Study of Christian Marriage Rites* (New York: Oxford University Press, 1983), 13ff.

3. See Robin Lane Fox, *Pagans and Christians* (New York: Knopf, 1987), 308–10.

4. Ibid., 35ff.

5. Edward Muir, *Ritual in Early Modern Europe* (Cambridge: Cambridge University Press, 1997), 32, 41.

6. Christopher N. L. Brooke, *The Medieval Idea of Marriage* (Oxford: Oxford University Press, 1989), 251–52.

7. Muir, *Ritual in Early Modern Europe*, 32.

8. Bossy, *Christianity in the West*, 22–23.

9. Muir, *Ritual in Early Modern Europe*, 39–41.

10. Ibid., 23–24.

11. See Steven Ozment, *Protestants: The Birth of a Revolution* (New York: Doubleday, 1992), 152ff.

12. See Thomas Max Safley, "Marriage," in *The Oxford Encyclopedia of the Reformation*, ed. Hans J. Hillerbrand, 3:18–23 (New York: Oxford University Press, 1996).

13. See "The Babylonian Captivity of the Church," in *Three Treatises* (Philadelphia: Fortress Press, 1973), 226–32, or *Luther's Works*, American ed. [*LW*], 36:96–103.

14. *LW* 45:388–89.

15. *LW*, 45:392.

16. *LW*, 53:111.

17. See Bryan Spinks, "Luther's Other Major Liturgical Reforms: 3. The Traubüchlein," *Liturgical Review* 10 (1980): 33–38.

18. See Bryan Spinks, "The Liturgical Origin and Theology of Calvin's Genevan Marriage Rite," *Ecclesia Orans* 3 (1986): 195–210.

19. Muir, *Ritual in Early Modern Europe*, 41.

20. See Jeffrey Watt, "The Marriage Laws Calvin Drafted for Geneva," in *Calvinus Sacrae Scripture Professor*, ed. Wilhelm H. Neuser, 245–55 (Grand Rapids: Eerdmans, 1994).

21. Bossy, *Christianity in the West*, 25.

22. *The Canons and Decrees of the Council of Trent*, trans. and ed. H. J. Schroeder (Rockford, Ill.: Tan, 1978), 180ff.

23. *The First and Second Prayer Books of Edward VI*, Everyman's Library 448 (London: Dent, 1968), 252.

24. See Arnold van Gennep, *The Rites of Passage*, trans. Monika B. Vizedom and Gabrielle L. Caffee (Chicago: University of Chicago Press, 1960), 116–45.

14. Liturgy and Confessional Identity

1. See Bodo Nischan, "Becoming Protestants: Lutheran Altars or Reformed Communion Tables?" in *Worship in Medieval and Early Modern Europe*, ed. Karin Maag and John D. Witvliet, 84–114 (Notre Dame, Ind.: University of Notre Dame Press, 2004).

2. See Bodo Nischan, *Prince, People, and Confession: The Second Reformation in Brandenburg* (Philadelphia: University of Pennsylvania Press, 1994), 185ff.

3. This axiom appears in the so-called *Capitula Coelestini* 8 [*Patrologia Latina*, ed. J.-P. Migne (Paris, 1844–1855), 51:205–12], which was appended to a letter of Pope Celestine I (422–432) but is now held to be the work of Prosper, dating from between 435 and 442. The full text of this chapter is given in English translation in Geoffrey Wainwright, *Doxology: The Praise of God in Worship, Doctrine, and Life* (New York: Oxford University Press, 1980), 225–26, along with a discussion of its argumentation in historical context.

4. See Augustine, *Contra Julianum* 6.4.10–5.14 (Patrologia latina 33:889–91); *Sermon 174*, 7–9 (Patrologia latina 38:943–45).

Presented to Honor Albert Hyma, 2nd ed., ed. Kenneth A. Strand (Ann Arbor: Ann Arbor Publishing, 1964).

37. See Antoine Arnauld, *Oeuvres*, 27:87ff., 251, 289ff., 350, 466ff., 567ff., 589ff.

38. This historical argument is developed in the preface, ibid., 92–137.

39. Found in François Fénelon, *Oeuvres* (Paris: Firman Didot, 1854), 1:665–75.

40. Calvin, *Institutes*, 4:45–46.

41. See R. Po-Chia Hsia, *The World of Catholic Renewal 1540–1770* (Cambridge: Cambridge University Press, 1998), 199.

42. Ibid., 200.

43. See Günther Stiller, *Johann Sebastian Bach and Liturgical Life in Leipzig*, trans. Herbert J. A. Bouman, Daniel F. Poellot, and Hilton C. Oswald (St. Louis: Concordia, 1984), 131ff.

44. See Doug Adams, *Meeting House to Camp Meeting: Toward a History of American Free Church Worship from 1620 to 1835* (Austin: Sharing Company, 1981), 80ff.

16. Worship Awakening

1. Thus Peter Gay, *The Enlightenment* (New York: Simon and Schuster, 1973).

2. See Dorinda Outram, *The Enlightenment*, New Approaches to European History (Cambridge: Cambridge University Press, 1995), 34.

3. See Ted Morgan, *Wilderness at Dawn: The Settling of the North American Continent* (New York: Simon and Schuster, 1993), 265ff.

4. See *The Journals of Henry Melchior Muhlenberg*, ed. and trans. Theodore G. Tappert and John W. Doberstein, 3 vols. (Philadelphia: Muhlenberg Press, 1942–1958); and Charles Woodmason, *The Carolina Backcountry on the Eve of the Revolution* (Chapel Hill, N.C.: University of North Carolina Press, 1953).

5. Jonathan Edwards, *The Religious Affections* (New Haven: Yale University Press, 1959).

6. Doug Adams, *From Meeting House to Camp Meeting: Toward a History of American Free Church Worship from 1620 to 1835* (Saratoga, Calif.: Modern Liturgy–Resource Publications, 1981), 90–97.

7. See Sydney E. Ahlstrom, *A Religious History of the American People* (New Haven: Yale University Press, 1972), 269–70.

8. See John Pollock, *George Whitefield and the Great Awakening* (London: Hodder and Stoughton, 1972).

9. See James F. White, *Protestant Worship: Traditions in Transition* (Louisville: Westminster John Knox, 1989), 130.

10. Barton W. Stone, "A Short History of the Life of Barton W. Stone Written by Himself," in *Voices from Cane Ridge*, ed. Rhodes Thompson, facsimile ed. (St. Louis: Bethany Press, 1954), 69–72.

11. Ahlstrom, *A Religious History*, 433.

12. Charles Grandison Finney, *Lectures on Revivals of Religion*, ed. William G. McLoughlin (Cambridge: Harvard University Press, 1960).

13. See White, *Protestant Worship*, 171–91.

14. See David W. Kling, *The Bible in History: How the Texts Have Shaped the Times* (Oxford: Oxford University Press, 2004), 193–229.

15. See Melva W. Costen, *African American Christian Worship* (Nashville: Abingdon, 1993).

16. See Ahlstrom, *A Religious History*, 735ff. on responses to the city, 743ff. on the great revivalists.

17. Ibid., 747–48.

18. See Jay Dolan, *The American Catholic Experience: A History from Colonial Times to the Present* (Garden City, N.J.: Doubleday, 1985).

19. J. William Frost, "Christianity and Culture in America," in *Christianity: A Social and Cultural History*, 2nd ed. (Upper Saddle River, N.J.: Prentice-Hall, 1998), 462.

20. Wade Clark Roof, *A Generation of Seekers: The Spiritual Journeys of the Baby Boom Generation* (San Francisco: HarperCollins, 1993), 55ff.

21. Quoted in Edgar S. Brown, "The Worship of the Church and the Modern Man," in *Liturgical Renewal in the Christian Churches*, ed. Michael J. Taylor (Baltimore: Helicon, 1967), 199.

22. Rick Warren, *The Purpose-Driven Church: Growth without Compromising Your Message and Mission* (Grand Rapids: Zondervan, 1995).

23. Timothy Wright, *A Community of Joy: How to Create Contemporary Worship* (Nashville: Abingdon, 1994).

24. See Lester Ruth, "*Lex Agendi, Lex Orandi:* Toward an Understanding of Seeker Services as a New Kind of Liturgy," *Worship* 70 (1996): 386–405.

25. Roof, *A Generation of Seekers*, 46.

26. William Strauss and Neil Howe, *Generations: The History of America's Future* (New York: Morrow, 1991). 63.

27. See Kling, *The Bible in History*, 251–59.

28. See Harvey Cox, *Fire from Heaven: The Rise of Pentecostal Spirituality and the Re-shaping of Religion in the Twenty-First Century* (Reading, Mass.: Addison-Wesley, 1995).

29. *Los Angeles Times*, April 18, 1906; quoted in Philip Jenkins, *Mystics and Messiahs: Cults and New Religions in American History* (New York: Oxford University Press, 2000), 65–66.

30. See Robert Mapes Anderson, *Vision of the Disinherited: The Making of American Pentecostalism* (New York: Oxford University Press, 1979).

31. White, *Protestant Worship*, 200.

32. Denominational statements regarding the charismatic movement have been collected in Killian McDonnell, ed., *Presence, Power, Praise: Documents on the Charismatic Renewal*, 3 vols. (Collegeville, Minn.: Liturgical Press, 1980).

33. See Donald E. Miller, *Reinventing American Protestantism* (Berkeley: University of California Press, 1997).

34. As summarized by Barry Liesch, *The New Worship: Straight Talk on Music and the Church* (Grand Rapids: Baker, 1996).

35. See Robb Redman, *The Great Worship Awakening: Singing a New Song in the Postmodern Church* (San Francisco: Jossey-Bass, 2002), 47–71.

17. Liturgical Restoration

1. See Immanuel Kant, *Religion within the Limits of Reason Alone*, trans. Theodore M. Greene and Hoyt H. Hudson (New York: Harper and Row, 1960), 182–89.

2. See Jaroslav Pelikan, *Bach among the Theologians* (Philadelphia: Fortress Press, 1986), 35–41.

3. See Günther Stiller, *Johann Sebastian Bach and Liturgical Life in Leipzig*, trans. Herbert J. A. Bouman, Daniel F. Poellot, and Hilton C. Oswald, ed. Robin A. Leaver (St. Louis: Concordia, 1984), 133, 164.

4. See Georg Feder, "Decline and Fall," in *Protestant Church Music*, ed. Friedrich Blume (New York: Norton, 1974), 334–36.

5. See the samples that I provide from the Consistory of Hannover in *Christian Liturgy—Catholic and Evangelical* (Minneapolis: Fortress Press, 1997), 542–43.

6. W. R. Ward, *Christianity under the Ancien Régime*, New Approaches to European History (Cambridge: Cambridge University Press, 1999), 197–98.

7. Ibid.

8. See Volkmar Braunbehrens, *Mozart in Vienna 1781–1791*, trans. Timothy Bell (New York: Grove Weidenfeld, 1986), 413–24.

9. Ward, *Christianity under the Ancien Régime*, 198–99. See also Charles Bolton, *Church Reform in 18th Century Italy (The Synod of Pistoia)* (The Hague: Martinus Nijhoff, 1969).

10. One of the most magisterial studies of Christianity in the French Revolution is John McManners, *The French Revolution and the Church* (New York: Harper and Row, 1960).

11. See William M. Sloane, *The French Revolution and Religious Reform 1789–1804* (New York: Scribner's, 1901).

12. See Dorinda Outram, *The Enlightenment*, New Approaches to European History (Cambridge: Cambridge University Press, 1993), 114.

13. See Dom Louis Soltner, *Solesmes and Dom Gueranger 1805–1875*, trans. Joseph O'Connor (Orleans, Mass.: Paraclete, 1995).

14. See J. William Frost, "Christianity and Culture in America," in *Christianity: A Social and Cultural History*, 2nd ed., 455–64 (Upper Saddle River, N.J.: Prentice Hall, 1998).

15. See Luther D. Reed, *The Lutheran Liturgy*, 2nd ed. (Philadelphia: Fortress Press, 1959), 152–53.

16. James F. White, *Worship in Transition* (Nashville: Abingdon, 1976), 80–82.

17. See Yngve Brilioth, *The Anglican Revival* (London: Longmans, Green, 1925).

18. See James F. White, *The Cambridge Movement* (Cambridge: Cambridge University Press, 1979).

19. See Harold Bloom, *The American Religion: The Emergence of the Post-Christian Nation* (New York: Simon and Schuster, 1992).

20. See Martin F. Connell, "On the U.S. Aversion to Ritual Behavior and the Vocation of the Liturgical Theologian," *Worship* 78 (5) (2004): 386–404.

21. Robert F. Hayburn, *Papal Legislation on Sacred Music* (Collegeville, Minn.: Liturgical Press, 1979), 219–31.

22. See Stanley Hauerwas and William Willimon, *Resident Aliens: Life in the Christian Colony* (Nashville: Abingdon, 1989).

23. Noteworthy examples of "restoration" parishes (my term, not theirs) are the Church of the Ascension in Chicago, Saint Paul's on K Street in Washington, D.C., Grace and Saint Peter's in Baltimore, St. Clement's in Philadelphia, Resurrection in New York City, Saint John the Evangelist in Newport, R.I., the Church of the Advent in Boston, and Saint Bartholomew in Toronto.

24. This phrase refers to the use of incense and the ringing of Sanctus bells before, during, and after the consecration of the Eucharist.

25. See especially Joseph Cardinal Ratzinger, *The Feast of Faith: Approaches to a Theology of the Liturgy*, trans. Graham Harrison (San Francisco: Ignatius, 1986); and Aidan Nichols, *Looking at the Liturgy: A Critical View of Its Contemporary Form* (San Francisco: Ignatius, 1996).

26. Among them we may note Saint John Cantius in Chicago, Saint Agnes in Saint Paul, Minn., Saint Martin of Tours in Louisville, Ky., Saint Alphonsus in Baltimore, Md., and Holy Family in Toronto.

18. Liturgical Renewal

1. See Bernard Botte, *From Silence to Participation: An Insider's View of Liturgical Renewal*, trans. John Sullivan (Washington, D.C.: Pastoral Press, 1988).

2. Ernest B. Koenker, *The Liturgical Renaissance in the Roman Catholic Church* (St. Louis: Concordia, 1966; first published by the University of Chicago Press, 1954).

3. Evidence of this in a number of areas of liturgical research is exposed in Paul F. Bradshaw, *The Search for the Origins of Christian Worship: Sources and Methods for the Study of Early Liturgy*, 2nd ed. (Oxford: Oxford University Press, 2002).

4. See Donald Myrvik, "A Letter from Donald Myrvik: Former Executive Secretary of the Lutheran Society for Worship, Music, and the Arts," *Liturgy* 19 (2) (2004): 49–53.

5. James F. White, *Christian Worship in Transition* (Nashville: Abingdon, 1976), 104.

6. See Frank C. Quinn, "Forty Years and Counting: Vatican II and the Transformation of the Liturgy in the Roman Catholic Church," *Liturgy* 19 (2) (2004): 3–10.

7. John Fenwick and Bryan Spinks, *Worship in Transition: The Liturgical Movement in the Twentieth Century* (New York: Continuum, 1995), 66–68.

8. Robb Redman, *The Great Worship Awakening: Singing a New Song in the Postmodern Church* (San Francisco: Jossey-Bass, 2002), 86–92.

9. See Gabe Huck, "Implementing the Constitution on the Sacred Liturgy: Forty Years Is a Start," *Liturgy* 19 (2) (2004): 11–22.

10. A whole series of Renewing Worship resources have been published by Augsburg Fortress, leading up to the resource that will be the successor to *Lutheran Book of Worship*. Renewing Worship has been guided by *Principles for Worship* (Minneapolis: Evangelical Lutheran Church in America, 2002).

11. I here follow the "ecumenical ordo" that Gordon Lathrop has popularized in his writings. See *Holy Things: A Liturgical Theology* (Minneapolis: Fortress Press, 1993). It should be emphasized that this is the ordo of liturgical renewal, not necessarily of liturgical restoration, and certainly not of the awakening traditions.

12. Gregory Dix, *The Shape of the Liturgy* (London: Dacre, 1945), exerted a profound influence on liturgical renewal. Bradshaw, *The Search for the Origins of Christian Worship*, 6ff., 122ff. discusses the methodological and historical flaws in Dix's theory.

13. See Anscar J. Chupungco, *Liturgies of the Future: The Process and Methods of Inculturation* (New York: Pueblo, 1989).

14. Anscar J. Chupungco, *Liturgical Inculturation: Sacramentals, Religiosity, and Catechesis* (Collegeville, Minn.: Liturgical Press, 1992), 37–44.

15. Pierre-Marie Gy, "The Inculturation of the Christian Liturgy in the West," *Studia Liturgica* 20 (1) (1990): 8–18.

16. Chupungco, *Liturgical Inculturation*, 47–51.

17. See *The Gregorian Sacramentary under Charles the Great*, ed. H. A. Wilson, Henry Bradshaw Society 49 (London: Harrison and Son, 1915).

18. See Mark R. Francis, *Liturgy in a Multicultural Community*, American Essays in Liturgy Series (Collegeville, Minn.: Liturgical Press, 1991).

19. Mitchell Stephens, *The Rise of the Image and the Fall of the Word* (New York: Oxford University Press, 1998), 21.

20. Joseph Brodsky, "The Nobel Lecture: Uncommon Visage," *New Republic*, January 4 and 11, 1988.

21. Walter Anderson, *The Future of the Self* (New York: Putnam, 1997), 35–45.

22. Aidan Kavanagh, "Scriptural Word and Liturgical Worship," in *Reclaiming the Bible for the Church*, ed. Carl B. Braaten and Robert W. Jenson (Grand Rapids: Eerdmans, 1995), 135.

23. Walter J. Ong, *Orality and Literacy* (London: Routledge, 1984 and 2002), 133.

24. Victor Turner, *The Ritual Process: Structure and Anti-Structure* (Chicago: Aldine, 1969), 131–65.

Epilogue: Postmodern Liturgical Retrieval

1. See Frank C. Senn, "Four Liturgical Movements: Restoration, Renewal, Revival, Retrieval," in *Liturgy* 19 (4) (2004): 69–79.

2. Robert Webber, *Ancient-Future Faith: Rethinking Evangelicalism for a Postmodern World* (Grand Rapids: Baker, 1999).

3. For a description of the worship of one emerging-church congregation in Melbourne, see Nathan Nettleton, "'Free Church Bapto-Catholic': A Story of Possibilities Embraced," in *Liturgy* 19 (4) (2004): 57–67.

4. See Stanley J. Grenz, *A Primer on Postmodernism* (Grand Rapids: Eerdmans, 1996).

5. See Philip Jenkins, *The Next Christendom: The Coming of Global Christianity* (Oxford: Oxford University Press, 2002), 107–39.

Index